THE CIRCULAR ECONOMY AND LIVEABLE CITIES

Edited by

ROBERT C. BREARS
Our Future Water

AF621458

CAMBRIDGE
UNIVERSITY PRESS

CAMBRIDGE
UNIVERSITY PRESS

Shaftesbury Road, Cambridge CB2 8EA, United Kingdom

One Liberty Plaza, 20th Floor, New York, NY 10006, USA

477 Williamstown Road, Port Melbourne, VIC 3207, Australia

314–321, 3rd Floor, Plot 3, Splendor Forum, Jasola District Centre, New Delhi – 110025, India

103 Penang Road, #05–06/07, Visioncrest Commercial, Singapore 238467

Cambridge University Press is part of Cambridge University Press & Assessment, a department of the University of Cambridge.

We share the University's mission to contribute to society through the pursuit of education, learning and research at the highest international levels of excellence.

www.cambridge.org
Information on this title: www.cambridge.org/9781009249454

DOI: 10.1017/9781009249492

© Cambridge University Press & Assessment 2025

This publication is in copyright. Subject to statutory exception and to the provisions of relevant collective licensing agreements, no reproduction of any part may take place without the written permission of Cambridge University Press & Assessment.

When citing this work, please include a reference to the DOI 10.1017/9781009249492

First published 2025

A catalogue record for this publication is available from the British Library

A Cataloging-in-Publication data record for this book is available from the Library of Congress

ISBN 978-1-009-24948-5 Hardback
ISBN 978-1-009-24945-4 Paperback

Cambridge University Press & Assessment has no responsibility for the persistence or accuracy of URLs for external or third-party internet websites referred to in this publication and does not guarantee that any content on such websites is, or will remain, accurate or appropriate.

For EU product safety concerns, contact us at Calle de José Abascal, 56, 1°, 28003 Madrid, Spain, or email eugpsr@cambridge.org

Contents

Contributors

Robert C. Brears an internationally recognised author and consultant, has dedicated his career to advancing water security, green growth, and comprehensive environmental stewardship. He is the Founder of Our Future Water, addressing urgent water-related challenges, and Global Climate Solutions, which explores cutting-edge ideas and actionable insights across multiple areas such as renewable energy, sustainable agriculture, and resilient urban development. Robert also contributes to global efforts through his role with the United Nations' Green Climate Fund, where he serves on the Roster of Experts (Water). Here, he assesses and ensures that water security projects align with broader environmental policy standards, promoting sustainability across various sectors.

Vanessa Carlow studied architecture and urban design at the Technical University of Berlin and at Delft University of Technology. She holds a joint MA in urban management from five European universities and a PhD in strategic planning from the Royal Danish Academy of Fine Arts, Copenhagen. She is a licensed architect and planner and the co-founder of COBE in Copenhagen (2005), currently practising under her own name. Since 2012 Vanessa has been heading the Institute for Sustainable Urbanism (ISU) at the Technical University of Braunschweig and the recently opened Spatial Analytics and Cross-Disciplinary Experimentation Lab (SPaCE Lab at the ISU) – a dedicated team and infrastructure for multidisciplinary post-digital urban research. Vanessa has lectured and taught at universities worldwide, including The Pennsylvania State University and Cornell University. In 2022 she was appointed to the Board of Trustees of Volkswagen Foundation.

Deborah Nabubwaya Chambers is a public health program coordinator who manages diverse undergraduate and graduate public health and healthcare administration programmes. She is also a health promoter and global health researcher. Deborah is currently pursuing a doctorate in health administration at National University,

San Diego. She earned a BA degree in psychology from Daystar University, Kenya, an MA in public health, and an MA in healthcare administration degree from National University, San Diego. She focuses part of her time on qualitative health research in Kenya and the United States while collaborating with healthcare administrators at the American Public Health Association (APHA) as a section member of the Engagement and Mentoring committees, incoming co-chair, and campus liaison under the APHA Student Assembly. She also leads the Daystar University Alumni Association, her alma mater diaspora chapter, as the current chair.

Tanya Clark is a writer whose research focuses on the ways in which the natural and built environments impact and influence mental health and well-being. She earned a PsyD in psychology from California Southern University, an MA in humanities from California State University, Dominguez Hills, and a second MA in psychology from Pepperdine University. She is a former clinician and professor now focused on investigating and communicating mission-critical human health and welfare issues to professional and lay audiences alike.

Dan Clinci is an architect and urban regeneration expert at the Institute for Research in Circular Economy and Environment 'Ernest Lupan' (IRCEM). With a rich experience in project management, Dan works on numerous projects focused on the systemic implementation of the circular economy in the urban environment and on the development of strategies for the transition to resilient and sustainable systems. His research activity is based on the study of blue–green infrastructure and its potential to develop circular cities adapted to the climatic and economic challenges of this century.

Vladut Vasile Constandoiu began his academic journey at a technical institute for surveyors before advancing to the University of Trento. There, he specialised in construction engineering and architecture, culminating in a thesis that emphasised the valorisation of river landscapes and the circular economy. After graduation, he joined ARS Engineering, where he honed his expertise in architectural design and became proficient in Autodesk Revit and building information modelling (BIM) methodology. This experience paved the way for his role at the ENG Group. Here, Vladut expanded his skill set, overseeing construction sites and pioneering the company's adoption of the BIM method. Currently, he is making strides as a researcher at IRCEM, where he continues to apply and broaden his vast knowledge in the fields of engineering and sustainable construction.

Anna-Vera Deinhammer is a Vienna-based strategist, lobbyist, and integral engineering scientist. She holds a diploma in architecture and subsequently completed a doctorate in integral engineering in Vienna and Sydney in the field of holistic quality assessment of buildings. All her activities centre the creation of a healthy and liveable built environment. She follows the Quadruple Helix approach, which combines the perspectives of business, science, civil society, and politics. Her work focuses on the circular economy in construction, integral construction research, and engineering science, to which she is currently contributing as Director for Circular Cities & Regions in the Circular Economy Forum Austria. She represents the Austrian Sustainable Building Council at the World Green Building Council and the Climate Positive Europe Alliance in Brussels. She holds the Endowed Chair for Sustainable Real Estate Development at the University of Applied Sciences for Management and Communication, Austria.

Yoeri Dijkhof is a research consultant at Ecorys, where he works on various projects in the Dutch and European context, aimed at the analysis and assessment of (policy) measures for the energy transition and a circular economy. During his double degree master in economic development and growth at the University of Groningen and Lund University School of Economics and Management, he studied economic policies aimed at achieving the UN Sustainable Development Goals. In his work, he supports local and national governments as well as multiple European institutions in implementing circular and sustainable policies.

Nanco Dolman is a lead expert in Water Resilient Cities at Deltares, the Netherlands. From 2011 to 2016 he was a part-time lecturer in urban water management at the Rotterdam University of Applied Sciences. Internationally recognised as a front runner in Water Sensitive Urban Design, Nanco specialises in bridging water-resilient design and engineering. Between 2015 and 2020 he also served as a Resilient Cities advocate for the United Nations Office for Disaster Risk Reduction. Currently he is the editor of the International Water Association's *Journal of Water and Climate Change*.

Frances Furio is an assistant professor in the School of Social Work at California State University, Sacramento (CSUS). She received her PsyD at California Southern University and her MSW at CSUS. In addition to her work at CSUS, she provides mental health services in the community and remains active in research related to the topics of mental health, forensic social work, and social and environmental justice. As an instructor, licensed clinician, and qualitative researcher, she is interested in understanding people's lived experiences and highlighting the strength and resiliency of communities that continue to face barriers and injustice. She is passionate about the promotion of equity, inclusion, and peaceful and progressive social work practice.

Regine Gerike is Professor for Mobility System Planning at the Dresden University of Technology (TUD). Before joining TUD, she chaired the Institute for Transport Studies at the University of Natural Resources and Life Sciences in Vienna, Austria. Regine did her PhD at TUD in the field of modelling transport and its environmental effects. From 2008 to 2012 she was an assistant professor at the Technical University of Munich and the head of mobil.TUM, a research centre on mobility and transport. Her research interests focus on transport planning and empirical research on travel behaviour.

Hendrik Görner has been a research associate at TUD since 2015, where he also pursued his studies in traffic engineering from 2013 to 2020, with a focus on transport planning and traffic engineering. His special interests lie in the spatial analysis of environmental data in urban areas in the context of pedestrian traffic and the associated automation of processes and applications.

Sebastian Hantschel has been a research associate at TUD since 2023. Previously, he was a project manager at wegebund (Saxony bicycle and pedestrian association) and at LISt GmbH (transport consultancy within the Saxon administration). He obtained his PhD at TUD in the field of acceptance and traffic safety of cyclists in mixed traffic conditions. His research interests focus on traffic safety and the safety-related behaviour of vulnerable road users.

Karin Huber-Heim is Chair of the Austrian Task Force Circular Economy, advising the Federal Ministry of Climate, Innovation and Technology and the Federal Ministry of Labour and Economy on the implementation of the Austrian Circular Economy Strategy. She is President of the Board of the Circular Economy Forum Austria, a joint initiative of key players from business, science, design, politics, and society, which she co-founded to support the economy in the transition to a circular economy. She is a long-standing board member of the Global Compact Network Austria and Academic Programme Director for executive programmes at the University of Applied Sciences, Vienna, where she has designed curricula for sustainability and responsible management, circular economy and innovation, and sustainable finance. She lectures and publishes on sustainable business, circular economy, and stakeholder communication at various universities.

Caroline Koszowski has been a research associate and lecturer at TUD since 2015. From 2008 to 2012 she studied spatial planning at the Technical University of Kaiserslautern, and from 2012 to 2015 she studied urban and regional planning at the University of Kassel. Her research interests include walking, active mobility, integrated transport planning, and urban street design, with a particular focus on user needs and behaviour in public space.

Maria Kottari is Principal Consultant at Technopolis Group, where she specialises in project management/coordination and research in the green transition and innovation domains (e.g. EU Green Deal). During her career in the public sector (European Commission Joint Research Centre), academia (European University Institute), and consultancy, she has been involved in various initiatives related to the policy and socio-economic aspects of the energy transition (including labour market reforms, circular economy principles) and climate change mitigation and adaptation, in particular the green economy (e.g. sustainable finance, decarbonisation processes), technological and citizen-driven innovation, gender equality, and youth engagement.

Michael Krieg has been Managing Director of the 'Friedrich List' Faculty of Transport Sciences at TUD for four years, responsible for the strategic, personnel, and financial development of the faculty. In his 20 years of professional experience in almost all management functions of universities, he has worked at private institutions (Kuehne Logistics University, Frankfurt School of Finance and Management), public universities (University of Oldenburg, University of Passau), and outside Germany (INSEAD: Europe (France), Asia (Singapore), the Middle East (Abu Dhabi)). His research interests cover sustainability, transport and logistics, and higher education, among others.

Elena Simina Lakatos obtained her economist's diploma in 2007, after graduating from Babeş-Bolyai University in Cluj-Napoca, and her engineer's diploma in 2010, after graduating from the Faculty of Materials Engineering and the Environment at the Technical University of Cluj-Napoca. Later, she pursued doctoral studies at the Technical University of Cluj-Napoca and Oulu University in Finland, earning the title of Doctor of Engineering and Management with a dissertation titled 'Corporate Social Responsibility through Partnerships between Businesses and NGOs for Company Sustainability'. She is the author and co-author of more than 80 articles in conferences and journals, giving an H index of 10. Her professional focus is on her activity as the president of IRCEM, founded in 2012 with the objective of offering services aimed at enabling the shift to a circular economy. She is currently Vice President of the Advisory Board for Research, Development, and Innovation of the Ministry of Research, Romania, where she provides scientific support for policy development in the field of research, development, and innovation.

Alexander Laszlo is President of the Board of Directors of the Bertalanffy Center for the Study of Systems Science, Director of Research at the Laszlo Institute of

New Paradigm Research, Co-founder and Global Collaborator of Global Education Futures, Co-founding Member of EARTHwise Centre, and Founding Member of the Board of Directors of the Social Systems Foundation. He served as the 57th President and Chair of the Board of Trustees of the International Society for the Systems Sciences and was Director of the Doctoral Program in Management at the Graduate School of Business Administration & Leadership, Mexico, and as Founding Director of the Doctoral Program in Leadership and Systemic Innovation at the Buenos Aires Institute of Technology, Argentina, where he currently resides. As a professor of systems science and evolutionary development, his research and teaching focus on evolutionary leadership, collaboration, and systems thinking. He is on the editorial boards of seven internationally arbitered research journals, is the recipient of the Gertrude Albert Heller Award, the Sir Geoffrey Vickers Memorial Award, and the Förderpreis Akademischer Klub award, and is the author of over 100 journal, book, and encyclopaedia publications.

Matthias Medicus has been a research associate at TUD since 2018. Previously, he studied traffic engineering at TUD from 2012 to 2018. His research interests include traffic safety and traffic flow and behaviour in urban areas, with a focus on pedestrian traffic.

Andrea Orsag, a sustainability and circular economy evangelist, is the founder of MissionC, a strategy advisory based in Amsterdam on a mission to accelerate the green transition on a global scale through circular economy and environmental, social, and governance incorporation. She is an advisor with more than 15 years of experience combining risk management, strategy, and change management cross-industry, both for the commercial sector and for not-for-profit organisations internationally. She helps organisations bring their ideas to life by refining their sustainability strategies, adjusting business models towards circularity, delivering programmes, and engaging stakeholders. Andrea also acts as a speaker, guest lecturer, expert moderator, and facilitator on topics related to circular economy, sustainability, and impact.

Elena Cristina Rada graduated in environmental engineering in 2002 from the Polytechnic University of Bucharest with a specialisation in energy and economics. Since 2005 she has received three PhDs from Italian and Rumanian universities: a PhD in environmental engineering, a PhD in energy engineering, and a PhD in engineering and management. In 2013, she attained the Italian National Qualification to function as Associate Professor in the sector of environmental and sanitary engineering, confirmed in 2018 and valid until 2027. In 2023, she attained the Italian National Qualification to function as Full Professor in the same sector, valid until

2034. In 2016, she received the Eminent Scientist Medal from the Wessex Institute of Technology. She is a member of several scientific committees of international conferences and is the author or co-author of more than 300 articles in conferences and journals (more than 230 articles are indexed in the SCOPUS® database, giving an H index of 37). She has edited numerous special issues of international journals published by Elsevier and MDPI (Multidisciplinary Digital Publishing Institute), including those with high and medium impact factors. Presently she is a senior researcher in the University of Insubria, Italy. She was ranked in the top two per cent scientists list of the world ranking published by Stanford University.

Anabel Ternès is a futurist, keynote speaker, author, and founder of sustainable start-ups. As the managing director of the SRH Institute for Sustainability Management in Berlin and a professor of communication management, she brings extensive international leadership experience in business development, having worked for companies and founded start-ups such CoCarrier, HealthMedo, and Aeco Delta. Anabel is actively involved in several committees, boards, and advisory boards. She is President of the Club of Budapest in Germany and International Embassy for Economic Affairs, as well as a member of the Club of Rome. She has received multiple awards for her entrepreneurial and volunteer efforts. She has a track record in international leading positions in the consumer industry, such as with Samsonite, Triumph, and Fielmann.

Sameh N. Wahba is Regional Director for Sustainable Development at the World Bank's Europe and Central Asia region. He oversees all lending, technical assistance, partnerships, and policy advisory work in agriculture and food, climate change, environment, natural resources and the blue economy, social inclusion and sustainability, water, urban, disaster risk management, resilience, and land. Previously, he worked as Global Director for Urban, Resilience, and Land Global Practice. He holds a PhD in urban planning from Harvard University and has 25 years' experience and numerous publications on cities, housing, land, infrastructure, finance, and the Sustainable Development Goals. He is a member of the World Economic Forum's Global Future Cities Council and a commissioner in the Global Commission for Urban SDG Finance.

Tara Rava Zolnikov is a professor whose research focuses on aspects of culture in global health. Tara earned a PhD in developmental science from North Dakota State University, an MS in environmental health from Harvard School of Public Health, and a second MS in industrial hygiene from Montana Tech of the University of Montana. She also earned a BS degree in biological sciences from Montana Tech of the University of Montana. She is the editor of *Dialogues in Health*.

Acknowledgements

First and foremost, I wish to thank Matt and Maya for their wonderful help in ensuring books like these come to fruition. Second, I would like to express my gratitude to my mum, who has a keen interest in environmental matters and has supported me in this journey of developing the book. Lastly, I want to extend a special acknowledgement to Kate, my love, who enriches my life in countless ways and has been an inexhaustible source of inspiration and motivation during the creation of this work.

1

An Overview of Circular Economy and Liveable Cities

ROBERT C. BREARS

1.1 Introduction

Today's industrial economy operates largely on a linear model, characterised by a cycle of extracting resources, manufacturing products, consuming them, and then disposing of them. As it stands, global material usage is expected to surge from 79 gigatonnes (Gt) in 2011 to 167 Gt in 2060. Concurrently, total emissions are anticipated to reach 75 Gt CO_2 equivalent by 2060, with material management contributing to approximately 50 Gt CO_2 equivalent of that figure. Non-metallic minerals, such as sand, gravel, and limestone, represent the largest share of total materials use and are projected to grow rapidly from 35 Gt in 2011 to 82 Gt in 2060. Metal use is smaller in weight but is projected to grow more rapidly, resulting in significant environmental impacts from extraction and processing.[1]

With rapid urbanisation, it is predicted that by 2050, 66 per cent of the world's economy will be housed in urban areas, up from 54 per cent in 2015. Under a business-as-usual scenario, the annual resource needs of urban areas could escalate from 40 billion tonnes in 2010 to nearly 90 billion tonnes by the mid twenty-first century.[2] Given the escalating scarcity of materials, rising pollution levels, increasing material demand, and growing consumer demand for sustainable products, it is evident that our current economic approach is not sustainable. The circular economy, on the other hand, seeks to decouple economic growth from resource consumption and its related environmental effects.[3] It is projected that cities could reduce their energy use, greenhouse gas emissions, and metal, land, and waste usage by 36–54 per cent if they embrace circular practices in areas like transportation, commercial buildings, and heating/cooling of buildings.[4]

In response, there is growing emphasis on the need for our cities to become circular to meet these challenges while enhancing the health and welfare of their residents, where a circular economy city seeks to generate prosperity, increase liveability, and improve resilience of both the city and its residents.[5]

1.2 The Linear Economy

In our current economic model, manufactured capital, human capital, and natural capital all contribute to human welfare by supporting the production of goods and services in the economic process. Natural capital – the world's stock of natural resources (provided by nature before their extraction or processing by humans) – is typically used for material and energy inputs into production and acts as a 'sink' for waste from the economic process. This economic model can be best described as 'linear', which typically involves economic actors – who are people or organisations engaged in any of the four economic activities of production, distribution, consumption, and resource maintenance – harvesting and extracting natural resources, using them to manufacture a product, and selling a product to other economic actors, who then discard it when it no longer serves its purpose. As such, natural resources in the linear economic model:

- *Become inputs*: Material resources used in the economy come from raw materials that are extracted from domestic natural resource stocks or extracted from natural resource stocks abroad and imported in the form of raw materials, semi-finished materials, or materials embedded in manufactured goods.
- *Become outputs*: After use in production and consumption activities, materials leave the economy as an output either to the environment in the form of residuals (pollution, waste) or in the form of raw materials, semi-finished materials, and materials embedded in manufactured goods.
- *Accumulate in manufactured stocks*: Some materials accumulate in the economy where they are stored in the form of buildings, transport infrastructure, or durable and semi-durable goods such as cars, industrial machinery, and household appliances. If these materials are not recovered from waste, they flow back into the environment.
- *Create indirect flows*: When materials or goods are imported for use in an economy, their upstream production is associated with unused materials that remain abroad, including raw materials needed to produce the goods and the generation of residuals. These indirect flows of materials account for the life-cycle impacts of the production chain but are not physically imported. As such, the environmental consequences occur in countries from which the imports originate.[6]

1.3 The Circular Economy

The circular economy, in contrast to the linear 'take–make–consume–dispose' economy, aims to keep resources in use for as long as possible, extract value from them while in use, and recover and regenerate products and materials at the end of each service life. As such, the circular economy focuses on recycling, limiting, and reusing the physical inputs of the economy and using waste as a resource, leading to reduced primary resource consumption, with the ultimate aim being the decoupling of economic growth from resource use. In addition, the circular economy is powered by renewable energy, such as solar, hydro, wind, and biofuels. The notion of decoupling is that economic output shall continue to increase at the same time as rates of increasing resource use and environmental impact are slowed and in time brought into decline. There are two modes of decoupling that can be distinguished:

1) *Resource decoupling*, or 'de-materialisation', involves reducing the rate at which natural resources are used per unit of economic output.
2) *Impact decoupling* seeks to increase economic activity while decreasing negative environmental impacts from pressures such as pollution, carbon emissions, or destruction of biodiversity.[7]

1.3.1 Circular Economy Principles

The circular economy is based on the three main principles of eliminating waste and pollution, circular products and materials, and regenerating nature:

- *Eliminating waste and pollution*: Our current take–make–consume–dispose linear economy involves taking raw materials, making products from them, and eventually disposing of them as waste. The majority of waste ends up in landfills or incinerators. With resources being finite, the circular economy ensures that materials re-enter the economy at the end of their use, turning the take–make–dispose system into a circular system. Many products can be circulated by being maintained, shared, reused, repaired, refurbished, remanufactured, and recycled.
- *Circular products and materials*: The circular economy involves circulating products and materials at their highest value by keeping materials in use, either as a product or, when they can no longer be used, as components or raw materials. As such, nothing becomes waste and the intrinsic value of products and materials is retained. In the technical cycle of the circular economy, products are reused, repaired, remanufactured, and recycled. In the biological cycle, biodegradable materials are returned to the earth through composting and anaerobic digestion.
- *Regenerating nature*: The circular economy regenerates nature by shifting the focus of the economy from extraction to regeneration. In contrast to the linear economy, which continuously degrades nature, the circular economy enhances natural capital by employing practices that restore nature, increase biodiversity, and return biological materials to the earth.[8]

1.4 Circular Economy Cities

Circular economy cities embed the principles of the circular economy across all their functions, establishing an urban system that aims to eliminate waste, keeps assets at their highest value at all times, and is enabled by digital technology. Furthermore, a circular economy city seeks to generate prosperity, increase liveability, and improve the resilience of the city and its residents. At the same time, it aims to decouple economic growth from resource consumption. Circular economy cities include a range of elements, including:

- A built environment that is designed to be flexible, sources health materials that improve the quality of life of residents, and minimises material use.
- Energy systems that are resilient, renewable, and localised to allow effective energy use, reduce costs, and have a positive impact on the environment.
- Water systems that encourage water conservation and efficiency, are resilient to climatic extremes, restore nature, and recover resources from wastewater.
- Urban mobility systems that are accessible, affordable, and effective. Circular economy cities have multi-modal mobility structures that reduce air pollution and congestion.
- An urban bioeconomy that returns nutrients to the soil in an appropriate manner while generating value and minimising food waste. Nutrients are captured from the organic fraction of municipal solid waste and wastewater streams, processed, and returned to the soil in forms such as organic fertiliser. Through urban farming, cities can supply some of their own food.
- Production systems that encourage the creation of local value loops with more local production and increased and more diverse exchanges of value in local economies.[9]

1.4.1 Circular Economy and Liveable Cities

Liveability can be defined as the quality of life experienced by residents in a community or a city. The concept of liveability can be viewed as improving the economic, social, cultural, and environmental well-being of present and future residents.[10] The circular economy can enhance the liveability of cities in a number of ways. For example, a circular economy path for urban mobility systems can reduce time lost in congestion. In the built environment, circular economy principles can impact indoor air quality through the use of healthy materials in buildings. Furthermore, the circular economy reduces air pollution through effective mobility systems, reduces unprocessed waste in open-air dumpsites, improves water and wastewater treatment processes, and restores the urban environment through urban regenerative projects.[11]

1.4.2 The 5R Approach: A Core Strategy for Circular Economy Cities

The 5R Approach – Reduce, Reuse, Recycle, Restore, and Recover – is a framework that can be seamlessly integrated into the operational fabric of circular economy cities. This quintessential strategy advocates for:

- *Reduce*: implementing efficient product designs and systems to minimise resource consumption, in terms of both raw materials and energy
- *Reuse*: extending the life cycle of products and materials by either refurbishing them or by sharing among multiple users
- *Recycle*: transforming waste materials into new products or resources, ideally without degrading their quality
- *Recover*: extracting valuable elements from waste streams for future use, such as nutrient recovery from wastewater
- *Restore*: focusing on renewing and revitalising natural ecosystems, which could be integrated into urban spaces as green infrastructure.[12]

By following the 5R Approach, cities can manage waste more sustainably, foster innovation, and move closer to the objective of decoupling economic growth from resource consumption. This comprehensive framework encourages a mindset that views waste not as an end but as a part of a circular process. Moreover, the 5R Approach has synergies with each of the elements discussed under circular economy cities – from a built environment that minimises material use to energy systems that prioritise efficiency and sustainability.

1.4.3 Enablers of Circular Economy Cities

There are various enablers of the transition towards circular economy in cities, including the following:

- *The ability of city governments to shape urban planning and policy*: Local governments have a large and direct influence on urban planning, the design of mobility systems, urban infrastructure, local business development, municipal taxation, and the local job market. Therefore, local governments can play an active role in embedding the principles of the circular economy across all urban functions and policies. Experts estimate that on a global scale 60 per cent of the buildings that will exist in 2050 are yet to be built, and in emerging economies such as India, this figure reaches 70 per cent by 2030. Since these investments will largely need to be made in cities, it presents a large opportunity for local governments to use their influence to apply circular economy principles from the outset for this infrastructure, which will help to avoid the 'linear lock-in' currently seen in developed markets (where there is a need to transform large parts of existing, entrenched infrastructure systems). Local governments can use demonstration and pilot projects at the local level as showcases in order to engage national and business actors in the process as well. Where there is a lack of leadership on the national or regional level, local governments have been seen to step in. In addition, research suggests that local leadership is more trusted by citizens, indicating a stronger level of possible influence.

- *Proximity of people and materials in the urban environment*: One of the main characteristics of cities is a high concentration of resources, capital, data, and talent over a small geographic territory. This proximity can enable the circular economy in a number of ways. Reverse logistics and material collection cycles could be more efficient due to the geographical proximity of users and producers, creating more opportunities for reuse and collection-based business models. The proximity and concentration of people enable sharing and reuse models (where products or assets are used multiple times by different users, typically within a neighbourhood or smaller geographic unit).
- *Sufficient scale for effective markets*: New circular economy business models are more likely to emerge and succeed in the presence of both a large and varied supply of materials and a high potential market demand for the goods and services derived from them. Both conditions are most likely to be met in cities.
- *Digital revolution*: Digital technology has enabled a fundamental shift in the way the economy functions and has the power to support the transition to a circular economy by radically increasing virtualisation, de-materialisation, transparency on product-use and material flows, and feedback-driven intelligence. Through the collection and analysis of data on materials, people, and external conditions, digital technology has the potential to identify the challenges of material flows in cities, outline the key areas of structural waste, and inform more effective decision-making on how to address these challenges and provide systemic solutions. Technologies such as asset tagging, geo-spatial information, Big Data management, and widespread connectivity have been identified as enablers of circular economy activity in cities.[13]

1.4.4 Benefits of the Circular Economy in Cities

The circular economy generates multiple benefits for cities, including:

- *Environmental protection*: The reusing and recycling of products slow down the use of natural resources, reduce landscape and habitat destruction, and help limit biodiversity loss. Another benefit of the circular economy is a reduction in greenhouse gas emissions. Creating more efficient and sustainable products will help reduce energy and resource consumption; it will also reduce the amount of waste.

- *Reduced raw material dependence*: The world's population is increasing, resulting in increased demand for raw materials. However, the supply of raw materials is limited. Finite supplies also mean some countries are dependent on others for their raw materials. Recycling raw materials mitigates the risks associated with supply, such as price volatility, availability, and import dependency. This applies particularly to critical raw materials needed for the production of technologies crucial for achieving climate goals, such as batteries and electric engines.
- *Cost savings*: Moving towards a circular economy increases competitiveness, stimulates innovation, boosts economic growth, and creates jobs. Redesigning materials and products for circular use increases innovation across different sectors of the economy. Consumers are provided with more durable and innovative products that increase the quality of life and save them money in the long term.
- *Relief of pressure on municipal services and budgets*: Reducing primary material consumption will reduce spending on waste management. In addition, public expenditure on products to run public facilities could be decreased by procuring products or services offered through new innovative business models.
- *Increased job opportunities*: The circular economy can generate employment opportunities in cities. For example, by 2036, a circular economy could provide London with 12,000 net new jobs in the areas of reuse, remanufacturing, and materials innovation. Employment opportunities would not be limited to remanufacturing, however; the circular economy can generate jobs across industrial sectors, within small and medium enterprises, through increased innovation and entrepreneurship, and in a new service-based economy.
- *Technological innovation*: The aspiration of the circular economy to replace one-way products with goods that are circular by design and increase local production will spur new ideas and enhance innovation in cities. Finding new ways of keeping components and materials at their highest value will encourage the development of new business modes, creating vibrant urban communities centred around repair cafes and sharing and exchange platforms.
- *Reduced waste*: Transitioning to a circular economy is crucial for sustainability, ensuring a stable supply of materials and reducing environmental impact. This model supports better waste and material management, addresses pollution problems like microplastics, and encourages recycling and reuse. It also advocates for longer product-use and sharing economy practices. The primary goals are to maximise value from circulating materials, minimise material consumption, prevent waste generation, and reduce hazardous waste components.
- *Reduction of biodiversity loss*: The circular economy reduces biodiversity loss by reducing the amount of land needed to provide resources for the economy and by designing out pollution at every stage of a product's life cycle. In circular economy liveable cities, urban areas are designed to be compact,

integrate with nature, consist of buildings and construction materials that are kept in use, and rely on renewable materials that are regeneratively produced. By planning compact and biodiverse urban environments that optimise the use of space, the sector can leave room for nature within and beyond urban areas. For example, in Europe, up to 30,000 square kilometres of fertile land could be saved by 2050 by planning cities with higher densities instead of encouraging urban sprawl.
- *Mitigation of climate change*: The circular economy reduces greenhouse gas emissions – for instance, it is projected that a circular economy development path in Europe could halve emissions by 2030.[14]

1.4.5 Barriers to the Circular Economy in Cities

There are various barriers to the development of circular economy in cities, including the following:

- *Attitude and knowledge*: The development of the circular economy faces the barriers of lack of understanding and awareness of the concept. This knowledge gap, coupled with the risk-averse nature of many businesses that prefer incremental changes over disruptive ones, hinders progression towards a more circular model. Furthermore, companies often exhibit inertia when considering new business models, strategic sustainability issues, or transitioning from a product-centric approach to a product-service-system orientation, which are essential aspects of the circular economy.
- *Lack of consumer interest*: The success of a circular economy is hindered by a lack of consumer interest and awareness. Mainstream consumer habits, characterised by rapidly changing preferences, are perceived to pose a challenge to businesses that focus on producing durable products designed to outlast fleeting fashion trends. There is a consensus among businesses that a shift in consumer demand could significantly propel the adoption of a circular economy. However, there's an overall recognition that such demand is presently scant.
- *Lack of information*: The removal of toxic material and separation of biological from the technical substance are lacking. Often there is a shortage of information regarding green suppliers. Furthermore, product design currently gives less attention to the end phase of products' life cycles.
- *Economic barriers*: Transitioning to a circular economy promises long-term sustainable growth, but the journey there is fraught with significant short-term hurdles. Major challenges include substantial upfront costs associated with adapting existing infrastructure, such as machinery retrofitting, factory relocation, building new logistics networks, and staff retraining. Additionally, financial constraints

often limit budget allocation for necessary circular economy innovations. The lack of industrial symbiosis, a costly yet essential component of circular economy, and the high expenses involved in ensuring quality control for recycled materials further complicate the transition.

- *Financial barriers*: The transition to a circular economy is often hindered by prevailing product-focused orientations and financial uncertainties in businesses. Concerns about revenue generation from new business models like product-service systems, the perceived low value of enhanced sustainability, and the disregard of sustainability in business model discussions contribute to these barriers. Moreover, the wide-ranging organisational changes needed for this transition, which demand considerable time and investment, conflict with the prevalent financial focus on quick returns and cost savings. This makes convincing stakeholders about long-term systemic change, particularly with uncertain future revenue streams, a significant challenge.
- *Complex supply chains*: Given that production and consumption frequently occur across different nations, supply chains may require restructuring to support reuse and remanufacturing. For companies to prioritise sustainable materials, durability, and reparability, incentives across the supply chain are essential. For a seamless transition to the circular economy, the current network must facilitate mode-switching in transportation.
- *Technological barriers*: Technological hurdles to the implementation of a circular economy arise from anticipated major modifications to both products and their production or recovery systems. Such modifications often raise concerns about feasibility, cost implications, and potential impacts on product quality. Specifically, apprehensions exist around the possible decline in quality when products are redesigned for improved circularity or when they include recycled materials or have undergone refurbishment.
- *Lack of capacity*: A barrier towards the implementation of circular economy is the lack of skills in small and medium-sized enterprises, which do not realise the benefit of implementing more advanced technologies that reduce the negative impacts on the environment and offer them cost savings.[15]

1.4.6 Policy Levers and Instruments to Develop Circular Economy Liveable Cities

Cities have a range of policy levers and instruments available to establish the conditions for circular economy transitions, including the following:

- *Urban management*: City authorities have a strong influence over the physical development of the city, the management of its assets, and the procurement of public goods and services. Urban planning shapes the physical development of a city. It has an impact on how people and goods move around a city and determines whether materials, products, and nutrients can be recovered and kept in use:

- *Urban planning*: Urban planning refers to the physical shaping and development of a city. It assesses physical, social, and environmental factors that determine the allocation, development, and usage of urban structures, such as parks, buildings, and infrastructure. With rapid urbanisation, decisions in urban planning contribute significantly to how materials, products, and nutrients flow between people and sites in the city. They can also influence how people work and travel. A circular approach to urban planning can unlock circular economy opportunities by creating a regenerative system that minimises waste, stimulating the circulation of valuable resources and making productive use of city assets to create new value and liveable cities.
- *Asset management*: Asset management is the management of city-owned physical assets, including land, buildings, and water and sewage systems. A significant portion of public investment is used to maintain costs associated with these assets. However, many cities have insufficient funds to maintain or replace them. At the same time, many city assets are underutilised, leaving revenue-generating opportunities untapped. A circular economy approach to asset management can help address these challenges. For instance, it can increase the utilisation of current assets and increase resource and cost savings during an asset's management. For example, operational costs can be reduced by increasing the asset's energy efficiency or making use of predictive maintenance.
- *Public procurement*: Public procurement is the purchasing of goods and services by the public sector, ranging from everyday office goods and services to infrastructure projects. Integrating the circular economy approach in public procurement policies and practices can stimulate circular design, provision, management, and servicing of goods. Cities can integrate circular economy criteria into public procurement policies and tenders for goods and services. Doing so incentivises circular economy market innovation and stimulates the increased use, reuse, and repair of products. Circular economy criteria in purchasing criteria can encourage the market to develop more durable products while ensuring the materials used are non-harmful, repairable, and reusable. Circular economy criteria can be incorporated into the renovation and maintenance of city-owned and operated buildings and infrastructure, ensuring the use of high-quality, renewable, and even prefabricated materials. The circular economy approach can also stimulate circular economy building developments on city-owned land.

- *Fiscal tools*: Cities can implement a range of fiscal measures, such as taxes, charges, or fees, to facilitate the shift towards a circular economy. Fiscal tools incentivise behaviour change among residents and businesses to encourage the use of recycled materials, reduction in waste, and recovering of resources.
  - *Tax credits*: Tax credits provided by local governments can incentivise circular economy products, businesses, and projects, such as a tax credit for businesses that donate their food waste.
  - *Charges and tariffs*: Cities can use charges and tariffs to incentivise behavioural change. For example, charges can be applied to single-use bags to reduce waste, or congestion charges set to encourage the use of public transportation during peak hours.
  - *Fines*: Fines can be used to discourage the under-use of assets or discourage harmful, polluting activities. For instance, cities can penalise companies that fail to sort their waste effectively, such as businesses that throw away recyclable and compostable items.
- *Legislation and regulation*: Legislation and regulation refer to bylaws, standards, rules, and requirements that city governments can set. Cities can implement regulations that guide the development of the circular economy while underpinning other policy levers. Legislation and regulation can be developed to promote the reuse and recovery of resources, limit the creation and disposal of waste, and facilitate sharing platforms. Cities can use legislation and regulation to stimulate circular economy activities in various ways, including:
  - *Shaping bylaws that facilitate circular economy practices in the city*: Local bylaws can be adapted and developed to enable and regulate conditions for circular economy practices in cities. For example, local bylaws can be developed to ensure that organic food waste from commercial food retailers and food service establishments are diverted from landfill. In the building sector, circularity can be incorporated into zoning plans, building standards, building codes, and land tenders.
  - *Banning the circulation of goods and materials harmful to society and the environment*: Cities can impose bans on goods and materials that have adverse impacts on people and the environment. For instance, cities can ban valuable resources going to waste or introduce stricter regulations on urban zones, such as polluting vehicles being banned from entering low-emission zones.
- *Capacity-building*: Capacity-building is the training and advisory support cities can provide to individuals, companies, and organisations. Cities can partner with local organisations to develop training and business capacity-building programmes to mainstream the circular economy. Workshops, training programmes, and skills development are tools cities can implement to develop

circular economy practices. Cities can also develop incubator programmes and material exchange platforms to give individuals and businesses the ability to engage in and implement circular economy initiatives:

  - *Skills development*: Cities can work with organisations to train young people in circular economy areas, such as refurbishment, repair, and reuse of electronics.
  - *Capacity-building networks and developing guides*: Cities can set up sector-specific workshops that provide city officials, vendors, and suppliers with information on circular procurement. Cities can also develop zero-waste design guidelines that inform architects, planners, and developers on how to design out waste in various sectors.
  - *Support of innovation and repair hubs*: Cities can help create community hubs that build skills among residents and businesses in innovation, repair, and reuse.

- *Awareness-raising*: Raising awareness of circular economy opportunities is crucial in supporting local transitions. Knowledge-sharing and communication campaigns can enable cities to increase awareness of circular economy best practices, initiatives, and market opportunities. Cities can raise awareness in various ways, including:
  - *Making information on circular economy city plans accessible online*: Cities can develop websites and webpages that inform the public on circular economy city plans and strategies. These plans provide an opportunity to showcase local best practices.
  - *Hosting and supporting awareness-raising events*: Cities can host circular economy events to showcase local activities and reach a wider audience. For instance, they can host water conservation events to encourage residents and businesses to conserve water and enhance efficiency through retrofits.
  - *Using communication campaigns*: Awareness campaigns can support behavioural change. They can help encourage waste reduction, reuse, and responsible consumption.
  - *Sharing information on local services to support circular economy practices*: Cities can share information on local sharing, reusing, and repair services. They can create websites that connect businesses, schools, universities, and non-profit organisations seeking to donate and receive donated goods. Digital mart maps can inform residents of where they can rent, share, borrow, give, and exchange items.
  - *Developing demonstration projects that inspire and showcase the potential of the circular economy*: Cities can implement demonstration projects that showcase what is practically possible and the opportunities a circular economy provides. For example, experimental modular buildings can showcase new material consumption and construction techniques.[16]

1.5 Case Study Examples of Circular Economy Liveable Cities

There are numerous case study examples of cities implementing initiatives to become circular economy liveable cities, including the following.

1.5.1 Singapore's Building Retrofit Energy Efficiency Financing Scheme

The Building Retrofit Energy Efficiency Financing (BREEF) scheme was a programme in Singapore that provided loans for energy efficiency retrofits of existing buildings. This was facilitated by the Building and Construction Authority and participating financial institutions and could cover the cost of equipment, installation, and professional fees. Key details of the BREEF scheme included a maximum loan amount of up to SGD $4 million or 90 per cent of costs (whichever was lower), with an interest rate determined by the participating financial institution. The maximum loan tenure was five years. To qualify, the credit facilities had to be used for energy efficiency retrofits that met at least a minimum Green Mark Certification standard, which had to be maintained throughout the loan tenure. The scheme was available until it closed on 31 March 2023. Eligibility for the BREEF scheme was extended to owners or joint owners of non-residential buildings in Singapore, management corporations under the Land Titles (Strata) Act for residential and non-residential buildings, energy performance contracting firms accredited by the Singapore Green Building Council, energy services companies (ESCOs) accredited by the ESCO Accreditation Committee, and special purpose vehicles set up to deliver, perform, or provide energy performance improvements for residential or non-residential buildings.[17]

1.5.2 San Francisco Public Utilities Commission's Onsite Water Reuse Grant Program

The San Francisco Public Utilities Commission (SFPUC) Onsite Water Reuse Grant Program is a funding initiative aimed at reducing reliance on the SFPUC's water supply. It encourages retail water users to collect, treat, and utilise alternate water sources such as rainwater, stormwater, greywater, foundation drainage, air conditioning condensate, and blackwater for non-potable uses, like toilet flushing, irrigation, and cooling tower makeup. Grant funding is provided for three types of projects:

1. *Voluntary Projects*: Installing on-site water systems without a mandate.
2. *Above and Beyond Projects*: Installing on-site water systems as per the Non-potable Water Ordinance, surpassing the baseline Non-potable Water Ordinance compliance.
3. *Brewery Process Water Projects*: Installing on-site treatment and reuse of brewery process water.

The eligibility for grant funding is based on the amount of SFPUC water a project can replace annually:

1. Projects replacing at least 450,000 gallons can get up to USD $200,000.
2. Projects replacing at least 1,000,000 gallons can get up to $500,000.
3. Projects replacing at least 3,000,000 gallons can get up to $1,000,000.

Applicants must demonstrate a reduction of SFPUC water supplies by utilising alternate water sources. Funded activities include the installation of collection systems, treatment systems, and storage of the treated water. Grant applications are reviewed and evaluated on a case-by-case basis, and funding is available on a first-come, first-served basis. Projects that are undertaken to comply with the City and County of San Francisco's ordinances, such as the Non-potable Water Ordinance, are not eligible for grants, except for Above and Beyond Projects.[18]

1.5.3 City of Toronto's Electronic Waste Programme

The City of Toronto collects unwanted electronics for free to ensure they are disposed of safely, recycled, and kept out of landfill. Electronic items can be put out on garbage day for pickup, brought to a drop-off depot on Community Environment Day, or donated for reuse. Items that are accepted as electronic waste are:

- Cell phones and home phones
- Computer cables
- Laptop computers and accessories
- VCRs/DVD players
- Video cameras
- TVs
- Desktop computers and monitors
- Printer and fax machines
- Accessories
- Cameras
- Receivers and speakers
- Stereos, tuners, and turntables

The City of Toronto also provides the TOwaste app to help residents never miss their garbage or recycling day again. The app lets users know what waste items go where, what bins to put out when, and where to donate used items or find a city drop-off depot from their smartphone or tablet. The key features of the app are:

- Waste Wizard – the City's quick and easy search tool with information on how to properly sort over 2,000 items

- Collection schedules and the ability to set reminders and opt-in for alerts about service changes
- A map of drop-off depot locations where residents can properly dispose of items such as hazardous waste
- A map of locations where residents can donate or buy used items.[19]

1.5.4 City West Water's Stormwater Harvesting Partnering Fund

In 2018, City West Water in Melbourne, Australia, launched its Stormwater Harvesting Partnering Fund to work with communities to develop meaningful projects that promote sustainable water management and reduce demand for potable water. The utility co-funded six projects that harvest up to 108 million litres of stormwater per year for the irrigation of sports grounds and public open spaces. In October 2020, the utility launched round two of the fund. The Dempster Park Stormwater Harvesting Scheme in Sunshine North is the first project to be co-funded in this new round. The scheme saves 11 million litres of stormwater run-off per annum as part of a new project to irrigate the park. The scheme captures stormwater in a 1.2-million-litre below-ground storage tank, where it is treated before irrigating the park and surrounds. A rain garden helps clean and filter the stormwater when it rains. The project is co-funded by various sources, including City West Water, the Brimbank City Council, the Victorian Government, and Melbourne Water.[20]

1.5.5 Berliner Wasserbetriebe Recovering Resources from Wastewater

Berliner Wasserbetriebe's Schönerlinde sewage treatment plant is turning sewage sludge into sewage gas to generate power and heat. Additionally, the utility has constructed three wind turbines, with a capacity of 2 MW each, as well as two micro gas turbines to complement the plant's combined heat and power unit. Overall, around 84 per cent of the energy required by the plant is produced internally, saving up to 13,000 tonnes of carbon emissions per year. Berliner Wasserbetriebe has also developed a patented process for recovering phosphorus from its sewage treatment plants. The recovered phosphorus is sold under the brand name Berliner Pflanze (Berliner Plant) to horticulture and agriculture producers in the surrounding areas of the city. Several years ago, Berliner Pflanze won the GreenTec Award for environmentally friendly recycling products. Berliner Plant is now available for purchase from the utility's customer centre in various sizes, with prices ranging from €2.50 to €28.00.[21]

2

Circular Urban Agriculture

Strategies for Sustainable Food Production in Growing Cities

ROBERT C. BREARS

2.1 Introduction

One of the largest challenges of the twenty-first century will be to feed an estimated nine billion people, many of whom will be residing in cities, while reducing the agricultural sector's footprint at the same time. Already, cities are dependent on large supplies of exogenous products, energy, and materials. Rapid urbanisation will further increase demand for basic goods, such as food products. Even with efficiency improvements within the food supply chain, the environmental footprint of food consumption in cities is expected to increase significantly. As such, urban agriculture, the growing of crops within cities for human consumption, could be one of the means for increasing global food supply without relying on further land clearing, utilising already cleared urban land and potentially preserving land in more natural rural areas.[1] Nevertheless, if urban agriculture follows the traditional linear model of resource use, it will lead to negative environmental impacts – including high concentrations of organic toxins, microbial contamination, and inorganic pollutants such as pesticides and heavy metals – in plants, soil, and irrigation waters. In addition, vertical farms are often energy-intensive.[2] In circular cities, urban agriculture can enhance resource efficiency, utilise waste streams, and limit the use and exhaustion of resources such as soil, energy, and fertiliser.[3] This chapter will first define the term urban agriculture before discussing the various technologies and best practices available that promote a circular city that ensures a safe and affordable supply of food while protecting and enhancing natural resources and ecosystem services and strengthening community relationships.

2.2 Urban Agriculture

Urban agriculture can be located within (urban) or on the fringe (peri-urban) of a town, city, or metropolis. Urban agriculture and peri-urban agriculture has been defined by the American Planning Association as 'the production, distribution, and marketing of food and other products within the cores of metropolitan areas (comprising community and school gardens; backyard and rooftop horticulture; and innovative food-production methods that maximise production in a small area) at their edges (including farms supplying urban farmers markets, community supported agriculture and family farms located in metropolitan green belts)'.[4] Urban agriculture includes:

- Crop production, animal raising, and fish-farming in and around cities
- Food production as well as non-food production (flowers, trees, pot plants, etc.)
- The processing and marketing of food and non-food products produced in and around the urban area
- Use of compost and (treated or untreated) urban wastewater as resources
- Use of open land areas in the city as well as backyards or rooftops.

2.2.1 Stakeholders in Urban Agriculture

There are numerous stakeholders who play a role in the production, processes, and marketing of food and other farming products within or near urban areas. Stakeholders in urban agriculture include:

- Urban farmers and all those involved with them in the production process and those who depend in any way on the results of this production
- Those who supply inputs, resources, and services to urban farmers
- Processors, distributors, marketers, and recyclers who deal with the outputs of urban farmers' activities
- Those who establish, modify, or implement the various frameworks (judicial, regulatory, political, economic, socio-cultural) that enable or hinder the activities of urban farmers, such as non-governmental organisations, community-based organisations, research institutes, local and national governments.[5]

2.2.2 Types of Urban Agriculture

There are various types of urban agriculture, including the following:

- *Community gardens*: These are smaller-scale urban agriculture sites (often serving a neighbourhood) where individuals and families grow food primarily for personal consumption or donations.
- *Forest gardening*: This is the practice of having gardens grown within an urban forest. Forest gardening is achieved by having different crops, vegetables, and fruits grown within urban settings. Forest gardens can be part of afforestation efforts.

- *Greenhouses*: This involves the practice of agriculture in residential, commercial, and communal urban spaces in greenhouses, which can require a substantial size of land depending on the crops being planted. Greenhouses give farmers the ability to grow a crop all year round as they provide a controlled environment where the crops can be subjected to specific conditions required for their growth.
- *Green walls*: The green wall can encompass the growing of vegetation or food crops on the external or internal surface of a wall. It does not require a lot of space as the mechanism used helps to supply the food with adequate water and it uses soil present on the walls.
- *Home gardens*: These are food-producing spaces on private residential property (multi-family or single-family occupancy) that are used primarily by the property's residents or guests.
- *Hydroponics*: Hydroponics is any system for growing plants without soil. Instead, nutrients are added to water that plants are immersed in, or that regularly washes over the roots of the plants. Gravel or other materials can be used to provide more physical support for the plants. Hydroponic systems can use chemical fertilisers or organic matter such as manure. As water in hydroponic systems is recycled and reused, it can save on water usage for growing crops.
- *Large*-scale *agro-enterprises*: Large-scale farms and agro-enterprises contribute to local economic development and urban food security at the city level. Large-scale agro-enterprises are either run by traditional farmers or by urban investors hiring a manager and labour to work the farm. Large-scale agro-enterprises consist of poultry, pigs, dairy, vegetables, mushrooms, nurseries, flowers, or aquaculture produced in large units. Production is fully geared towards the local, national, or even international market. They are mainly located in peri-urban areas around cities, in areas with good transport facilities, both for input supply and for marketing produce.
- *Micro-farming*: This is the growing of mainly vegetables, herbs, or medicinal plants on small areas in or on the house, such as a balcony, windowsill, cellar, barn, rooftop, or kitchen. Participating households include low- as well as medium- and high-income families, who grow their food or herbs for either subsistence or leisure or out of environmental awareness and interest in growing their own food.
- *Multifunctional farms*: Multifunctional urban agriculture combines different functions within an area. For instance, an urban farm may offer recreational and leisure services, such as pick-your-own farms, while in peri-urban areas, wineries and accommodation may be offered nearby. Social farming integrates social and healthcare services with agricultural activity, such as farms offering training and educational services; examples include children's education programmes and training for community residents, youth, women, and other groups.

- *Rooftop gardens*: Rooftop spaces can be easily utilised for cropping vegetables, fruits, and herbs. Rooftop gardens can also reduce the urban heat island effect, improve air quality, and beautify recreational facilities.
- *Small-scale farms*: Small-scale farms consist of land within city limits or on the edges of towns and cities that is owned, rented, or leased to farmers. They may be charitable or educational in nature or urban market gardens – commercial operations that grow food for sale.
- *Street landscaping*: This is the landscaping of streets for different uses such as community gardens, which are tended by the people in the neighbourhood. Their added advantage is their capability to reduce urban stormwater run-off.
- *Tactical gardens*: This involves using the limited space available to practise agriculture. For instance, an urban dweller may make a keyhole garden to cover a space that was intended for car parking in the street; putting the land to use that could have potentially gone to waste and instead creating an activity for leisure or to produce food.
- *Urban farms*: These are larger-scale, more intensive sites where food may be grown by an organisation or private enterprise, and often include entrepreneurial opportunities such as growing food for sale.
- *Vertical farms*: These involve farming upwards to reduce the agricultural land footprint. Green walls can be used as for vertical farms as they use minimal space.
- *Zfarming*: Zfarming, or zero-acreage farming, involves farming in or on urban structures. It is a recent trend that combines food production into the urban building design. Zfarming can take the form of rooftop gardens, edible walls, indoor farms, or vertical greenhouses.[6]

2.2.3 Multifunctionality of Urban Agriculture

Urban agriculture can provide multiple ecosystem services beyond the supply of food that it provides. Urban agriculture has the potential to prevent soil erosion, buffer against flooding and storm run-off through water retention by leaves and permeable surfaces and enhance pollination and seed dispersal by providing nutrients for bees and other pollinating insects. Urban agriculture can buffer against the urban heat island effect, with the temperature reduction depending on species composition and the leaf area. From the social perspective, urban agriculture enhances social inclusion, empowerment, and employment opportunities, reducing social inequalities exacerbated by urbanisation. Urban agriculture can improve human health and well-being, for instance, by providing leisure and recreational space for walking in urban agriculture landscapes and opportunities for education and youth development. Economically, urban agriculture provides market expansion for farmers, decreases food expenditures, and increases home values nearby.[7]

2.3 Water Conservation

Water use has been growing at more than twice the rate of population growth over the past century. In rapidly expanding urban centres, water has become scarce from climatic extremes and rising competition from various sectors. At the same time, substantial amounts of potable water in cities are lost to evaporation and run-off due to a lack of sustainable water management.

Lowering demand for water in urban agriculture reduces dependence on municipal water supplies and infrastructure and their related operational costs. In particular, sustainable water practices, such as drip irrigation, the recycling of wastewater for irrigation, and the capturing of rainwater and reuse of greywater decreases reliance on public water systems by providing supplemental water for non-potable uses. It also decreases the energy and chemical costs of treating potable water for non-potable uses. In addition, using the landscape to capture run-off fertilises the soil and creates sustainable gardens.

2.3.1 Improving Water Efficiency in Irrigation

Climatic conditions, soil type and structure, plant type, and irrigation techniques are some of the main factors that influence the efficiency and effectiveness of irrigation practices. The efficiency of water irrigation practices can be improved through crop type, irrigation scheduling, irrigation method, soil enhancement measures, and water source. More particularly:

- *Crop Water Needs*: Crops differ in terms of their daily water needs and the duration of their total growing period (crops with high daily needs and a long growing season require more water). As such, irrigation water needs can be reduced by selecting crop varieties with lower water demand that still provide sufficient added value.
- *Irrigation Scheduling*: Irrigation scheduling helps remove or reduce instances where too little or too much water is applied to crops. The timing and amount of water applied in irrigation is based on the water content in the crop root zone, the amount of water consumed by the crop since it was last irrigated, and the crop development stage.
- *Weather-based irrigation*: It is important to irrigate based on plant water needs. Weather-based irrigation controllers manage watering by automatically controlling how much and how often water needs to be delivered according to local

weather conditions. The systems sense precipitation and high humidity and will automatically shut off irrigation systems when they are not needed.

- *Irrigation Methods*: Three main irrigation methods can be selected to use available water effectively:
  - *Surface (or Gravity) Irrigation*: This involves the application of water by gravity flow to the surface of the field. There are different forms of surface irrigation, including basin irrigation, where the whole field is flooded with water, and furrow or border irrigation, where water is fed into small channels or strips of land.
  - *Sprinkler Irrigation*: Sprinkler irrigation systems imitate natural rainfall. Water is pumped through pipes and then sprayed onto the crops through rotating sprinkler heads. These systems are more efficient than surface irrigation, but they are more costly to install and operate because of the need for pressurised water. There are two main types: conventional sprinkler systems spray the water into the air, losing considerable amounts to evaporation, while low-energy precision application delivers water to the crops from drop tubes that extend from the sprinkler's arm, saving both water and energy compared to conventional systems.
  - *Drip Irrigation*: In urban and peri-urban agriculture, locally adapted small-scale irrigation methods are possible solutions for conserving water. Drip irrigation is the slow and accurate application of water to plants. Drip systems comprise a network of tubes and emitters that allow water to drip straight to plant roots at low volumes. They can be constructed from existing local products, such as pipes with holes in which water is dripped onto the soil above the root zone only. Potential irrigation efficiencies for drip systems are high, ranging up to 90 per cent. They also consume half as much water as sprinklers. Drip systems can be operated manually or with automatic scheduling controls. It is a highly efficient method because only the immediate root zone of each plant is wetted. The system also allows precise application of water-soluble fertilisers and other agricultural chemicals.
- *Soil Enhancement Measures*: Several soil enhancement measures can be considered to improve the efficiency of irrigation practices:
  - *Proper Field Levelling*: This allows the water to travel at an optimum speed, assisting in the uniform distribution of water and reducing run-off.
  - *Furrow Dyking*: This involves the capture of irrigation or precipitation water in small earthen dams within furrows.
  - *Crop Residue Management and Conservation Tillage*: Management of the amount, orientation, and distribution of crop and plant residues on the soil surface can lead to water savings. Such practices improve the ability of the soil to hold moisture, reduce run-off from the field, and reduce surface evaporation.[8]

2.3.2 Recycled Water

Wastewater is water polluted and degraded by several forms of waste, mainly coming from homes, industries, and agriculture. Domestic wastewater includes household materials, while industrial wastewater includes food pulps, papers, pharmaceuticals, chemicals, and heavy metals enriched with organic and inorganic contents. However, it can be reused in irrigation by eliminating pollutants, when it is called recycled water.[9]

The increased availability of wastewater from population growth and urbanisation, along with increased competition for water supplies, provides an opportunity to develop this resource for urban agriculture, particularly during times of drought when regular water supplies are limited or non-existent. The use of recycled water for irrigated crop production is controlled by regulations that govern the treated water quality, with lesser standards required for forage crops compared with those for food crops.

Overall, recycled water provides a year-round supply of water for urban agriculture, providing food, income, and employment opportunities to cities, while:

- Improving the urban landscape
- Reducing nutrient and contaminant loads in oceans and rivers
- Increasing the amount of potable water available for domestic uses, by replacing it in irrigation of crops and amenity horticulture
- Reducing stress on groundwater and rivers through the provision of alternative water supplies.[10]

2.3.2.1 Reuse of Wastewater

The reuse of municipal wastewater for irrigation is dependent on its chemical composition, which determines the methods and degree of treatment required. Furthermore, there are risks to human health and the environment due to the presence of pathogens. As such, effluents from municipal wastewater should undergo secondary treatment before use for irrigation.

Primary treatment involves the removal of suspended solid material from wastewater. Floating material such as wood, paper, and oil are removed first; otherwise, it will block the filters and pipes. Wastewater is then pushed into a grit chamber where sand and small stones settle to the bottom of the chamber. This process is common in areas with combined stormwater drainage and sewer systems because in these systems sand and gravel often wash into sewers after storm events. Following this, wastewater proceeds into primary settling tanks, where suspended solids settle as sludge for removal.

The secondary treatment process involves the removal of oxygen-demanding organic matter. This involves two types of processes: trickling filters and activated sludge systems. Wastewater is passed through trickling filters, which are beds filled with coarse material comprising rocks and gravel. As the wastewater passes through the beds, a microbial filter develops on the surface of the rocks and gravel trapping oxygen-demanding organic matter as the wastewater passes through. In the activated sludge system stage, the effluent is constantly agitated and aerated so that sludge forms. This sludge contains aerobic organisms that digest any remaining organic material. By this stage, the secondary treatment process has removed approximately 85 per cent of the organic matter in the wastewater, leaving only around 15 per cent before it is safely discharged into waterways.[11]

2.3.2.2 *Low-Cost Treatment Methods*

There are also many low-cost treatment methods for treating wastewater for reuse in urban agriculture, including small-bore sewerage systems. In low-density, unconnected neighbourhoods, small-bore sewerage provides an opportunity for evacuating waste at 20–50 per cent of the cost of traditional infrastructure. It also requires less water to function compared to conventional systems. Small-bore sewerage systems use 10-centimetre-wide plastic tubing to collect household waste and can collect as much as 80 litres per household per day.[12]

2.3.2.3 *Principles for the Safe Use of Wastewater for Urban Agriculture*

The development of programmes for the treatment and use of wastewater in urban agriculture means being able to manage health risks and to facilitate the adoption of appropriate technologies at the neighbourhood and municipal level. A set of principles should be followed for developing safe urban agricultural programmes that include the use of wastewater:

1. *Apply risk management strategies*: In many situations, wastewater is the only source of water for irrigation. When this is realised, guidelines and mechanisms should be put in place for reducing the health risks associated with the use of non-treated wastewater and at the same time promoting wastewater treatment:
   a. *Running education and political campaigns*: Educational campaigns targeted at awareness-raising and providing information to different actors are the most affordable and efficient way of disseminating information about strategies for managing health risks. These strategies include monitoring water quality, selecting appropriate crops, managing irrigation techniques effectively, and treating produce.
   b. *Monitoring water quality*: An ongoing process for monitoring water quality, soils, and products should be established.
   c. *Selecting crops*: It is important to consider the quality of wastewater to be used for irrigation when selecting crops to be planted, as there are many ways plants that can become contaminated with pathogens and heavy metals.

d. *Applying proper techniques for irrigation and treating products*: Appropriate irrigation practices include irrigation to roots to avoid direct contact with leaves and drip irrigation rather than flood irrigation to avoid excessive irrigation and the contamination of groundwater. Washing the products with clean water prior to their sale and avoiding contamination during food processing, transportation, and sale is of equal importance.

2. *Adopt appropriate technologies for the treatment of wastewater*: Wastewater treatment for farming or recreational uses should be promoted. The selection and investment in suitable technology for water treatment should result from an evaluation process that considers minimising pollution, costs, the scale of the operation (household, neighbourhood, city) and the quality of water needed for specific purposes.

   a. *Separating industrial outflow from household outflows*: The separation of household outflows from industrial flows reduces the contamination of water by heavy metals. Industrial parks need to have their own special treatment plants. The adoption of some industrial processes should be promoted (avoiding contamination during the process), as well as treatment at the source before discharging the water to the sewerage network in the city. Low-cost wastewater treatment technologies should also be explored to ensure effective on-site treatment for industries, minimising the burden on municipal wastewater systems and reducing overall environmental impact.

   b. *Selecting the technology for wastewater treatment*: The most interesting treatment options are those designed to eliminate pathogens while keeping nutrients, as do, for example:

      i. *Waste stabilisation ponds*: Waste stabilisation ponds use natural influences (wind, sun, gravity, and biological processes) to provide primary and secondary treatment over a period of days. Well-designed waste stabilisation ponds can achieve very high biological oxygen demand (BOD), nitrogen, and phosphorous removal rates. They provide a financially feasible and ready source of irrigation water. Their investment costs are as much as 80 per cent lower and the operation costs 90 per cent lower than more sophisticated technologies, such as aeration plants or those activated with mud. Nevertheless, these ponds are more suitable for peri-urban areas due to the large space required.

      ii. *Household greywater treatment and constructed wetlands*: Alternative sanitary treatments could also be used for treating sewage and greywater at the household or neighbourhood level. Constructed wetlands are an effective method for treating greywater and using the water as an irrigation supplement. A wetland is composed of a small pond in which water plants are grown. The plants use a combination of anaerobic and aerobic processes to break down organic matter. Constructed wetlands have an effective removal rate of BOD, total suspended solids, and nitrogen. There are many types and sizes of constructed wetlands depending on their purpose; however, the most appropriate in urban areas are sub-surface wetlands. In a sub-surface wetland, water drains into rocks and soil before being treated by the roots of a series of plants. Reed beds are best for use in wetlands as they are simple to maintain.

3. *Develop an enabling political framework*: The treatment and use of wastewater should be included in a coherent and pertinent legal and regulatory framework linked to physical planning. Developing new or reforming existing regulations (national or local) should be considered, such as sanitation, environmental, and agricultural legislation:
   a. *Coordinating the actors involved*: It is important to create mechanisms and opportunities for coordination and concentration between institutions in charge of regulations, the management of wastewater, and the final users.
   b. *Including wastewater treatment and use in municipal planning*: The location of water treatment systems should be determined in coordination with the planning and land management departments, taking into account:
      i. The quantity of land required
      ii. The relationship between where water treatment takes place and where it is used
      iii. Future urban development.
4. *Determin the financial sustainability of wastewater treatment and use*: For water treatment plants to be financially sustainable, wastewater treatment and use systems need to be integrated. All the costs involved in the implementation of these systems need to be calculated, as well as their direct and indirect benefits. Finally, it is important to determine who will be responsible for covering the cost of the treatment and use of wastewater:
   a. *Conducting a cost–benefit analysis*: It is necessary to consider installation, operation, and maintenance costs of the water treatment systems, as well as the benefits of using treated water. The benefits could be direct (income generated through farming) and indirect (savings from using less potable water and fewer fertilisers).
   b. *Determining the cost of wastewater treatment and use*: The application of the 'polluter pays' principle should be adopted as a priority. The industry and the urban population should assume the cost of treating the wastewater they produce. Farmers, on the other hand, should pay for the use of treated water, just as they pay for potable water.[13]

Table 2.1 *Queensland Urban Utilities' recycled water pricing*

Class (all regions)	Price per kL (AUD)
Class A	$1.401
Class B	$1.293
Class C	$0.120

2.3.3 Case Study: Fit-for-Purpose Recycled Water in Queensland

Queensland Urban Utilities' recycled water programme is a fit-for-purpose programme that offers various qualities, or classes, of recycled water to meet customers' requirements, with the price per kilolitre (kL) decreasing with quality (Table 2.1). Examples of different purposes include irrigation of sporting fields or golf courses with controlled public access, washing down of hard surfaces in agriculture industries, irrigation of pastures or fodder crops, irrigation of other non-food crops, irrigation of nurseries or forestry plantations, and below-ground irrigation of above-ground food crops. Under the programme there are four classes of recycled water:

- *Class A+ recycled water*: This is very highly treated recycled water. This class is usually only required for industrial process water or for the irrigation of minimally processed food crops.
- *Classes A and B recycled water*: This usually requires additional treatment processes above the normal sewage treatment processes that are sufficient to allow effluent to be discharged to the environment.
- *Class C recycled water*: This is the lowest quality of recycled water supplied by Queensland Urban Utilities. This quality is generally produced as a result of the requirements for effluent discharge to the environment, as contained within the sewage treatment plant environmental licences. This class can often be supplied directly without any additional treatment.[14]

2.3.4 Case Study: Whittlesea Community Farm

Yarra Valley Water in Victoria, Australia, is currently planning the development of the Whittlesea Community Farm alongside its Aurora recycled water treatment plant at Wollert. With a Victorian Government grant of AUD $1.5 million, Yarra Valley Water is providing land, recycled water, and renewable energy for the farm, which is being developed in partnership with the City of Whittlesea, Melbourne Polytechnic, and Whittlesea Community Connections.

The vision is to create a farming enterprise and community food hub which uses best practices in sustainable agriculture and demonstrates the circular economy in action. In particular, the hub will provide food for distribution into the local emergency relief network and provide volunteering, education, and employment opportunities in best practice sustainable agriculture systems for peri-urban areas.[15]

2.4 Water Harvesting and Greywater

Water harvesting captures rainwater and stormwater run-off for later use, decreasing the need to use costly and energy-intensive potable water. Rainwater harvesting provides water for various uses, including irrigation. In addition, greywater (water from sinks, showers, and washing machines) can be used for landscapes.

2.4.1 Rainwater Harvesting

Rainwater harvesting systems collect and store rainfall for later use. When designed appropriately, they slow down and reduce run-off and provide a source of water. There are two main types of rainwater harvesting systems:

- *Passive harvesting systems*: They are typically small volume (190–380-litre) systems designed to capture rooftop run-off. Rain barrels are usually used in residential applications where the flow from rain gutter downpipes is easily captured for outdoor use, for example, garden and landscape irrigation.
- *Active harvesting systems*: They are larger-volume (typically 3,800–380,000-litre) systems, for example, cisterns, which capture run-off from roofs or other suitable surfaces. Rainwater collected in active systems is typically used for irrigation.[16]

2.4.2 Greywater

Greywater refers to the wastewater generated from household uses such as washing clothes. This wastewater is distinguished from 'black water', or sewage, from toilets. Typically, greywater is combined with sewage in a single domestic wastewater stream. However, greywater can be of higher quality than sewage due to its low level of contamination and higher potential for reuse. When greywater is used on-site, it reduces the demand on new supplies of water. A greywater system captures water that has been lightly used but has not come into contact with high levels of contamination, for example, sewage or food waste. Water used for showers, clothes washing machines, or bathroom sinks can be diverted for outdoor irrigation. As a result, demand for potable water for irrigation is reduced.[17]

2.4.3 Swales and Basins

Swales and basins can facilitate water capture. A site's topography can be assessed for low-lying areas that can collect run-off. Developing swales and basins requires digging trenches and at times moulding raised beds (berms) along the contour of the landscape. When it rains, water is captured in the trenches and remains on the surface for a few hours while it slowly percolates into the soil. Swales and basins provide a less complex system for rainwater capture and can be dug between garden beds and trees. The harvested water is filtered as it seeps into the soil and recharges the groundwater in the garden. The slowing and retention of water on-site promotes increased root growth, improving plants' drought tolerance and increasing crop yields.[18]

2.4.4 Case Study: San Francisco Public Utilities Commission's Laundry-to-landscape Graywater Program

San Francisco Public Utilities Commission (SFPUC) has developed a laundry-to-landscape (L2L) greywater programme and a rebate to encourage the uptake of greywater systems.

SFPUC's L2L Graywater Program, in partnership with Urban Farmer Store, offers residents a USD $125 discount off the purchase of an L2L greywater kit (retail cost $175). The kit includes the basic components to divert water from washing machines to gardens, with participants also receiving:

- A copy of the *San Francisco Graywater Design Manual for Outdoor Irrigation*
- Optional on-site consultation with a greywater expert
- Mandatory training to review the design, installation, and maintenance requirements of an L2L greywater system
- Access to a free tool kit for do-it-yourself installation.

For greywater projects that require a permit from the Department of Building Inspection (required for all other greywater systems except L2L), SFPUC's Graywater Permit Rebate Program offers a rebate up to $225 to help cover the costs of the permit. The rebate is available for residential greywater systems with sub-surface irrigation.[19]

2.4.5 Case Study: New York City's Largest Rooftop Garden

Brooklyn Grange recently opened its third rooftop farm to date, which is also the largest rooftop farm in New York City. The 13,000-square-metre farm is located on the rooftop of the Liberty View building in Sunset Park, Brooklyn, and has the capacity to manage over 660,000 litres of stormwater in a single rainfall. The farm produces around 13,600 kilograms of vegetables each year, and the project was made possible with a USD $1.38 million grant from the New York City Department of Environmental Protection's Green Infrastructure Grant Program. Brooklyn Grange has been a leader in the integration of green infrastructure into the city, with a focus on using green roofs and rooftop farms to improve local waterways. The Sunset Park farm includes 5,100 square metres of cultivated space and features bluestone paved walkways, Skypaver brick pathways made from 95 per cent post-consumer recycled materials, and a 450-square-metre greenhouse fitted with a hydroponic growing system. The second phase of the project will include a 560-square-metre indoor events hall and sustainability centre.[20]

2.5 Resource Recovery and Urban Agriculture

Cities depend on regional and global areas for the supply of water, energy, nutrients, and materials, and the disposal of waste, making them hotspots of resource conversion. Currently, this conversion follows a linear model, and few resources are recovered for reuse. As such, there is potential for cities to reduce resource consumption and recover resources from wastewater for urban agriculture.[21]

2.5.1 Phosphorous and Struvite

Phosphorous is a macronutrient essential for plant growth. Since only a small fraction of phosphorous content in soil is readily available to plants, it needs to be artificially added through mineral fertilisers to sustain global food production. Currently, phosphorous is obtained from phosphate rocks, with 80 per cent of the available stock used in the production of fertilisers. As phosphorous is renewed in a scale of geologic time, mineral phosphorous resources are likely to be depleted in the twenty-first century. Since 2014, the European Union has recognised phosphorous as a critical resource and encourages phosphorus recovery from local sources.[22]

Humans excrete around three million metric tonnes of phosphorous per annum, the equivalent of 20 per cent of annual global phosphate fertiliser consumption. In urban areas, wastewater treatment plants are beginning to recover phosphorous, which can be applied to urban agricultural land. Phosphorous can be recovered from wastewater in different forms, with magnesium ammonium phosphate, commonly called struvite, being the most prominent. Spontaneous struvite crystallisation is problematic in wastewater treatment plants, particularly after anaerobic digestion, with it commonly creating a layer on the surface of pumps, centrifuges, and pipes, reducing operational efficiency and increasing maintenance costs. Studies have shown that struvite's fertiliser efficiency is like conventional fertilisers.[23]

2.5.2 Sewage Sludge to Biosolids

A challenge of urban agriculture is compromised soils from disturbances, including compaction, topsoil removal, or loss of vegetation. The result is urban soil softening, resulting in reduced water-holding capacity and infiltration, low organic matter and nutrient availability, modified microorganic activity, and higher pH values from additives in cement and road salts. Also, urban soils often contain elevated concentrations of lead due to historic use of leaded gasoline and lead paint.

Organic amendments, such as biosolids, can help restore urban degraded soils and improve plant-growing conditions. Biosolids usually have around four per cent nitrogen, which is released slowly over time. Biosolids also contain phosphorous and many micronutrients that are beneficial to crop growth. Also, increasing soil organic matter using soil amendments increases the water-holding capacity and infiltration rates and reduces bulk density. Furthermore, biosolids typically have concentrations of lead in an order of magnitude lower than those present in urban soils.

Exceptional Quality (EQ) is a term used in the wastewater industry to describe biosolids that have undergone advanced treatment to eliminate pathogens, reduce vectors, and lower concentrations of pollutants. Common processes include composting, thermal drying, pasteurisation, and thermal hydrolysis in addition to anaerobic digestion, resulting in Class A biosolids. Some EQ biosolids are mixed with sources of dry organic material, a mineral matter, or both to reduce moisture content, enhance structure, and improve ease of spreading in urban areas. Biosolids have been used successfully for many years in agriculture and forestry. Table 2.2 provides an overview of the applications of biosolids in urban soils.[24]

Table 2.2 *Applications of biosolids and urban soils*

Biosolids application		Examples

Soil improvement	Carbon	• Increased soil organic matter
		• Improved physical properties
		  o Decreased bulk density
		  o Increased water-holding capacity

	Nutrients	• Increased nitrogen and phosphorous • Long-term release
	Contaminants	• Reduced concentrations of lead • Reduced bioaccessibility of lead, arsenic, etc.
Growth media/ response – biosolids blends/composts	Urban trees	• As a soil amendment • As a container media
	Vegetables	• Reduced contaminant (lead) • Equal or superior growth response

2.5.3 Case Study: City of Saskatoon's Nutrient Recovery Facility

The City of Saskatoon's Nutrient Recovery Facility at the Wastewater Treatment Plant, which began operations in 2013, is the first Canadian site to feature the patented Ostara technology. This technology eliminates the build-up of cement-like material (struvite) in wastewater treatment equipment and pipes, preventing significant recurring maintenance and repair costs. The facility recovers phosphorous and nitrogen from wastewater and converts them into a highly pure, slow-release, environmentally friendly fertiliser called Crystal Green®. The city produces 240–350 tonnes of fertiliser annually, which is distributed by Ostara, generating an ongoing revenue stream. Crystal Green® is an all-in-one fertiliser containing magnesium, phosphorous, and nitrogen, with slow-release properties that reduce leaching and run-off. It can be blended with other fertiliser products and soil types for application on turf grass, golf courses, and high-value crops including berries and fruit trees.[25]

2.5.4 Case Study: DC Water's Bloom Initiative

Bloom is brand name for the District of Columbia Water and Sewer Authority's (DC Water) EPA-certified EQ biosolids product. At DC Water's Blue Plains Advanced Wastewater Treatment Plant, solid materials are separated from liquid and sent to DC Water's new state-of-the-art thermal hydrolysis process and anaerobic digesters. From there, heat, pressure, and helpful bacteria remove harmful pathogens and reduce odour. The output is Bloom, a biosolid product that can be used in any area, from large farms to backyard gardens and lawns. Currently, Bloom is on sale for USD $3.50 per cubic yard, providing additional revenue for DC Water, which helps offset the need for tariff increases for its customers. There are various varieties of Bloom available:

- *Fresh*: Fresh Bloom is DC Water's Class A EQ biosolids product. It has been dewatered and contains about 30 per cent solids. Considered a favourite of farmers, soil blenders and contractors, Fresh Bloom is sold in bulk by DC Water.
- *Woody Blend*: The Woody Blend, made at the Blue Plains facility, is 50 per cent Fresh Bloom and 50 per cent hardwood fines, and is an all-purpose soil amendment.
- *Sandy Blend*: Sandy Blend is an all-purpose, high performing blend for top-dressing lawns and more, sold in bulk from Blue Plains and select resellers.
- *Cured Bloom*: This is the same high-quality product as the other Bloom varieties but dried to a potting soil-like consistency, making it easier to handle. It is available in bags and bulk through select retailers in the Washington metropolitan area.[26]

2.6 Conclusion

As the twenty-first century faces the immense challenge of feeding an estimated nine billion people amidst rapid urbanisation, urban agriculture emerges as a potential solution for increasing global food supply without further land clearing and potentially preserving natural rural areas. However, adopting a circular approach is crucial in order to avoid the negative environmental impacts associated with traditional linear resource-use models.

Urban agriculture, encompassing a wide array of practices, holds significant promise for sustainable urban development, offering various environmental, social, and economic benefits. Effective water management practices and the use of recycled water can greatly enhance sustainability, reducing dependence on municipal water supplies and operational costs. Ensuring the safe use of wastewater in urban agriculture requires risk management strategies, appropriate treatment technologies, and enabling political frameworks.

Examples such as Queensland Urban Utilities' recycled water programme and the Whittlesea Community Farm demonstrate innovative approaches to sustainable water use in urban agriculture. Furthermore, rainwater harvesting and greywater systems present valuable water management solutions for urban agriculture, as showcased by the Brooklyn Grange rooftop garden.

Lastly, the recovery from wastewater of resources such as phosphorous and biosolids can contribute to sustainable resource management in urban agriculture. Initiatives like the City of Saskatoon's Nutrient Recovery Facility and DC Water's Bloom project exemplify successful resource recovery and the creation of environmentally friendly fertilisers for urban agriculture.

In conclusion, urban agriculture has the potential to play a crucial role in addressing the challenge of feeding a growing global population while minimising the agricultural sector's environmental footprint. By adopting circular approaches and implementing best practices, cities can harness the power of urban agriculture to ensure a safe and affordable food supply, protect and enhance natural resources, and strengthen community relationships.

3

Urban Water Demand Management

ROBERT C. BREARS

3.1 Introduction

In traditional water resources management, urban water managers forecast population growth and economic development to determine future levels of demand. If there is a projected supply deficit (demand outstripping supply), traditional water management relies on large-scale water supply projects consisting of dams, reservoirs, and pipelines to transport water over large distances to bridge that gap or store it to balance allocation across wet and dry seasons. Over time, however, these supply-side solutions can generate cost overruns and large environmental costs; for instance, dams and reservoirs impact the quantity and quality of water available for ecosystems, adversely impacting the numerous services on which both humans and nature rely for their survival. There are also significant economic costs involved in supply-side solutions; in particular, the reliance on more distant water, often of inferior quality, to meet rising demand increases not only the costs of transportation (energy costs) but treatment (chemical) costs too. Politically, water scarcity is likely to lead to inter-user, inter-sectoral, inter-regional, and international competition, or even conflict over scarce water resources as aquifers, rivers, lakes, and even entire river basins frequently cross internal and external political boundaries. Without ongoing dialogue and cooperation between municipalities, regions, and states, unilateral actions, such as water abstractions, can significantly impact water resources in neighbouring local, regional, or national jurisdictions. In addition to these challenges, traditional water resources management faces significant challenges arising from the deep uncertainty in supply from climate change extremes (floods and droughts) and changing weather patterns (spatial and temporal changes in precipitation). As such, with increased demand for water from urbanisation and variability of supply from climate change, traditional water management practices have become outdated, impacting urban water security.

While urban and industrial use accounts for a relatively small proportion of total water use in comparison to agriculture, urbanisation and socio-economic development are expected to increase urban industrial and domestic water demand by 50–80 per cent over the next three decades. In addition, climate change will affect the spatial distribution and timing of water availability. As a result, there is a need to improve the management of this and reduce the demand,[1] as a failure to do so may comprise the achievement of the United Nations Sustainable Development Goals (SDGs), particularly SDG11 Sustainable Cities and Communities and SDG6 Clean Water and Sanitation.[2] In addition, urban water scarcity will increase competition between cities and agriculture for water.

As such, urban water managers can implement demand management to radically change people's culture, attitudes, and practices towards water and manage consumption patterns, with the eventual goal of decoupling water consumption from economic and population growth. Urban demand management will thus be integral to coordinating water use across the urban and agricultural sectors and preventing conflicts over allocation of water resources. This chapter discusses the concept of water security and the challenges of achieving it in an urban context. The chapter then discusses what a transition to a new water system is. Finally, it reviews the various urban demand management instruments available.

3.2 Water Security

The United Nations has defined water security as the 'capacity of a population to safeguard sustainable access to adequate quantities of acceptable quality water for sustaining livelihoods, human well-being and socio-economic development, for ensuring protection against water-borne pollution and water-related disasters, and for preserving ecosystems in a climate of peace and political stability'.[3] Nonetheless, achieving water security is not a static goal; instead, it is an ever-changing continuum that alters with numerous challenges.[4] Therefore, future water security depends on meeting increased demand and how effectively humans can use limited water resources to meet these needs.[5] However, urban water security is at risk worldwide (Table 3.1).[6]

Globally, 933 million (32.5%) of urban residents lived in water-scarce regions in 2016. Of the world's 526 large cities (with a population of over 1 million), 193 (36.7%) were located in water-scarce regions. Of the 30 mega-cities (urban areas with a population of 10 million or more), 9 (30%) were located in water-scarce regions. By 2050, the urban population facing water scarcity is projected to increase rapidly to 2.065 billion people, a 121.3% increase from 2016. By the same point, the number of large cities facing water scarcity is projected to increase

Table 3.1 *Climatic and non-climatic challenges to urban water security*

Challenge	Trend
Climate change	• For each 1 degree Celsius of global warming, 7% of the world's population is exposed to a decrease in renewable water resources of at least 20%. • Already, more than two billion people live in countries experiencing high water stress.
Population growth	• By 2050, the world's population is expected to reach 9.7 billion, up from 7.7 billion in 2019. Already, 47% of people live in areas that suffer water scarcity at least one month a year. By 2050, it is estimated that this figure will rise to 52%. • During the mid-2010s, 1.9 billion people lived in potentially water-scarce areas. In 2050, this number will increase to between 2.7 and 3.2 billion. • Groundwater is under pressure from rising populations, with more than 30% of the world's largest groundwater systems already in distress.
Urbanisation	• Globally, 55% of the world's population resided in urban areas in 2018, up from 30% in 1950. By 2050, it is projected that 68% of the world's population will be urban. • Urbanisation has already led to increased competition between cities and agriculture for water, with 69 cities, representing a total population of 383 million people, currently receiving around 16 billion cubic metres of reallocated water per annum, and 21 cities relying on multiple water reallocation projects. • Around 40% of the land in urban source watersheds of the world's largest cities show moderate to high levels of degradation, impacting the present and future quality and reliability of water flows.
Rapid economic growth	• Global gross domestic product is projected to quadruple between 2011 and 2060. By 2050, global demand for water for manufacturing, thermal electricity generation, and domestic use will have increased by 400%, 140%, and 130%, respectively. • Overall, 78% of all jobs in the world are dependent on water.
Water–Energy Nexus	• The energy sector currently accounts for around 15% of global water withdrawals. Global energy demand is projected to increase by approximately 27% between 2017 and 2040. • By 2040 the amount of energy used in the water sector will more than double, with the most substantial increase coming from desalination, followed by large-scale water transfer and increasing demand for wastewater treatment, as well as higher levels of treatment.
Water–Food Nexus	• With the world's population expected to reach nine billion people by 2050, demand for food will increase by 60% from 2025 levels. • Currently, agriculture accounts for 70% of all water withdrawn from aquifers, streams, and lakes. • The global area equipped for irrigation is expanding by 0.6% per annum. Almost 40% of the irrigated area relies on groundwater as either a primary source or in conjunction with surface water.

to 292 (55.5%), and the number of mega-cities facing water scarcity is likely to increase to 19 (63.3%).[7] Growth in urban population and water demand are the main factors contributing to the increase in urban water scarcity. Between 2016 and 2050, population growth, urbanisation, and socio-economic development are projected to increase water demand and contribute to an additional 0.990 billion people facing urban water scarcity. Climate change is projected to increase the urban population subject to water scarcity by 52 million people.[8]

3.3 Urban Demand Management

Urban demand management is a process in which ideas, norms and innovations of water conservation are communicated across water users in a community so as to change water users' attitudes, culture, and practices towards water and reduce consumption patterns to achieve a targeted level of water consumption.[9] Overall, demand management involves the better use of existing water supplies before plans are made to increase supply by promoting water conservation during times of both normal conditions and uncertainty.[10] While urban demand management promotes water conservation and water efficiency, it can also support other high-level goals, such as improving livelihoods in low-income communities, reducing energy consumption and greenhouse gas emissions, or improving the environmental flows of water bodies. In addition to the environmental benefits of preserving ecosystems and their habitats, urban demand management is more cost-effective than supply-side management. It allows the more efficient allocation of scarce financial resources (which would otherwise be required to build expensive dams and water transfer schemes from one river basin to another). Finally, urban demand management ensures the equitable use of water by all users (homes, industry, recreation, electricity, agriculture, nature, etc.).[11]

Urban demand management increases urban water security by:

- Reducing the loss and misuse in various water sectors (intra-sector efficiency)
- Optimising water use by assuring a reasonable allocation between various users (cross-sectoral efficiency) while taking into account the supply needs of downstream ecosystems and in situ uses of water such as recreation, fisheries, agriculture, and energy production
- Facilitating significant financial and infrastructural savings for countries, cities, companies, and users by minimising the need to meet increasing demand with new water supplies
- Reducing the stress on water resources by reducing or halting unsustainable exploitation of water resources
- Developing alternative water supplies as a means of diversification.[12]

3.3.1 Demand Management Strategies

Urban water managers can use two types of demand management strategies to modify attitudes, culture, and practices towards water: Antecedent strategies attempt to influence the determinants of target behaviour prior to the performance of the behaviour. Consequential strategies attempt to influence the determinants of target behaviour after the performance of the behaviour. This assumes that positive and negative feedback of the consequences of that behaviour will influence the likelihood of the behaviour happening or not happening in the future.[13]

3.3.2 Demand Management Instruments

Water managers can use two types of demand management instruments to influence the norms and values of society towards water resources (Table 3.2):

- *Regulatory and technological instruments:* Regulatory instruments are frequently used to manage water and involve setting allocation and water-use limits. Regulatory instruments are frequently combined with technological instruments to incentivise all water users to conserve water, use it efficiently, and avoid pollution.
- *Communication and information instruments:* These encourage a water-oriented society. Information is an important tool for changing behaviour through public awareness campaigns, school curricula, university water courses, and professional training. Transparency of water resources data and product labelling of water efficient appliances and practices are other key social change instruments.[14]

Table 3.2 *Demand management instrument examples*

Demand management instruments	Examples
Regulatory and technological	*Regulatory* • Direct controls, including regulations, land-use plans • Economic instruments, for example, prices, tariffs, subsidies, fees, taxes • Self-regulation, for instance, transparent benchmarking, product labelling *Technological* • Research and development • Efficiency guidelines • Improving water supply infrastructure
Communication and information	Raising awareness of the need for water conservation Informed stakeholder participation

3.4 Regulatory and Technological Urban Demand Management Instruments

Regulatory and technological instruments are frequently used in water management and involve setting allocations and water-use limits. In addition, regulatory and technological instruments provide incentives for all water users to conserve water and use it efficiently.

3.4.1 Pricing

Pricing water and water-related services is an essential mechanism for managing demand, promoting the efficient use of water, and allocating water among competing uses. Various pricing structures are available, including the following:

- *Fixed tariff*: A flat fee, independent of consumption. It can be uniform across customers or linked to a customer characteristic, for example, property value. There is no need for metering, and it does not encourage water-use efficiency.
- *Volumetric tariff*: Customers pay a fixed per-unit price, multiplied by the volume of water consumed in a charging period. It requires metering and encourages water-use efficiency. Nevertheless, the poor may not be able to moderate water demand, and a decrease in consumption reduces the revenues of water utilities and may hamper cost recovery.
- *Volumetric rates combined with recurrent fixed charges*: A single rate per cubic metre is applied regardless of volume consumed. It requires metering and data on household income. The fixed charge can be uniform or differentiated. It secures recovery of utilities' fixed costs and enables coupons to be provided to low-income families. However, the complexity can make it more costly to administer than a simple volumetric tariff.
- *Increasing block tariffs*: The volumetric charge changes in steps with volume consumed. It requires metering at the household level, data on household wealth, composition, and water use to design tariff blocks and subsidies. Theoretically, it promotes water-use efficiency and ensures that poor households have access to a basic amount of water at free or affordable rates. Nevertheless, poorer households are often larger and may consume more water than wealthier ones, potentially placing them in higher tariff blocks. Lack of metering at the household level or insufficient household data can hamper successful design. Furthermore, households often have difficulty understanding the tariff structure, hindering the expected reaction to the price signal.[15]

3.4.2 Water Trading

Water trading is a policy tool for reallocating water to higher-value uses. Globally, water markets are well established and operate in a number of water systems. For instance, surface-water trading can take place in the form of annual leases of irrigation water, particularly during times of drought to meet municipal industrial water supply deficits. Groundwater trading can reallocate water away from water-intensive agriculture and toward meeting growing urban demand.[16] In urban settings, hybrid water systems utilise locally occurring water sources for collecting and using water within a discrete boundary, reducing potable water demand. Alternative water technologies, such as greywater and rainwater collection systems, reduce pressure on groundwater resources and essential infrastructure, and on the maintenance costs of existing water systems. Hybrid water systems can bring about the creation of a water trading market, with excess water traded with peers, either physically or via a 'credit–debit' scheme.[17] Overall, some of the hydrological, institutional, and economic preconditions for the effective and efficient trading of water include:

- The consumptive share of a system is close to full allocation or is fully allocated, and this cap is able to be enforced
- Hydrological and system type, which covers
  The availability of water (for example, rainfall variability, groundwater level)
  - Connectivity – the number of users for whom trade is hydrologically feasible and the degree that a system is primarily surface water, groundwater, or an interconnected combination of both
  - Presence of structures such as dams, weirs, and offtakes that regulate flows and store water
- Existing institutional, planning, and property right arrangements, including seasonal allocation processes and enforceable access rights
- Favourable economic factors that influence the possibility for trade, including:
  - Sufficient numbers of users and heterogeneous water use
  - Changes in other markets that lead to adjustments in the activities of businesses using or trading water.[18]

3.4.3 Water Metering

Before water users can be charged for the amount of water they use, the dwelling or building must have water meters to measure the volume of water consumed. Automatic meter readers are 'one-way' automated meter readers that send usage data back to the utility. In comparison, advanced metering infrastructure (AMI) is a 'two-way' solution that creates a network between the meters and the utility's information system. Data flow both ways, facilitating not only remote meter reading but also, for example, enhanced conservation awareness programmes. Specifically, AMI smart meters target the management and extraction of useful information from large amounts of high-resolution consumption data. From the utility side, smart meters provide many benefits, including leakage detection/energy reduction, demand forecasting, enhanced conservation awareness campaigns, promotion of efficient appliances, variable water pricing/tariffs, a case for investment, and performance indicators. On the customer side, smart meters provide many benefits, including information on where/when water is used, comparing water consumption against other customers, leakage detection, and calculating associated energy consumption. Consumption-based feedback encourages water conservation behaviours via smart meters with in-home displays, reducing water consumption by around six to eight per cent.[19] For example, in 2021 the Punjab Public Private Partnership Authority in Pakistan approved the installation of smart meters for water users in the provincial metropolis. The partnership model was approved at 17 per cent less than the estimated cost and will involve the installation of 711,265 water meters. Currently, most water customers receive fixed bills. Installing meters will significantly lower the average consumer's water bill, which will, in turn, reduce electricity costs and help conserve groundwater.[20]

3.4.4 Active Leak Detection

In many distribution systems, up to half of the water supplied by the water treatment plant is lost to leakage. A significant proportion of the leaks occurring in a water distribution network do not reach the ground surface. These leaks can be detected by applying a range of active leakage control strategies, including:

- Analysing changes in minimum night flow
- Setting flat-line alarm levels at crucial monitoring locations in a water distribution network, allowing near real-time identification of, usually, large bursts
- Using hydraulic sensor technology with utilities deploying many pressure and flow devices, with data coming from such devices; when used in combination with predictions of the water distribution network behaviour by hydraulic modelling, this has the potential to enable fast detection and location of pipe bursts
- Using machine learning – a subset of artificial intelligence that helps derive meaning from data generated by people, devices, and smart systems, etc. – to predict pipe failure.

A water utility can improve the management and rehabilitation of its water distribution network with a well-planned maintenance programme based on sound knowledge of the distribution network. This knowledge is usually embodied in a distribution system database that includes the following data:

- An inventory of the characteristics of the system components
- A record of regular inspections of the network, including the condition of the mains and degree of corrosion
- An inventory of soil conditions and types, including the chemical characteristics of the soils
- A record of the quality of the product water in the system
- A record of any high- or low-pressure problems in the network
- Operating records, such as pump and valve operations, failures, leaks, and maintenance and rehabilitation costs
- A file of customer complaints
- Metering data.[21]

For example, the Phnom Penh Water Supply Authority (PPWSA) has a non-revenue water (NRW) rate of around seven per cent, which is one of the lowest rates in the world. To reduce leakage, as well as energy required in treating water to potable standards – nearly 45 per cent of the PPWSA's operating cost is attributed to energy consumption – the Authority has installed a telemeter system that detects high leakages and illegal connections in different zones of the water supply system. To detect leakages more efficiently, the city has been divided into 58 sub-zones, each with its own local leak detection system. To ensure leaks are fixed rapidly, the utility has leak repair teams on standby that operate 24/7, with the response time being two hours after a leak is detected. To ensure the utility is proactive in detecting leaks, the PPWSA has established leak detection teams that are offered incentives to find leaks throughout the water supply system; to become more efficient in its operations, incentives have become an important element of the PPWSA's staff remuneration. At the end of each year the PPWSA's NRW Committee reviews all leakage work and analyses each leak detection team's performance. The most efficient teams – based on the ratio of leaks at the start of the year compared with the end of the year – are rewarded monetarily, with some technicians having received rewards of up to 25 per cent of their annual salaries.[22]

3.4.5 Subsidies

Subsidies are a subset of funding flows between governments, service providers, and customers. Subsidies occur when a user/customer pays less for a product or service than the service provider's cost, leaving a third party, such as a government, responsible for covering the difference. Subsidies can take the form of explicit financial transfers (for example, between a utility and a customer) or implicit transfers (when products, services, or inputs are underpriced). Governments subsidise water supply and sanitation (WSS) services to achieve various policy objectives, mainly advancing equitable access to affordable WSS services and to harness the positive externalities associated with WSS services.[23] Nonetheless, around the world, water-related subsidies commonly fail to achieve their objectives due to poor design; they tend to be pervasive, only serving political interests, expensive, poorly targeted, non-transparent, and distortionary.[24] Therefore, the following principles should be followed to ensure subsidies result in all people benefitting from WSS services:

- *Subsidies should achieve the intended policy outcome*: Subsidies require a smart design and clarity about what the policy objectives and short- and long-term objectives are.
- *Subsidies should reach the intended target groups*: They require clarity on who is the intended target group and how they can best be reached. They also require rigorous monitoring to track how they are reaching the intended groups.
- *Subsidies should be clearly communicated*: It is essential that a communications strategy is developed to help people understand the benefits of the subsidy and how these link to their own lives.
- *Subsidies should be financially sustainable*: A thorough understanding of the programme's potential costs is required. Costs include both upfront capital costs and long-term operational and maintenance costs.
- *Subsidies should integrate local peoples' needs*: To guarantee the sustainability of the subsidised water technology, it is of prime importance to facilitate the integration and participation of the local beneficiaries and to develop a sense of ownership towards the new infrastructure.
- *Subsidies should be implemented clearly and transparently*: As subsidies involve public funds, subsidy programmes need to be clear and transparent, enabling eligible households or communities to access them and providing clear recourse mechanisms in cases where there is a suggestion of impropriety.[25]

3.4.6 Water Restrictions

There are two types of water restrictions available to mitigate water source depletion and degradation and ensure environmental water needs are met:

- *Temporary restrictions*: These are enacted to restrict certain types of water use during specified times and/or restrict the level of water use to a specified amount. These programmes are usually adopted during times of severe water shortages and cease once the shortage has passed.
- *Permanent water restrictions*: These include amendments to building codes or ordinances requiring the installation of water-saving devices in new developments or retrofits.[26]

3.4.7 Source Water Protection

Source water protection includes a variety of actions and activities that aim to safeguard, maintain, or improve the quality and/or quantity of sources for drinking water and their contributing areas. Examples of source water protection include riparian zone restoration; land protection/conservation easements; best management practices for agriculture and forestry activities or stormwater control; local ordinances to limit certain activities in source water or wellhead protection areas; and educating the local industry, businesses, and communities on pollution prevention and source water protection.[27] Protecting source water from contamination helps reduce treatment costs and may avoid the need for developing new sources of supply.[28] For example, if the current scale of forest restoration is increased three-fold in California, there could be up to a six per cent increase in the mean annual streamflow for individual watersheds. In the Feather River, the watershed that is the major source of the state's water needs and that provides nearly all the water delivered by the California State Water Project, forest restoration may produce between approximately 120 million and 352 million cubic metres of additional run-off.[29]

3.4.8 Developing Alternative Supplies

Developing alternative water supplies enables water utilities to provide a reliable, climate-resilient, and economically sound source of water for non-potable and potable uses.[30] At the building level, the use of alternative supplies can lead to a nearly 70 per cent reduction in demand for municipal water if supplementary water is used for non-potable uses.[31] Alternative water supplies include:

- *Rainwater harvesting systems*: These systems collect precipitation running off roof surfaces into cisterns or other storage vessels. They are particularly valuable in arid regions as they can reduce demand on already limited water supplies. The systems are commonly used for non-potable uses, including toilet/urinal flushing, laundry, irrigation, fire suppression, and building cooling.
- *Stormwater harvesting systems*: These systems involve collecting, storing, and treating stormwater from urban areas, which can be reused for various purposes, including irrigating public parks, gardens, sports fields, and golf courses.
- *On-site non-potable reuse systems*: On-site non-potable water systems capture and treat water sources generated from within or surrounding a building, such as roof run-off, stormwater, domestic wastewater or blackwater, and greywater. It is treated and then reused on-site or locally for non-drinking purposes. The potential uses of the water are irrigation, cooling/heating applications, process water, and clothes washing.

- *Water recycling systems*: Recycled water, which is harvested water used for another purpose after treatment, can be used for a range of purposes, including in urban environments (households and recreational parks), industry (washing and cooling in power stations and mills), agriculture (horticulture, forestry, pasture, flowers, viticulture), and other possible uses, including firefighting, groundwater recharge, irrigating municipal landscapes, 'dual-pipe' urban uses, and maintaining environmental flows and wetlands.[32]

3.4.9 Retrofits

Retrofit programmes involve the distribution and installation of replacement devices to physically reduce water use in homes and offices. For example, the most common retrofits are toilet retrofits involving customers having their older toilets replaced with newer low/dual flush toilets, replacement of showerheads, and installation of faucet aerators (devices that reduce the flow when inserted into water taps). The overall benefits of retrofit programmes are that they are: relatively inexpensive; easily installed by homeowners or plumbers with little or no disruption to users; effective in reducing water use, waste flows, and energy consumption; and permanent.[33]

3.5 Communication and Information Urban Demand Management Instruments

Communication and information instruments encourage the development of a water-conserving society. In particular, communication and information instruments aim to change behaviour through public awareness campaigns around the need to conserve scarce water resources.

3.5.1 Education in Schools

Schools use large volumes of water each day for heating and cooling systems, toilets, taps, cafeterias, laboratories, outdoor playgrounds, swimming pools, and landscaping. Water efficiency programmes in schools provide an opportunity for students to regard water conservation as the norm, making it more likely that there will be a change in how water is used across society. Water efficiency initiatives can also become part of the school curriculum, with students not only seeing the process of conservation and saving water in action but also participating in helping to collect data on the savings achieved through the installation of new water-efficient devices. Students can also participate in field trips that enhance awareness of the water cycle, such as trips to water treatment plants and waterways.[34]

3.5.2 Public Education and Awareness

Water utilities can influence an individual's attitudes and behaviours towards water resources by increasing their knowledge and awareness of environmental problems associated with water scarcity. Furthermore, public acceptance of alternative water sources can be increased through information provision. Water utilities can use multiple tools and formats to increase environmental awareness and water conservation, including the examples shown in Table 3.3. For example, Essex and Suffolk Water has found that behaviour-change messages – which the utility defines as water-saving hints and tips, expression of volumes of water or money saved, and certain behavioural materials – provided to customers after home visit appointments led to water savings of seven litres per property per day.[35]

3.5.3 Competition between Water Users

Water managers can increase participation rates in water conservation programmes by promoting competition among water users to achieve specific water consumption targets. Examples of competitions include eliciting commitments to water-savings targets and promoting competition through the water bill. Regarding eliciting

Table 3.3 *Public education and awareness tools*

Tool	Description
Public information campaigns	Television commercials, newspaper articles, and advertisements can provide conservation hints and tips. Water managers can partner with private companies to conduct joint campaigns.
Internet campaigns	Internet and social media campaigns, such as YouTube videos, and Twitter, Instagram, and Facebook campaigns can provide conservation hints and tips.
Public events	Public events such as conservation workshops, and public exhibitions can educate customers on water-saving devices and how to detect leaks at home.
Billing inserts	Information can be included in water utility bills, such as leaflets on water conservation tips.
Water-saving kits and devices	Distribution of water conservation kits and provision of rebates can encourage physical water savings.

commitments, water managers can obtain verbal or written commitments from individuals and communities to achieve specific water-saving targets. Competitions can be formed to compare one community with another and offer winners recognition or prizes for their water-saving achievements.[36] The water bill can also be used as a tool for competition between water users. For example, water bills can show a household's water consumption compared to the average household in the neighbourhood, city, province, or state.[37] Water managers can also 'reference' other communities' water savings as models to emulate or mimic. Alternatively, water managers can use water-saving role models such as community leaders or winners of water-saving competitions as reference points for ideal behaviour.[38]

3.5.4 Water Labelling

Water managers can promote water efficiency product-labelling schemes covering water-using devices such as taps, showers, and toilets. The labelling of household appliances according to their degree of water efficiency is essential in reducing household water consumption by eliminating unsustainable products from the market, provided the labelling scheme is clear and comprehensible and identifies both the private and public benefits of conserving water. There are two main types of labelling schemes:

- *Endorsement labels*: The label indicates that a product has met a certain minimum standard.
- *Rating labels*: The label indicates the level of efficiency by rating the product on a performance scale and/or by stating the product's actual water consumption or flow rate figures.[39]

3.5.5 Demonstration Projects

Demonstration projects illustrate the feasibility and commercial viability of water conservation and water efficiency initiatives. They can also showcase the various economic, environmental, and social benefits to the community, including water utility customers, private building owners, and developers. Furthermore, demonstration projects can pilot new policies for municipal or regional governments and build local and institutional capacity and confidence.[40]

3.6 Portfolio of Urban Demand Management Instruments

Price alone cannot be relied on in demand management to achieve water conservation targets, for three reasons. First, pricing alone to achieve water conservation is economically and politically sensitive. In particular, water pricing raises the day-to-day costs of households and businesses. This can be inflationary and attract opposition.[41] In addition, water managers need to take note of the price elasticity of water, as it indicates the likely revenue impacts from price changes: If demand is elastic, price increases will decrease demand to the extent the water suppliers' total revenues will decrease. Conversely, inelastic demand will mean revenues from a price increase will outweigh the losses associated with a decrease in demand. Furthermore, water pricing is politically sensitive, as people are often sceptical about whether price increases for water are really for environmental reasons or are simply an additional revenue source for the water utilities or government. As such, price is seldom relied on as the main instrument in demand management. Second, studies have shown that when pricing is introduced, individuals may modify their behaviour in the short term, but people revert to their old habits in the long term. Third, it is usually difficult to assess the effectiveness of pricing alone, as it is frequently used in conjunction with other demand management instruments (metering, education, regulations, installing water-saving devices, etc.).[42] Nonetheless, if water managers rely too much on non-price conservation programmes to reduce demand, revenues could decline significantly, impacting the financial sustainability of providing water supplies (the costs being for pumping, treating, and distributing water, as well as operating and maintaining the water infrastructure). As a result, water managers may be forced to increase the price of water substantially following 'successful' non-price conservation programmes as a way to prevent water utilities from suffering unsustainable losses.[43]

Therefore, water managers should use a portfolio of demand management instruments (regulatory, informational, market-based, etc.) to achieve specific water conservation targets.[44] However, the portfolio cannot be a random collection of demand management instruments; instead, each instrument must complement and support the overall strategic vision (water conservation target).[45] Furthermore, when deciding on which demand management instrument to incorporate into the portfolio, a cost–benefit analysis should be conducted for each instrument before its inclusion in the overall demand management strategy, as non-price water conservation programmes incur numerous financial costs, such as advertising, billing inserts, monitoring, and enforcement.[46]

3.7 Conclusion

In conclusion, traditional approaches to urban water management have centred around supply-side infrastructure projects, which have proven to be both costly and environmentally damaging and can also create political tensions. It is necessary to shift the focus towards managing the actual demand for water. This involves setting water conservation goals and implementing various regulatory, technological, and communication-based demand management instruments. A carefully chosen portfolio of demand management instruments can complement and support the overall water conservation target, resulting in greater urban water security. Ultimately, it is society's attitudes and behaviours towards water that determine the amount of water that needs to be supplied, making demand-side management a crucial aspect of sustainable urban water management.

4

Vibrant Streets

Characteristics, Success Factors, and Contributions to Sustainable Development

REGINE GERIKE, VANESSA CARLOW, HENDRIK GÖRNER, SEBASTIAN HANTSCHEL, CAROLINE KOSZOWSKI, MATTHIAS MEDICUS, AND MICHAEL KRIEG

4.1 Introduction

Streets in urban areas have three main functions, namely:

1. *Movement function*: people and vehicles should get safely, comfortably, and efficiently to their destinations.
2. *Place function*: streets are destinations on their own, as people come here to access adjacent properties or to carry out activities directly in the street.
3. *Environmental function*: streets play a role in climate adaptation or water management.[1]

There are many interdependencies within and between these three functions. For example, pedestrians, cyclists, buses, cars, and goods vehicles compete for space to move along the street. Green space in the street supports place and environmental functions. General targets differ between the three groups. Streets are like 'conduits' for the movement function; they are successful when movements are smooth, fast, safe, and undisturbed. Streets are like 'sites' for the place function; they are successful when many persons come to the street, stay there for a long time, and perform higher-level place activities, like having conversations rather than just waiting for a bus. Streets are like green spaces, corridors regulating air quality and temperature, or facilities for water management in the environmental function.

Vibrant streets are streets that are full of life, energy, and enthusiasm. Interestingly, this vague definition based on the meaning of the term 'vibrant' as found in standard dictionaries has no commonly accepted standard specification in the street context. It is applied to communities and neighbourhoods[2] rather than to specific street sections, where concepts of complete streets,[3] liveable streets,[4] and, to a lesser extent, vital streets[5] are more common. The literature identifies several characteristics of vibrant streets, including their active use, the functional yet distinct design of the street itself and of the adjacent properties, and successful businesses and other uses in the street and the neighbourhood.[6]

For this chapter, we choose the definition of vibrant streets close to the more general meaning of the term 'vibrant'. Being full of life means that there are many people in the street; being full of energy means that these people do not just wait to cross the street but linger out of pleasure in the location and the activities provided there; being full of enthusiasm means that these people feel comfortable and develop a sense of place and community in the street. In this chapter, the first characteristic (being full of life) is defined as the main characteristic of vibrant streets, whereas the last two characteristics of vibrant streets (being full of energy and full of enthusiasm) are treated as correlates with an interdependent relationship. Streets with many people attract businesses which in turn become profitable; successful businesses attract people and customers. Pleasant street and building designs attract people and businesses; successful businesses can afford more sophisticated designs for their properties.

Comparing these characteristics with the three groups of street functions as introduced above, more activities in the place function of a street clearly increase its vibrancy. Activities in the movement function might have positive or negative effects on vibrancy. Vibrancy reduces with higher volumes of motorised vehicles but increases with higher volumes of people walking as pedestrians along the street directly to destinations or to public transport (PT) stops. Cycling also brings people to the street, with positive effects on vibrancy when they get to destinations or stop for place activities within the street, and with neutral or even possibly negative effects when cyclists only move along the street on facilities that are close to or mixed with pedestrian spaces. Kerbside activities such as parking, loading, or drop-off/pick-up events might have positive or negative effects on vibrancy and are included here under place activities (although they might also be subsumed under the movement function). Trees and plants as part of the environment function offer higher street quality and contribute to vibrancy, but at the same time compete with the other functions for space.

The number of people in the street as the core characteristic of vibrant streets is a combination of people walking along the street to destinations or to PT stops as pedestrians and of people coming to the street as place users. These two types of people's movement and place activities in the street are called street activities from now on. They have very different determinants, but at the same time they can hardly be separated from each other. In the movement function, pedestrians walk along the street to destinations because these are within walkable distances, because they feel safe, or because they decide that this is the most suitable transport mode for their specific trip purpose. Pedestrians walk along the street to PT stops because PT is the fastest, cheapest, most suitable transport mode for their specific trip. In the place function, people walk along the street without any specific destination or stay at one point for a while in order to get fresh air, to stroll, to window shop, or to meet people. Nice destinations and a pleasant environment are the main determinants of these place activities. Mode choice decisions as the basis for movement activities are shaped by transport planning; the two modes of walking and PT are of particular interest for vibrant streets because they bring people to streets. Decisions on place activities are made by both urban and transport planning. Urban planning is responsible for the overall width of the street, and for the location, size, usage, and design of buildings or parks. Urban and transport planning, together with environmental planning, are responsible for street design, providing functional yet pleasant designs for movement and place activities.

It is evident that interdisciplinary approaches are needed to consider all these aspects in order to understand and purposefully design vibrant streets. Currently, the professional communities of urban and transport research and those of planning practices are disconnected. There is a long tradition in transport research on mode choice decisions[7] which is mainly based on surveys on revealed or stated behaviour. Studies rarely consider specific street designs or place activities, because their focus is on individuals with their specific preferences, needs, and travel behaviour. There is a wealth of literature on the impact of the built environment on pedestrian volumes, which interestingly comes from either urban research[8] or transport research.[9] These so-called walkability studies focus on specific street sections; they investigate pedestrian volumes, including movement and place functions,[10] and, in some cases, more detailed characteristics of place activities such as their type (e.g. talking, eating), postures (e.g. standing, sitting), or duration.[11] These studies do not consider individual variables of the street users (e.g. age, gender) or characteristics of the transport systems.

This chapter purposefully includes literature from transport and urban research, literature investigating individuals' preferences and mode choice behaviour, as well as literature on the walkability of the built environment and its impacts on the activities in specific street sections. The aim of this chapter is to give an interdisciplinary introduction into the determinants and effects of the entire set of street activities as the core characteristic of vibrant streets. The term street activities as used in this chapter covers pedestrians walking along the street to destinations or PT stops (movement function), and on-site place activities where streets are not conduits that enable movement but destinations in their own right (place function).

Benefits of vibrant streets for sustainable development are of particular interest, from two main aspects. Streets act as one core element of transport systems that enable people to move to their destinations to meet their needs; they are thus a prerequisite for social participation and successful societal development. At the same time, these movements cause substantial negative effects in the social, economic, and environmental dimensions, with greenhouse gas (GHG) emissions being one prominent example. In the EU-27, the transport sector accounts for more than 25 per cent of all GHG emissions; it is the only sector where these emissions are still growing in absolute terms.[12]

Vibrant streets support both aspects of sustainability in promoting walking, cycling, and PT use as the most accessible and inclusive transport modes which, at the same time, have the lowest negative environmental effects. In terms of the 5R approach (see Section 1.4.2), this chapter focuses on the dimension 'reduce', including reducing resource consumption for transport; emissions of air pollutants, noise, and greenhouse gases; and the spatial footprint of transport infrastructure. The other dimensions of reuse, recycle, restore, and recover could mainly be addressed in the provision of infrastructure manufacturing of vehicles over their entire life cycle. However, these sustainability impacts are not the main focus of this chapter, which concentrates on the usage of streets and vehicles rather than how they are built.

In this chapter, the presentation of the determinants and effects of vibrant streets is organised as follows. Studies from urban and transport planning investigating the determinants of street activities at specific street sections are introduced in Section 4.2, followed by literature on the determinants of travel behaviour in Section 4.3. Studies on the effects of community building on street activities are presented in Section 4.4. Section 4.5 summarises the relevance of vibrant streets for sustainable development. Based on the insights gained on determinants and effects, strategies for fostering vibrant streets are developed in Section 4.6, followed by good practice examples in Section 4.7. The chapter closes with conclusions and avenues for future research and policymaking in Section 4.8.

4.2 Built-Environment Factors of Walking and Place Activities at Street Level

4.2.1 Neighbourhood Level

Neighbourhood characteristics classified by the typical '5 Ds' (density, diversity, design, distance to PT, and destination accessibility) or even '7 Ds' (add demand management and demographics) are consistently significant and influential for pedestrian volumes in research.[13] Ewing *et al.*[14] demonstrate that density is of particular relevance, measured in their example as floor area ratio and population density within 400 metres of the investigated commercial streets. Diversity describes the mixture of land uses in a neighbourhood; it is usually captured by entropy measures describing the number and variety of different land-use types in a given area.[15] Ewing *et al.*[16] find this statistically significant in one study but not in another.[17] Lower distances, particularly to rail PT, consistently and significantly increase pedestrian volumes.[18] Design variables describe the characteristics and, more specifically, the connectivity of the street network, measured, for example, as intersection density or as the share of four-way intersections.[19] Mixed findings exist for these design variables, which are significant in some studies but not in others.[20] Destination accessibility describes the level to which relevant activities can be reached.[21] Destinations are operationalised, for instance, by the number of nearby amenities and stores weighted by their distance; these are hardly significant[22] and show an overlap with diversity.

Some authors work with Cs instead of the Ds to investigate the influence of the built environment on pedestrian volumes: these include connectivity, convenience, comfort, conviviality, conspicuousness, coexistence, and commitment.[23] These Cs are a mixture of variables on the neighbourhood and street levels; they show a substantial overlap with the Ds, and findings on their impacts on pedestrian activities are consistent with the findings already summarised.

4.2.2 Street Level

The Ds as introduced in the previous section also apply to the street level. This holds true particularly for design but also for the other Ds. Ewing *et al.*[24] demonstrate the significant influence on pedestrian volumes of floor area ratios of the streets themselves (computed as the total building floor area for parcels abutting the street, divided by the total area of tax lots) and of the proportion of retail frontage along the block face. Ewing and Handy[25] rank more than 100 features of selected streetscapes based on expert input and identify the following five urban design qualities as most relevant for pedestrian volumes at specific street sections:

1. *Imageability*: the quality of a place that makes it distinct, recognisable, and memorable, measured by the proportion of historic buildings and of buildings with non-rectangular silhouettes, as well as identifiers such as major landscape features
2. *Enclosure*: the degree to which the streets are visually defined by buildings, walls, trees, and other vertical elements, measured by the proportion of street walls, of sky visible across and ahead, and by long sight lines
3. *Human scale*: the size, texture, and articulation of physical elements that match the size and proportions of humans and correspond to the speed at which humans walk, measured by long sight lines, street furniture, proportion of first floor with windows, building height, and small planters
4. *Transparency*: the degree to which people can see, hear, or smell what is beyond the edge of a street, measured by the proportion of first floor with windows and active uses on street level
5. *Complexity*: the visual richness of a place, measured by the number of buildings, building colours, public art, people in the street, and presence of outdoor dining.

These criteria are validated against counted pedestrian volumes in subsequent studies.[26] Controlling for the D variables at neighbourhood level (as introduced in the previous section), on the street level only transparency was found to significantly influence pedestrian volumes. This is consistent with findings from other studies.[27] Additionally, Ameli *et al.* highlight the significance of imageability.[28]

Ewing *et al.*[29] refine the above concepts and analyse the influence of around 20 further and more detailed variables measuring physical features of streetscapes, resulting in the three significant variables: proportion of windows, street furniture, and active uses. These three variables significantly increase the explanatory power of the statistical models explaining pedestrian volumes, compared to models with only the D variables on the neighbourhood and street levels. Street furniture is defined as a variety of signs, benches, parking meters, trash cans, newspaper boxes, bollards, and street lights, and includes anything at the human scale that increases the complexity of the street. Public seating is found to be of particular relevance. Active uses are defined as shops, restaurants, public parks, and further uses that generate significant pedestrian traffic. Inactive uses include blank walls, driveways, parking lots, vacant lots, abandoned buildings, and offices with no apparent activity.

Kang[30] and Kim *et al.*[31] focus on the street layout itself. They find significant positive impacts on pedestrian volumes of sidewalk widths, crosswalks, and trees, and negative impacts of slope. The number of traffic lanes is significantly positive but highly correlated with the distance to PT. Lai and Kontokosta[32] compute a composite variable streetscape as the product of sidewalk coverage, pavement quality, and street amenity. If this variable is significantly improved, pedestrian volumes increase on weekends only.

Few research groups and studies have investigated the number and characteristics of place activities.[33] These activities are operationalised either by the sheer number of people who perform these activities[34] or by the liveliness index as the product of the number of people with place activities and the duration of their activities.[35] Mehta and Bosson[36] classify the recorded place activities into activity types (e.g. talking, eating, reading, sunbathing) and postures (e.g. ambling, standing, sitting, lying, sleeping).

For the determinants of these place activities, there is a substantial overlap with the determinants of movement activities (pedestrian volumes). The existence of community places such as stores (which are places to meet neighbours, friends, strangers, etc.) is most relevant for the liveliness index, followed by the provision of seating, both commercial and public. Personalisation is also significant: it describes how the interface of the businesses with the street (building facade, entrances, shop windows) is embellished with personal touches such as displays, decorations, signs, banners, planters, or flowerboxes. The variables of permeability and variety of businesses are only significant in one study each.[37] Sidewalk width is only significant in Metha;[38] it seems to be a mediating variable that is less important on its own but rather enables installing facilities that foster place activities on the sidewalk, such as seating. No significant influences on the liveliness index have been identified for shade provided, the existence of street furniture besides seating, the articulation of facades, or the degree of independence of the adjacent stores.

Gehl[39] composes 12 quality criteria for pedestrian facilities and spaces for place activities, grouped into three categories:

1. *Protection*: the variables are prerequisites for movement and place activities; they include objective and subjective (perceived) safety against traffic and traffic accidents, security against crime, and protection against unpleasant sensory experiences.
2. *Comfort*: after taking into account protection, the provision of comfortable spaces has to be ensured to invite people to come to the street. For pedestrians walking along the street to destinations, sidewalks should offer sufficient space void of obstacles (e.g. with a dedicated footway clear zone) and good surface quality. Providing space for place activities invites place users to spend time in the street.
3. *Delight*: to ensure the well-being of pedestrians and place users, the human scale needs be taken into account, with street and building dimensions and proportions being the most relevant variables. Thoughtful design – especially attention to detail, materials, and green structures – enhances the walking experience and encourages people to enjoy the street.

Gehl[40] does not provide any quantitative validation for these criteria based, for example, on a comparison with empirically measured volumes of pedestrian movement or place activities. However, he lists various examples for the successful application of these criteria in projects for redesigning streets and public spaces all over the world.[41]

4.3 Determinants of Individual Travel Behaviour

The travel behaviour of persons living, working, or being in the neighbourhood around the street under investigation is relevant for street activities: Generally speaking, more environmentally friendly travel behaviours increase street activities. Walking and PT, with people walking to/from PT stops, are of particular importance for street activities; cycling also brings people to the street. Car use should be low in vibrant streets because higher car volumes consistently reduce street activities.[42]

Literature on the determinants of transport mode choice is extensive.[43] Relevant determinants can be grouped into person-related factors (e.g. socio-demographic and socio-economic factors, availability of mobility tools, socio-psychological factors), built-environment factors (e.g. access to destinations), and transport infrastructure and services (e.g. PT supply, parking facilities, facilities for walking and cycling).

Some studies claim that younger and older person groups have higher walking frequencies compared to persons aged in between,[44] while others claim that the age variable is not significant.[45] Women tend to walk more and also use PT more often than men.[46] Gascon *et al.*[47] find less walking with higher education levels, but no effect of education was found in most other studies.[48] People with lower income use PT services more often, whereas for walking the role of income is inconclusive. For example, Brüchert *et al.*[49] find more walking with higher income, whereas Wang *et al.*[50] find the opposite effect. People not working walk more compared to working people.[51] For PT, the role of employment is not that clear.[52] People with access to a car consistently walk less[53] and also use PT less often.[54] The same holds true for access to bicycles.[55] People who are physically active in their leisure time walk more than people who are not,[56] and healthy people walk more than people who have any difficulty in walking.[57]

Socio-psychological factors such as perceptions, preferences, attitudes, habits, perceived controls on behaviour (e.g. linked with the ability to carry luggage or to walk certain distances), and social and personal norms are consistently correlated with individual mode choice, including walking and PT. Kroesen *et al.*[58] demonstrate the bidirectional causal relationship of these correlations: attitudes influence mode choice and mode choice influences attitudes, with the latter effect being the dominating one. This means that travellers with dissonant (non-aligned) attitude–mode choice patterns tend to adjust their attitudes to align them with their behaviour rather than vice versa.

For built-environment factors, the 5 Ds are as influential for residents' walking behaviour and PT use as they are for street activities as described in Section 4.2.[59] Density and diversity are again of highest relevance.[60] Distance to PT facilities and particularly to rail-based services consistently increase residents' walking activities[61] and PT use.[62] Destination accessibility shows an overlap with diversity but is shown as significant in many studies.[63] Blue and green infrastructures are relevant, particularly for recreational walking.[64] Christiansen *et al.*[65] use Generalised Additive Mixed Models (GAMMs)-models and geographic information system (GIS) data to find a linear relationship between residents' weekly walking time and land-use mix, but not for residential density. This leads to the question whether tipping points might exist for some of the correlates of walking.

Koszowski *et al.*[66] analyse the impact of perceived built-environment characteristics on walking behaviour based on survey data. They find that the relevance of the built environment is higher for frequent walkers than for less frequent walkers, and higher for leisure walking than for utilitarian walking. Following the classification of street characteristics from Gehl,[67] protection variables (e.g. safety, security) are ranked high for leisure walking, followed by comfort (e.g. space, surface quality) and by delight (e.g. attractive buildings, greenery). Distance is key for utilitarian walking. Significant differences between frequent and less frequent walkers are identified mainly for the delight variables, namely attractive buildings and greenery for utilitarian walking, and space availability and street furniture for leisure walking.

Besides the built-environment characteristics, the quality of networks and services is of particular relevance for PT mode choice. Travel time and travel cost are consistently significant in the choice models. Further relevant variables include reliability, comfort, and accessibility.[68] These transport system characteristics are always relative. For example, prices for PT compete with prices for parking or sharing services. Framework conditions for car use therefore belong to the most important determinants of walking, cycling, and PT mode choice. The same PT systems, and the same conditions and facilities for walking and cycling lead to completely different uses of these environmentally friendly modes depending on how fast, costly, and reliable car use is.[69]

4.4 Community Building

Studies in urban design, and particularly the projects published by the groups around Mehta *et al.*[70] and Gehl *et al.*,[71] demonstrate convincingly that successful provision for walking and place activities needs more than tailor-made and pedestrian-focused designs. Designing and managing vibrant streets is an interdisciplinary ambition that can only be achieved if far more stakeholders collaborate than just urban and transport designers.

Cities have a prominent role in initiating and coordinating such collaboration and in supporting the various community-based stakeholders to engage in improving and actively using the streets in their neighbourhood. Incentive schemes are one potential instrument for initiating or strengthening independent businesses, especially those that are perceived as community places. Longer and more flexible opening hours for local businesses might be considered and encouraged, as they contribute to active street usage over the entire day, week, and year. Cities might transfer some control to local businesses and users to enable and invite them to (re) claim street space, for example, by providing movable street furniture or by allowing businesses to use parts of the street for their activities and facilities. Incentives and support might also be provided for the organisation of events such as street closures, festivals, open classroom projects, or other activities that strengthen the community. Temporary modifications of the design and regulation of streets, such as allowing parklets in summer, closing lanes, or taking out parking lots on select weekends, might also encourage street activities and give a different perspective on the street space.

Local building codes might support permeable and articulated facades at the street level. Nooks, alcoves, small setbacks, steps, and ledges serve multiple purposes for people to find shelter, get out of the pedestrian flow, or stop and rearrange their belongings.

Streets are ecosystems; their users and usages constantly evolve. Streetscapes that are perfect for today might not be suitable even in the near future. In addition, vibrant streets are well-maintained streets; street management should be considered as important as design. Regular monitoring of street users and usages are necessary to respond to changing requirements and to modify the street accordingly. Regular street management includes the operation of removing trash, sweeping and keeping the street space clean, repairing and replacing furniture, maintaining trees and plants, and so on. Local stakeholders might engage in some of these activities, and they can be supported and incentivised by small and flexible funding schemes.

4.5 Contributions of Vibrant Streets to Sustainable Development

Sustainable development has been a prominent societal ambition for decades; it has become the guiding political principle worldwide since 2015, when the Sustainable Development Goals (SDGs) were adopted by the United Nations.[72] Sustainability is an anthropocentric concept focusing on human needs and on the responsibility for today's generations to only use the resources available to an extent that leaves sufficient resources for future generations to satisfy their own needs. The so-called Brundtland definition summarises this basic principle: 'Sustainable development is development that meets the needs of the present without compromising the ability of future generations to meet their own needs'.[73]

Transport has a dual responsibility for supporting the sustainability ambition.[74] Transport enables people to get to destinations; it is a means of satisfying human needs and a driving force of economic and societal progress. At the same time, transport generates substantial negative effects which hamper progress towards sustainability. Sustainability in transport will therefore always be a balance. It has to respect limits, for instance, in terms of available resources or maximum emissions. Within these limits, accessibility and mobility should be optimised towards the satisfaction of evolving human needs. These core principles can be summarised as follows: sustainable transport is about providing access to destinations where needs can be satisfied, for all parts of society, today and in the future, while at the same time minimising negative effects that result from movements between the destinations.

Transport is included in most strategic policy documents in the sustainability discourse but hardly receives full attention in the cross-sector documents. There is no dedicated SDG for transport, but several of the 17 SDGs are related to this domain instead, for example SDG11 Sustainable Cities and Communities.[75] Possible reasons for this limited consideration of transport in the typical cross-sector indicator systems are that they focus primarily on the impacts of human activities rather than on strategies to promote sustainable societies and, in our case, sustainable transport systems. Indicator systems for sustainable transport address this problem by adding domain-specific indicators that describe the scope and quality of transport infrastructure and mobility services for providing accessibility.[76]

Vibrant streets contribute to both responsibilities of sustainable transport. They provide access to destinations and social participation, and, with their focus on walking and on the environmentally friendly modes, support the reduction of the negative effects of transport. Various relevant pathways have been identified in the literature. Most of them investigate the relationship between the built environment and effects in the different sustainability dimensions without considering street activities as a mediating variable in between. For example, higher walkability is related to better public health,[77] social health,[78] and fitness,[79] and it contributes to quality of life.[80] In their study, van den Berg *et al.*[81] find a positive relationship between walkability and place attachment.

Rashidfarokhi und Danivska[82] review the relationship between detailed characteristics of the built environment, including urban form, accessibility, architecture, technical infrastructure, and functionality with individual and community resilience, and find the typical walkability indicators such as the 5 Ds being of particular relevance. Pathways from greenspace and urban ecosystems to public health (as shown, for example, in Browning *et al.*[83] and Elmqvist *et al.*[84]) also matter because greenspace is one success factor of vibrant streets and often gets higher priority and more space in these streets than in typical urban streets.

Nieuwenhuijsen[85] describes in more detail the pathways between urban design, which includes streets and transport services, via physical activity to public health. Suitable urban designs promote the active modes walking and cycling, which have positive effects on stress and social contacts and reduce the negative environmental effects of transport. The combination of increased physical activity and decreased transport emissions reduce the risk of non-communicable diseases (morbidity) and premature mortality.

Vibrant streets are in the middle of these complex causal relationships. The number of people and street activities results from walkable built environments including greenery in the street, which in turn generates positive effects for community building, public health, and the environment. Table 4.1 compiles indicators that are suitable to directly assess specific street sections in terms of vibrancy and sustainability. Adding these indicators to future studies that investigate pathways between the built environment and sustainability outcomes might help better understand the pathways in their entirety and the role of vibrant streets within.

Table 4.1 shows that vibrant streets are highly synergetic with the sustainability ambition. Vibrant streets focus on street activities and on walking in the movement function. Sustainability is more neutral between the transport modes for the movement function; it aims at finding the optimal balance between accessibility provision including all modes and the minimisation of negative effects. Table 4 1 also shows that vibrant streets contribute to both responsibilities of transport for sustainability because walking to destinations means satisfying human needs with minimum negative effects for transport. In addition, the scope of the sustainability concept is broader and includes all effects from providing and maintaining infrastructure and transport services which are not of primary interest for vibrant streets and are therefore not listed in Table 4.1.

Table 4.1 *Indicators for street assessment in terms of vibrancy and sustainability (source: authors' own compilation)*

Theme	Indicators	Relevance for vibrant streets	Relevance for sustainable development
Place function			
Place activities	Activity number and duration by type Liveliness index (number of activities multiplied by their duration)	Core characteristic of vibrant streets	Positive in the provision of accessibility and in minimising negative effects
Kerbside activities	Number and duration of parking, loading, drop-off/pick-up events by location and time	Potentially bring place activities to the street Need space, might reduce safety	Positive in the provision of accessibility For motorised modes, negative in emissions and safety
Movement function			
Pedestrian volumes	Volumes per time (e.g. per hour) at one location (e.g. by age group, use of mobility aid, walking along, and crossing the street)	Core characteristic of vibrant streets	Positive in the provision of accessibility and in minimising negative effects
Public transport (PT) passengers	Number of passengers boarding/alighting buses or trams at one PT stop	Core characteristic of vibrant streets, but might also be challenging because of their local and temporal concentration	Positive in the provision of accessibility and in minimising negative effects

Table 4.1 (*cont.*)

Theme	Indicators	Relevance for vibrant streets	Relevance for sustainable development
Cyclist volumes	Volumes per time (e.g. per hour) at one location by type of bicycle	Cyclists are people in the street and thus support vibrancy Space for cyclist facilities competes with space for street activities	Positive in the provision of accessibility and in minimising negative effects
Volumes of motorised vehicles	Volumes per time (e.g. per hour) at one location by vehicle type	Should be low in vibrant streets because of their negative effects	Positive in the provision of accessibility Negative in emissions (noise, air pollutants, greenhouse gases), resource consumption, safety
Characteristics of movements in the street	Speed, delays, travel times, waiting times	High levels of service have low priority in vibrant streets Slow movements reduce emissions, improve safety, allow for space-efficient designs	High levels of service improve accessibility but increase negative effects
Environmental function			
Emissions	Vehicle emissions (air pollutants, greenhouse gases, noise)	High emissions reduce street activities; vibrant streets reduce emissions	Core sustainability indicator
Safety	Number of accidents and conflicts by type, severity, and involved street user groups	Insufficient (perceived) safety as one main barrier for walking (and cycling)	Core sustainability indicator
Security	Number of street crimes	Bidirectional relationship: deficits in security as one barrier to come to a street; higher levels of street activities improve security	Less prominent in sustainability indicator systems but highly relevant
Public health	Morbidity, mortality	Improved public health as one core outcome of vibrant streets	Core sustainability indicator

4.6 Strategies for Fostering Vibrant Streets

Strategies for promoting vibrant streets can be directly derived from their determinants in the built environment, individual travel behaviour and community building. Urban planning strategies for high-density and mixed land-use are the basis of walkable built environments. People living and working in the neighbourhood are prime candidates to visit local streets. Shops, services, and other relevant destinations in the neighbourhood allow them to satisfy their needs locally and within walkable distance. Highest densities should be provided around PT stops, based on the coordination of urban and transport planning from the earliest planning stages. The design of architecture, infrastructure networks, and streets comes next. Highly connected networks are of highest relevance for walking as the most distance-sensitive transport mode, but also for cycling and the motorised modes. Street design and operation need to provide for comfortable and safe movements for all street user groups. In addition, streetscapes should be attractive in order to encourage people to visit and spend time there.

Integrated packages of measures in transport planning complement these efforts. They can be categorised as the '4 Es': engineering (infrastructure design and operation, PT services etc.), enforcement (legal framework such as speed limits or rights-of-way and their surveillance), economy (monetary incentives, prices, taxes, etc.), and education (information, training, social marketing, etc.).

Buehler *et al.*[86] stress the importance of push-and-pull-strategies: pull measures strengthen certain transport modes, such as PT, with the provision of dense and high-quality PT services. Pull measures for the environmentally friendly modes are core components of sustainable transport systems. They need to be complemented by push measures that reduce the attractiveness of the individual motorised transport modes (mainly car and motorcycles) in order to actually achieve the sustainability ambition. The reallocation of street space from the motorised modes to walking, cycling, and place activities is, besides monetary incentive schemes, the most prominent example for push-and-pull strategies. Space for the motorised modes is reduced (push) but increased for walking, cycling, and place activities (pull). Parking management implemented as reduced parking capacities and/or changed prices is another highly effective push measure for the individual motorised transport modes.

Neither of these measures directly addresses street design, but they are both vital drivers or barriers of vibrant streets (Figure 4.1). People tend to use their car when this is the fastest mode and parking facilities exist at the destination at

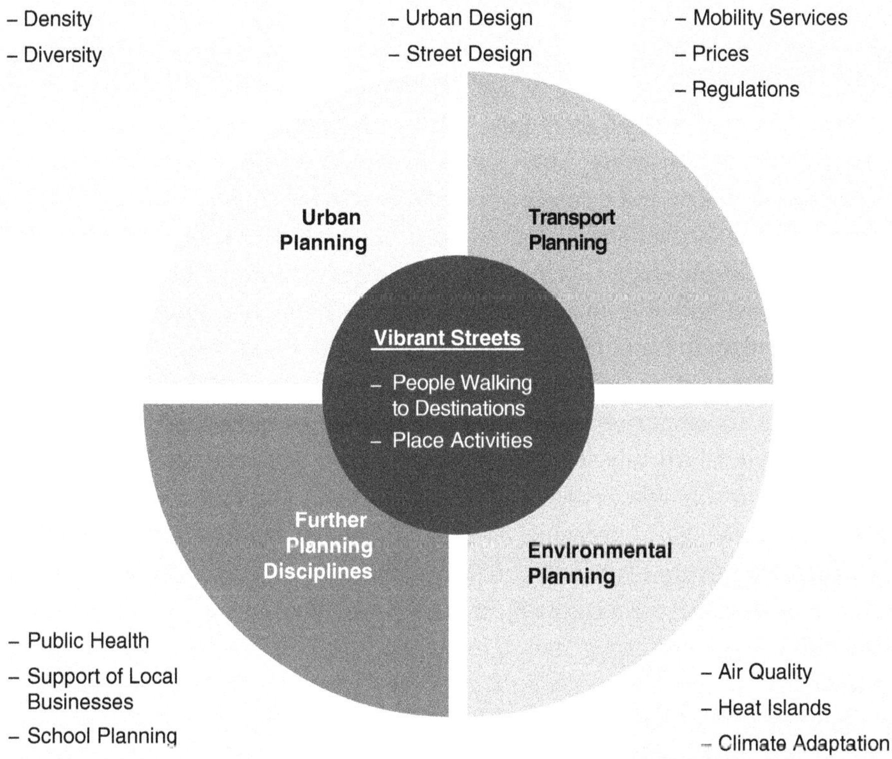

License:CC BY-SA 4.0

Figure 4.1 Success factors, characteristics, and effects of vibrant streets (source: authors' own figure)

reasonable prices; people tend to prefer the environmentally friendly modes when these are competitive in travel time, cost, reliability, and when parking space is scarce and/or expensive. Higher shares of the environmentally friendly modes and particularly of walking and PT in the local modal split increase the number of street activities with everything else being equal in urban planning.

Vibrant streets are in constant change: neither people's preferences, abilities, and knowledge nor the framework conditions are static. New needs arise with new opportunities, such as innovative mobility services or digitisation. Other needs such as owning a private car might reduce in importance. Constant monitoring of street user groups and usage are therefore needed to detect changed requirements and to adapt street design or further measures and services accordingly.

4.7 Good Practice Examples

Cities strive for vibrant streets and neighbourhoods because their success factors in transport and urban planning as well as in community building synergetically contribute to various other ambitions, such as economic success, public health, liveability, and sustainability. Many cities worldwide work actively on improving the built environment and transport systems to provide more walkable cities; the German cities of Kassel and Cologne could be mentioned here.[87] The Mayor of London[88] has developed a transport strategy which commits to making London the world's most walkable city and subsequently implements various measures for improving walkability and the attractiveness of streets and public places. Streets have been redesigned in many cities,[89] but rarely are any of the initiatives to redesign streets or to support walkable neighbourhoods systematically and transparently monitored; hardly any success story can be fully told, and hardly any insights can be gained to help other cities learn from successes and failures.

The redesign of the Limmatquai in Zurich is one of the few examples that has been comprehensively evaluated.[90] The Limmatquai is located in the inner city of Zurich next to the river Limmat. In 2004, individual motorised vehicles were banned from this street; only trams, buses, bicycles, and delivery and taxi vehicles have been allowed ever since. In 2006, the street was redesigned with wider and more attractive facilities for walking and place activities, and the maximum allowed speed was reduced to 30 kilometres per hour. As a result, by 2008 the number of pedestrians had increased by 17 per cent, with the most significant growth in the afternoon hours; cyclist volumes had increased by 18 per cent and place activities by 100 per cent. This example demonstrates the importance of street design matters: reallocating road space, widening facilities for walking and place activities, providing safe crossing facilities, and adding greenery and further equipment that makes the street more attractive.

It is commonplace, and common sense, to include citizens in the decision-making processes of urban and transport planning. One may also consider, however, that citizens can play a very active role themselves: A neighbourhood initiative may host a street party, local urban activists invent a pop-up park, street artists reclaim street space to display their art, and so on. These short-term projects might lead to long-term projects adopted by municipalities, and therefore to a fundamental change in the approach of creating liveable cities.[91]

All these initiatives potentially increase the number of people and thus the vibrancy of a street, even if nothing else is changed. Interestingly, reducing space for motorised vehicles or even banning them locally does not lead to a collapse of the transport system. People, streets, and cities adapt. Mobility and transport look different afterwards; they might be slower, but it is very likely that they are more sustainable.

4.8 Avenues for Research and Planning Practice

Vibrant streets as places with life, energy, and enthusiasm are of high relevance for sustainable development. They prioritise the environmentally friendly modes, particularly walking, in the movement function and thus provide access to destinations with the minimum possible resource consumption and emissions. They assign high priority to street activities in the place function, with various positive effects including public health, community building, and the economic success of local businesses. Causal relationships are complex and bidirectional. Street activities as the core characteristic of vibrant streets are shaped by the built environment, street design, and transport systems, but at the same time, they also shape these framework conditions.

Vibrant streets are about people in the street who come on foot, by bicycle, or with the motorised modes for movement activities and for place activities. These two types of activities follow different mechanisms and need different strategies for their support. Compared to complete streets, vibrant streets are less neutral in their priorities for the different street user groups; they are clear in their focus on people. Compared to liveable streets with their focus on place activities, vibrant streets are about a mixture of movement and place activities which both need to be understood in their complexity and correlation. There is a substantial overlap of vibrant streets with vital streets, which could be used as synonyms.

Urban and transport research approaches need to be combined to fully understand the success factors and effects of vibrant streets. Urban research provides insights into the influence of the built environment on street activities, including the location and type of destinations and more generally of urban structure and design. Transport research provides insights into the determinants of the travel behaviour of local residents and of people travelling through a street or coming there as a destination. Minor extensions of each disciplinary approach would already generate great benefits for the interdisciplinary understanding of vibrant streets. For example, on-site street user surveys in walkability studies from urban research could also ask about typical mode choice behaviour, off-street travel behaviour surveys (e.g. of local residents in transport research) could collect more detailed data on walking trips and distinguish between walking to destinations and place activities as two components of walking trips.

We will hardly succeed in on-site observations (e.g. based on video recordings) to clearly classify street users into pedestrians walking to destinations (movement function) and place users; people might even change their function while walking. However, we can distinguish between movement and place activities. We should investigate in far greater detail what people do where in the street and for which reasons, because movement activities on foot and place activities need very different types of strategies for their support. The same holds true for off-site travel surveys, which will never be able to trace respondents' movements in specific street sections in detail, but already more detailed data collection on walking trips would be highly beneficial to better understand where respondents perform which place activities at which time.

Similar to research, urban and transport planning strategies also need to be aligned to promote vibrant streets. Further relevant disciplines include environmental planning, public health initiatives to support physical activity, and community engagement. The coordination of these different planning disciplines is challenging but indispensable for successfully implementing vibrant streets.

Overall, the concept of vibrant streets is deeply rooted in the Western world; most studies come from the USA, followed by Europe and Asia. Further studies all over the world would help to better understand the transferability of the existing research methods and results, and to intensify the exchange in research and practice in order to further enrich the toolbox for vibrant streets, which will always need tailored solutions.

5

Sustainable Built Environment in Circular Economy Liveable Cities

ELENA SIMINA LAKATOS, DAN CLINCI, VLADUT VASILE CONSTANDOIU, AND ELENA CRISTINA RADA

5.1 Introduction

Cities, in their dynamic and intricate nature, face the intricate task of contextualising and defining the circular economy (CE) paradigm in the realm of urban resilience. These urban systems, with their multifaceted interdependencies, not only encompass economic aspects but also bear significance in a wider array of sectors and disciplines, underscoring the importance of integrating the CE into urban strategies.[1] The term 'resilience' delineates a system's ability to revert to its original equilibrium following disturbances. By fostering stability and ensuring the future generations a sustainable habitat, the CE becomes a bedrock for urban resilience. Arguably, resilience introduces a renewed lens for interpreting sustainability, making it an indispensable element of sustainable urban planning.[2] Drawing its origins from disciplines such as industrial ecology, environmental economics, and corporate sustainability, the CE paradigm provides an innovative alternative to conventional urban planning methodologies. Its implementation has witnessed varied scales since its inception in 1989, with countries like Germany, Japan, and China integrating it into their developmental strategies.[3] CE, by emphasising the principles of sharing, renting, reusing, and recycling, seeks to prolong product life cycles, thereby reducing waste and promoting sustainable consumption.[4] Amidst current environmental predicaments and economic uncertainties, CE has been recognised as an efficacious alternative to the prevailing linear economic models.[5]

Various global stakeholders, including the Ellen MacArthur Foundation, the European Union, China, and Google, are fostering policies, technological innovations, and research efforts aligned with CE principles. It is essential to understand the CE not just as an isolated concept but as a holistic system that interlaces diverse economic activities along the value chain, impacting both societies and ecosystems, especially in developing nations.[6]

The application of CE principles can potentially enhance the quality of life for urban inhabitants and ensure ecological equilibrium. Increasing industrial and municipal waste not only threatens the organic functionality of cities but also exacerbates socio-economic issues stemming from inefficient waste management. Effective circular waste management can deliver socio-environmental benefits by reintegrating materials into the supply chain, contributing to both sustainability and social well-being. Given the accelerating urbanisation rate, with cities accounting for approximately 70 per cent of global greenhouse gas emissions and an estimated 66 per cent of the global populace projected to reside in urban settings by 2050,[7] the push for urban sustainability is paramount. The CE model, in this context, offers a promising approach, aiming to orchestrate closed material and energy loops, thus preserving resource value.[8]

The RESOLVE framework outlines six key actions towards achieving a CE. These include:

1. *Regenerate*: focusing on restoring and renewing resources
2. *Share*: encouraging shared use of products and services to maximise their utility
3. *Optimise*: improving resource efficiency and minimising waste in production processes
4. *Loop*: ensuring materials are reused and recycled
5. *Virtualise*: aiming to shift physical activities into the digital realm to reduce material usage and environmental impact.
6. *Exchange*: involving the substitution of non-renewable materials and products with renewable ones.

These actions collectively drive sustainable practices by maintaining the value of products and resources for as long as possible.[9]

A sustainable economic growth, often termed 'growth from within', is an envisaged outcome of CE. However, its realisation necessitates collaborative efforts, transparency among firms, and an informed and agile society.[10] Its potential impacts on economic and environmental landscapes are profound, as seen in projections for the European Union. Various analytical tools, including the butterfly diagram, RESOLVE, Mass Flow Analysis, and Life Cycle Analysis, offer insights into circularity, even if they were not specifically conceptualised for urban applications.

With escalating urban populations, the merger of urban resilience and CE is crucial. The conception of 'circular city' embodies this union, offering a model for cities that is sustainable, resilient, progressive, and innovative. The envisioned attributes of such cities, driven by CE, include reduced raw material consumption, sustainable consumption avenues, effective waste management, the fostering of multidisciplinary innovations, and the augmentation of human and societal well-being.

Realising a CE at the city scale necessitates concerted efforts from various stakeholders, including governments, businesses, and citizens. Such a transition embodies community maturity and autonomy and envisages a harmonised developmental trajectory.

In order to amplify the value of the CE, a reconceptualisation of its application at the project or action level is vital. A well-informed populace, understanding both the potential advantages and challenges of a CE, is paramount for its successful implementation.[11]

5.2 Assimilating the Needs of a Liveable City by the Urban Community

The concept of a liveable city is nuanced, suggesting that achieving an optimal urban environment, given the multifaceted nature of urban ecosystems, is challenging. An ideal urban setting entails a comprehensive equilibrium between citizens' needs and the city's capacity to cater to these. Factors such as population density, service quality, transportation efficiency, environmental quality, cultural offerings, safety, and others comprise a delicate balance that is not easily attainable.[12]

Modern urban challenges like high population density, reduced access to natural landscapes, pollution, and noise highlight the complexities in urban development. The trajectory towards sustainable urban development may necessitate some sacrifices in individual comfort. For instance, the ambition to create smart and resilient cities – emphasising reduced emissions and climate change adaptability – might stress societal norms by proposing shifts away from personal vehicles.

Crafting effective public policy that facilitates urban health while preserving elements of comfort necessitates negotiation and compromise. A key question arises: how can public administrations execute stringent environmental policies while retaining public support for subsequent elections? Identifying strategies to subtly enforce these policies and ensure a city's sustainable progression that garners community backing is pivotal.[13]

Effective communication between environmental advocates and a community accustomed to its conveniences must be grounded in comprehensive community engagement, necessitating an intensive process of public awareness and active societal participation.

Transitioning cities from unconstrained growth models to sustainable ecosystems has been a recent focus for municipal leadership. Comprehensive urban regeneration should address both the physical urban infrastructure and its inhabiting community. Collaborative efforts, as encouraged by macro-entities like the European Union, between local or regional administrations, research bodies, and community institutions are crucial.

Romania presents a unique case in this discourse. Post-1990, Romania transitioned from a centralised state-driven urban development model to one that seemed devoid of comprehensive planning.[14] Over three decades, urban areas, irrespective of their size, largely catered to the immediate requirements of developers and citizens. While certain cities experienced economic downturns leading to depopulation and social restructuring, others, seen as economic hubs, faced immense pressures of population and function accumulation, resulting in a dense urban environment.

The dynamics between these contrasting urban growth trajectories have created challenges in both declining cities and thriving ones. Layering these existing challenges with contemporary sustainable imperatives amplifies the intricacy of the situation. Grappling with these complex urban issues, while ensuring the harmonious integration of sustainability measures without imposition, necessitates a synergised network of stakeholders committed to crafting and implementing adaptive urban solutions.[15]

5.3 Sustainable Built Environment: Definitions and Core Aspects

The ongoing discourse on climate change, fossil fuel exhaustion, and energy stability underscores the imperative for resilient environmental strategies. An ecologically sustainable built environment plays a pivotal role in mitigating greenhouse gas emissions and is instrumental in fostering holistic health for individuals, urban locales, and the broader ecosystem.

The processes involved in the construction, utilisation, and decommissioning of our built environment either directly or indirectly contribute to several paramount environmental challenges. These range from eutrophication to soil degradation, acid precipitation, global temperature rise, and stratospheric ozone diminution. For context, the built environment accounts for approximately 40 per cent of all primary energy consumption in several EU countries and about 30 per cent in the USA. Consequently, edifice operations significantly impact energy sourcing and processing, power plant construction and management, transmission infrastructures, and logistics. The geographical dispersion of the built environment also substantially influences the life cycle impacts of vehicular production, operation, and decommissioning. Thus, the environmental footprint of buildings extends well beyond their immediate physical boundaries. Notably, around 40 per cent of all extracted resources in the USA are deployed for infrastructure development or maintenance. Concepts such as sustainable construction, eco-architecture, and green design converge to articulate the sustainable built environment paradigm, which is often equated with green building. The notion of sustainability encompasses a spectrum of practices aimed at engendering environmental resilience.

Sustainable construction, recognised globally since 1993, is defined as the realisation of a built environment that aligns with ecologically grounded tenets. This encompasses the comprehensive life cycle of the built environment from conceptualisation to decommissioning, including material end-of-life strategies. Sustainable architectural principles guide this trajectory, emphasising judicious resource utilisation spanning land, water, energy, and construction materials.[16]

It is noteworthy that the evolution of the built environment is not solely influenced by conventional demand-side perspectives and governance structures, both local and central. The financial sector wields considerable influence across the design, construction, management, and refurbishment phases. Pertinent to facets such as energy optimisation, material life cycle management, design quality, and urban planning, it substantially impacts the realisation of sustainable development tenets.[17]

The core principles of sustainable construction emphasise reducing resource consumption and utilising resources as much as is feasible. Recycling waste from the built environment and employing recyclable materials are key strategies, alongside protecting natural systems and their functions in all actions. Moreover, it is vital to remove harmful elements and by-products from the built environment. These principles are supported by various entities, including the National Association of Home Builders, the US Green Building Council, and governmental bodies across different levels in the United States, all of which champion sustainable construction initiatives.

A compendium of policy instruments is available for stakeholders, including individuals and governmental entities, to support the transition towards sustainable practices, including:

- *Regulatory Mechanisms*:
  - *Technological standards*: mandates that delineate approved methodologies for certain industrial procedures or environmental challenges, with a pronounced focus on the adoption and implementation of preventive strategies
  - *Outcome-driven standards*: directives that define an organisation's responsibilities concerning the challenges to address or goals to achieve, emphasising the desired outcome rather than specific methods
- *Financial Mechanisms*:
  - *Emission-based levies and taxes*: direct financial charges determined by the volume and quality of a specific pollutant released
  - *Pollution product charges*: financial impositions on items that generate contamination during their manufacturing, utilisation, or disposal stages, such as batteries, pesticides, and fertilisers
  - *Service fees*: amounts paid to offset the expenses associated with communal services, predominantly used to support municipal operations like solid waste

collection or wastewater treatment; in natural resource governance, these fees are charges for accessing and utilising resources like parks, fishing docks, or hunting zones

- *Tradable permits*: set environmental allowances, entitlements, or upper limits granted to business entities by an authoritative agency
- *Deposit-return schemes*: upfront charges levied during the purchase of specific products, like packaging; upon returning the item to the retailer or a designated processing centre, the initial deposit is either wholly or partly refunded

- *Informational Resources*:
  - *Environmental awareness initiatives:* endeavours aimed at enhancing the public's knowledge about environmental issues
  - *Technology dissemination programmes*: schemes provided to manufacturers with the objective of guiding them towards eco-friendlier production methodologies; include demonstrative sessions and informational services
  - *Eco-certification schemes*: the provision of information regarding the environmental credentials of products, either verified by independent entities or self-attested by the producers, in alignment with established criteria
- *Voluntary Policy Instruments*:
  - *Unilateral commitment*: a self-initiated pledge or declaration by a business entity, crafted without the participation of any public institution
  - *Negotiated commitment or agreement*: a framework that encompasses a formal accord between a governmental body and a business or corporate consortium
  - *Discretionary regulation* (commonly referred to as a public opt-in scheme): characterised by governmental authorities defining policy parameters but leaving participation at the discretion of the businesses.[18]

Shaping and influence on the built environment extend beyond traditional demand-side and governmental entities, both local and central. The financial sector plays a pivotal role in the design, construction, management, and renovation stages. This sector's involvement is crucial concerning energy efficiency, closure of material cycles, design quality, and urban development, as it significantly influences the realisation of sustainable development principles. Hence, incorporating financial stakeholders is essential due to their profound influence on the dynamics and outcomes of the real estate and construction sectors.[19]

5.4 Circular Cities: Fundamental Aspects

Cities are vibrant and multifaceted hubs shaped by diverse entities, networks, and individuals. Some argue that their role in transitioning to a sustainable society is ever-increasing.[20] The essence of urban sustainability centres on people and their future well-being. Any vision of a circular city must acknowledge this priority. However, the complexities of public governance often hinder clear actionable paths.[21] For example, navigating smart, circular cities can lead to compounding biases, especially if these models sideline societal well-being. Yet, the prominence of the CE, its inclusivity, and the increasing recognition of urban areas in sustainability necessitates understanding the potential of future circular cities.[22]

Embracing circular management of city resources like materials, energy, water, and land could drastically reduce global resource consumption. This approach can address challenges like waste management, greenhouse gas emissions, climate extremes, and more. It also presents solutions to urban socio-economic issues, from affordable housing to fostering communal ties, ultimately enhancing urban life.[23]

Currently, cities account for a substantial proportion of resource consumption and environmental impact. With urban populations set to rise sharply, transitioning to circular economies within cities becomes paramount. According to McKinscy's projections, by 2050, the majority of the global populace will be urban residents, and the world's urban footprint is projected to triple by 2030.[24] Interestingly, McKinsey predict a marked increase in oyster consumption by 2030, reflecting broader trends in rising material and energy demands. This pattern highlights how urban environments are becoming significant reservoirs of accumulated resources – often referred to as 'urban mines', underscoring the continuous demand for materials and energy. In an era of dwindling resources, tapping into these urban material stocks presents a viable pathway for sustainable growth by reducing reliance on the extraction of new resources.[25]

Much of Europe's municipal waste currently ends up in landfills in Asia or is processed there, leading to environmental and health concerns. While some countries, like China, have tightened regulations, this has often resulted in the diversion of low-quality waste to other nations. The shifting dynamics have posed disposal challenges for European cities and affected their recycling needs.[26]

Cities face mounting resource security concerns, especially around food, water, and energy. A significant number of cities are in water-scarce regions, and urbanisation pressures farmlands, affecting local food supply. The rising reliance on global food sources, heavy fossil fuel dependency, and climate change exacerbate these concerns, jeopardising resource security.[27]

From an urban ecology perspective, a city is a human-created, heterotrophic ecosystem, intricately woven with natural, architectural, and socio-economic elements.[28] In this web, the economy plays a significant but not overriding role. Cities, as described by urban ecologists, are intricate organisms processing resources through a vast network of interconnected stakeholders. Maintaining resource loops is vital for urban health and sustainability on multiple scales.[29]

The principle of urban self-sufficiency emphasises staying within local resource capacities, mindful consumption, and resource recovery. This integrated view stresses localising resource flows, with urban ecosystem health directly impacting its sustainable capacity.[30] Cities are flexible urban ecosystems, and the circular city model epitomises their adaptive nature.[31]

Thus, envisioning cities as intricate ecosystems underscores the importance of resource recycling, ecosystem conservation, and, ideally, localisation of resource flows. This bolsters urban sustainability.

As urban demographics evolve, it will affect the lives, social activities, and consumption patterns of city inhabitants. Addressing these consumption habits is essential for realising a circular society. Urban infrastructure is also a significant resource reservoir, with its creation and maintenance consuming vast amounts of resources. Thus, in the vision of a circular city, infrastructure recycling should be a priority.[32] In summary, a circular city transcends merely incorporating circular economies or business models; it seeks to rejuvenate complex urban ecosystems.[33]

5.5 Innovation in Circular Cities

Circularity, symbolising the shift towards a sustainable city through circular economic practices, is emerging prominently in policy innovations, urban planning, and sustainability goals. Representing this concept, circular cities delve deeper than merely implementing urban circular economies. While businesses are frequently the focus, circular initiatives fostering economic, environmental, and social resilience at city levels require more attention.[34]

A truly circular city is not just about embedding a CE, but about rejuvenating complex urban ecosystems. The technological advancements of the 2010s and early 2020s make cities the prime venues for transforming concepts into reality. These include innovations like sensor technology, cloud computing, ultra-broadband networks, the Internet of Things (IoT), Big Data, and artificial intelligence (AI). They further manifest in applications such as smart transport systems, smart grids, electric vehicles, and renewable energy infrastructures.

The ascendancy of the CE model is buoyed by the widespread adoption of sustainable development by businesses, institutions, and societies. Concurrently, the smart city concept, propelling urban sustainability and CE projects, gains traction. Well-organised resource management bolstered by digital capabilities can magnify sustainability.[35] Similarly, the intersection of smart homes and CE emphasises data-driven resource consumption enhancement.

The momentum towards circular cities is increasing, with technological innovations in energy systems, water supplies, waste management, and infrastructures like transport, healthcare, and education. While the IoT plays a significant role in integrating smart city functions, its use is not imperative in order for a city to be sustainable. However, blending technology and CE principles can lead to cities functioning sustainably and efficiently. Circular city development necessitates innovative strategies for energy and material management.[36] Whether it's energy systems, waste management, or circular planning, innovation remains the linchpin. With an abundance of technological and human resources, cities can be innovation hubs for the urban CE, embracing the '10 Rs' of circularity.[37]

It's pivotal for cities transitioning to circularity to innovate in consumption and production systems. Upcoming research should elucidate sustainable consumption and production dynamics, especially with cities grappling with resource constraints. As urban hubs significantly influence resource consumption, waste production, and global gross domestic product (GDP), they can also be powerhouses for innovation and socio-economic evolution.[38] When activated in cities, innovation fosters a circular approach to resource management, aligning both supply and demand cycles.

5.6 Case Studies: Circular Cities

In this section, we delve into the insights gathered from case studies spanning five cities: Amsterdam, Rotterdam, Barcelona, Glasgow, and The Hague. These insights encompass the perspectives of the respondents and enumerate the distinct efforts and initiatives observed in each city.[39]

5.6.1 Amsterdam

Amsterdam has capitalised on investment avenues in CE activities through the 'Nederland Circulair' programme initiated in 2015. Its sustainability framework intertwines CE with concerns like energy, climate resilience, and air quality. The city's encompassing action programme signifies circularity as its core. Policies are comprehensive, and a balance is evident in initiatives from procurement and infrastructure to collaboration, knowledge-sharing, and commercial support programmes. A notable entity, the AMS Institute, champions research on sustainable urban solutions. A Dutch expert on the circular economy offers key insights on executing CE at the urban scale, sharing recommendations on resource management. Although CE is a nascent realm for Amsterdam, city officials recognise its potential and the need for experimentation. The city is also experimenting with innovative approaches such as 'De Ceuvel', a fully circular section of the city, and waste collection models in areas including Buiksloterham. Their spatial planning emphasises waste clusters, residual heat utilisation, and green space conservation, all fostered through programmes like the 'Learning by Doing' initiative.[40]

5.6.2 Rotterdam

Rotterdam's policymakers envision CE as a catalyst for sustainable business innovation. Visible initiatives have spurred a ripple of innovative solutions. The city collaborates closely with businesses to bring about a fresh and vibrant vision, using the success stories to draw in more stakeholders. Examples include Better Future Factory's recycling tool and City Lab 010's collaborative platform. A significant alliance with the Port of Rotterdam aims at bio-based initiatives. Efforts like the Bio-based Delta Alliance encapsulate the city's dedication to a green transformation, and grassroots projects like the Blue City and 'green waste stream' are pivotal to this vision.[41]

5.6.3 Barcelona

Barcelona envisions a self-reliant future by 2050, embarking on this journey with a top-down smart city blueprint. Major overhauls have been made to transit, lighting, and temperature control systems, resulting in significant resource savings. The intertwined nature of smart and circular city projects is epitomised in the Fab City concept. This idea champions sustainable, interconnected urban blocks. Despite an initial top-down approach, there's a palpable shift towards more citizen-centric planning. An intriguing aspect of Barcelona is its commons movement, advocating collaborative economic activities. Community-led groups actively explore the CE, aiming to amalgamate digital innovations with sustainable economic models. This community-driven ethos is pivotal to the city's identity, with cooperatives constituting a significant portion of the city's economy.[42]

5.6.4 Glasgow

Scotland initiated its sustainability journey in 2002 and further solidified it in 2007 by aiming to reduce greenhouse gas emissions by 80 per cent by 2050. The Climate Change (Scotland) Act, passed in 2009, coupled with Scotland's Zero Waste Plan of 2010, gave birth to Zero Waste Scotland, an institution dedicated to a waste-free society. Glasgow is at the forefront, focusing on garnering expertise and knowledge to usher in this change. Glasgow's main aim is to gather data and foster knowledge for businesses to adopt circular models. For this, they teamed up with Circle Economy, a consultancy from Amsterdam, for a City Scan that links with Glasgow's Digital Plan. By 2013, the city introduced Future Glasgow, a platform using data and technology for smarter urban solutions, such as renewable energy potential and energy consumption patterns. Glasgow emphasises enhancing the quality of life for its residents, integrating better waste management, and effectively utilising resources. This is echoed by the Strategic

Advisor from the Chamber of Commerce, who underscores the role of businesses in the city's circular vision. To help companies transition, the Glasgow Chamber of Commerce and the city set up the Green Business Network. Additionally, the University of Strathclyde launched the Scottish Institute for Remanufacturing in 2015, emphasising reutilisation and remanufacturing, vital for Scotland's industrial landscape.[43]

5.6.5 The Hague

With a vision of achieving zero climate impact by 2040, The Hague's municipal council recognises the significance of sustainability. However, a consistent commitment across departments seems elusive. Despite this, in 2016 the city revamped its employment programme, appointing a director deeply rooted in sustainability and keen on urban metabolic processes, providing a top-down impetus to the CE movement. Research to ascertain the feasibility of becoming carbon-neutral by 2040 suggested that heavy financial injections would be necessary. This led to a shift, making businesses central to the city's sustainability journey. The primary role evolved to facilitating rather than solely funding CE initiatives, emphasising collaboration between residents and larger stakeholders. Even with this momentum, The Hague grapples with defining a concrete vision for CE. The city lacks a clear strategy, partly due to the relatively recent emergence of the CE vision and partly because of differing interpretations of this concept among politicians. The programme manager expressed the need for tangible examples of a circular city to provide guidance, influence key municipal figures, and engage with broader stakeholders. While the marketplace is deemed crucial in shaping a circular city, articulating its role remains a challenge.[44]

5.7 Example of Good Practice in Strategic Planning: Enel Group's Strategy for Circular Cities

Because of the declaration of sustainable development as a paradigm and common aim of businesses, institutions, and civil society, the CE has become a reference model. For numerous years, Enel's strategy has prioritised innovation and sustainability. This alternative presents itself in a variety of ways, ranging across an inclusive and transparent strategy for creating mutually beneficial outcomes to the development of highly modern facilities and the continued spread of renewable energy and innovative solutions powered by electricity. Cities are areas in which we integrate clean power sources, electric transportation solutions, creative infrastructure (smart grids, fibre optics, smart public lighting), customer and company apps, and conservation of energy.

Enel's commitment to the circular city also includes programmes like circular procurement, which measures the circularity of its suppliers, and Future, which converts no longer competitive thermal power plants for new purposes.

Many old economic industries have vanished or are struggling to resurface, producing considerable employment and societal problems. The establishment of a new economic model based on the CE has the potential to provide new possibilities and jobs. The emphasis on existing asset management and accompanying services might create new employment that cannot be removed through automation or delocalisation, as is the case with many industrial operations.[45] Furthermore, new technologies are enabling a phenomenon known as e-government: the accessibility of huge quantities of knowledge, reviewed based on specific needs, allows for rapid decision-making, quick and assertive communication with citizens, and the conversion of substantial quantities of accessible data into improvements in standard of living and competitiveness.

The concept of circularity management becomes dynamic as a result of continuous changes, necessitating an open and adaptable strategy. This is compatible with what happens at a company, for instance, with the open innovation model, in which innovation no longer happens in a planned and 'closed' way, but rather grows through the development of an ecosystem in which start-ups, tech collaborations, and partnerships with academic institutions connect and contribute to new approaches.

Enel's strategy prioritises innovation and sustainability, and the CE is an effective combination of the two. Since it has been concretely used in all sectors of the company, from renewables to electrification and infrastructure, Enel's approach to the CE has become a worldwide point of reference.[46]

6

Dynamic Water Resource Management for Regenerative Cities

NANCO DOLMAN

6.1 Introduction

Only 0.5 per cent of the Earth's water is available fresh water. Although 3.0 per cent of the Earth's water is fresh, all but a small proportion of it is unavailable: locked up in glaciers, polar ice caps, atmosphere, and soil; highly polluted; or too deep beneath under the Earth's surface to be extracted at an affordable cost.

For tens of thousands of years, early human settlements and small cities would rely on water supply that the natural water cycle provided. The construction of aqueducts, introduced by the Romans over two thousand years ago, made it possible to move water over longer distances through gravity alone, along an overall downward gradient. This led to the development and growth of the first major cities in the world, in the Mediterranean region.

Today, more than half of the world's population, over 3.5 billion people, live in urban areas. And almost 50 per cent of people (827.6 million) in urban areas live in slums, often lacking adequate water and sanitation services.[1] At the same time, large areas of the world, from California to the Middle East, face water shortages, and a billion people have no access to safe drinking water. Water supply and sanitation is vital when it comes to health and quality of life. Conflicts over water, in particular water shortages, can exacerbate and trigger conflicts.

In recent history, some of the largest cities have faced water shortages. In June 2018 Cape Town launched an official 'day zero' countdown to highlight the impending cuts to domestic water supply for its more than 3.7 million inhabitants. A prolonged drought raging since 2015 meant that Cape Town's reservoirs had not been able to recover their reserves over the winters of 2015, 2016, and 2017, leading to a steady decline in water storage rates.

Numerous regions worldwide have experienced water supply crises in recent years. São Paulo, the financial capital of Brazil and one of the 10 most populated cities in the world, went through a Cape Town-like situation of water crisis in the year 2015, when the water level in its main reservoir dropped to below four per cent of its capacity. It is thought that a drought that affected southeastern Brazil between 2014 and 2017 was to blame. In 2008, Barcelona was forced to transport water in tankers and, in 2009–2010, Melbourne residents lived under the threat of water cuts following an extraordinarily long drought (1998–2010). The same drought also forced Sydney to implement water restrictions, reducing consumption by 20 per cent.

This chapter outlines strategies, concepts, and best practices to help water-scarce cities to develop resilient strategies for long-term water security. Cities can enhance self-sufficiency in their own fresh water supply by revaluing water as a natural resource. Merging of the urban water balance with urban planning plays a key role in addressing water scarcity among a wide range of climate-related water challenges. This is illustrated by best practices from Tokyo's water-saving city, Singapore's closing the water loop, China's Sponge City Revolution, and Rotterdam Water City 2100.

6.2 Towards a Water-Saving City

Cities are experiencing the impacts of climate change through water-related disasters, while the sustainable management of water resources remains crucial for urban climate resilience. Accordingly, frameworks that integrate urban water management with climate change adaptation become increasingly relevant. Based on a historical analysis of the technical and institutional arrangement in urban water management over time, this is captured by the Urban Water Management Transitions Framework, shown in Figure 6.1.[2]

The first three city states of the framework describe the evolution of the water system to provide essential services: single-purpose and engineered 'grey infrastructure'. These are followed by three city states which describe the anticipated evolution of the urban water system in order to deliver higher-order services ('blue–green infrastructure') such as social amenity and environmental protection, provide reliable water services under constrained resources, and ensure intergenerational equity and resilience to climate change.

The water cycle city forms the central city state in the path towards greater water sensitivity, between waterways city and water sensitive city. According to Brown, Rogers, and Werbeloff, the water cycle city represents an evolution in urban water management where water is conserved and sourced from a variety of supplies, each used according to its suitability. This stage reflects a strong societal commitment to sustainability and marks a shift from the traditional hydro-social contract – where government alone was responsible for delivering safe water – to one of co-management involving government, businesses, and community.[3]

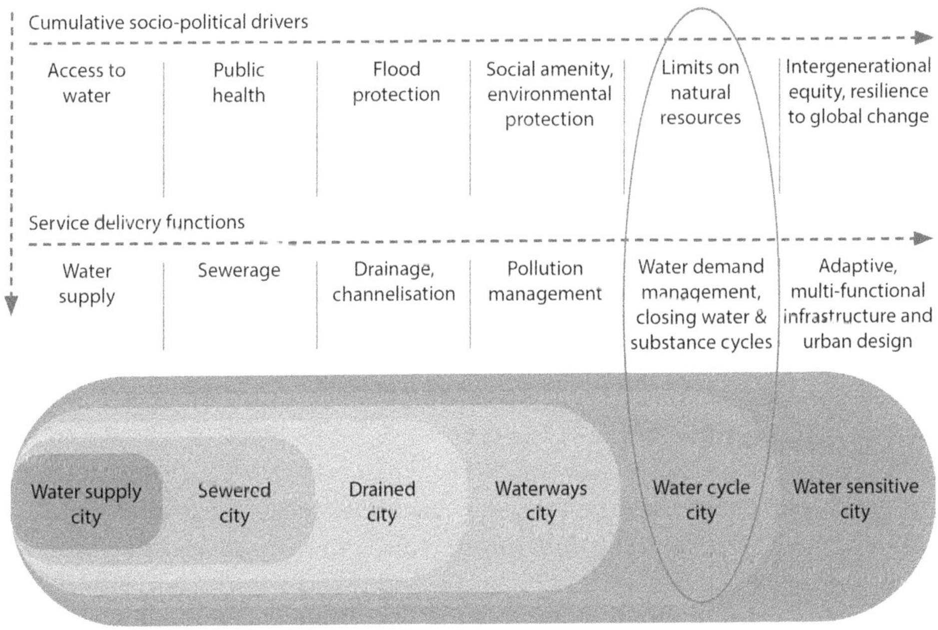

Figure 6.1 Urban Water Management Transition Framework, illustrating the transition to water sensitive cities and resilience through a new hydro-social contract (Credit: Adapted from Rebekah Brown *et al.*, Proceedings of the 11th ICUD, 2008. Reproduced with permission).

To operationalise this water sensitive city vision, Wong and Brown[4] proposed three principles for practice: cities as water supply catchments, cities providing ecosystem services, and cities comprising water sensitive communities. The first principle for practice, cities as water supply catchments, espouses that cities access a range of water sources that include but go beyond surface water sources that capture rainfall run-off from rural and forested catchments or groundwater.

A water cycle city has a supply strategy built around multiple water sources and diverse infrastructures for water harvesting, treatment, storage, and delivery. And this portfolio of sources imposes the least cost, including environmental impacts and other externalities. These alternative water sources include managed aquifer (groundwater) recharge schemes, urban stormwater (catchment run-off), rainwater (roof run-off), recycled wastewater, and desalinated water. Many of these sources are provided within city boundaries and each has its own reliability, environmental risk, and cost profile.

There is a distinct difference between reuse and use. Assuming there are several types of water in cities (and regions) – surface water, rainwater, groundwater, drinking water, and wastewater – reuse implies using water again within the same type of water, apart from a difference in quality. For example: greywater systems for reuse of drinking water in non-potable water demand (e.g. toilet flushing). On the other hand, use is the utilisation of a type of water for another type (of use), like harvesting of rainwater for non-potable water use or utilising effluent from a wastewater treatment plant for influent drinking water production.

Although many developed cities implement blue–green infrastructure (BGI) projects, they are lacking 'cities as water supply catchments' practices concerning sustainable water resource management. Cities have historically invested heavily in single-purpose systems, and consequently in the maintenance of these systems. Besides, the price of (potable) water is low. Against these challenges, Dolman and Ogunyoye[5] adapted the Urban Water Management Transition Framework to examine water infrastructure projects and 'leapfrog' the path towards greater water sensitivity possibilities in cities (Figure 6.2).

The framework indicates that cities with single-purpose infrastructure are in the early phase of the transition process, while multifunctional infrastructure is part of more advanced water management stages. It also shows that, in developing cities, leapfrogging can support cities skipping more stages than developed cities because the developing cities have not yet heavily invested in single-purpose systems and, consequently, the upkeep of these systems.

Our understanding of water challenges in cities, gained from looking back into history and at our current systems, is that they are more complex and multifaceted than engineered grey infrastructure. We need to recognise that many current systems are products of single-purpose, infrastructure-driven solutions. It is therefore important that we first evolve and adapt our systems into those that are resilient in the face of complex and changing conditions, as opposed to just maintaining an increasingly failing system.

With the above in mind, Dolman and Ogunyoye[6] focused on the understanding of the broad water challenges and how we can start a transition into more integrated management of the functions, as well as the social and political contexts. They looked specifically at freshwater scarcity in cities and how different water challenges, such as flood risk, can shape future cities.

With regards to water security in a changing climate, we need to change our view of water use. This means the redesign of urban water management in cities from 'water supply city' to 'water cycle city', in which cities are considered as water supply catchments and promote self-sufficiency. Taking a longer run, leapfrogging towards greater water sensitivity could also be possible for developed cities. A step-by-step approach for the developed cities has been proposed in three 'waterways city' sub-states (Figure 6.2). Additionally, the sustainable water usage and water sensitive city transition in developed cities can be promoted in coherence with other transitions, such as clean energy and circular economy.

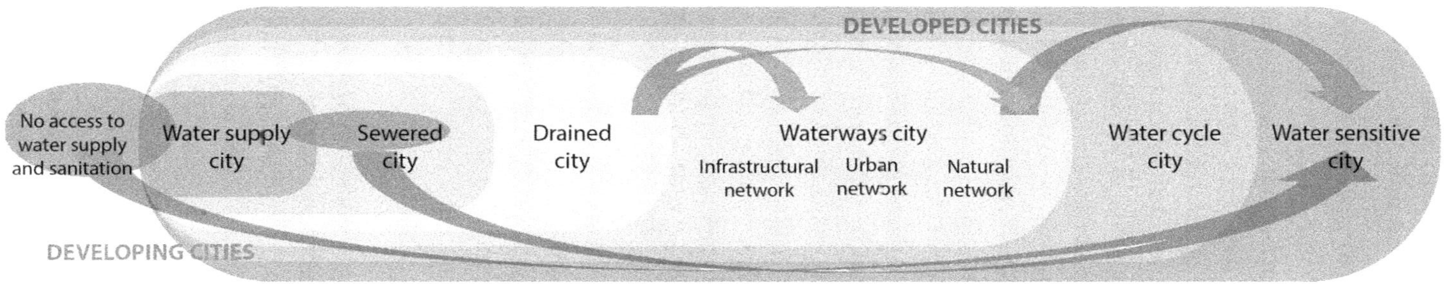

Figure 6.2 Step-by-step approach and potential of leapfrogging of developing cities in the Urban Water Management Transitions Framework (source: author).

6.3 Associated Benefits: Synergy with Water, Energy, and Food Nexus and Net Zero

Water security, energy security, and food security are very much linked to one another in the water, energy, and food security nexus, according to the Food and Agriculture Organisation (FAO) of the United Nations,[7] meaning that the actions in any one area can often have effects in one or both other areas. Water, being a finite resource but also the most abundant resource of the three sectors, is the most exploited. Water is primarily used in forestry, fisheries, and agricultural production (in its entire agri-food supply chain) and is used to create or transfer energy in varying forms.

Water can provide cooling in hot weather, using energy to extract heat. If this principle is reversed, then energy can be extracted. Other energy-generation techniques are energy from water movements (flow through weirs and sluices and from waves and the tide), energy from salinity gradients[8] and aquatic biomass, or energy from the thermal properties of water (temperature gradients between water and the environment, underground thermal energy storage, and geothermal heat).

Urban farming can contribute to urban needs by connecting local food and energy production to community goals, such as improving a liveable urban environment, room for recreation in urban areas, mental and physical health benefits, or educational possibilities. Urban farming can be a garden on a rooftop or balcony, an allotment for amateur gardeners, or professional urban food production and processing at the edges of a city. Urban farming may help to reduce the urban environmental footprint.

Another synergy is BGI, which can be defined as planned and interconnected networks of natural and semi-natural areas (including water bodies and green and open spaces) that provide different ecosystem services (own definition, drawing on EU Commission,[9] Voskamp and Van de Ven,[10] and Ghofrani *et al.*[11]). As illustrated in Figure 6.3, BGI is in the centre of the climate change mitigation–adaptation nexus,[12] by:

- Helping reduce greenhouse gas emissions through more sustainable usage of water resources and associated energy
- Reducing atmospheric carbon through sequestration (carbon offsetting)
- Helping cities adapt to the impact of climate change by
  - Managing flood risk
  - Mitigating the urban heat island effect
  - Reducing drought risk.

For example, by reducing or attenuating run-off, BGI leads to lower volumes of water in combined systems, reducing the flows to sewage treatment works. This leads to energy savings from reduced pumping and treatment.

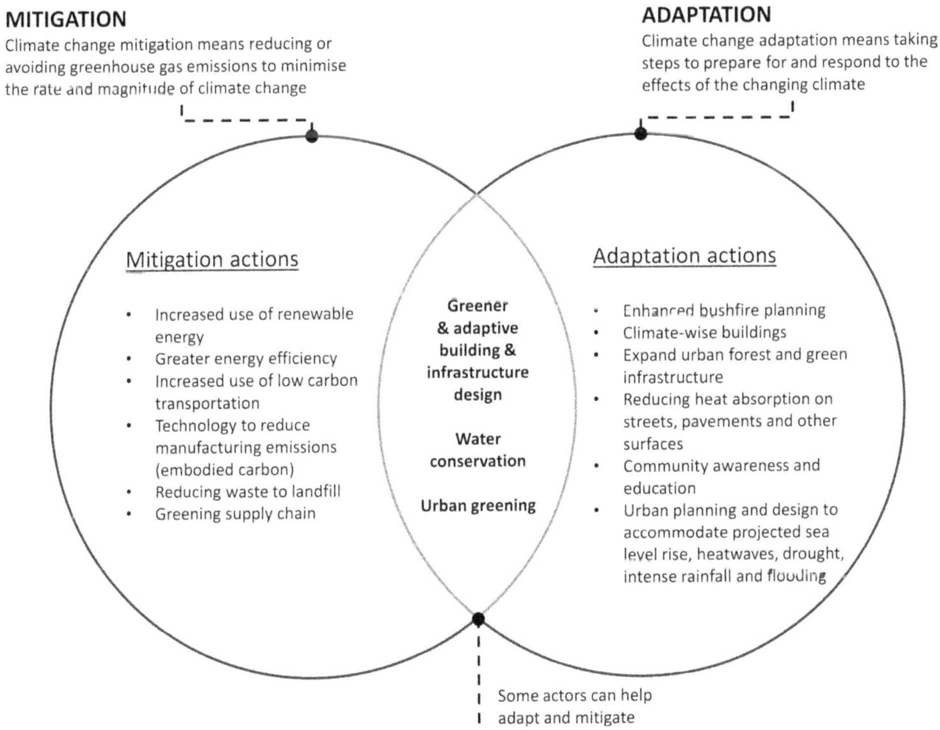

Figure 6.3 Mitigation–adaptation nexus and opportunities for blue–green innovation, highlighting pathways for low-carbon living
(Credit: Adapted from Peter W. Newton *et al.*, Decarbonising the Built Environment: Charting the Transition, Palgrave Macmillan Singapore, 2019. Reproduced with permission).

Managing rainwater at source avoids the large-scale infrastructure to transport the surface water, therefore reducing the carbon footprint. BGI typically has a smaller whole-life carbon footprint compared with grey drainage infrastructure.

The challenge now is to align BGI with net zero initiatives and ensure that BGI is a key part of the drive to make cities carbon neutral and able to manage future impacts of climate change.

6.4 Integration of Water Supply–Demand Balance in Planning Principles and Solutions

A water-regenerative or water-positive city means that it aims to close its water cycles within the limits the natural water system can provide. The starting point for the design of any urban water system is an overview of all the functions and functionalities that the water system – surface water and groundwater – must fulfil, now and in a sustainable future. These ‘dynamic water resource management’ functions and

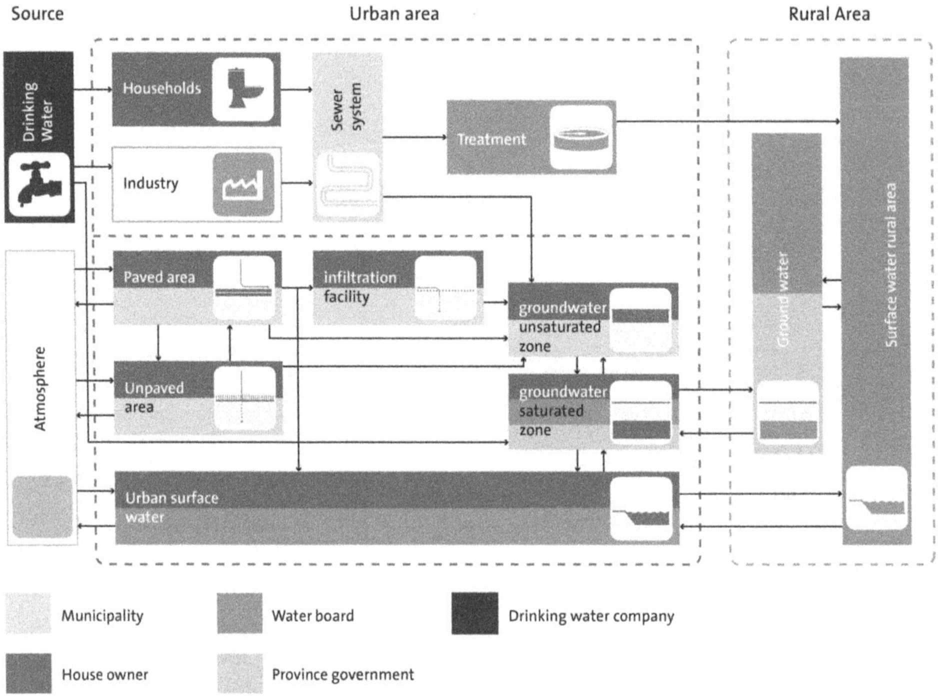

Figure 6.4 Urban water cycle and responsibilities, illustrating key roles and processes in sustainable urban water management
(Credit: Adapted from R. E. de Graaf, PhD dissertation, 2009. Reproduced with permission).

functionalities are the basis for the design standards that are to be applied.[13] Such an overview of functions and functionalities – ecosystem services (benefits to humans provided by the natural environment and healthy ecosystems) – are to be composed for all the five sorts of urban water; that is, for rainwater, surface water, groundwater, drinking water, and wastewater, as well as for the urban soil and subsurface, with each having its own water tasks and responsibilities,[14] as shown in Figure 6.4.

A balance of water resources supply and demand explores the relationship between water availability under natural conditions and demand for water in socio-economic environments. According to the characteristics of incoming water and water consumption, Wang *et al.*[15] describe a water balance formula based on the available data:

$$P + R_{in} - R_{out} - \sum WDi = \Delta SDG$$

where P is precipitation, mm; R_{in} is the inflow from surface water, m^3; R_{out} is the outflow of water volume from the area; ΣWDi is the amount of water demand (required), i represents the water use by ecology, industry, and municipality; and ΔSDG means 'supply–demand gap' and is the residual term of the water balance.

Positive values represent surplus within a closed watershed and vice versa: the ΔSDG can be considered as the volume of groundwater change.

Water scarcity is defined as a situation where insufficient water resources are available to satisfy long-term average requirements.[16] Several methods have been developed to assess water scarcity according to water quantity and water quality, for example, the Falkenmark index,[17] criticality ratio, International Water Management Institute indicator,[18] water poverty index,[19] blue water availability, and green water availability.[20] In general terms, water scarcity represents the overexploitation of water resources when water demand is higher than water availability. Therefore, the Water Scarcity Index (WSI) describes the ratio of water supply to water demand and has been widely used to calculate the dynamic relationship between water supply and water demand:[21]

$$\text{WSI} = \frac{Wd}{Ws}$$

where Wd is water demand, m^3; Ws is water supply, m^3. The classifications for WSI are shown in Table 6.1.

Based on the water resources supply–demand balance, a more holistic – yet conceptual – balance of the urban water cycle can be described as follows:

$$P(t)+G(t)+D(t)=R(t)+S(t)+Q(t)$$

where $P(t)$ is precipitation, mm; $G(t)$ is seepage and infiltration of groundwater, mm; $D(t)$ is production and consumption of potable water, m^3; $R(t)$ is retention and losses [delay] (e.g. rainwater infiltration and groundwater recharge), m^3; $S(t)$ is

Table 6.1 *Classifications of Water Scarcity Index, detailing water supply and demand changes under future climate projections in arid regions of northwestern China*

Range of WSI*	Category of water stress	Level of water shortage
0.0<WSI≤0.1		Surplus
0.1<WSI≤0.2	Low stress	Slight shortage
0.2<WSI≤0.4	Moderate stress	Moderate shortage
0.4<WSI≤1.0	Medium stress	Serious shortage
1.0<WSI	High stress	Awful shortage

* The value of WSI must be greater than zero.
Credit: Adapted from Guo and Shen, *Agricultural Water Supply/Demand Changes under Projected Future Climate Change in the Arid Region of Northwestern China*, 2016. Reproduced with permission.

storage capacity [store] (e.g. surface water), m^3; $Q(t)$ is discharge capacity [drain], including effluent from wastewater treatment plants.

Dynamic water resource management functions and functionalities are to be considered in the supply–demand gap side of the balance, following the living water principles[22] of 'delay (and retain), store (and reuse), drain, only when necessary'. Some practical measures and optional alternatives, both at system and site scale, are: (re)use of water, surface drainage (delay), retention (streets, parks etc.), infiltration (swales etc.), green infrastructure, storage surface water, and adaptive and water-positive building. These functions and functionalities will have to be addressed during the design process by at least considering separately a fast surface and piped run-off component and a slow run-off component through the soil or subsurface drainage system. It should be considered to incorporate these in best-practice guidelines or in a manual.

The current blue–green solutions in the city are mainly aimed at climate adaptation but can contribute much more to other sustainable goals in the city. Nature-based solutions are central to the connection between climate adaptation and mitigation. The transition to a more sustainable, circular, and clean future is also linked to the spatial urbanisation transition and is promoted by nature-based solutions. These solutions aim to restore the balance between the natural and urban water systems by providing ecosystem services to make cities self-sufficient.

Table 6.2 *Type of water infrastructure in connection with urban network and planning, exploring the integration of water infrastructure with urban design and development*

Water infrastructure		Urban planning	Explanation
Hard	Adaptive solutions (e.g. grey infrastructure)	Follows infrastructural network (e.g. utilities, roads)	Strongly dominated by engineers, such as rainwater sewerage and related interventions, e.g. underground buffer facilities (crates, etc.) and water squares that collect rainwater.
	Hybrid solutions (e.g. blue–grey, green–grey infrastructure)	Co-organizing in city network (occupation)	The hybrid intervention is co-organizing in the urban network by increasing multifunctional shared use, for example in a flood defence as an elevated park.
Soft	Nature-based solutions (e.g. blue–green infrastructure)	Retro-fit natural network (soil and water systems)	Nature-based solutions and the 'regenerative' development of the natural network in the city. Examples are urban water buffers, rain gardens and water parks.

Credit: Adapted from Dolman and Brolsma, Water Governance, 01/2023. Reproduced with permission from Water Governance editorial board.

In addition to more urban green spaces, a change in our water management and water use is required. The intensive exploitation of the urban landscape has led to a gradual deterioration of the natural water system to the detriment of the surrounding region. The aim is to restore the water balance between urban areas and the surrounding countryside. This means redesigning urban water management from a 'surface water city' to a 'water cycle city', in which cities are regarded as self-sufficient super sponges. Closing the water cycles in the city is one of the strategies to ensure sufficient freshwater of good quality in the future. Instead of adaptive cities, we prefer to talk about regenerative or water-positive cities. This requires a different approach to the replacement task of the often-grey infrastructure. In connection with landscape, soil, water, and ecology, Table 6.2 proposes a distinction between three types of infrastructure in connection with urban development networks.[23]

6.5 Case Studies: Experience from Practice

Some major cities in Asia have seized the opportunity to transform towards water-saving cities and greater water sensitivity: Tokyo, Singapore, and the Sponge Cities Program in China.[24] Besides the challenge of water scarcity, an associated high price of (potable) water, and related effects like droughts, salination, and land subsidence, these Asian regions have a comparable hierarchical, effective, and strong institutional governance in common. While the government of the People's Republic of China is an authoritarian one-party political system, Japan and Singapore are governed through a coordinated 'whole-of-government' approach. The transformation to water cycle or water-saving cities took between 30 years (Singapore) and 50 years (Tokyo).

Outside Asia, other cities are exploring the holistic approach to develop resilient strategies for long-term water security. One of these cities is Rotterdam in the Netherlands, which used 'research by design' to aim to become a water sponge city in 2100.

6.5.1 Tokyo's Water-Saving City

Solutions to limit land subsidence are to be found in the implementation of dynamic water resource management in the built environment. This means achieving the self-sufficiency of cities by considering the reuse of supplied (potable) water and the use of alternative water sources to limit groundwater extractions. This is an attractive ambition and is further justified by the first pillar of the Water Sensitive City Framework: building flexibility and adaptability in our water sources – cities as water supply catchments.[25]

A city where this has been achieved is Tokyo, the world's largest metropolitan area, with a population of 38.8 million people (2017). In the past the land subsidence experienced by Tokyo was similar to that experienced by Jakarta today.[26] In the 1970s the Japanese managed to slow down and even stop the Tokyo subsidence rate. This was only possible through an extreme decision: to end groundwater extractions and transfer to other water sources,[27] like rain, sea, and surface water. Besides strict legislation and regulation, the Tokyo success in limiting land subsidence was also made possible by the importance of discipline in Japanese culture.

6.5.2 Singapore's Closing the Water Loop

When Singapore became independent in 1965, it was a city challenged by pollution and dependent on agreements with neighbouring Malaysia for the supply of water. Holding limited land and no natural resources, it was ranked first among countries with the greatest risk of high-water stress by 2040 by the World Resources Institute.[28] In 1969, the then Prime Minister Lee Kuan Yew intervened in the matter of cleaning highly polluted watercourses and developing Singapore's sustainable use of its water sources.[29] While the Public Utilities Board (PUB) – Singapore's national water agency – has diversified Singapore's water sources and closed the water loop with reclamation, Singapore isn't yet self-sufficient. In a short period of 50 years, Singapore has become a clean, modern metropolis with a diversified economy and reliable infrastructure.

Singapore is considered a forefront city in Asia and is working on being sustainable in both water demand and supply. Since 2011 two-thirds of the island has been used as water catchment to collect rainwater on a large scale for its own water resources. ABC Waters Programme was launched in 2006 to improve the quality of water and life by harnessing the full potential of its water bodies. By integrating the drains, canals, and reservoirs with the surrounding environment in a holistic way, the ABC Waters Programme creates active, beautiful, and clean streams, rivers, and lakes with community spaces for all to enjoy. Singapore's water management transition is built on four pillars:[30]

1. Four national taps strategy
2. Collaborations with the private sector and population
3. Enhanced international cooperation
4. Water demand management, including:
    i. pricing water to reflect its scarcity value
    ii. mandating water efficiency standards
    iii. encouraging water conservation practices.

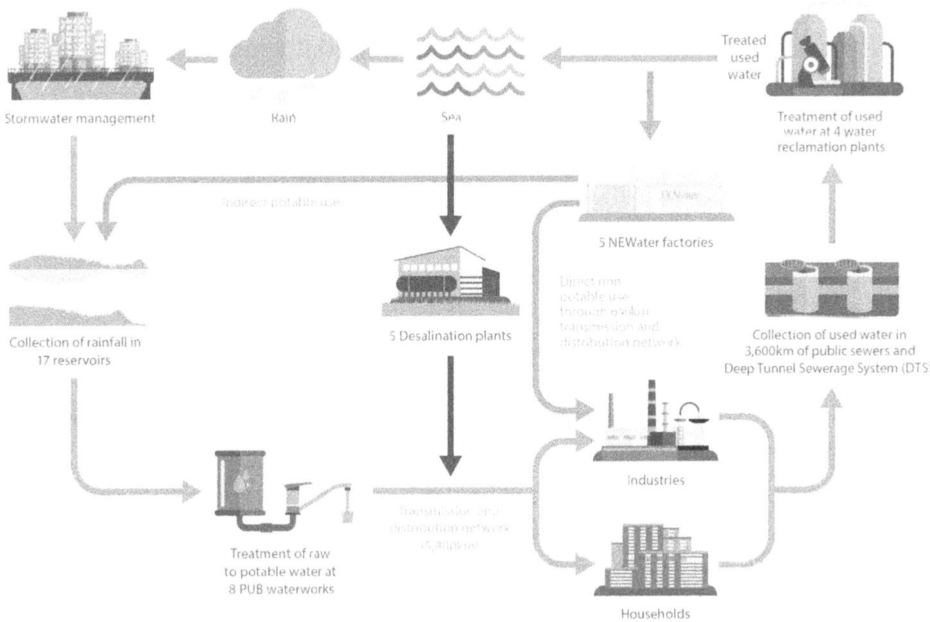

Figure 6.5 Closing Singapore's water loop

With two-thirds of the island utilising water catchment methods, Singapore is one of the few countries in the world to harvest urban stormwater on a large scale for potable consumption. And by reclaiming used water into high-grade reclaimed 'NEWater', PUB is closing Singapore's water loop (Figure 6.5). Despite the current success, Singapore remains a water-stressed nation. Besides rainwater from local catchments (first national tap), Singapore is still importing water from Malaysia (second national tap). To contribute to its own water availability, Singapore is investing in NEWater (third national tap) and desalinated water (fourth national tap).[31]

NEWater is Singapore's own brand of ultra-clean, high-grade reclaimed water. By reclaiming every drop of water so that it can be used again, the water supply can be increased substantially. Although the technology for producing reclaimed water was feasible, initially the cost was too high. It wasn't until the 1990s, when reverse osmosis (RO) membrane technology became more affordable and reliable, that reclaiming water on a large scale became feasible. In 2003, Singapore's first two NEWater plants successfully commenced operation following three decades of development from studies of technology feasibility to full-scale operation.

As an island nation surrounded by sea, desalination is a potential option. Like NEWater, it was not until the early 2000s that desalination finally became a technically and financially viable option for Singapore. Again with RO membrane, the first desalination plant commenced operation in 2005. And Singapore is currently proactively supporting research into more energy-efficient desalination technology, such as electro-deionisation, which would potentially further halve the energy consumption for desalination.

6.5.3 China's Sponge City Revolution

China is transforming urban surface water management systems and promoting water-resilient, low-impact development integrated with urban planning. They are building BGI to improve the city's ability to act as a 'sponge' – absorbing rainwater to manage flood risk, and storing and purifying water for future reuse. The Sponge City Program (SCP) was initiated by the Chinese Government in 2013 to tackle urban water challenges, rapid urbanisation, and reduction in permeable greenspace. The sponge city construction guidance by China was published in 2014. It targets 20 per cent sponge features (e.g. rain gardens, swales, wetlands) by 2020 and up to 80 per cent by 2030. A total of 70–85 per cent of annual precipitation will be managed within urban areas.[32]

As of 2022, this programme has led to SCP projects in 30 pilot districts all over China. In China, the national government, which has responsibility for stormwater management, is a key driver of BGI implementation and has provided funding for the 30 pilot sponge cities. In the hierarchical Chinese governance system, the national government is responsible for developing mandatory standards and clearer maintenance responsibilities to enable barriers to BGI to be overcome.

The sponge city campaign has also taken on an ideological character. As a catchy slogan for eco-urbanism with Chinese characteristics, it has become a symbol for one of Xi's most cherished projects: to establish China as a post-industrial, 'ecological civilisation' (*shengtai wenming*). As a result, visionary urbanists have been empowered to push for an aggressive greening of China and represent a new vanguard of Chinese environmentalist thought and practice.

An example is the starting area in Xiongan New District, Hebei Province, tasked to relieve urban pressure on Beijing. This new sponge city[33] will transform urban water management systems to promote water-resilient, low-impact development integrated with urban planning to improve the city's capacity to function 'like a sponge' by absorbing rainwater to mitigate flood risk while storing and filtering water to meet future use (Figure 6.6).[34]

In other regions, like Europe, many local-scale, low-impact design projects at street or neighbourhood level are implemented. But China is implementing these projects on the district and city scale, such as urban wetlands or eco-corridors. It is showing that ecological design can be about more than just green roofs and rain gardens – it can be a revolutionary rethink of the very texture of a city. China could leapfrog Europe by 2035.[35]

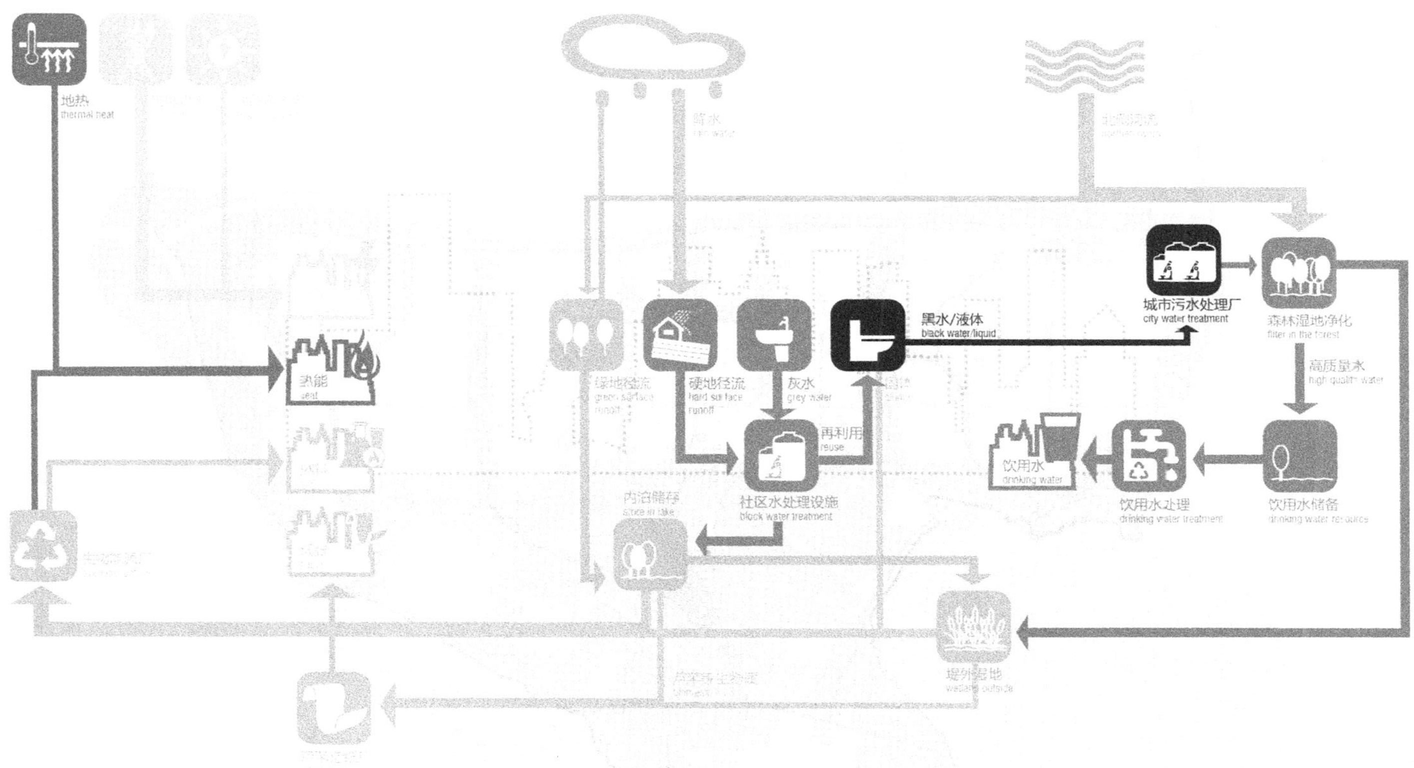

Figure 6.6 Chinese sponge city – water strategy example, illustrating innovative water management approaches in the Xiong'an project
(Credit: Courtesy of West 8, co-author of the Xiong'an project. Reproduced with permission).

6.5.4 Rotterdam Water City 2100

During the last 20 years some very hot and dry summers affected Europe, including five summers in the past six years (2018–2023). This resulted in regionally record-breaking high temperature or low precipitation values. Long-term changes of such extremely hot and dry summers are of great relevance for our society, as they relate to a manifold range of negative impacts on human society, natural ecosystems, and diverse economic sectors. But even if precipitation levels stay the same, climate change will reduce water availability across swathes of Europe.

In 2022 Deltares published a study[36] that confirms climate change will have adverse consequences for the Dutch drinking water that is extracted from the Meuse: during periods of low water discharge the river will be exposed to more contamination incidents or (industrial) discharges as it will lose its capacity to dilute pollutants. This can lead to situations whereby drinking water companies are forced to temporarily stop the intake of water from the Meuse more frequently in the future. A prolonged interruption of water intake endangers the drinking water supply of seven million people. Furthermore, the drinking water sector is currently already facing several challenges, such as an anticipated growth in the demand for drinking water due to population growth as well as an increased concentration of harmful substances in the Meuse water that also threatens the quality of drinking water.

Lastly, extended periods of low water discharge in the Meuse will also affect many other sectors, such as shipping, agriculture, and industry located along the catchment, as well as vulnerable and protected ecological areas that depend on the Meuse.

One of the major cities that is depending on the intake of water from the Meuse is Rotterdam. Both as a port city and a delta city, Rotterdam has a close and essential connection with water. As a low-lying city situated in the deltas of the Rhine and Meuse rivers, about 85 per cent of the city lies up to seven metres below sea level. The remaining 15 per cent of the city, besides the main port area, lies in outer dyke areas. As evacuation is almost impossible, adaptation to climate change is a serious business for Rotterdam. Without climate change, Rotterdam already faces water-related challenges. After a series of different water plans (2001, 2007, 2015), the city presented the Programme Framework Rotterdam WeatherWise[37] in 2019. A year later, the city announced that it was investing heavily in new green public spaces in seven iconic urban projects. The blue and green measures have been brought together in the 2023–2026 Implementation Agenda.[38]

At the same time, Rotterdam is developing a hopeful perspective for the blue–green sponge city of the future.[39] Rotterdam Water City 2100 is built on three pillars: (i) flood protection – closing off Rotterdam from the open water, (ii) flexible integration of land in water: wide, habitable higher landscapes along the large waters, and (iii) sponge city: a water-resilient strategy for long-term freshwater security.

The aim for Rotterdam as a sponge city is to restore the water balance between the urban area and its environment. Thinking in terms of optimal use of space and multifunctional water and liveable city solutions, for example, offers the concept of the city as a sponge: the collection, storage, and use of water, to relate all water and climate challenges. The city as a sponge contributes to the resilience of the landscape in which it lies, including the quality of the living environment and biodiversity.

The city gets a delta dyke protection and becomes a self-sufficient and circular freshwater sponge city with the New Meuse River as its central water body closed off by two double locks (Figure 6.7). This will produce a freshwater lake within the city water system, which allows the city also to further grow and to use the potential of this central water body. Due to the closure of the New Meuse, more housing is possible in former port areas outside the dykes, such as canals and houseboats. Commercial shipping that is currently moving towards the hinterland will be moved more south. Waterfronts can be softened and made more accessible and greener, and an intelligent fresh urban water system supports the city as a sponge. The polders around the city will allow for wetter conditions, enabling it to cope with floods and droughts much better.[40]

As a sponge city, Rotterdam needs to absorb a storm event of 70 millimetres within two hours on all paved surfaces (by means of e.g. green polder roofs, wadis, rain gardens, water squares, soil improvement, and storage under roads). Additionally, the collected rainwater can be buffered locally in the city, such as using the so-called ‘urban water buffers’. Collecting rainwater (rainwater harvesting) has great potential and can meet the water needs of the city of Rotterdam (residents and companies) in both a wet and average year. In a dry year, the amount of rainwater is insufficient to meet the water requirement.

During a peak rain event, the city collects all its rain via a connected open water system, and this is transported to the New Meuse as a central water buffer that can handle approximately nine million cubic metres of water. After the rain, this water is redistributed to the open water network and stored in underground seasonal water buffers in the deeper aquifers under the city. Along the New Meuse, there will be a larger concentration because of the filter capacity of the outer dyke areas, which mainly consist of sandy soils.

In dry periods, the water in these buffers in the aquifers is pumped up again and redistributed through the open water system into the entire city. This was tested in a conceptual water balance considering the WSI in 2100 in a very dry year (serious shortage), in an average year (slight shortage), and in a very wet year (surplus). In an average and very wet situation, Rotterdam can supply its own water demand by

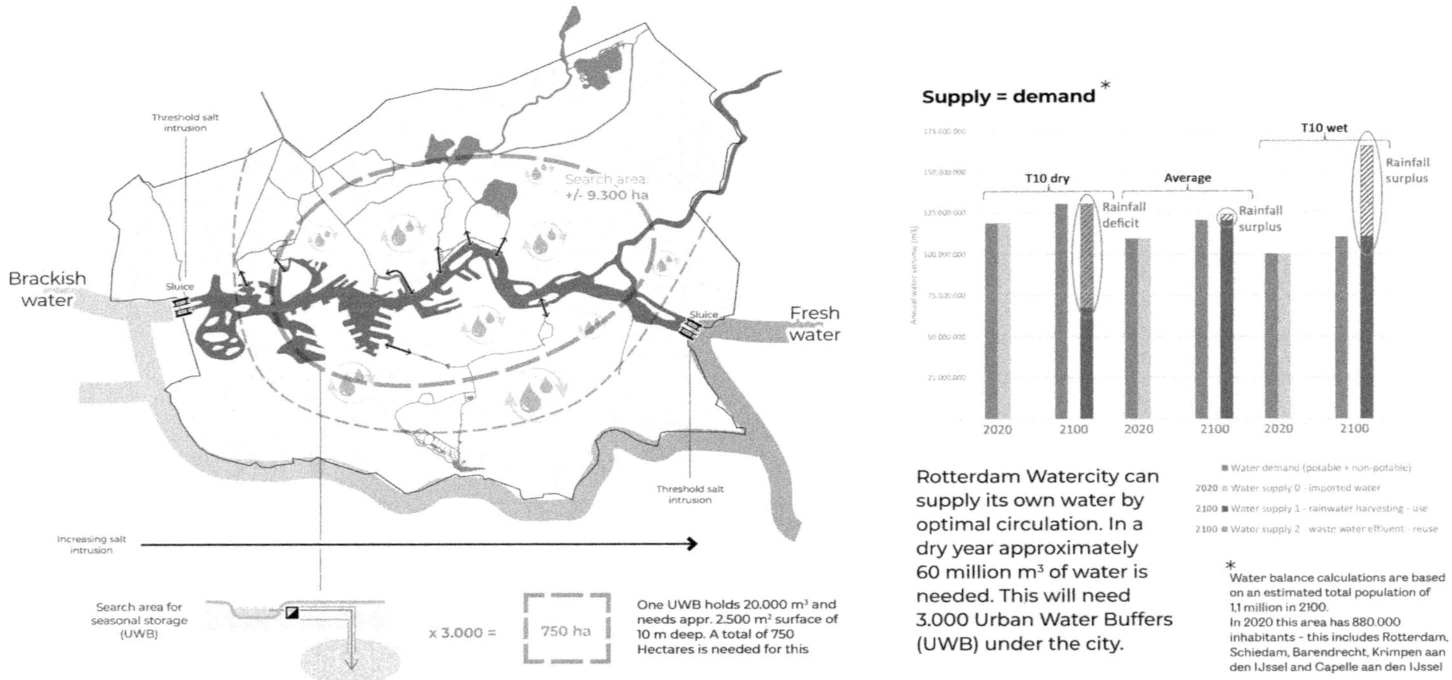

Figure 6.7 Illustration showcasing a circular water strategy for liveable cities (Credit: Courtesy of De Urbanisten. Reproduced with permission).

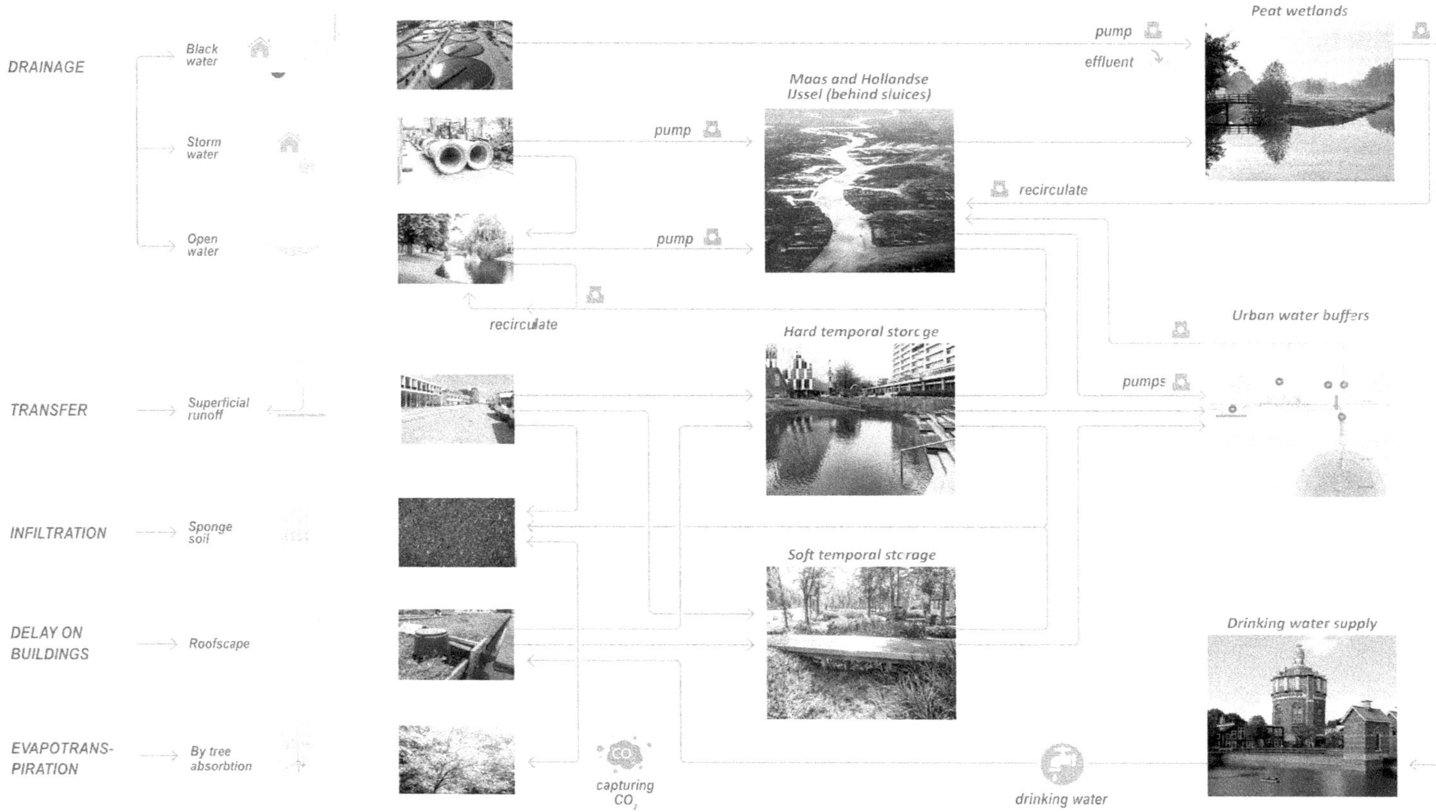

Figure 6.8 Illustration highlighting urban design concepts for sustainable and liveable cities (Credit: Courtesy of De Urbanisten. Reproduced with permission).

optimal circulation. In a very dry year the city is short of 60 million cubic metres of water. This would be provided by storing the surplus in a wet year and then actually transporting that back up into the city.

To retain water from previous wetter years and seasons, Rotterdam needs about 3,000 urban water buffers (as shown in Figure 6.7 within the oval dotted line), which all can store up to 20,000 cubic metres each within the area with the least salt intrusion. Interestingly, the salt intrusion will be less in the future after partly isolating the New Meuse, making it the most central freshwater buffer in Rotterdam.

The region can also help with supply of fresh water during long periods of drought. Potentially, the polder of Krimpenerwaard can become vital for Rotterdam to become self-sufficient in its freshwater demand and supply by using it as a pre-treatment ecosystem service. If needed, the effluent of the wastewater treatment can also be transported there. This will stimulate peat growth through peat-forming vegetation serving as pre-treatment of fresh water and subsequently stimulate carbon sequestration, since wetland soil appears to be the most effective (on land) in CO_2 storage.

The scheme in Figure 6.8 shows how the complete closed freshwater cycle of Rotterdam could look, with the existing base layers on the left, the modalities to collect and recirculate in the middle, and the long-term storage, cleaning, and supply on the right.[41]

6.6 Best Practices

Based on the theory and experience presented in this chapter, best practices follow the three As: 'analysis, ambition, action' as key elements for transforming water-scarce cities into water-secure cities.[42] In addition, 'assessment' should be considered as fourth A that addresses monitoring and evaluation.

6.6.1 Analysis: Good Understanding of Urban Water Cycle and Integration with Urban Planning

Cities can achieve self-sufficiency in their own fresh water supply by considering water as a valuable resource. For this, understanding of the urban water balance is important, by differentiating five sorts of water in cities (rain, surface, ground, drinking, and waste) into demand, use, and quality of water. We must make sure that we reduce our water use, that we reuse every drop and recycle it in our system, and that we utilise other fresh water sources such as by collecting rainwater and storing effluent of wastewater treatment.

Urban planning plays a key role in addressing water scarcity among a wide range of climate-related water challenges. Both in urban retrofit projects as well as new urban development, integration of water management in the different phases of design and development is important.[43]

6.6.2 Ambition: Water-Resilient Strategy Development and Strong Governance to Support Transition

Many cities are struggling to implement measures to safeguard freshwater resources, in synergy with other climatic issues like flood risk reduction and urban heat stress regulation. Transformation towards sustainable and resilient societies, such as water cycle, water-saving, and sponge cities, is only possible when the following conditions apply: (i) there is a collective issue or challenge, (ii) there is consensus on solutions and (future) perspective, and (iii) the momentum and urgency is acknowledged, for example, after experiencing climatic extremes.

Often there is not enough sense of urgency and political commitment to build the required capacity and generate the necessary funds. Yet, the front-runner water cycle cities (Tokyo, Singapore, China's sponge cities) have a comparable hierarchical, effective, and strong institutional governance in common. Safeguarding our freshwater resources asks for raising awareness and a change in behaviour. In culture and heritage, water has been valued but largely been neglected in the modern era.

6.6.3 Action: Implementing the Right Combination of Grey, Hybrid, and Nature-Based Solutions

To achieve improved health outcomes, sustainable livelihoods, and enhanced environmental quality, water security needs to be part of climate-resilient water management, which emphasises solutions and measures that are both robust (able to perform well across a range of possible futures) and flexible (capable of responding to unexpected shocks and long-term uncertainty). This includes considering both nature-based solutions and grey infrastructure, and source water resilience (like rainwater harvesting). Nature-based solutions, such as wetland restoration and preserving flood plains, can increase water availability and quality and reduce the risks from water-related disasters. They can also play a dual role in tackling climate change, supporting both mitigation and adaptation outcomes.

6.7 Discussion and Conclusions

Across the globe, we are already experiencing the widespread negative impacts of variability and unpredictability; from Melbourne residents living under the threat of water cuts following an extraordinarily long drought (1998–2010) to Cape

Town's 'Day Zero' water crisis in 2018. Water scarcity will be further exacerbated by climate change. The UN estimates that by 2050, 5.7 billion people will be living in areas experiencing water scarcity for at least one month per year.[44]

The pressure on freshwater resources will continue to grow, increasing the urgent need to invest in water infrastructure assets. To achieve water-resilient and climate-proof cities, we need to get started immediately. A holistic and integrated approach is required. Many transition strategies are available, such as the water cycle city, water-saving city, and sponge city.

A water-regenerative or water-positive city means that it aims to close its water cycles within the limits the natural water system can provide. We must make sure that we reduce our water use, that we reuse every drop and recycle it in our system, and that we utilise other fresh water sources such as through the collection of rainwater and the storing of effluent from wastewater treatment. By involving design, engineering, and governance in the spatial planning process, we have the potential to bring the built environment and natural environment into balance.

Often there is not enough urgency awareness and political commitment to build the required capacity and generate the necessary funds. The policies, leadership, and investments that get this rapid urbanisation right hold the key to a resilient and sustainable development. Importantly, cities can build on successful case studies such as Tokyo, Singapore, and China's sponge cities, applying the knowledge of those before them and combining these insights with home-grown innovations.

Planning for water-secure cities is always customised. Achieving a water-resilient and climate-proof city is above all about achieving a healthy and liveable city. Involving our living environment and social values is vital. After all, we are all part of the urban ecosystem or 'Ecopolis'.[45]

7

Renewable Energy and Energy Efficiency in Circular Economy Liveable Cities

MARIA KOTTARI AND YOERI DIJKHOF

7.1 Introduction

The research discussed in this chapter is situated within the energy transition and climate action studies at the city or local level through a multiple-actor governance perspective and the just transition principles globally, but more specifically as these have been set up within the European Commission's Green Deal.[1] Academia needs to thoroughly examine the practical implementation of energy-related circular economy (CE) solutions at the city level. Limited research exists on renewable energy and energy efficiency and their connection with the CE. Various schools of thought have studied CE,[2] but not directly within climate change mitigation and adaptation studies, or within energy transition as the critical enabler of greenhouse gas emissions reduction. To date, economists and industrial ecologists dominate the analyses around circularity at the global or city level.[3] However, there is a significant shift towards studies that explore the nexus of urbanisation trends, sustainability, and the CE paradigm.

The chapter does not aim to perform an exhaustive analysis of the CE concept. However, it is necessary to provide a comprehensive overview of the critical CE principles, together with an attempt at a definition based on the most frequently repeated elements while putting it into a local, city-level perspective and within the scope of the energy transition.

Broadly, and assuming the elements found in most CE definitions,[4] such a model aims to minimise the use of raw resources, promote cleaner technologies, and sustain the value of materials and products for the most extended period possible, thus reducing eliminating waste generation. This closed-loop economic system aims to reuse raw resources for as long as possible, eventually replacing the current take–use–dispose linear model. At an optimal phase, the CE could decouple economic growth from resource consumption and ecosystem depletion by keeping materials and energy in a continuous reuse cycle,[5] hence contributing positively to climate change combat by addressing one of its main drivers. Still, the assumption of a decline in resource consumption is not exclusively bound to monetised costs and benefits, but also to consumers' behaviour and encouraging sustainable consumption patterns.[6]

A CE model can be implemented at various levels. Those range from the macro or national level – China[7] and the European Union (EU),[8] for instance, have already adopted CE programmes; to the meso-level, such as in an industrial district or a city, which this chapter focuses on; and the micro-level, such as a company or a household.

The concept of a circular city and the contextualisation of a CE at the city level, in general, is relatively recent. However, the benefits of a CE model in cities are diverse. These include employment opportunities in new industrial sectors or synergies between existing ones, reductions in carbon emissions and air pollution, health improvements,[9] and overall enhancements in liveability and citizens' welfare – particularly in sectors such as the built environment and mobility.

This chapter seeks to further enhance the understanding of circularity at the city level as part of a more comprehensive climate action plan concerning practical implementation. The focus will be on deploying renewable energy and energy efficiency schemes in the buildings and transport sectors.

The transition to a CE is unequivocally linked to the energy transition on various levels. A CE model is more resource- and energy-intensive than the conventional linear economy model. Simultaneously, the energy transition requires more resources, such as rare earth materials, minerals, and metals.[10] Thus, it is crucial to consider critical elements in the relationship between energy and circularity for both transitions to succeed.

Circular design and innovation require a change and increase in the current use of energy. Sufficient energy must be available. Hence, there is a direct link to renewable energy. Furthermore, circularity aims to reduce the consumption of natural resources and materials and minimise waste production. Hence, focusing on resource and energy efficiency is a central component of a CE model.

This chapter takes the framework of circularity strategies within the production chain from Potting *et al.*[11] and applies it to the link between energy and circularity. This framework consists of nine strategies that order circularity strategies by the level of circularity. It therefore defines strategies to reduce resource and material use and maximise the lifetime of products and materials. The nine strategies include: refuse, rethink, reduce, reuse, repair, refurbish, remanufacture, repurpose, recycle, and recover. This so-called '9R framework' is applied to local cases to show the relevance and applicability of a CE model on a city level.

There needs to be more research on renewable energy and energy efficiency and their connection with the CE application at the city level. Various schools of thought have studied CE,[12] but without providing an in-depth analysis of the interrelation between CE and the energy transition process. Following these introductory remarks, the chapter will explore the concept and contextualisation of CE application at the city level. Furthermore, it will attempt to dive deep into the relevance between the CE and the energy sector and inquire into the effectiveness of this synergy in climate change combat. The chapter will present a criteria matrix to reflect on the choice of case studies. Finally, it will conclude by drawing lessons from the case studies while identifying gaps and areas for further research.

7.2 The Circular Cities Concept

As stated in the introductory remarks, the allocation of CE in cities has gained attention among scholars. However, it remains an academic area that requires further investigation concerning the practical implementation of CE solutions. Given their high rates of resource consumption, and significant emissions and waste footprint, it is imperative for cities to adopt CE solutions and practices.[13] With the expected acceleration of urbanisation[14] and the growing accumulation of world population in urban environments, we also expect a significant rise in the demand for material flow and services (such as energy, infrastructure, or accommodation) that would subsequently increase the waste deposit. In addition, the scarcity of resources, coupled with the fact that the acceleration of climate change threatens the security of existing ones, calls for circular approaches in managing the resources produced and consumed at the city level to tackle their finite nature while reducing waste and emissions.

Cities, regions, and circular territorial agents (such as public authorities, industries, small and medium-sized enterprises, the research community, and civil society) can act as potential engines for the transition towards a CE by providing a fertile environment for implementing, demonstrating, and replicating innovative circular solutions. The implementation of the CE solution at the city scale is quite promising from a governance point of view, particularly regarding the role public authorities can play due to the concentration of human talent and capital.

More specifically, the role of the municipality or regional authorities in accelerating the circular transition involves, amongst others, four main domains:

1. *Policy design and application:* Local and regional authorities hold core competencies for most policy areas underlying the CE, such as waste and water management, mobility, built environment, and land use. In the context of the built environment, for example, authorities can operate buildings and housing and enforce regulations on commercial and residential buildings in favour of heating, cooling, and efficient energy performance. For solid waste, authorities

exercise powers in collection, treatment, and cleaning, as well as communication and information. Local and regional authorities have powers over water management, operating infrastructures, and incentivising water efficiency. Authorities can approve land use planning and policies, including zoning, redevelopment, and regeneration, encourage farmers' markets and commercial food production, harness untapped resources in terms of energy and buildings (e.g. abandoned buildings), and develop climate adaptation and resilience plans.

2. *Monitoring and evaluation:* As an integral part of the policy design and application of the CE solutions, the local and regional authorities also have the capacity to define targets and develop key performance indicators to put in place monitoring and evaluation tools assessing the progress of the CE solutions, including the performance of the different actors involved in the process.
3. *Fostering collaboration:* Local and regional authorities can facilitate cross-thematic and cross-sector collaboration; for example, by promoting a culture of cooperation, knowledge exchange, and creation. Cities have always been magnets for creative potential and, thus, facilitators of societal transformation towards more sustainable practices in the public and private sectors.
4. *Access to funding:* Local and regional authorities' public procurement and access to funds can play a key role in driving demand and successful implementation and replication of circular products and services. First, local and regional authorities can increasingly implement circularity criteria as part of their public procurement procedures. Setting this example creates demand for circular products and services, thus supporting circular business models and other initiatives. Second, authorities can support local initiatives and innovative circular products through funding or setting up platforms or networks where funders and entrepreneurs meet.

A vast majority of CE initiatives at the urban level have been reported in the EU[15] in cities known under names such as 'smart cities', 'green cities', or 'eco-cities'. Several cities have recently established strategies and plans to create sustainable circular ecosystems and to design participatory community-based innovation schemes in their localities. A CE strategy mainly focuses on the vision and roadmap towards the circular transition at the city level. At the same time, an action plan should elaborate further on the details of the specific city's or region's 'metabolism' (e.g. material and energy streams, bio-sources, and sinks), identify critical actors and drivers of the transition to circularity, at a minimum, and set up an action agenda. It should analyse and quantify the economic, social, and environmental benefits and challenges related to its implementation and demonstration in its territory. It should include monitoring and evaluating the transition towards a CE, as well as identifying its strengths, weaknesses, and their underlying causes. It should analyse regulatory obstacles and drivers and provide clear and precise policy recommendations to promote the CE through regulatory mechanisms (including, when relevant, inputs on standardisation and certification) at the national, local, or supranational level (EU overarching CE policy framework, for instance). Furthermore, it should analyse the effectiveness of available financial schemes for urban or regional CE solutions and propose concrete options for their improvement. Last, it should include monitoring and evaluation tools that measure the progress of the CE actions based on quantified equity criteria and targets, and it should ensure safeguards. The example of the city of Amsterdam highlights the importance of developing and implementing a coherent CE strategy and action plan. Amsterdam has identified itself with the concept of CE since 2013[16] and is a European pioneer in transitioning to circular models in various economic sectors.[17] The city council has launched the Circular Innovation Programme 2016–2018,[18] encouraged innovations, and accelerated the transition to a CE in order to rebuild the city after the COVID-19 pandemic and mitigate climate change. Inspired by the concept of Doughnut Economics developed by the British economist Kate Raworth,[19] according to which an economy can only be sustainable and prosperous if social and economic goals are achieved without exceeding the ecological ceiling, Amsterdam's new vision for urban development will be based on the principles of CE, reassessing the impact of the current economic system.[20] In the Circular Amsterdam 2020–2025 programme,[21] the city aims to adopt a more innovative approach to the use of raw materials (the aim is to halve the use of new raw materials by 2030 and to achieve a fully circular city by 2050), to avoid waste or use it as fuel, and to 'close' the production circles for products and buildings. Circularity will target three value chains responsible for the scope-3 emissions: food and organic waste, consumer goods, and buildings. The municipality has developed a monitoring framework, the so-called Monitor for Circular Economy,[22] based on input indicators related to the three prioritised value chains (which are expressed in weight and will be further broken down into CO_2 emissions and environmental cost). This model is constantly updated with more accurate data to identify areas that need further intervention, determine the social and ecological impact of the circular transition, and define the ultimate feasibility of the circularity goals. The monitor is not socially blind. Amsterdam's ambition is to keep its residents inside the 'doughnut circle', safeguarding their broad prosperity without putting more pressure on the planet than is sustainable.[23]

As already specified in the previous section, this chapter is approaching CE intervention within the context of the 9R framework. Table 7.1 elaborates on these CE principles while providing examples of the application of these principles at the city level and references to the energy sector.[24]

Table 7.1 *The 9R circular framework, showcasing strategies for circular economy implementation.*

Circular economy principles	Description	Relevant energy sectors and stakeholders at city level
Refuse	Making products redundant by abandoning their use or offering the same with a radically different product	Uptake of renewable energy (removing the need for fossils)
Rethink	Using products more intensively	Mobility as a Service
Reduce	Increasing efficiency or using fewer natural resources and materials	Biobased buildings
Reuse	Reusing products by multiple consumers	Circular solar panels
Repair	Repairing and maintaining defective products so that use in their original function can be maintained	'Repair cafés'
Refurbish	Restoring an outdated product and bringing it up to date	Amac Premium Apple Reseller
Remanufacture	Using parts of discarded products in a new product with the same function	Fairphone: a modular and repairable phone
Repurpose	Using discarded products or their parts in a new product with a different function	Use of products or parts in city design
Recycle	Process materials to obtain the same (high-grade) or lower (low-grade) quality	Recycling stations
Recover	Incineration of materials with energy recovery	Waste incinerator

Credit: Adapted from the original 9R framework by Potting *et al.*, with permission. Note: Original source properly cited as per approval.

7.3 Circular Economy and Energy at City Level

Today, cities account for about 75 per cent of global energy use, which is expected to increase considerably as the proportion of the global population in cities is also expected to rise from 50 per cent to 70 per cent in 2050.[25] Local governments have a unique opportunity to reduce green energy demand while retaining continuous development within their cities. Creating favourable circumstances for circular design in the energy system allows cities to cope with growing demand while reducing their environmental footprint. Cities are excellent testing places for innovative circular design, as the boundaries of policies and changing consumer patterns define the playing field. Simultaneously, cities give advantageous stimuli for scaling initiatives to successful implications on the (energy) system level. Circularity can help the energy system integration at the city level through sharing energy resources and shifting consumption patterns. The further uptake of renewables and including different actors is crucial in any case. The operation of energy communities is expected to be an essential driver of CE solutions at the city level.[26] It could significantly impact household energy behaviour, cascade energy use, introduce new business models (e.g. urban mining for critical resources) and product design, and stimulate citizen-driven innovation while bringing additional social benefits such as circular green job creation in the installation and maintenance sectors. Selecting case studies within cities was based on three criteria:

1) The cases needed to be located in developed regions and, therefore, affluent cities. This was based on the assumption that these affluent cities were the hotspots of consumption and waste and had appropriate resources for successfully implementing and scaling CE initiatives.
2) The city needed to be within a country that has adopted a national strategy towards CE. An overarching circular policy framework provides ground for the circular city principles and development of a circular ecosystem on a city level.
3) The city needed a specific CE strategy or plan that promotes a circular way of living in the local community.

This chapter covers case studies entirely from cities in the EU, which has set an overall goal of becoming a complete CE by 2050.[27]

The cases show front-runner initiatives in affluent European cities. Key to these cases is the involvement of local stakeholders, including authorities, citizen initiatives, businesses, and other organisations. The cities are backed by ambitious local and national policies aimed at supporting the transition to a CE. Furthermore, the initiatives are often supported by local, national, and even European funding. The case studies do not go into the strategies in depth but gather give an overview of the on-the-ground implementation of circular activities.

7.3.1 Renewable Energy and Circular Economy Cities

A circular economic model is more energy and resource intensive than the current linear model. Hence, sufficient availability of renewable energy is crucial to cities' sustainable development and growth. Energy from renewable sources, such as solar photovoltaic (PV), solar thermal, energy recovery from waste, or geothermal, offer opportunities to cities to narrow, slow, and close the loop of fossil fuel consumption. Simultaneously, the circular design of energy systems maximises the lifespan of system components and the recycling and recovery of critical materials.

The Leiedal intermunicipality association in Zwevegem, Belgium, proves a valuable case for the design of a circular and closed energy system on a city level. The RE/SOURCED project[28] ('Renewable Energy SOlutions for URban communities based on Circular Economy policies and Dc backbones') has a circular design to optimise the uptake and use of renewable energy. It is sited in a former 1912 power station, which offers a unique environment for a closed circular renewable energy system. The project is a unique collaboration between the local authority, the grid operator, knowledge institutes, businesses, and citizens.

The backbone of the project involves a DC (direct current) power grid resulting in energy savings (higher energy efficiency, as fewer conversions from DC to AC are required) and resource efficiency (higher capacity of the grid with a similar amount of resources required). In its design, the project makes use of retrofitted solar PV panels and energy storage solutions.

The project's ownership, management, and consumption are shared in an energy cooperative. Through energy cooperatives, citizens can participate in initiatives promoting renewable energy production and consumption. Cooperatives offer cities an instrument to implement a decentralised energy policy.[29] Energy cooperatives, therefore, play a unique role in involving local communities and cities in the design and transition to a more circular energy system.

Moreover, innovative technologies in mobility further provide opportunities for the sustainable use of renewable energy in a circular system. Charging and recharging vehicles to the local electricity grid facilitates an efficient uptake and use of renewable energy. Shared mobility systems strengthen a city's circularity by reducing vehicle ownership and enhancing service-oriented activities. Sharing services (e.g. electric moped scooters) have grown enormously recently, particularly in European cities. In Berlin, these services are considered a space-efficient and eco-friendly alternative for mobility in cities,[30] potentially having a similar environmental impact on global warming mitigation as public transport.[31]

Circularity, furthermore, facilitates innovative technologies supporting the development of renewable energy. For instance, circular solar panels reduce the need for virgin resources and harmful materials, reducing their carbon footprint compared to conventional panels. This improves the overall environmental footprint of the energy system and, thus, of cities. Moreover, such developments open a new array of green and sustainable jobs through producing, installing, maintaining, and recycling panels.

In conclusion, circular cities and the production and consumption of renewable energy are undoubtedly interlinked. The circular design of energy production, transmission, and storage offers the potential for expanding the life cycle of the energy systems and making optimal use of resources and materials on a city level. This goes hand in hand with other circular city-level developments, such as shared mobility systems, and other circular jobs and business models.

7.3.2 Circular Economy and Energy Efficiency: Spotlight on Buildings

A research gap remains for a comprehensive and multidisciplinary review of concrete applications of CE in the built environment to understand the complexity of sustainable development in the field and to support the development of successful policies and planning practices.[32]

The built environment plays a crucial role in global climate emissions. Still, because of high resource consumption in both phases – construction and use – climate efficiency cannot be improved by simply replacing the existing cities with new ones. To decrease the environmental impact in the construction industry, Krausmann *et al.*[33] suggest more intensive utilisation of existing building stocks, longer service life, and more efficient design and technologies. Hara *et al.*[34] suggest implementing the concept of industrial symbiosis, including urban waste utilisation as energy and material sources, especially in the steel and cement industries. Esa *et al.*[35] consider CE concepts such as waste hierarchy and 3R (Reduce, Reuse, Recyle) in their waste management strategy for the construction industry and note that waste prevention strategies are applied to the design and planning stage, while recycling and reuse are used during procurement, construction, and demolition.[36]

Multiple improvements have been suggested for the buildings' Life Cycle Analysis. One direction for recent development is considering any compensating elements on the property, intending to promote renewable energy and green infrastructure as a carbon sink (Renger *et al.*).[37] A significant part of operation-phase energy consumption in a building's life-cycle emissions requires harnessing upcoming renewable energy techniques that apply to an urban environment.[38]

The awareness and behaviour of consumers inhibit the successful implementation of the CE. For instance, this is visible in the construction sector, where consumers' critical demand for circular buildings or building materials is low. For example, new Dutch house owners focus more on the gas issue and the degree of isolation and less on circular construction. However, using biobased materials in the insulation and renovation of buildings provides opportunities for developing local resource loops while at the same time improving the energy efficiency of buildings.

Whereas in most cases the use of biobased materials in the built environment is limited to individual buildings, in Stockholm, an urban construction project will solely make use of wooden structures. The Stockholm Wood City project extends over 250,000 square metres, including 7,000 office spaces and 2,000 houses. Construction will commence in 2025, with the first building expected to be finalised in 2027. The area combines residential, working, recreational, and shopping functions of daily city life. Wooden constructions can offset carbon emissions during construction compared with conventional structures such as concrete foundation works.[39]

New and more energy-efficient buildings improve urban emissions, but construction materials production in new construction may offset the savings.[40] Energy-intensive facilities and settlement patterns cannot be easily replaced because of material-intensive construction and slow regeneration of the built environment.[41] Therefore, buildings' circular or modular design offsets the need for replacing buildings with new energy- and material-intensive construction. The function of buildings can change throughout their lifespan, particularly in vibrant and quickly developing cities. Modular design provides an answer to changing needs in the functionality of buildings, with minimal waste of materials and resources. The city hall of Brummen, a small municipality in the Netherlands, was renovated using a modular design. The city sought a building that could serve its purpose for at least 20 years. As buildings are typically built to last longer, the renovation was designed so that the building could be disassembled after its primary use. This resulted in a city hall that could be dismantled while reusing or recycling 90 per cent of its components.

7.4 Conclusions

Between 2015 and 2020, the European Commission issued two non-binding Circular Economy Action Plans to support the transition to the CE. These plans included various measures to enable innovation and investment in CE solutions. By now, almost all the EU Member States (MSs) have adopted or are in the process of adopting national, and in many cases regional and city-level, CE strategies and plans. During the same period, the European Commission made available a significant amount of funding, which reached €10 billion, to foster green innovation and help private businesses transition from a linear to a CE. Still, little progress has been identified in the overall circularity performance of the EU MSs. In addition, the European Court of Auditors has drawn attention to the fact that the MSs spend most of the available funds on managing waste rather than preventing it through circular product design.[42]

The transition to new sustainable growth models incorporating CE solutions comes with numerous challenges. The CE may best be realised at the city level, where cities and their metropolitan regions are at just the correct scale to make the shift. There is no one-size-fits all solution for a circular city; the municipality/region authorities should spend much time with their citizens and consult with relevant stakeholders in order to understand how they would like to see their city in the future. A clearly spelled-out roadmap, accompanied by a targeted action plan with guiding principles, would ensure that society develops in the right direction during its implementation. It is imperative to focus on critical areas of a city. With understanding the limitations of a city, it is vital to narrow down the sectors which could also be measured and monitored. As Joensuu, Edelman, and Saari rightly point out,[43] the cities should focus on collecting valid and accurate data, which is the critical enabler for developing evaluation methods for the objectives of CE in the future. Evaluating sustainability in CE innovations differing from business-as-usual practices calls for developing hybrid methods built by combining well-established scientific methods. More attention also needs to be paid to social aspects, which call for developing evaluation methods for social acceptability and inclusive easy-to-understand methods for presenting the results. Appropriate evaluation methods would help start a self-correcting process and establish the next broadly shared CE strategic plan.

The energy transition is taking shape in European cities. The uptake of renewable energy has seen fast-growing numbers in the last few years and will continue to grow in the coming years and decades. However, this surge in the uptake of renewable energy technologies poses new challenges, such as the availability of sufficient resources. Therefore, the transition must take a circular approach, where the use of materials and components is maximised. Only this creates a sustainable, future-proof energy system. Circular innovations supporting energy efficiency are taking place but need further scaling. Individual cases are known where circular, energy-efficient applications have been successfully implemented in the built environment. Cities should involve architects and designers, construction companies, and future homeowners to boost circular initiatives in the built environment.

8

Urban Nature-Based Solutions to Create Circular and Liveable Cities

ROBERT C. BREARS

8.1 Introduction

Urban nature-based solutions (NBSs) address multiple climatic and non-climatic challenges, including extreme weather events, biodiversity loss, water and food security, human health, and socio-economic development. The International Union for Conservation of Nature describes NBSs as measures taken to preserve, manage sustainably, and rejuvenate either natural or altered ecosystems. These solutions are devised to respond to societal issues in a flexible and efficient manner, while concurrently offering advantages to both humans and biodiversity. In urban centres, NBSs is considered an umbrella concept of approaches, including green infrastructure, blue–green infrastructure, and natural capital. Irrespective of the terminology, NBSs can help enhance climate change adaptation and mitigation and improve liveability, all the while generating multiple environmental, economic, and social co-benefits. Examples of these co-benefits include reducing run-off and associated impacts of flooding, creating job and business opportunities, and promoting healthy lifestyles through increased outdoor recreation opportunities.[1]

8.2 Urban Nature-Based Solutions

Urban NBSs vary in both scale and scope and include the levels of buildings, public spaces, water bodies, drainage systems, and green corridors. Urban NBSs provide three main opportunities. First, they support economic development in urban areas, which is dependent on the amount and quality of natural resources available. Second, urban planning that incorporates urban NBSs has a positive environmental impact, such as mitigating emissions through increased carbon storage, and increased resilience to floods, droughts, and heatwaves. Third, urban NBSs contribute to the social dimension of urbanisation, such as green space increasing people's happiness and general health. By working with nature, cities can deliver a range of ecosystem

Table 8.1 *Ecosystem services provided by urban NBSs*

Ecosystem service	Examples
Provisioning	Fresh water
Regulating	Carbon sequestration
Cultural	Inspiration for culture, art, and design
Supporting	Habitats for species

services to residents (Table 8.1). Through the delivery of these services, cities become more competitive, resource efficient, resilient, and liveable.

The planning and designing of urban NBSs can be guided by six principles:

1. *Multifunctionality*: Urban NBSs can perform several functions and provide several benefits within the same spatial area by, for example, harnessing the interrelationships between vegetation and the water cycle to improve living conditions in the city, thus enhancing both sustainable development and ecosystem services.
2. *Connectivity*: Urban NBSs form an interconnected network across the urban landscape. For example, a natural reserve that is connected to others by green corridors provides more ecosystem services than one surrounded by urban development, as it allows for wildlife movement between different habitats.
3. *Habitability*: Urban NBSs provide an outdoor habitat for people, flora, and fauna, providing multiple benefits to humans and nature, including improved air and water quality, increased opportunities for outdoor recreation, and restoration of native habitats.
4. *Resilience*: Urban NBSs can increase resilience to climate change across various scales. For example, green roofs can reduce the urban heat island effect at the city level while reducing the cooling needs of individual buildings.
5. *Identity*: Urban NBSs can contribute to the visual definition of a place. For example, it can include vegetation of significance to the area.
6. *Return on investment*: Urban NBSs need to demonstrate how they can reduce costs and yield positive financial outcomes. Urban NBSs can generate monetary benefits by increasing land value, catalysing economic development, lowering energy demand, and reducing grey infrastructure costs.[2]

8.3 Types of Urban Nature-Based Solutions

There are numerous types of urban NBSs that can be applied to restore and enhance the natural environment while providing multiple environmental, economic, and social benefits, including the following.

8.3.1 Green Roofs

Green roofs are essentially roofs with plants. Also known as ecoroofs and living roofs, green roofs manage stormwater by releasing it gradually, and they contribute to a reduction of the urban heat island effect. Green roofs improve the long-term performance of roof structures due to the protection they provide against ultraviolet radiation and extremes of temperature. The plants in green roofs also provide habitat for animals in urban environments. There are various types of green roofs:

- *Extensive green roofs*: These have a shallow substrate, with overall depths between 100 and 180 millimetres. Their main purpose is stormwater mitigation. Typical vegetation on extensive green roofs includes moss, herbs, and grasses. Because a lighter supporting structure is required, extensive green roofs are more economical; however, the thin substrate means it can store very little water, necessitating irrigation and the selection of appropriate plants.
- *Intensive green roofs*: These have a deeper soil profile, with overall depth around 200 to 760 millimetres, and therefore a greater range of plants can be considered. Typical vegetation includes lawns, perennials, shrubs, and trees. Their main purpose is stormwater mitigation, biodiversity, and amenity space. A heavier structure is required to support the weight of deeper soils and plant material, and so there is higher initial cost. Intensive green roofs are often used for landscaped terraces and over underground carparks.
- *Semi-intensive green roofs*: Semi-intensive green roofs form a transition from extensive to intensive green roofs. They are usually around 150 to 250 millimetresin depth and characterised by herbaceous plants, perennials, ground cover, grasses, and even small shrubs. Their purpose is typically stormwater mitigation and biodiversity enhancement. They require moderate maintenance and occasional irrigation. These green roofs can retain more stormwater than extensive types and host a richer biodiversity. Semi-intensive roofs have higher weights than extensive green roofs.
- *Solar green roofs*: Solar green roofs integrate solar photovoltaic (PV) systems with a green roof. The application of a PV-green roof is effective for two reasons, first, the use of a green roof creates new habitats for biodiversity, and second, the combination of a green roof with a PV system is used for cooling the surface of the PV system, producing energy more efficiently in urban areas. In various studies conducted in different locations, incorporating green roof vegetation in PV systems has been shown to increase power output by up to 8.3 per cent, reduce surface temperatures, and enhance energy efficiency.
- *Blue–green roofs*: Blue–green roofs efficiently manage stormwater volume by retaining and detaining water in an engineered drainage media layer. They are controlled by smart drains and a smart flow control system, ensuring precise management of stormwater release. The advantages of blue–green roofs include

maximising stormwater management, enhancing evapotranspiration, controlling flow rates, boosting biodiversity, reducing potable water usage, and providing educational opportunities. They are versatile and can be implemented on roofs without greenery. Blue–green roofs have the potential to eliminate stormwater fees and contribute to flood prevention when connected in a citywide system.[3]

8.3.1.1 Case Study: Subsidies for Green Roofs in The Hague

The Hague's climate adaptation subsidy, which was available until 31 December 2023, offered homeowners, tenants, businesses, schools, neighbourhood centres, housing associations, and homeowner associations in specific neighbourhoods the opportunity to get a refund of 50 per cent of the costs for harvesting rainwater. Subsidy recipients could receive between €500 to €50,000 per application. Rainwater could be harvested by constructing a green roof, placing a rain barrel or a rainwater fence, disconnecting the downspout from the sewer system, or replacing paving stones with grass or plants. However, certain costs would not be reimbursed, such as costs paid by the municipality for a green roof, costs for structures such as roof constructions or a roof cover, costs for removing and replacing existing plants or permeable surfaces, or costs for the applicant's labour.[4]

8.3.2 Green Walls

The term green wall is used to describe and refer to all forms of vegetated wall surfaces. Green walls come in various configurations, ranging from simple to complex. Green walls deliver multiple benefits, including reducing interior temperatures by delaying solar heat transfer, which lessens the demand for air conditioning, mitigating outdoor and surface temperatures, contributing to the reduction of the urban heat island effect, and decreasing noise pollution, particularly at low to middle frequencies, due to the sound-absorbing effect of the substrate. According to the type of vegetation and the supporting structure used, green walls can be divided into two main groups: green facades and living walls.

8.3.2.1 Green Facades

Green facades are based on the behaviour of climbing or hanging plants that can grow along the wall, either upwards or downwards. Green facades can be classified into two categories: direct greening systems and indirect greening systems:

1. *Direct greening systems*: In these systems, plants are attached directly to the wall itself, attaching themselves due to their adhesive properties. No additional structures are used to support the plants, and their roots are either placed in the ground or in a planter box.

2. *Indirect greening systems*: Some plants do not have adhesive properties and therefore require a supporting structure system to maintain their position and develop their growth along the wall. These systems create a gap between the building surface and the vegetation. The plant's rooting system is either laced at the bottom of the facade or at multiple intervals along the height of the building. The most common supporting structure systems are cable and wire rope net systems, metal mesh, or modular trellis panels.

8.3.2.2 Living Walls

Living walls differ from green facades in that their vegetation is rooted to the wall itself rather than being rooted at the base of the wall. Living walls allow for the integration of various plant species. There are two main types of living walls:

1. *Continuous systems*: The continuous living wall system is composed of two layers of synthetic fabric with pockets filled with growing media and plants. The fabric walls are supported on a framework and backed by a waterproof membrane against the facade. Nutrients and water are delivered to the plant roots through an irrigation system at the top of the wall.
2. *Modular systems*: These systems are composed of modular containers that can be in the form of trays, flexible bags, framed boxes, or other receptacles, with pre-cut holes or panels. The containers hold the growing media to support the plant material. They are usually pre-vegetated, providing instant cover after installation. The system requires regular irrigation and fertilisation, using gravity to distribute water and nutrients along the growing media.[5]

8.3.2.3 Case Study: Barcelona's Grants for Party Walls

Barcelona's city council announced a grant programme for party walls – dividing walls between properties that sometimes become exposed due to urban planning changes. These exposed walls can detract from a city's appearance and cause thermal and constructive deficiencies in homes. The grant aimed to address these issues and enhance landscape integration, sustainability, and biodiversity. Key requirements and details included:

- Optional improvements included new window openings, ground floors, PV power generation, and naturalisation.
- The grant was open to owners, communities of owners, and licensees of activities in buildings that meet the general requirements.
- Grant applications could be submitted until 15 November 2023.
- The works to qualify for the grant had to be in buildings over 10 years old, cost at least €750, and respect the conditions established in the granting of the subsidy for a minimum of 5 years.

The subsidy percentage and limit depended on the type of improvements made, ranging from 35 per cent of the action with a limit of €120 per square metre for basic landscape integration and thermal insulation, up to 70 per cent of the action with a limit of €580 per square metre for more comprehensive improvements, including new openings, vertical vegetation, and photovoltaic panels.[6]

8.3.3 Community Gardens

Community gardens represent unified parcels of land that are tended to and overseen cooperatively by a community of individuals. They can be either permanent or temporary. Community gardens come in various shapes and sizes, varying between neighbourhoods. Each is developed according to the needs of the participants who come together to grow fruit, vegetables, flowers, herbs, and ornamental plants. Community gardens can be in schools, parks, housing projects, places of worship, vacant lots, and private properties. There are various types of community gardens, including:

- *Plot gardens (divided into individual plots)*: A common strategy is to subdivide gardens into family-sized plots. Occasionally, a designated area within the garden is set aside for the communal cultivation of larger crops like corn, pumpkins, berries, and so forth, which might be too expansive for personal plots.
- *Cooperative gardens*: In a cooperative garden, the entire space is managed as one large garden through the coordinated efforts of many community members. Produce from the gardens can be distributed among the member gardeners. These gardens are typically associated with communities of faith, civic groups, or service organisations.
- *Youth gardens*: With increasing interest in science and nutritional education, many schools are planting gardens to serve as outdoor classrooms. In the garden, every student becomes a scientist participating in research and discovery. In addition to providing a hands-on setting for teaching skills, the garden is a place for students to learn responsibility, self-confidence, and critical thinking.
- *Entrepreneurial gardens*: Gardeners acquire commercial acumen and abilities through the cultivation and sale of produce to nearby markets and dining establishments. In the context of enterprising market gardens, young individuals not only learn the art of growing food but also master the skill of marketing it at local farmers' markets or grocery outlets.

Community gardens provide multiple benefits in urban environments, including promoting habitat for plant species. They can make significant contributions to human health and well-being, with the main benefits coming from contact with nature and the social opportunities these places provide. Community gardens are drivers of social cohesion by providing environmental education, intergenerational learning, and understanding of climate change. They encourage the sharing of common values, aims, and behaviours, and facilitate social connections through social bonds and networks.[7]

8.3.3.1 Case Study: Brisbane's Cultivating Community Gardens Grants Programme

The Cultivating Community Gardens Grants programme in Brisbane offers funding to non-profit community groups to establish and maintain community gardens that grow food. Grants can be used for tools, materials, services, facilities, educational initiatives, publicity, and operating expenses for these projects. Eligibility requires the applicant to be a non-profit organisation based within Brisbane's local government area, with no outstanding debts or overdue grants with the council, and the project must be accessible and beneficial to the broader community. Schools are also eligible if their gardens are accessible, involve community participation, and are linked to curriculum outcomes. The grant ranges from AUD $1,000 to $2,500 and may cover the full or partial cost of a project. The applications are assessed on specific criteria, each given a percentage weighting: alignment with Brisbane Vision (essential), sustainable project delivery (25 per cent), promotion to the broader community (20 per cent), value for money and budget soundness (20 per cent), project management capabilities (20 per cent), effective consultation and networking (15 per cent), and compliance with necessary permit approval criteria (essential).[8]

8.3.4 Permeable Pavements

Porous pavements, which include materials such as open pore pavers, asphalt, or concrete, are unique in their design, featuring a permeable surface atop a stone reservoir. This innovative construction enables them to capture rainwater and surface run-off, storing it temporarily in the reservoir. Subsequently, the stored water gradually seeps into the underlying soil or is channelled out through a drain tile. The stone or gravel acts as a natural filter and clears the water of pollutants. Permeable pavements are commonly used in parking lots, low-traffic roads, sidewalks, and driveways. There are three common types of permeable pavement, including:

- *Traditional concrete/asphalt*: The standard mix minus the fine particles, which are left out to make it more porous.
- *Plastic pavers*: The plastic grids have a honeycomb shape that allows vegetation, such as grass, to grow through the holes.
- *Concrete pavers*: There are spaces between the concrete blocks which aid better drainage and water permeability.

Permeable pavements provide various benefits, including the following:

- *Hydrologic balance and run-off reduction*: Permeable pavements restore hydrologic balance and lower run off volume by trapping and gradually releasing precipitation, preventing rapid, large-volume water discharge into stormwater systems.
- *Pollutant minimisation*: Permeable pavements reduce certain pollutants through physical entrapment, chemical decomposition via microbes, and biological uptake by plants.
- *Urban run-off temperature moderation*: Permeable pavements slow run-off, cooling its temperature and reducing environmental impact on streams and lakes.
- *Efficiency in surrounding NBSs*: Permeable pavements can lessen the need or size of surrounding NBSs, such as detention ponds, offering cost and effort savings.[9]

8.3.4.1 Case Study: Atlanta's Permeable Paver Retrofit Project

In 2015–16, Atlanta's Department of Watershed Management and Belgard Hardscapes embarked on North America's largest permeable paver retrofit project. They installed over six kilometres of permeable interlocking concrete pavement (PICP) across neighbourhoods near Turner Field to address the persistent flooding issues resulting from impervious urban surfaces and heavy rain. The PICP system, consisting of concrete pavers filled with permeable aggregate, mimics natural processes for managing stormwater run-off, reducing flooding and erosion, and controlling sewer overflows. As part of the USD $16 million project, they chose Belgard's Aqualine™ L-Stone permeable paver, which surpasses Environmental Protection Agency stormwater requirements and endures harsh climates. By 2016, this initiative had provided over 7.6 million litres of storage capacity, helping to mitigate flooding during heavy rains. Atlanta has since adopted stringent post-development stormwater management ordinances, with over 2,000 green-infrastructure-incorporating construction projects permitted since 2013, eliminating approximately 1.3 billion litres of polluted run-off annually.[10]

8.3.5 Rain Gardens

Rain gardens are depressed areas of the landscape that collect rainwater from a roof, driveway, or street and allow it to soak into the ground. They are planted with grasses and flowering perennials and are cost effective in removing pollutants, slowing down stormwater flows, and recharging water bodies. They also provide a habitat for wildlife and increase the visual attractiveness of urban spaces. Typically, rain gardens absorb and filter contaminants before the stormwater flows to surrounding pipes, drains, and water bodies. They are suitable for most locations, including individual sites, roads, and new property developments. Rain gardens can be applied in various settings:

- *Urban areas*: Developers can install rainwater gardens in densely developed areas with few permeable surfaces. They can fit into existing parking lot islands, along roads, at intersections, or in other areas as part of a retrofit, redevelopment, or new construction.
- *Stormwater hotspots*: These are areas where land uses can generate highly contaminated discharges with pollutant concentrations exceeding those typical of stormwater. Examples include petrol stations and some industrial areas.
- *Coldwater streams*: Some wildlife species in cold water streams are sensitive to temperature changes. Impermeable surfaces can increase the temperature of stormwater discharge as it flows into nearby surface waters. Rain gardens can decrease the temperature of stormwater by temporarily detaining stormwater discharge beneath the ground surface.[11]

8.3.5.1 Case Study: King County's RainWise Program

King County's RainWise Program in Washington State, USA, provides rebates, averaging around USD $4,400, to cover most or all the cost of installing cisterns and/or rain gardens on private properties within eligible combined sewer overflow basins. To secure a rebate, property owners are required to collaborate with RainWise-trained contractors, design a suitable installation, undergo pre-construction and final inspections, and submit a completed RainWise package. Upon approval, rebates are typically received within four to eight weeks. The programme places emphasis on maintaining installed systems, and property owners are guided to either self-maintain or arrange maintenance contracts with their contractors. To broaden accessibility, the RainWise Access Grant offers an additional $1,000 to eligible homeowners and non-profit community organisations, including religious groups, in income-limited and underserved communities, thus bridging the gap between the rebate amount and actual project costs. Furthermore, a vendor payment option is offered by select contractors, who cover the upfront installation costs and directly receive the rebate, easing the financial burden on the homeowner.[12]

8.3.6 Bioswales

Bioswales are planted or mulched channels along streets and parking lots that slow down and allow stormwater to infiltrate into the soil. They use soil and vegetation to filter out contaminants before the water is discharged into waterways. Bioswales provide a range of benefits, including reduction of run-off volumes from local roads, pollutant removal through filtering by vegetation and soils, and groundwater recharge if a high level of infiltration is achieved. Bioswales are well suited to treating highway or residential road run-off due to their linear nature. They can also be used to replace existing drainage ditches that are typically designed to only convey stormwater away from roads. There are several types of bioswales:

- *Grassed channels*: These are like typical drainage ditches, with the main difference being flatter side slopes and longitudinal slopes, and a slower design velocity for water quality treatment. The best application of grassed channels is a pre-treatment of stormwater before other stormwater treatment practices.
- *Wet swales*: These swales have a shallow permanent pool and vegetated wetland vegetation to provide stormwater treatment. Wet swales are not typically used in residential settings because of the shallow standing water.
- *Dry swales*: These include a constructed soil layer embedded in the channel base. The original soil is replaced with a mixture of sand and soil that meets minimum permeability standards. Additionally, an underdrain mechanism is installed beneath the soil layer. This usually entails a layer of gravel surrounding a pipe with holes. The soil bed processes stormwater, which then flows into the underdrain. This system subsequently channels the treated stormwater back into the storm drain network.[13]

8.3.6.1 Case Study: Bioswales in New York City

The New York City (NYC) Department of Environmental Protection (DEP) has installed four bioswales on Dean Street in the Boerum Hill section of Brooklyn to manage stormwater run-off and reduce combined sewer overflows into the Gowanus Canal. This forms part of the NYC Green Infrastructure Plan, proposing a total investment of USD $2.4 billion over 20 years to enhance harbour water quality by managing stormwater before it enters the sewer system. Greenstreets crews, funded by the DEP, are tasked with the maintenance of the bioswales. These installations are designed to detain stormwater, which would typically enter the combined sewer system, thereby improving water quality by reducing the intensity of combined sewer overflows. The project is expected to divert over 27,000 litres of stormwater away from the sewer system with each rainfall. Bioswales are vegetated tree pits that allow stormwater run-off to seep into the ground, thus decreasing sewer overflow into nearby bodies of water. Each bioswale on Dean Street can handle 7,000 litres of stormwater per storm.[14]

8.3.7 Green Urban Parks

City parks are often characterised by their expanses of open space, functioning as natural sponges that absorb rainwater. However, their benefits extend far beyond this, touching upon several essential aspects, including water quality enhancement, habitat

Table 8.2 *Opportunities to enhance park features with NBSs*

Park infrastructure	Nature-based solutions
Parking lots	• Bioretention in landscaped areas, medians, and roundabouts • Permeable pavement in parking stalls and walkways • Trees in landscaped areas
Visitor centres	• Bioretention demonstration gardens • Pollinator gardens that treat stormwater • Green roofs • Rainwater barrels and cisterns • Planter boxes in space-limited areas
Playing fields	• Temporary detention storage • Permeable pavement in parking stalls and walkways
Wetlands and drainage systems	• Natural areas along stream channels • Constructed wetlands created in existing drainage areas • Wildlife habitat areas that serve as stormwater run-off areas
Paved trails, walkways, and roads	• Permeable pavement walkways, parking, and fire lanes • Trees planted along roadsides and pathways

conservation, and the enrichment of the surrounding aesthetics. The infrastructure embedded within these parks is varied, ranging from parking facilities and roadways to buildings and sports arenas, as well as courts and other human-made surfaces. Each of these structures offers an opportunity for the integration or retrofitting with NBSs (Table 8.2). The focus of this NBS is primarily on efficient stormwater management, channelling it in the direction of enhanced permeable surfaces for better absorption. This infusion of NBSs into park infrastructure generates multiple advantages:

- *Educational enhancement*: By restoring degraded areas or leaving them to revert to their natural state, parks can become thriving wildlife habitats. These spaces provide practical learning experiences, contributing to outdoor education programmes. They offer first-hand insights into nature's intricate workings, allowing visitors to witness the symbiotic relationships within ecosystems and the importance of biodiversity.
- *Social and environmental equity*: Parks incorporating green infrastructure play a crucial role in enhancing public health and well-being, particularly in resource-strapped or disadvantaged communities. They provide an accessible avenue for physical activity, from jogging and cycling paths to open spaces for yoga or group exercises. Moreover, they act as community centres, where residents can gather for communal activities, thereby fostering stronger community bonds and shared stewardship of the environment.
- *Cost-efficient maintenance*: The introduction of green infrastructure within parks also brings significant maintenance benefits. Improved drainage systems enhance

vegetation health, meaning less effort and resources need to be expended on the care and upkeep of green spaces. For example, plants are less likely to suffer from water-logged roots in a well-drained environment, reducing the likelihood of disease and death. This not only preserves the park's aesthetic appeal but also lowers the overall cost of park maintenance.[15]

8.3.7.1 Case Study: NYC Parks' Green Infrastructure

The Green Infrastructure initiative by the NYC Department of Parks and Transportation, established in 1996, aims to transform unused, impervious areas into functional green spaces. These engineered landscapes, known as Greenstreets, enhance neighbourhood aesthetics, improve air quality, reduce air temperatures, and calm traffic. Since the initiative's inception, the city has built over 2,500 Greenstreets. In 2010, the programme expanded its focus to actively capture stormwater, in partnership with the NYC DEP. This shift aims to build cost-effective stormwater capture systems, particularly in DEP-designated priority sewersheds, where the effect of combined sewer overflow is most pronounced. To decide on the locations for stormwater Greenstreets and right-of-way bioswales, DEP considers various factors, such as hydraulic analysis, site survey, existing conditions, and traffic safety standards. Soil borings and soil permeability tests are also carried out to ensure the subsoil's suitability for stormwater infiltration.[16]

8.3.8 Green Streets

The concept of greening streets represents a comprehensive district-level initiative that utilises vegetation and permeable surfaces to manage excessive stormwater while simultaneously introducing nature into communities. NBSs in streets primarily serve two purposes: to capture stormwater run-off in vegetated areas and to facilitate water percolation into the ground. For the capturing of stormwater, strategies include the use of buffer vegetation and lawns, stormwater planters, bump-outs, and tree trenches. On the other hand, permeable pavement, de-paved areas, and gravel trenches aid in letting water soak into the ground. However, greening the streets provides more benefits beyond managing excess stormwater. For instance, vegetation acts as a natural air filter against pollution; serves as a noise barrier, thus improving local acoustic quality; offers shade; and lessens the urban heat island effect. Moreover, it fosters the use of alternative means of transportation like walking and cycling. Typical NBSs used in green streets include the following:

- *Buffer vegetation and lawns*: Vegetative buffer strips can replace traditional methods that divert stormwater into open trenches alongside roads, pavements,

and squares. Stormwater flowing directly from roads can gather in nearby lawns, reducing street and footpath flooding.
- *Stormwater planters*: These are typically rectangular structures installed in the footpath area. They manage run-off by providing storage, infiltration, and evapotranspiration.
- *Stormwater bump-outs*: These vegetated kerb extensions can be placed mid-street or at intersections. They allow for stormwater storage, infiltration, and use for evapotranspiration by plants.
- *Stormwater tree trenches*: This system connects trees via an underground infiltration structure. The run-off is stored in the porous stone or gravel, providing water for the trees and slowly infiltrating the ground.
- *Permeable pavement*: This special pavement system prevents water from becoming run-off by allowing infiltration through the pavement into an underground reservoir before it seeps into the soil.
- *De-paved areas*: Removing paving from underutilised areas makes way for trees and plants, providing a habitat for wildlife and allowing stormwater to infiltrate where it falls.
- *Gravel trenches*: These non-vegetated trenches filled with stones create an underground reservoir for stormwater run-off, which gradually seeps into the subsoil through the bottom and sides of the trench.[17]

8.3.8.1 Case Study: Toronto's Development-Led Green Streets Projects

In May 2022, the Toronto Green Standard Version 4 required all new street constructions to incorporate green infrastructure for maximal stormwater capture and control. Stanley Greene Boulevard, a residential street located south of Downsview Park, exemplifies this initiative. Completed in 2020, its design was proposed by a development applicant and approved by city staff. The project involved constructing a new street, featuring a sidewalk on the west and a multi-use trail on the east. These two pathways were separated by a bioswale, providing several benefits such as reducing the quantity of stormwater entering the sewer system, thereby boosting resilience to extreme weather events. The bioswale design also eliminated the need for catchbasins on the west side, as it could capture significant volumes of stormwater. In addition, the bioswale facilitated enhanced water quality through filtration and served as a safety buffer between the trail and the roadway. Maintenance responsibilities of the bioswale were initially taken up by the development applicant for an extended period of five years, ensuring the bioswale was well established, considering it was among Toronto's first. After this five-year period, the city will assume the maintenance responsibilities.[18]

8.3.9 Constructed Wetlands

In their natural state, wetlands slow down water flow, allowing suspended solids to settle out as they are trapped by vegetation. They also facilitate the transformation of pollutants into less soluble forms, which are either absorbed by plants or rendered inactive. Additionally, wetlands offer suitable conditions for the existence of microorganisms, which assist in transforming and eliminating pollutants from the water. Nutrients, such as nitrogen and phosphorus, find their way into wetlands via stormwater run-off, with surplus nutrients being absorbed by wetland soils and taken up by plants and microorganisms. Engineered wetlands are generally constructed on upland areas and outside floodplains or within a floodway to prevent damage to infrastructure from excess stormwater. The construction process typically involves excavation, backfilling, grading, dyking, and the installation of water control structures to create the desired hydraulic flow patterns. In cases where the site is situated on highly permeable soils and impermeable compacted clay, a liner is usually installed, with the original soil placed over it. Following these steps, wetland vegetation is planted or allowed to grow naturally. Thus, through careful design and construction, these constructed wetlands mimic natural ones, providing similar benefits while controlling stormwater run-off.

Constructed wetlands generate co-benefits in multiple areas, including:

- *Water quality improvement*: Constructed wetlands use vegetation and biota to filter pollutants from stormwater run-off. They are also capable of soil absorption and gravitational settling but are only moderately effective at removing nitrogen and phosphorus.
- *Water quantity and hydrology*: These wetlands effectively control run-off rates by temporarily storing water, providing significant benefits for channel protection and flood mitigation.
- *Energy conservation*: Constructed wetlands contribute to energy savings, primarily through wastewater treatment, and to a lesser extent through the reduction of heat islands via evapotranspiration.
- *Climate resilience*: Constructed wetlands enhance ecosystem services, alleviate water shortages, provide flood control, and potentially sequester carbon, thus contributing to climate resilience.
- *Air quality*: The impact on air quality is mainly indirect, primarily through carbon sequestration, although improperly maintained wetlands may release methane.
- *Habitat improvement*: Constructed wetlands create excellent habitats for various wildlife species due to the permanent water pool they retain.
- *Community liveability*: These wetlands increase community liveability by creating aesthetically pleasing, recreational landscapes. However, their integration into urban landscapes can be challenging due to space requirements.

- *Health*: Green spaces, like constructed wetlands, may contribute to improved mental and physical health for residents, and potentially reduce crime.
- *Economic benefits*: Properly designed and maintained constructed wetlands provide life-cycle cost savings and can enhance property values.[19]

8.3.9.1 Case Study: Sydney Park Wetlands

The City of Sydney, in collaboration with the federal government, undertook an AUD $11.2 million water reuse project at Sydney Park, a former brick-making site and rubbish dump. This project has not only transformed the park into a flourishing wetland ecosystem but also offers environmental, social, and economic benefits. Key components of the project include stormwater diversion and treatment, wetland revitalisation, landscape improvement, and information dissemination about the wetlands' water treatment and ecological functions. The project is expected to capture and treat approximately 850 million litres of stormwater annually, thereby providing a sustainable water supply to the wetlands and potentially other local users. Environmentally, the project has greatly improved water quality, with up to an 85 per cent reduction in various pollutants observed. There has been an increase of 6 per cent to 49 per cent in the number of water samples meeting local quality criteria across four wetlands. The improved conditions have also supported a 24 per cent increase in bird species and a 119 per cent increase in freshwater wetlands habitat area. On the social front, the project has enhanced public awareness and interaction with the park, as evidenced by an increase in visitor interaction and positive feedback on social media platforms. An estimated 62 per cent of surveyed visitors reported a better understanding of water management processes because of the project. Economically, the project aims to help the city achieve its 2030 target of reducing sediment and nutrient run-off from stormwater and meeting 10 per cent of water demand through local water capture and reuse. This water reuse project demonstrates a successful transformation from a wasteland to a thriving wetland, delivering multiple benefits across different sectors and setting a high benchmark for similar initiatives.[20]

8.3.10 Urban Forests

Urban forests and vegetation present a myriad of benefits. They intercept and filter stormwater run-off, absorb airborne pollutants, and act as windbreaks to safeguard buildings from wind damage. Moreover, they regulate the urban heat island effect through shading and evaporation, provide habitats for wildlife, offer ecosystem services, and combat climate change by storing carbon dioxide.

Urban forest programmes strive to plant trees in public spaces such as parks, along streets or alleys, or in any available open areas managed by local government. For instance, these may include areas around public buildings, along stream rights of way, or in city-owned vacant lots. Urban forests can also stretch to green belts that buffer waterways and manage urban development around cities. Additionally, they can involve the acquisition and management of lands to conserve urban watersheds, thereby safeguarding the quality and supply of drinking water. The urban forests generate multiple co-benefits, including the following:

- *Reduced stormwater run-off*: Trees intercept rainfall and enhance infiltration, and through transpiration, they minimise soil moisture, thus reducing run-off. Simultaneously, they can eliminate nutrient pollutants and heavy metals from stormwater.
- *Increased groundwater recharge*: Trees contribute to the recharge of local aquifers.
- *Reduced energy use*: By providing shade that cools air temperatures, trees lessen the energy needed to cool buildings. They also reduce wind speed, which can lower the energy required for heating buildings in winter.
- *Improved air quality*: Trees absorb pollutants and intercept particulate matter. They also reduce carbon emissions associated with the heating and cooling of buildings.
- *Reduced atmospheric carbon emissions*: Trees directly sequester carbon dioxide from the air.
- *Reduced urban heat island effect*: Trees offer shade, thereby reducing local temperatures.
- *Improved community liveability*: By providing shade, enhancing recreational spaces, and reducing local noise and pollution levels, trees foster a sense of well-being.
- *Improved habitat*: Trees, especially those native to the region, increase wildlife habitat.
- *Enhanced public education*: Community tree-planting activities provide opportunities to boost awareness about the benefits of NBSs.[21]

8.3.10.1 Case Study: Vancouver's Urban Forest Strategy

Vancouver's Urban Forest Strategy aims to create a diverse, resilient, and beautiful urban forest on both public and private lands across the city. The strategy includes every tree within city limits, recognising their crucial role in air purification, rainwater absorption, providing habitat, and improving human health and well-being. Since 2010, 150,000 trees have been planted in alignment with the goal set for 2020. To sustain the urban forest, the strategy has clear objectives: protecting trees during development, planting new trees, managing trees for health and safety, engaging citizens, and monitoring the urban forest's status and condition. Urban forest targets included increasing the urban forest canopy to 22 per cent by 2050, restoring or enhancing 25 hectares of natural areas by 2020, and doubling street tree density in certain neighbourhoods by 2030. The strategy was instigated as a priority item under the Greenest City 2020 Action Plan and was approved in 2012. Research has shown that Vancouver's urban forest is shrinking, particularly on private property, leading to the implementation of an amendment to the Protection of Trees Bylaw. This amendment is aimed at preventing the unnecessary removal of healthy and mature trees on private property.[22]

8.3.11 Green Corridors

Green corridors are nature's highways, facilitating the movement of not only people but also wildlife, seeds, and at times, water. They serve numerous roles, including providing habitats, aiding daily and seasonal movement, and enhancing dispersal capacities. By connecting trees, parks, green spaces, and drainage areas through vegetated walkways, cycling paths, and transport routes, green corridors increase biodiversity and allow wildlife to thrive. Moreover, they bolster resilience against floods, droughts, heatwaves, and climate change. The specific benefits that green corridors offer in urban settings are numerous:

- *Ecological*: Green corridors foster high-quality habitats and ecosystems, especially natural passages such as riparian corridors, waterways, and aquatic habitats. They help prevent soil erosion and absorb rainwater, thereby improving drainage systems. They also shield against the urban heat island effect, thus mitigating climate change impacts.
- *Social*: From a social perspective, green corridors offer recreational benefits as places to play, meditate, gather, or rest. They contribute to a sense of place, identity, and belonging while promoting cultural growth and fostering community spirit. By integrating nature into the urban environment, they elevate the quality of life.
- *Environmental*: Environmentally, green corridors create a network of routes and greenways that enhance accessibility, shaping the urban form by delineating land use. They also encourage sustainable transportation, providing pathways for walking, cycling, and other eco-friendly travel modes. Hence, green corridors not only beautify urban landscapes but also serve essential ecological, social, and environmental roles.[23]

8.3.11.1 Case Study: Medellín's Green Corridor Project

Medellín, Colombia's second-largest city, is utilising NBSs to combat the rising temperatures exacerbated by the urban heat island effect. With the Green Corridor project, which won the 2019 Ashden Award for Cooling by Nature Award, the city authorities have transformed 18 road verges and 12 waterways into green spaces that mitigate the heat island effect. This initiative has resulted in a more than 2°C reduction in temperature. Urban parks can typically reduce ambient daytime temperature by about 1°C on average. The Green Corridor project emphasises the significant role nature can play in urban design. The project not only mitigates the effects of climate change but also adapts to it. The Cool Coalition, comprising governments, businesses, civil society, and international organisations, works to minimise emissions from cooling sectors. It aims to avoid active cooling by implementing NBSs and smart city design, shifting cooling to renewable energy, increasing the efficiency of conventional cooling, protecting vulnerable people from heat extremes, and fostering cooperation.[24]

8.4 Best Practices

From the preceding case studies, the chapter identifies a range of best practices in urban NBSs that can be emulated by other cities worldwide in becoming circular and liveable.

8.4.1 Creating Financial Incentives for Rainwater Harvesting and Green Infrastructure

Based on The Hague's climate adaptation subsidy, cities across the globe can emulate this approach by establishing financial incentives that encourage the implementation of rainwater harvesting systems and green infrastructure. These incentives can take the form of subsidies or rebates that are accessible to a broad range of stakeholders, including homeowners, tenants, businesses, schools, neighbourhood centres, housing associations, and homeowner associations. The incentives could be used to cover part of the costs of developing green infrastructure, such as green roofs, rain barrels, rainwater fences, and permeable surfaces, to replace traditionally impervious ones. By doing so, cities can stimulate the wider adoption of these sustainable measures, bolster their resilience against the impacts of climate change, ensure a sustainable water supply, and promote better management of urban water systems. The initiative will necessitate clear guidelines on subsidy eligibility and application processes, and may exclude costs related to specific tasks or structures. Such a financial incentive programme can contribute to making cities greener and more sustainable, fostering a more environmentally conscious mindset among residents and businesses alike.

8.4.2 Providing Grants for Urban Aesthetic Improvement and Sustainability

Barcelona's party wall grant programme offers a viable blueprint for cities aiming to harmonise aesthetic appeal with sustainability. With this strategy, cities can put forth grants to assist property owners in refurbishing exposed party walls, which are often a consequence of urban planning changes. Such grants could financially support the incorporation of green elements on these walls, such as vertical vegetation, the installation of energy-producing PV systems, or the creation of new window openings for natural light and ventilation. This dual-purpose approach not only enhances the city's aesthetic appeal by transforming otherwise unattractive elements of the urban fabric, but also bolsters sustainability by encouraging energy efficiency and promoting urban biodiversity. To ensure success, the grant programme should have clear guidelines regarding eligibility, deadlines, and minimum investment requirements, while encouraging compliance with the subsidy conditions for a specified duration. This initiative can thereby contribute to creating a visually engaging and ecologically vibrant urban environment.

8.4.3 Encouraging Community Gardening through Grant Programmes

By following the blueprint provided by Brisbane's Cultivating Community Gardens Grants Programme, other cities can create funding mechanisms to encourage non-profit community groups, and even schools, to establish and maintain community gardens. These grant programmes could cover costs associated with garden tools, materials, services, facilities, educational initiatives, publicity, and operating expenses. This initiative, while promoting local food production, also fosters a sense of community by bringing people together to work on a shared project. Moreover, community gardens can serve as powerful tools for instilling environmental stewardship and raising awareness about sustainability issues. Implementing such programmes would require clear guidelines for eligibility, ensuring that the projects benefit a broad community and that they align with the city's broader environmental and sustainability vision. This approach not only strengthens communities but also promotes a greener, more sustainable cityscape.

8.4.4 Implementing Large-Scale Permeable Paving Projects to Manage Stormwater

Cities around the world can learn from Atlanta's implementation of the permeable paver retrofit project to address their own challenges related to stormwater management. Large-scale permeable paving projects can be effective in reducing flooding and controlling sewer overflows by mimicking natural processes to manage stormwater run-off. The use of PICP systems, such as the one used in Atlanta, allows water to infiltrate through the paved surface into an underlying stone reservoir, from where it slowly infiltrates into the soil or drains away. This strategy significantly reduces the volume and rate of stormwater run-off, thereby lessening the burden on existing sewer systems and decreasing the risk of overflow. Additionally, these measures enhance the city's resilience to climate change by improving its capacity to handle extreme weather events. These projects require substantial investment and collaboration with expert companies, but the long-term benefits to urban sustainability and resilience can justify the costs.

8.4.5 Offer Rebates for Rain Garden and Cistern Installation

Drawing inspiration from King County's RainWise Program, other cities could introduce similar initiatives to motivate homeowners to install rain gardens and cisterns. Such practices serve to effectively manage rainwater run-off on private properties and lessen the strain on municipal sewer systems. Providing substantial rebates could cover most or all of the installation costs, making these solutions more attractive to homeowners. To ensure equity and widespread adoption, cities can establish programmes that offer additional financial assistance to homeowners in income-limited and underserved communities, bridging the gap between the rebate amount and actual project costs. Moreover, implementing vendor payment options can further ease the financial burden on homeowners, as the contractors cover the upfront installation costs and directly receive the rebate. By easing access to these rebates and facilitating installations, cities can encourage broad-based participation in their rainwater management efforts, significantly reducing the risk of combined sewer overflow and contributing to overall urban sustainability.

8.4.6 Invest in Green Infrastructure for Stormwater Management

Based on the bioswales initiative by the NYC DEP, other urban areas can invest in similar green infrastructure solutions. These could include the creation of bioswales or vegetated tree pits for efficient stormwater management. Bioswales are an effective way to reduce the amount of stormwater run-off entering the sewer system, thus mitigating the risk of sewer overflow, which can be particularly problematic during heavy rainfall. By design, these infrastructures also contribute to urban greening and biodiversity. They absorb water run-off, provide habitat for local fauna, and aesthetically enhance urban spaces. For optimal outcomes, cities may need to ensure regular maintenance of these installations and undertake public education campaigns to increase awareness about their function and benefits. By doing so, cities can effectively manage stormwater, improve water quality, and create more resilient and aesthetically pleasing urban environments.

8.4.7 Transform Unused Spaces into Functional Green Spaces

Learning from the NYC Parks' Green Infrastructure initiative, cities can repurpose unused or underutilised areas into functional green spaces. These reimagined spaces not only improve neighbourhood aesthetics but also offer a plethora of environmental benefits, including improved air quality, stormwater management, and potential habitat for urban wildlife. To successfully implement such transformation, interdepartmental cooperation is key. Departments responsible for environmental protection, parks and recreation, urban planning, and transportation can collaborate to identify potential sites for transformation and to ensure the necessary infrastructure changes are made. For maximum efficacy and longevity, these sites should be carefully selected based on their potential to effectively manage stormwater and their accessibility to local communities. Through sustained efforts, cities can turn concrete jungles into green havens, contributing to the overall well-being of residents and the environment.

8.4.8 Revitalise Urban Spaces through Wetland Restoration and Water Reuse

As demonstrated by Sydney Park Wetlands, cities worldwide can invigorate their urban spaces by restoring wetlands and adopting water reuse systems. Wetland restoration enhances biodiversity and ecological health, while water reuse systems improve water quality and conserve resources. Furthermore, these innovative urban projects can serve as educational and recreational platforms for residents and visitors alike. They can raise public awareness about the importance of environmental sustainability, foster a greater appreciation for nature within the urban context, and encourage the adoption of more sustainable practices within the broader community.

8.4.9 Establish Urban Forest Strategies to Increase Green Cover

Based on Vancouver's Urban Forest Strategy, cities can establish a comprehensive plan to augment their green spaces. The strategy involves regulatory measures to protect existing trees during urban development projects. Alongside safeguarding current trees, cities should also invest in planting new ones, focusing particularly on urban areas with insufficient greenery. Additionally, encouraging citizen engagement through initiatives such as tree-planting programmes or 'adopt a tree' schemes can foster community participation and environmental stewardship. Finally, the urban forest's health should be periodically monitored through partnerships with local research institutions, providing data to enable proactive management and ensure the long-term vitality of these green spaces. With such a strategy, cities can enhance air quality, reduce urban heat effects, and offer recreational benefits to their residents.

8.4.10 Implement Green Corridors to Combat the Urban Heat Island Effect

Drawing from Medellín's Green Corridors Project, cities can transform urban areas such as road verges, waterways, unused land, and other public spaces into green corridors to mitigate the urban heat island effect. The first step in this strategy would be to identify suitable areas that could be transformed into green corridors. Detailed city mapping and environmental assessment would be necessary to determine the viability and potential benefits of each proposed location. It is also crucial to consider the types of vegetation used in these corridors. Native and climate-resilient plants would be preferred due to their low maintenance and higher adaptability. Cities could reallocate existing environmental budgets, apply for environmental grants, or set up specific fund-raising initiatives to fund these corridors. Public–private partnerships could also be considered, where local businesses sponsor the creation or maintenance of green corridors in exchange for recognition or other benefits. Once established, green corridors need regular maintenance, which could involve citizens, schools, and local community groups in maintaining these spaces, fostering community bonding and raising environmental awareness.

8.5 Conclusion

Overall, urban NBSs, such as green spaces, urban forests, and green corridors significantly contribute to urban sustainability, resilience, and the overall quality of life in cities. Urban greening strategies provide multiple benefits ranging from health improvements for city dwellers to environmental enhancements, including reduction of heat island effects and carbon sequestration. Urban NBSs foster human well-being by providing recreational areas and fostering social cohesion. For instance, urban forests, as discussed, enhance cities' environmental performance by filtering stormwater run-off, absorbing pollutants, reducing energy use, and storing carbon dioxide. These urban green areas, in public and private domains, are vital in combating climate change and preserving biodiversity. These green initiatives, however, are not limited to stationary areas but can extend to linear patterns like green corridors. Green corridors serve as nature's highways, improving biodiversity, bolstering resilience against climate-related risks, and offering numerous social and environmental benefits, such as recreational areas and sustainable transportation paths. It is important to note that these initiatives require comprehensive planning, management, and regular evaluation to ensure effectiveness and sustainability. The case studies of urban greening efforts in cities demonstrate the transformative power of NBSs when they are successfully implemented. In conclusion, urban NBSs represent a viable and beneficial approach to sustainable urban development. They contribute to the overall resilience of cities to climate change and foster a healthier, more liveable environment for their inhabitants. Moreover, their effectiveness has been demonstrated in various cities around the world, emphasising the value and need for these NBSs.

9

Environmental Justice, Circular Economies, and Green Living

TARA RAVA ZOLNIKOV, FRANCES FURIO, TANYA CLARK,
AND DEBORAH NABUBWAYA CHAMBERS

9.1 Environmental Justice

Environmental justice is defined as 'the fair treatment and meaningful involvement of all people regardless of race, color, culture, national origin, income, and educational levels with respect to the development, implementation, and enforcement of protective environmental laws, regulations, and policies'.[1] Throughout history, minority and low-income communities have been disproportionately impacted by cases of environmental injustice.[2] Recently, we have seen examples of environmental injustice with the Flint, Michigan water crisis and the Dakota Access Pipeline protests.[3] And still, cases of environmental injustice continue to affect minority and low-income communities every day.[4] Historically, dominant groups have influenced patterns of development in the environment that benefit them while simultaneously burdening marginalised groups and promoting environmental inequities and injustices. Environmental injustice is clearly rooted in social stratification, including racial, ethnic, and class-based systems of stratification.[5] Vulnerable communities, such as groups experiencing homelessness, have been shown to face increased health impacts.[6]

9.2 Problems within Environmental Justice

There has been increasing research interest over the last several decades in the impact that the environment has on health and well-being.[7] According to Wyes, 'the environment was neglected for a long time because it was considered an unlimited resource for exploitation, growth, and well-being'.[8] Today, we are seeing the consequences of fossil fuels, air pollution, and waste disposal practices. In the next several sections, these topics will be further explored, with an emphasis on adverse health impacts and social and environmental injustice.

9.2.1 Fossil Fuels

The primary contributor to the release of greenhouse gases is humanity's energy production and, specifically, fossil fuel combustion.[9] According to Höök and Tang, these authors, fossil fuels have significantly contributed to economic growth throughout the industrial revolution.[10] According to the Natural Resources Defense Council (NRDC), 'using fossil fuels for energy has exacted an enormous toll on humanity and the environment – from air and water pollution to global warming'.[11]

Fossil fuels, like coal, crude oil, and natural gas, have been used as sources of energy for over 150 years.[12] These fossil fuels have a high carbon content, which is said to be due to their origins: the fossilised and decomposed remains of both plants and animals from millions of years ago.[13] When burned, these fossil fuels produce carbon dioxide.[14] The United States Department of Energy explains how fossil fuel industries drill or mine for these energy sources and then proceed to refine them for use as fuel or burn them to produce electricity.[15]

In the United States, the burning of fossil fuels has provided us with our primary energy source for more than a century. More specifically, 80 per cent of energy needs in the United States are sourced from gas, oil, and coal.[16] As evidenced by the opening statement by the NRDC, there are many significant costs for this practice of using fossil fuels for energy. These costs include, but are not limited to, emissions, land degradation, air pollution, water pollution, global warming, and ocean acidification.[17]

9.2.2 Air Pollution

Sun *et al.*[18] assert that 'air pollution is one of the five most critical issues threatening the survival and development of human beings'. In addition to being a major contributor to climate change, the burning of fossil fuels and release of carbon and greenhouse gases also significantly contributes to air pollution.[19] The primary sources of outdoor air pollution include ozone, ammonia, particulates, sulfur dioxides, and nitrogen oxides. Particulates include, but are not limited to, soot, dusts, metals, spores, and endotoxins.[20] When it comes to air pollution, fine particulate matter, particularly, is a significant concern due to its associated adverse health effects. Even further, there is still much to be understood about how the simultaneous exposure to various and multiple pollutants affects human health.

Air pollution is linked to a variety of acute and chronic health effects and millions of premature deaths each year around the world.[21] Even lower levels of air pollution can result in adverse health effects and increased rates of mortality.[22]

Because air pollution impacts various systems of the body, a variety of health issues can result, including physiological impacts, cognitive impacts, and behavioural impacts.[23] Air pollution is linked to cardiovascular damage, non-communicable diseases, metabolic conditions like cancer, and other adverse impacts on the immune system.[24] It has also been linked to asthma, allergy development, respiratory morbidity, deficits in lung development, and poor birth outcomes.[25] Today, research largely focuses on the impacts of longer-term, lower-level exposure to a variety of pollutants.[26]

Since the passage of the 1963 Clean Air Act in the United States, air pollution levels have decreased. However, the regulation of air pollution remains an important health and environmental issue in the United States and beyond.[27] In many developed nations, these problems with air quality are only worsening.[28] To this day, research continues to demonstrate trends in inequality of exposure to air pollution by class and race.[29] This continues to occur even in the context of decreasing emissions.[30] This finding clearly justifies additional research and exploration regarding the effectiveness of policies and efforts related to the pursuit of social and environmental justice.[31]

9.2.3 Waste

According to Sarigiannis, 'assessment of the health impacts related to hazardous waste is a major scientific challenge with multiple societal implications'.[32] The production and disposal of hazardous waste is a significant concern and risk for environmental and public health.[33] In fact, waste is a priority area outlined for the Member States of the World Health Organization (WHO).[34]

There are a variety of health problems that can result from improper hazardous waste disposal practices, including increased risk of disease and disability.[35] Studies have demonstrated an association between cancer and the prevalence of incinerators, as well as an association between proximity to landfills and adverse health outcomes at birth.[36] In addition to health concerns, there are also concerns about ecological damage, expensive clean-up costs, and depreciated property values.[37]

Research has demonstrated that positionality likely plays a role in the disproportionate distribution and location of hazardous waste facilities. People of colour, ethnic minorities, and low-income communities face an increased burden of environmental contamination.[38] Studies have shown that ethnic and socio-economic minorities are at an increased risk of exposure to hazardous substances. These groups are often concentrated in areas that are close in proximity to toxic waste and result in increased exposure to hazardous substances.[39] Populations residing near hazardous waste sites are more likely to report increased rates of birth defects, cancer, illness, and mortality.[40]

9.3 Solutions and Barriers

Over the past two decades, the majority of human-caused emissions were a result of burning fossil fuels. Helm argues that 'another century dominated by fossil fuels would probably be disastrous'.[41] Hunter asserts that in both urban and rural areas, and in both indoor and outdoor settings, air pollution levels need to be further reduced.[42] According to the NRDC, now is the time to pursue a future of clean energy.[43] Over the last decade, the United States has made significant progress towards pursuing renewable energy sources and energy efficiency.[44] This is largely the result of policies at local, state, and federal levels geared towards improving the efficiency of energy use and growing the clean energy economy. Renewable energy sources, like solar and wind, are predicted to become less expensive sources of energy than fossil fuels.[45]

However, further research related to future climate change is essential. One article noted that 'examining likely and possible trajectories of the future energy systems are vital for understanding future climate change caused by mankind'.[46] Research has also suggested that providing the public with general information related to the health implications associated with fossil fuels and air pollution may not only educate communities, but also may increase support for transitions to cleaner sources of energy.[47]

The Environmental and Energy Study Institute asserts that these cleaner technologies, in combination with improved energy storage and efficiency, will support goals towards cleaner energy and an increasingly sustainable energy system.[48] With sustained efforts, including coordinated policy efforts, the reliable renewable energy sources and options that we have today can lead us towards a clean energy future.[49] Measures to reduce air pollution and curb emissions have resulted in improved health outcomes.[50] Not only is there an opportunity to save hundreds of billions of dollars in pollution control costs, there is also an opportunity to save and extend lives.[51]

Policies that address environmental inequity are also needed.[52] Not only could climate change mitigation policies benefit air quality, but also the disadvantaged and marginalised communities experiencing significant and disproportionate air pollution.[53] We must pursue environmental justice, specifically, and address the fact that low-income minorities and ethnic minorities disproportionately face a variety of environmental burdens.[54] Recently, environmental justice efforts have been focused on providing equal protection from hazards in the environment, particularly for those groups that have been historically and traditionally disadvantaged and marginalised.[55]

9.4 Circular Economy

As Earth's life-support systems continue to be jeopardised by environmental problems, experts are looking more towards ideas about accessing cleaner energy sources, increasing sustainability, restoratively utilising resources, and pursuing a more circular economy.[56] One of the most discussed terms among those in the environmental sciences field is the circular economy. This was even a focus of the European Union Horizon 2020 strategy.[57] The term and larger topic of sustainability are growing in popularity within industry fields, academic fields, and among policymakers.[58] It is promoted by a variety of businesses and governments around the world.[59]

This cyclical concept is an alternative to our current unsustainable energy flow model ('extract, produce, use, dump').[60] A circular economy is defined as 'an economic system that is based on business models which replace the "end-of-life" concept with reducing, alternatively reusing, [and] re-cycling [...] materials in production/distribution and consumption processes'.[61] The aim of a circular economy is to restoratively use resources.[62] More specifically, the goal of a circular economy is 'to accomplish sustainable development, which implies creating environmental quality, economic prosperity and social equity, to the benefit of current and future generations'.[63] Not only is the pursuit of a circular economy better for the environment, it can also create new job opportunities, save costs from materials, and promote economic growth.[64]

9.4.1 Case Study 1: Urban Initiative to Promote Positive Health and Well-Being

The Thriving Cities Initiative represents a national circular economy intervention adapted to a city level implementation. The initial benefits of a circular economy were touted as antidotes to wasteful spending and degradation of the environment.[65] Increasingly, policymakers and academics recognise the need to include health as a driver of a circular economy.[66] The decimation of health and well-being wrought by COVID-19 greatly accelerated the need for a circular economy to include mechanisms addressing physical and psychological health.[67]

The Thriving Cities Initiative uses economic researcher Kate Raworth's Doughnut Economics as a model to introduce a circular economy in three major cities: Amsterdam, Portland, and Philadelphia.[68]

9.4.1.1 The Doughnut Model Explained

Over the last three years, circular economy theory has gained traction as a viable alternative to existing linear economy models due to the ravages of climate change coupled with the devastating effects of the COVID-19 pandemic. The accelerated need to put in place mechanisms that conserve and sustain the Earth's resources while minimising the damage done in producing and using these resources make circular economy models attractive alternatives – some would say necessary replacements – for linear economies.

It is with this new reality in mind that progressive municipalities have begun to adopt circular economies with policymakers, business leaders, researchers and academicians recognising the primacy that circular economy strategy has in the attainment of equitable and circular outcomes for the environment and the life forms that reside in it.

Amsterdam's vision of a circular economy is based on British economist Kate Raworth's Doughnut Economics template. This model demonstrates how societies and businesses can apply circular economic theory to build and sustain an equitable social and environmental future.[69]

9.4.1.2 City of Amsterdam Circular Economy Particulars

Amsterdam elected to implement a City Doughnut in April 2020, becoming the first municipality in the world to do so. The Amsterdam Circular Strategy 2020–2025 explains the transition process to a circular city using Kate Raworth's Doughnut Economics-based philosophy and toolkit.

With the implementation of a doughnut economy, the city aspires to take the first steps towards a new holistic vision that incorporates a circular strategy to drive policy decisions. This holistic systems approach recognises the state of the environment's health on the human health condition and seeks to engage multiple stakeholders to drive transformative change.[70]

Amsterdam's plan is ambitious yet well documented. The city has set a target date of 2050, by which time it expects to be a functional circular city. The next three decades will serve as a road map for other cities looking to reach the same circular civic destination: using resources for as long as possible, obtaining the maximum output from them while in circulation, and reclaiming goods at their end of life.

The Amsterdam Circular Strategy 2020–2025 details a 2-year initial practical action plan and a medium-term objective of a 50 per cent reduction in primary resources within 10 years (2030). The strategy outlines the methods by which the city aims to become 100 per cent circular and climate neutral by 2050.

The circular strategy focuses on three priority value chains, which incorporate three action ambitions. In each case, the first ambition focuses on interventions at the beginning of the value chain, the second ambition addresses usage, and the third ambition focuses on ways to make the most of waste streams.[71]

9.4.1.3 Priority Value Chains

The first value chain addresses food and organic waste streams:

Ambition 1: Short food chains provide a robust sustainable food system.
Ambition 2: Healthy and sustainable food for the people of Amsterdam.
Ambition 3: High-quality processing of organic waste streams.

The second value chain focuses on the cycle of consumer goods:

Ambition 1: The City sets the right example by reducing its consumption.
Ambition 2: Using what we have more sparingly.
Ambition 3: Amsterdam makes the most of discarded products.

Lastly, the third value chain takes aim at the built environment:

Ambition 1: The transition to circular development requires a joint effort.
Ambition 2: The City sets the right example by formulating circular criteria.
Ambition 3: A circular approach to the existing city.

Within the city of Amsterdam these three value chains are at the top of the hierarchy due to their vast and documented strain on the area's economy and ecology. For example, it is estimated that a third of the city's food is wasted. Additionally, food production has been shown to be a major cause of greenhouse gas emissions while at the same time requiring massive land and water consumption. Studies show that modification of present-day food consumption and production can potentially benefit the environment and human health.[72] Additionally, the city has identified the use of consumer goods as being responsible for an inordinately large ecological footprint. Finally, nearly half (40 per cent) of the city's overall waste products are tied into the built environment.

The initial phase encompasses the first 2 years with the goal of activating 200 projects that are to be implemented by a range of entities: the city administration, the private sector, and the citizens at large. Specifically, the city anticipates a target goal of a 10 per cent city procurement that is fully circular by 2022. The following year, the city expects to reach a goal of having all tenders in the built environment categorised as circular.[73]

In conclusion, Amsterdam has chosen to incorporate a City Doughnut scheme as the means of achieving a circular economy that results in an equitable economic, environmental, and health landscape for all within its borders. This historic decision is driven by data that show that human-driven stressors are responsible for environmental change that impacts human health and well-being.[74]

9.4.2 Case Study 2: Urban Initiative to Promote Positive Health and Well-Being

Glasgow, Scotland is making fundamental changes to its economy and society by tackling the climate change emergency by transitioning to a circular economy. This city's economy innovates and designs new resources to last by repairing and reusing while minimising waste as much as possible.

The circular economy reflects how much value can be created when Glasgow makes an effort to build a healthier city. Glasgow's effort to promote positive health and well-being is beneficial for the communities, economy, and the planet. By limiting waste and promoting collaboration between cities in Scotland, it contributes to the circular economy – a USD $4.5 trillion dollar economic opportunity.[75]

The COVID-19 pandemic brought about a shift in people's thinking. More individuals saw the importance of adopting sustainable development, enacting pre-ecological reforms, and embracing nature more. National environmental policies and the global Sustainable Development Agenda can enhance the importance and scale of circular economy development in the future.[76]

The city of Glasgow is making great strides towards becoming a carbon-neutral city by 2030. A circular economy is fuelled by a beneficial partnership model which is promoted by the collaboration between the Glasgow Chamber of Commerce (through its Circular Glasgow initiative), Zero Waste Scotland, and Glasgow City Council.

9.4.2.1 Partnership Model Explained

The partnership between these three bodies has continued to promote several activities. These include identifying consumer footprints through studies that track inflows and outflows of materials in the city and facilitate collaborations through events on the circular economy. The Glasgow Chamber of Commerce launched the Circular Glasgow Network in 2019. About 175 companies from diverse sectors cooperated to form this network. The *Circular Economy Route Map for Glasgow*[77] was produced in 2020 after five years of accrued information, preparation, and research.

A streamlined transition to a circular economy in Glasgow can be achieved by overcoming a number of policy, engagement, and capacity challenges. Municipal departments need to consciously adopt system thinking. It is highly recommended that strategic plans such as the *Resource and Recycling Strategy 2020–2030*[78] need to align with the *Circular Economy Route Map*. Additionally, residents and large corporations would make a difference if they actively participated in consultation proposals. Lastly, identifying efficient public officers who adopt efficient green public procurement and circular economy practices would bridge the gap.

9.4.2.2 Glasgow City Circular Economy Data

The circular economy in Glasgow aims to transition to tackling carbon-neutral goals by 2030. Glasgow has opportunities for addressing environmental, demographic, and socio-economic challenges. Glasgow anticipates its population to increase by 4.2 per cent by 2043. As a result, the city council aims to ensure that 25,000 new homes are provided in the city by 2025. Consequently, efficiency in the building sector will increase, and the net zero carbon targets from the planning phase will be exemplified. Moreover, plans to rehabilitate industrial areas into green spaces offer a meaningful prospect to improve the quality of life of local communities.

The economy will also be boosted by creating new job opportunities, thus addressing social challenges. The city can leverage digitisation to create material exchange programmes, monitor waste collection and recycling efforts, and promote open-access tools and applications that engage citizens and raise awareness. Additionally, businesses are linked across the value chain.

Glasgow is a key gateway to Scotland; therefore, opportunities produced by the tourism sector promote the economy. In 2018, 2.3 million tourists generated £662 million for the local economy and events industry. Other industries such as waste management, goods, transport, energy, and water collaborated in enhancing a more sustainable and low-carbon economy.

Small and medium-sized enterprises (SMEs) are becoming increasingly popular in Glasgow and have migrated from a linear to a circular economy, hence enhancing business creativity and collaborations. The city of Glasgow promotes, facilitates, and enables the circular economy through a collective and coordinated approach.[79]

9.4.2.3 Policy Recommendations and Approaches

The following recommendations and associated policies are adapted from the *Circular Economy Route Map for Glasgow*, which outlines strategic actions to advance the city's transition to a circular economy.

Recommendation 1: Promote the Circular Economy Across Sectors. This recommendation focuses on embedding circular economy principles within municipal operations and strengthening partnerships with key stakeholders:

Policy 1: Launch a transversal working group across municipal departments. Reinforce the relationship between the city, Zero Waste Scotland, and the Glasgow Chamber of Commerce.

Policy 2: Promote strategic leadership and uphold circular economy principles.

Policy 3: Establish a circular vision of key divisions with sturdy potential, such as tourism, food, and events industries.

Policy 4: Create awareness among residents and key economic actors through communication campaigns.

Policy 5: Use more labels and certification to encourage trust.

Recommendation 2: Strengthen Collaboration Across Sectors and Governance Levels. This recommendation highlights the importance of aligning efforts across public, private, and community sectors:

Policy 1: Associate local and regional targets into a coordinated vision across levels of government.

Policy 2: Include circular economy principles across strategic policy documents.
Policy 3: Engage stakeholders in establishing and establishing the circular vision of Glasgow.
Policy 4: Transform deprived neighbourhoods into circular areas by involving property developers and relevant actors in experimentation and pilot schemes.

Recommendation 3: Enhance Governance Mechanisms and Economic Conditions. This recommendation seeks to remove regulatory barriers and create enabling conditions for circular innovation:

Policy 1: Detect regulatory constrictions to circular economy practices and partner with the regional government to overcome them.
Policy 2: Incentivise effective implementation of green public procurement with circular economy efforts.
Policy 3: Discover fiscal tools and funding possibilities to boost the shift to a just circular economy.
Policy 4: Encourage capacity building for the circular economy in all municipal departments. Support training in circular business models for entrepreneurs and youth.
Policy 5: Develop an incubator to foster the creation of new business models and innovations pitched towards the circular economy.
Policy 6: Foster a digital marketplace, aligning tools and networking platforms to generate partnerships across large companies and SMEs embracing circular economy principles.
Policy 7: Improve digital maps and material flow analyses to realise material input and output.
Policy 8: Observe and evaluate progress on the *Circular Economy Route Map.*

Glasgow promotes strategic leadership and embedded partnerships between business, academia, and the public sector that make the difference in driving change towards a circular city.[80] Glasgow strives to be a pioneer of revolution and innovation. Its economic opportunities have created collaboration to create value between organisations, thus enhancing the economy and promoting positive health outcomes. The city incorporates digital technology to use new technology to enhance opportunities that promote job creation.

Glasgow strives to be a globally recognised city by working towards tackling the climate crisis through reducing its carbon output minimising waste, and decreasing loss of labour and natural resources. The city wants to tell a story of using its resources in productive and useful ways by improving its environment and quality of life, and by transforming communities through promoting meaningful lives and healthy lifestyles. The circular economy has the potential to employ many more individuals. More young people are evolving towards creating, learning, and pursuing more meaningful lifestyles that promote health.

In conclusion, a national focus on circular economy, innovation, and partnerships are highly promoted in Glasgow. Stakeholder engagement in businesses in various sectors and government agencies such as the Chamber of Commerce are finding ways to fill the existing gaps so that a circular economy continues to thrive in Glasgow.[81]

9.5 Conclusion

Environmental injustice occurs where certain populations do not have equitable access to a healthy environment and instead face poor sanitation or increased amounts of air pollution or waste, among other problems. One way to create a solution to this issue is through a circular economy within an environmental context. This is where the environment promotes sustainable interventions, like recycling and reusing, which is the foundation for economic growth. A circular economy can improve the environment and also create jobs while helping save the planet from continued resource depletion. Two cities have adopted models of circular economy in the environment. Amsterdam has incorporated the doughnut model, which focuses on reducing waste, which can eliminate excessive garbage and waste exposure. Glasgow has incorporated a circular economy and zero waste within its city limits, which seek to reduce waste and improve resource usage, all while employing more people and encouraging improved health outcomes. These strategies and policies can be used worldwide to achieve a more equal environmental platform for all populations, regardless of socio-economic status, race, ethnicity, or location.

10

Circular Economy as a Pathway to City Resilience and Sustainability

Challenges and Opportunities

SAMEH N. WAHBA

10.1 Introduction

The world is urbanising fast. By 2050, more than two in three persons globally will be living in cities.[1] Cities are also the place where an estimated 80 per cent of the world's gross domestic product (GDP) is generated.[2] This means cities – which barely cover two per cent of the global land area – are the centre of economic growth. This translates into cities being responsible for 70 per cent of greenhouse gas (GHG) emissions and 70 per cent of global material flows and final energy consumption.[3]

The scale and speed of global urbanisation trends pose a severe challenge to cities' ability to plan and deliver housing, infrastructure, and municipal services to such a growing population. Cities are at the frontline of the main environmental and sustainability challenges facing the world today, including climate change, depletion of natural resources, loss of biodiversity, and unsustainable production and consumption patterns that are resulting in unprecedented quantities of waste. Indeed, today, as much as 1.905 billion tonnes of municipal waste is generated daily, and this figure is expected to increase to 3.084 billion tonnes by 2050. This corresponds to a 70 per cent increase in waste generation in three decades, far outpacing the rate of global population growth.[4] Clearly, such global waste generation trends are unsustainable.

At the same time, the world is not on course to meet the Paris Agreement's 1.5 degrees Celsius target.[5] This places even more onus on cities, given their concentration of economic activities and GHG emissions. It's not surprising, then, that the United Nations Secretary-General described cities as the places 'where the battle against climate change will be largely won or lost'.[6]

How the world deals with the challenges of waste management and minimisation, optimisation of the use of materials, protection of natural resources from depletion, and rationalisation of consumption – whether of food, water, energy, or building materials – will be critical to tackle climate change, achieve a socially and environmentally sustainable development, and keep the global population living within planetary boundaries, all without sacrificing economic growth. At the heart of this process is the imperative of decoupling economic growth from unsustainable resource utilisation, environmental degradation, and waste generation, which have been central to the economic model that has prevailed to date.[7]

How to transition towards a circular economy (CE) model and mainstream it in the medium to long term is the key challenge for our generation. This imperative has been accelerated by the COVID-19 pandemic, which highlighted the links between environmental degradation through the loss of nature and biodiversity, and pandemics. And since the world continues to urbanise rapidly, the challenge of how to grow in a resilient and sustainable way is especially relevant for cities.

This chapter explores the link between the CE model and city resilience and asks in what ways a CE approach contributes to resilient, prosperous, and sustainable cities. The chapter starts by defining the concepts of CE and resilience and developing a framework linking both notions towards the achievement of sustainable and prosperous cities. The chapter then examines the different facets of a circular city, including both sectoral and cross-sectoral dimensions, with examples from cities from around the world, and analyses the challenges and opportunities associated with the transition from a linear to a CE model.

10.2 Circular Economy and Urban Resilience: Definitions and Linkages

The CE approach has gained traction as a new model for development that can balance economic growth with environmental and social sustainability, with increased adoption by nations and the private sector in the past 15 years. Leading public sector proponents of the CE include the European Union (the Commission and several member states), China (the first country to pass a regulatory framework for the CE, in 2009), and India.[8] In the private sector, a CE approach is increasingly adopted by companies in a range of sectors including furniture (e.g. IKEA), footwear (e.g. Adidas), and food (e.g. Waitrose supermarkets) linked to production, supply chains, distribution, and logistics.[9]

The CE concept, which can be traced back to the issue of resource limitations within the planet in the mid-1960s, has evolved considerably since then: from an early focus on waste management (cradle to grave), to the reuse of materials (cradle to cradle), and more recently, towards ideas of resource preservation and prolongment, life-cycle approach, and closing the material and energy loops.[10]

Kirchherr *et al.*[11] came up with the following definition of the CE based on an analysis of 114 different examples:

> circular economy describes an economic system that is based on business models which replace the "end-of-life" concept with reducing, alternatively reusing, recycling and

recovering materials in production/distribution and consumption processes, thus operating at the micro level (products, companies, consumers), meso level (eco-industrial parks) and macro level (city, region, nation and beyond), with the aim to accomplish sustainable development, which implies creating environmental quality, economic prosperity and social equity, to the benefit of current and future generations.

At the heart of it, the CE is about reducing, reusing, recycling, and recovering (known as the 4 Rs), with the aim of eliminating waste, optimising resources and materials utilisation, and stopping the depletion of natural resources and environmental degradation.[12] The CE concept emerged as a critique of the unsustainable model of economic development centred around 'extract–produce–use–dump', especially in relation to material use and energy flows.[13] CE replaces the 'end-of-life' concept based on the 'take–make–dispose' approach with restorative and regenerative design.[14] Specifically, the CE hinges on three premises: (1) eliminating waste and environmental degradation, (2) optimising and sustaining the use of products and materials, and (3) regenerating nature and natural systems.[15]

Transitioning towards a CE requires a systemic shift.[16] It requires a radical transformation to design, production, consumption, and waste management processes. In the context of a city, a CE approach entails structural changes to traditional spatial planning, urban development, and management processes; this includes the way urban form, land uses, and densities are planned; structures and infrastructure are built; and basic services such as water and sanitation, energy, transport, and waste management are delivered.

Mainstreaming a CE approach in cities represents an important dimension of resilience and is key to achieving long-term sustainability. Resilience is defined as the ability of entities – for example, individuals, cities, communities, or businesses – and systems to withstand, recover from, and adapt to shocks and chronic stresses, including disasters from natural and geological hazards, climate change, pandemics, conflict, and economic shocks.[17] A CE approach would enable cities to optimise the use of local materials, minimise the depletion of natural resources such as water, and eliminate waste. This would enhance city resilience by reducing potential disruptions to economic activities, production, supply chains and logistics, and improve sustainability by minimising GHG emissions, biodiversity loss, waste disposal, and other negative environmental impacts.

When managed well, the urbanisation process is expected to lead to resilient, inclusive, and sustainable development, and cities would fulfil their promise as an escalator out of poverty. Indeed, urbanisation and growth typically go hand in hand. Practically no country has reached middle-income status without urbanising to a level of 50 per cent, and no country has reached high-income status without thriving cities accommodating 70–80 per cent of the population.[18] Where strong rural–urban linkages exist, there are also spillover effects in terms of poverty alleviation in adjoining rural areas.[19]

For cities to achieve their promise of poverty alleviation, the benefits of urbanisation – agglomeration economies, improved productivity, innovation, and knowledge spillovers – need to be realised, while the negative externalities associated with poorly managed urbanisation (also referred to as congestion forces) – such as pollution, congestion, crime and violence, and lack of affordable housing – among others, need to be mitigated.[20]

Cities are critical actors to implement a CE approach, for various reasons.[21] First, waste management is typically the responsibility of local governments.[22] The ways in which cities approach waste management will range greatly between landfilling growing volumes of waste (basically a linear economy model) versus adopting a waste hierarchy approach that emphasises the principles of reduction, reuse, recycling, and recovery, and thus results in minimising residual waste for landfilling (a CE model). The choice of waste management approach will have major implications on cities' ability to achieve sustainable development. Second, cities are also typically responsible for the delivery of a range of municipal services such as water, wastewater, transport, and energy, where a CE approach helps achieve important social and environmental sustainability policy objectives, such as minimising air and water pollution, abating carbon emissions, and reducing utility bills. Third, because local and regional governments are responsible for a large share (37 per cent) of total public investments globally,[23] their expenditure and capital investment decisions – whether through public procurement or via public–private partnerships (PPPs) – will matter greatly for sustainable development. Fourth, the agglomeration effect within cities that brings a range of public, private, and civil society stakeholders in close proximity helps to facilitate the exchange of ideas and collaboration towards closing the materials and energy loops.[24]

On the other hand, a CE would contribute to resilient and sustainable urban development through two main channels. The first is by alleviating the negative externalities or congestion forces associated with poorly managed urbanisation, especially minimising environmental degradation and waste. The second is by strengthening the dividends of urbanisation in terms of growth and prosperity by reducing vulnerability to shocks and stresses that could set back the gains of poverty alleviation. This would happen through promoting the use of local materials and technology to minimise disruption from distant supply chains and protecting the use of water, natural resources, and biodiversity to strengthen cities' resilience to climate change and boost economic competitiveness and productivity. For instance, a CE approach to managing urban water resources would reduce risks of conflict, climate-induced migration, and erosion of city competitiveness due to stresses from water scarcity. Similarly, improvements to cities' transport, energy, and construction systems due to the adoption of a CE approach would also reduce GHG emissions.

10.3 The Making of a Circular City: Waste, Water, and the Built Environment

The past decade has seen increasing interest from cities to adopt a CE approach, with Chinese and European cities taking the lead following the enactment of China's CE legislation in 2009 and the increased momentum in Europe, where the European Commission issued a roadmap in 2011 to achieve resource efficiency (coupled with a scorecard that tracks progress in the areas of materials, water, land, and carbon), and followed it with an action plan towards the CE in 2015.[25]

To achieve a circular city requires comprehensive interventions to mainstream the CE approach across a range of sectors, including waste, water, natural resources, transport, energy, land uses, and buildings, as well as transversal interventions across systems of planning, management and governance, procurement, and finances to ensure CE implementation, mainstreaming, and results measurement.

Overall, cities transition towards the CE through a range of interventions intended to close the material loop (e.g. minimising waste, using sustainable and recycled materials in construction, together with reducing demolition waste) and/or the energy loop (e.g. via using renewable energy, optimising transport systems, improving energy efficiency in buildings, and through land-use planning to develop a compact and more sustainable urban form that reduces commuting patterns), together with optimising the use of natural and finite resources such as water, treating wastewater, and promoting nature-based solutions.[26]

Each city, however, approaches circularity in its own different way, based on a range of institutional, regulatory, economic, technical, and cultural factors. A study of how the Dutch cities of Amsterdam, The Hague, and Utrecht are implementing the CE highlighted the prominence of public procurement and zoning legislation as the leading instruments, combined with capacity building and knowledge dissemination, with construction and municipal purchases being the key application areas.[27] Amsterdam, a European leading city in terms of circularity, has set a target of cutting by half the consumption of primary raw materials, including metals and fossils, and separating nearly two-thirds of household waste by 2025.[28]

The city of Paris launched a road map in 2017 to achieve circularity, including a 15-point action plan. The key pillars of the city's strategy included the reuse and recovery of building materials, waste reduction, circular construction processes, increasingly the share of eco-products in public procurement, raising awareness among citizens, and connecting enterprises, among other things.[29]

Chinese cities have, on the whole, taken holistic approaches to transition towards a CE, including with regards to rationalising water consumption, wastewater discharge, pollution generation, energy consumption, and waste generation. The effort was underpinned by the ratification of national legislation mandating provinces and municipalities to develop CE targets and plans to prevent resources scarcity and abate environmental pollution, which was passed on 1 January 2009. As a result, a significant reduction of emission and discharge of key pollutants was registered across the board in several Chinese mega-cities, including Beijing, Shanghai, and Chongqing, with a more than 70 per cent decrease in chemical oxygen demand in wastewater, dust, and soot during the period 2005–2014.[30] Similarly, these cities witnessed a decrease in wastewater discharge per unit of GDP of over 30 per cent, and of industrial waste generation per unit of industrial value added of more than 50 per cent during the same period.[31]

In most developing countries and emerging economies, however, the prevailing channel for cities to transition towards a CE tends to be via municipal waste management. This is because municipal waste management is predominantly a local government responsibility.[32] In developing countries, municipal solid waste management systems are characterised by a significant informal sector role. Waste pickers sort waste in landfills or in city streets – often without organised systems – to extract valuable recyclable material such as metals, glass, high-grade plastics, and paper, which helps to reduce the waste amounts slated for landfilling. As such, transitioning towards a CE model in developing country cities will require formalising the role of the informal sector by organising waste pickers into cooperatives and incorporating them in recycling facilities, together with facilitating sorting either at the source (household) or in transfer stations.[33]

Other channels to advance circularity in developing country cities include sustainability improvements to the municipal energy, transport, and water and wastewater systems –, including energy efficiency, waste minimisation, resource reuse, and demand management – but the extent of actions that cities can take in these areas depends on the degree of decentralisation. Other promising approaches include spatial planning and land development regulations to encourage compact development, nature-based solutions, and building regulations to promote energy- and resource-efficient buildings that reduce waste and carbon emissions.

Yet, despite the existence of many channels to pursue circularity, on the whole, the transition towards CE globally can still be characterised as incipient, with much of the focus on material recycling rather than reuse.[34] At the city level, only a handful of cities within OECD countries can be considered as more advanced in their transition towards circularity.[35]

The following section analyses the main dimensions through which cities transition towards a CE with a focus on solid waste, water, and the built environment. These are illustrated with examples from cities across the world that have advanced the transition towards the CE, together with an analysis of challenges and opportunities.

10.3.1 Solid Waste Management

One of the most important channels to introduce or promote a CE within cities is solid waste management, given its nature as a local government responsibility. A key guiding principle for effective solid waste management is to follow the waste hierarchy. The latter is defined as a 'preferred order of waste management practice, subject to technical feasibility, affordability and financial sustainability constraints: prevention, (preparing for) reuse, recycling, recovery and, as the least preferred option, disposal, which includes landfilling and incineration without energy recovery'.[36]

In this preferred hierarchy, the first step to develop a sustainable waste management system is to promote the 3 Rs – reduce (which can be divided into prevent and minimise), reuse, and recycle waste. This is promoted through a range of interventions including: (1) strong engagement in awareness-raising through a whole-of-society approach to influence widespread behaviour change toward waste prevention and minimisation; (2) government regulations mandating waste separation at source, coupled with incentives for reuse and recycling; and (3) pricing policies reflecting the 'polluter pays' principle (applied to both producers and consumers) and regulations to disincentivise waste production, coupled with strong enforcement.[37] Then follows the fourth R, related to the recovery of energy – electricity and heat – from the incineration of waste and the generation of refuse-derived fuel (RDF), which can be produced in incineration facilities or in cement and steel plants.[38]

Obviously, not all waste can be recycled or reused. Some types of waste, including metals, high-grade plastics, and paper, have recycling value and a market. In many developing country cities, such as Cairo, Rio de Janeiro, Mumbai, and other large agglomerations, a substantial amount of waste collection and recycling is carried out by the informal sector. For instance, there are close to 100,000 waste pickers in Cairo, collecting and recycling 10 per cent of the city's waste, while Beijing has an estimated 200,000 waste pickers.[39] On the other hand, there are other types of waste for which it would be difficult to apply the waste hierarchy on technical or financial feasibility grounds, such as electronic waste in low-income countries and especially small states.[40] Similarly, not all types of waste are amenable for energy recovery and generation of RDF; factors such as moisture and organic content are significant.[41]

One of the leading cities in waste management and environmental sustainability is Kitakyushu, Japan. The city has managed to transform itself from a manufacturing centre with heavy polluting industries up until the 1960s to an environmentally sustainable city recipient of international environmental awards by the 1990s.[42] Today, average waste generation in Kitakyushu city is about 0.42 kilogrammes per person per day, less than half Japan's average rate of waste generation at 0.95 kilogrammes per person per day, and about a quarter of the average rate of waste generation in high-income countries at 1.6 kilogrammes per person per day.[43] In fact, Kitakyushu's per capita waste generation is below the average for sub-Saharan African countries, despite the major difference in income.[44] Between 2003 and 2015, as a result of recycling and waste reduction efforts such as composting organic waste and reusing, household waste generation dropped by over one-third.[45]

As part of its transformation towards environmental sustainability, the city championed an approach to waste management that emphasised reduction, reuse, and recycling, which were then complemented with recovery. The city introduced environmental education as early as 1969 and has shifted its waste management approach towards resource recycling and circularity since the 1990s.[46] The city mandates waste separation at source, in addition to significantly engaging citizens, who practice composting widely.[47] The city also introduced disincentives to waste generation by applying user fees, where waste is priced by volume. In addition, Kitakyushu invested in an 'eco-town' for recycling and material recovery, as well as to promote environmental awareness.[48] Industries have reformed their production lines towards resource re-extraction.[49]

In Europe, where there are comprehensive directives issued by the European Commission that govern the sector, municipal waste management systems operate in close alignment with the waste hierarchy. One example is the city of Malmö, Sweden. Priority is given to waste separation at source, with municipal facilities to process recycled waste distributed throughout the city. Organic waste is then converted into biogas for vehicle use (including by the municipal waste management fleet) and bio-fertiliser. Non-recycled waste is incinerated and recovered as energy and heat.[50]

In Ningbo, a city of over eight million inhabitants in China, a World Bank-supported project helped to improve municipal solid waste management and resource efficiency by setting up a waste separation, collection, transportation, and recycling system in eight urban districts, with a combined population of 3.1 million inhabitants.[51] The result was an impressive increase in waste recycling from zero to 17.54 per cent over an 8-year implementation period from 2013 to 2020, producing in the process 64,977 tonnes of recyclables in 2020.[52] In addition, as much as 175,261 tonnes of kitchen waste was separated in 2020 and processed in an anaerobic digestion treatment plant built under the project through a PPP for biogas production.[53] One of the main factors behind the success of the project, which involved over 900,000 households and all institutions, is a major awareness campaign to promote waste separation, which resulted in a 99 per cent awareness rate of waste separation at source and a 94 per cent satisfaction rate, measured through an external performance monitoring and evaluation system.[54] A tariff system is in the process of being rolled out, while the overall design of the project is being replicated in other Chinese cities.[55]

To incentivise behaviour change in Ningbo, an incentive system was set up at the neighbourhood level, using cash payments to reward communities that successfully separated waste into four streams: food, recyclables, hazardous waste, and all other waste.[56] Separated waste was evaluated according to quantitative targets as well as the quality of separated waste, including the purity of the organic content for anaerobic digestion and the proper separation of recyclables. A minimum score was established to receive incentive payments as well as a maximum reward amount.[57] The project involved the neighbourhood residents' committees, which generated strong community involvement and enabled the deepening of residents' awareness of waste separation. Combining regulations for waste separation with incentives, together with strong enforcement and independent performance evaluation, helped produce important results, including behaviour change.

Beyond municipal solid waste, tackling construction waste is an important pillar of achieving circularity in cities. In Denmark, construction and demolition waste represent 37 per cent of total waste volumes, and the recycling of such waste typically involves downcycling through reuse as road base and filling material.[58] Against this context, Bornholm municipality set up a fund to incentivise the creation of a circular value chain for demolition waste. The municipality's interest stemmed from its island geography and its ambition to be free of waste by 2032.[59] Buildings slated for demolition with material of high conservation value were identified, building materials sorted into batches for recycling versus downcycling, the resulting building material for recycling was stored, and the city connected with interested private developers and builders to close the loop for material reuse. This approach was not without challenges, as only a fraction of salvaged building materials had the quality to support reuse, but some material proved in high demand for historic renovation projects.[60]

In low- and middle-income countries where the informal sector prevails, initiatives to formalise such activities and organise waste pickers into cooperatives are critical to develop such an important part of the value chain and help transition municipal waste management systems towards a CE model. Brazil is leading the way in efforts to recognise and incorporate the informal sector in waste management activities in cities. In fact, waste pickers were organised in cooperatives and integrated into recycling systems in several metropolitan areas as early as the 1990s.[61] Waste pickers became increasingly organised with the creation of a national movement in 2001 and the inclusion of waste pickers as an occupational category in household surveys and censuses.[62] In 2010, waste pickers were formally recognised as stakeholders in the recycling value chain with the issuance of the Solid Waste Policy and Law.[63] Despite the lack of waste separation at source in almost four in five Brazilian cities, waste pickers' efforts result in the recycling of an estimated 97 per cent of cans and 67 per cent of cardboard produced.[64] Yet, according to Dias *et al.*,[65] the COVID-19 pandemic resulted in a full or partial suspension of 71 per cent of total waste picking activities, which highlights the precariousness of informal employment despite its relevance as essential work within cities.

Ultimately, what will differentiate countries and cities in their ability to transition towards a CE in waste is the issue of cost and affordability. In low-income countries, 90 per cent of the waste is either burnt or openly dumped, and yet, on average, as much as 20 per cent of local government revenue is dedicated for waste management services that collect a fraction of the waste and with limited cost recovery.[66] In particular, there are significant differences in waste management services' cost between countries and cities by income level, with a tonne of waste averaging USD $110 to collect, transport, treat, and dispose of in high-income countries, compared with $39 per tonne in low-income countries.[67] And the higher a country or a city goes up in the waste hierarchy – with more waste being reused, recycled, and recovered, in tandem with society-wide behaviour change efforts to prevent and minimise waste – the more expensive the cost of the service.

Not surprisingly, city and regional efforts to mainstream a CE in waste tend to benefit from important subsidies from national governments or, in the case of Europe, from the European Commission. For instance, Morocco provides a subsidy of up to 60 per cent of total cost for 5 years (consisting of full investment cost and up to 30 per cent of operating cost) for city and inter-municipal waste management systems that operate in line with national policy guidelines, including integrating informal waste pickers.[68] In Korea, the capital cost for Seoul's incineration facility was shared between national, provincial, and municipal government.[69] In other instances, such as in Japan and the Philippines, local governments subsidise households and cover waste management costs through the property tax system.[70]

However, adding more subsidies is no guarantee of more circularity. For instance, reducing plastics, which account for 12 per cent of municipal waste and are a major source of ocean pollution,[71] requires policies that pass on the cost of the resulting environmental pollution to those responsible for it, including both producers and consumers, as opposed to a system that allows negative externalities to be borne by the general public. To achieve this objective requires introducing policies such as a ban on plastics, which Rwanda introduced regarding plastic bags in 2008; the 'polluter pays' and 'extended producer responsibility' schemes to internalise environmental externalities such as waste and pollution, which are in force in the European Union and other countries; and landfill taxes, in place in the United Kingdom, in order to incentivise alternative waste treatment and disposal.[72] In other words, subsidies should not compensate for inefficient pricing policies that fail to charge consumers and producers for the (full) environmental costs associated with waste and pollution.

10.3.2 Water Management

Water resources management is a critical pillar of a CE approach within cities. This is because population growth, urbanisation, and climate change are exacerbating stresses related to water availability. The result is increasing water scarcity in many cities in the Middle East, North Africa, Central Asia, and South Asia, which are some of the most water-stressed regions in the world.[73] One-third of urban residents globally – 933 million – faced water scarcity in 2016, and this figure was projected to increase to 1.7–2.4 billion urban residents in 2050 under different socio-economic and climate change scenarios, corresponding to between one-third and nearly one-half of the global urban population.[74] In 2016, 37 per cent of the world's large cities – those with a population exceeding 1 million inhabitants – were found in water-scarce regions (193 out of 526 cities), and that figure is projected to reach nearly half of the world's large cities by 2050.[75] India's urban population is expected to fare even worse, with a projected 150 per cent increase in the share of urban population facing water scarcity, which would translate into India housing over one-quarter of the world's urban population affected by water scarcity.[76]

Some of the world's largest cities have faced a water scarcity crisis that was so acute as to undermine the city's existence, including by threatening a so-called 'day zero', when the taps would be shut off due to critically low reservoirs. Such crises are typically the result of several factors, including severe droughts and the impacts of climate change, compounding an already wasteful and inefficient water resources management system. In Cape Town, South Africa, day zero was predicted in 2017, which led to a series of strong rationing measures that in 2018 reached the level of 50 litres per person per day and required cuts to agricultural production.[77] These drastic reductions – which exceeded other efforts in similar circumstances in the USA and Australia among others – led to averting the crisis.[78] São Paulo, Brazil, also faced an acute water crisis during the 2013–2015 period. A combination of drought and high temperatures led water reservoir levels to drop to 5–15 per cent of capacity and caused water shortages for both urban residents and farmers.[79] To tackle the crisis, the utility SABESP resorted to incentives by offering discounts on water bills to users who reduced their consumption levels. The utility also decreased water pressure to reduce leakages, a measure that led to depriving poor people living in peripheral and hilly areas from water.[80]

In addition to its impact on exacerbating water scarcity, the combination of urbanisation and climate change is also exacerbating flooding, leading to complex scenarios with many cities facing either too much or too little water. In China, the sponge cities approach was developed as a national initiative in 2014 to tackle the challenges of pluvial flooding and stormwater management while contributing to improving the environment and natural ecosystems. A total of 30 cities, including Beijing and Shanghai, were selected as pilots for the initiative; these had levels of annual rainfall that ranged from less than 500 to over 1,700 millimetres.[81] This was designed as a strategic programme because in China 45 per cent of cities have insufficient water resources and nearly all metropolitan areas (30 out 32) have difficulties meeting new demand for water.[82]

In the face of rapid urbanisation, the approach focuses on conserving, restoring, and remediating ecosystems and natural landscapes to maintain or strengthen their ability to absorb and store rainwater, hence the reference to a sponge.[83] This top-down initiative is carried out through strategic and land-use planning as well as investments by a range of government entities at different levels.[84] Not surprisingly, given the complexity of urban stormwater management, which requires a holistic, multi-sector approach that extends beyond traditional engineering solutions and involves significant inter-departmental coordination, the sponge city approach was not without challenges.[85] Yet, at the same time, surveys point to community appreciation of the placemaking, liveability, and health benefits emerging from green stormwater infrastructure, indicating the importance of co-benefits.[86]

Policies to strengthen water resources management and reduce wasteful water consumption are critical to enhance the sustainability of such a valuable resource. These include pricing, regulation, and other water demand management approaches, improving the efficiency of utilities, reducing leakage and unaccounted-for water, pollution control, water harvesting, and nature-based solutions to protect and replenish the aquifers, among other measures. These interventions combine the regeneration of natural capital (through nature-based solutions), continued use of the resources (through treatment of wastewater), and the minimisation of waste (through pricing and other demand management measures together with pollution and leakage control to protect the supply side).

In the Barcelona Metropolitan Area, nature-based solutions were implemented with the construction of the nine-square-kilometre riverside Besos park and wetlands around the wastewater treatment plant.[87] The system was complemented with integrated river basin management and water reuse technologies, which collectively resulted in improving water quality and the hydraulic capacity, not to mention the recreational use and improved liveability of urban public space.[88]

The city of Chongqing, China, has achieved a reduction in water consumption per unit of industrial value added of 75 per cent in one decade between 2005 and

2014, while water consumption in relation to GDP also declined 65 per cent.[89] This said, if Chongqing were to expand the recycling of reclaimed municipal wastewater, its CE performance would be considerably enhanced.[90] With regards to wastewater reuse, Singapore, with its limited water resources and insufficient land area to store rainfall, has achieved considerable advances, including tertiary treatment allowing for reuse as potable water. The scheme, called NEWater and planned over decades and complemented with extensive communications and education campaigns, covers 40 per cent of Singapore's potable and non-potable water today.[91] Perception issues, cultural factors, and the quality and cost of treatment, however, tend to hamper efforts to reuse treated water for drinking purposes, limiting it to irrigation and industrial use only.

10.3.3 The Built Environment: Buildings, Land Uses, and Mobility

The built environment is a major source of generation of waste and GHG emissions, which makes it a natural starting place for the introduction of CE approaches to reduce energy and material flows and close their loops. Indeed, globally, urban areas are responsible for some 70 per cent of final energy consumption and over 70 per cent of global GHG emissions, despite housing a little over half of the global population.[92] This is because cities, which barely occupy two per cent of the total land area globally, house a disproportionate share of economic activities and are home to some 80 per cent of global GDP.[93] Specifically, construction, energy use in buildings (for heating, cooling, and operating), and transportation are major sources of GHG emissions globally, where they are responsible for 15 per cent, 25 per cent, and 21 per cent of total emissions, respectively.[94]

Yet, according to the Coalition for Urban Transitions, GHG emissions in urban areas could be cut by as much as 90 per cent by 2050 relative to a business-as-usual scenario, through technically feasible decarbonisation measures that are available today.[95] The study estimates that as much as 58 per cent of total emissions could be cut through decarbonisation of energy use in buildings, together with 21 per cent from interventions in the transport sector and 16 per cent from material efficiency in the construction sector.[96] Achieving these targets in cities requires the decarbonisation of electricity supply, together with measures to achieve energy efficiency and waste prevention, the expansion of mass transit, active mobility, and smart logistics, and planning compact cities with high liveable density and mixed-use developments.[97]

Arguably the most complex measure is the development of compact, high-density liveable cities that are reliant on mixed-use development and mass transportation systems, thereby limiting horizontal sprawl and GHG emissions from transportation. Several cities, such as Curitiba, Brazil; Bogotá and Medellín, Colombia; and Quito, Ecuador, have promoted such approaches, including through the development of mass transit systems (e.g. bus rapid transit system along dedicated corridors with high capacity, such as the TransMilenio in Bogotá or the underground metro in Quito) serving high-density developments (e.g. transit-oriented development in Curitiba). Cities such as Paris and Milan have taken this concept further with the adoption of the 15-minute city model, wherein all day-to-day activities such as work, leisure, shopping, and schools are to be located within a 15-minute distance from home.[98] While it was lauded for its positive impact on the environment and public health due to the anticipated reduction of commuting and air pollution, the major critique of the 15-minute city model is that it deprives the city of its most important attribute, namely a large labour market with access to economic opportunities, and can lead to socio-economic segregation.[99]

However, several of the mobility measures promoted through the 15-minute city model are important for sustainability. Most important is active mobility, namely through cycling and walking. Many cities, including Bogotá, Milan, Paris, and Washington DC, have added a significant network of cycle lanes as part of their post-COVID-19 recovery interventions. Other cities, such as Barcelona, have pedestrianised several roads in the city centre, while others, like Washington DC, New York City, and Paris, expanded sidewalks at the expense of the right-of-way of roads or parking spaces.[100] One such iconic project is the restoration of the Cheonggyecheong stream in Seoul after the dismantling of an elevated highway that had carried over 170,000 vehicles per day. The result was an improvement in liveability through the provision of an attractive public green space of 16.3 hectares, increased property values, a decline in air pollution, and an 18 per cent reduction in temperatures in the neighbourhood, coupled with an improvement of traffic conditions in the overall zone.[101]

In the construction sector, and in line with the waste hierarchy's prioritisation of waste reduction, the achievement of a CE approach could be achieved through approaches that minimise new, greenfield expansion of the building stock and expand the useful lifetime of existing buildings, including through adaptive reuse and retrofit.[102] Planning and building regulations promoting compact urban form would help in limiting sprawl and new horizontal expansion, while strict regulation of construction activity to promote green buildings and preserve historic properties could retain the existing building stock and reduce waste. As for new construction and retrofit, promoting a CE could be achieved through design approaches that allow for disassembly, repair, reuse, and reconfiguration.[103] At the same time, sustainability could be achieved through green buildings that enhance the efficiency of water, energy, and other resource consumption, and reduce waste and the resulting emissions and environmental degradation from the construction process.[104]

Several standards for green buildings have been developed to enable the measurement of environmental impact and allow the recognition and incentivisation of developments that achieve the required benchmarks. Widely used examples include Leadership in Energy and Environmental Design, developed by the US Green Building Council, and the Well certification, which prioritises health. An increasingly adopted system is the International Finance Corporation's Excellence in Design for Greater Efficiencies (EDGE) standard, where buildings are certified when they achieve a reduction of 20 per cent in energy, water, and embodied energy in materials.

There are multiple benefits to green buildings that are found compliant with rigorous construction and operation standards. These include energy and water cost savings, increased demand from corporate tenants concerned with sustainability, and the ability to access better lending terms through green mortgages. Indeed, the adoption of EDGE as a standardised approach in lieu of individual environmental assessments against country regulations allowed ProCredit group to expand operations in Southeastern and Eastern Europe and reach €1 billion in green loans, equivalent to one-fifth of its loan portfolio.[105]

As with all metrics, green building standards are not without their critics.[106] They are critiqued for a range of issues including their scope (e.g. limited emphasis on social sustainability), weighting, indicators, complexity, and measurement (e.g. measuring percentage reduction in energy and water use but not the actual performance). Some of the critics of green buildings call for a more holistic transformation of the built environment. One such approach is the practice of regenerative design, which goes beyond the engineering approach to green buildings to advocate for the use of ecological designs and building technologies that embrace natural heating, cooling, and energy systems and allow for their regeneration.[107] Another approach is to use sustainable building materials, especially cross-laminated timber, which allows timber to overcome the challenge of vertical construction.

10.4 Municipal Powers and Instruments to Leverage Circularity

In addition to their responsibilities over the management and delivery of local services including water, wastewater, and solid waste management, cities have several powers, instruments, and policy levers at their disposal to promote a CE, including most prominently their regulatory powers over planning and building, public procurement, and financing.

10.4.1 Planning and Building Regulation

The city's planning and regulatory powers are critical towards promoting a CE, specifically through planning and building regulations. Planning for more compact cities with high liveable densities and mass transit systems is important for combatting sprawl and reducing commuting. The comparison between two cities,

Barcelona and Atlanta, which had the same population but where the latter had 26.5 times the urbanised area of the former, is a particularly telling example.[108]

Planning for cycle lanes, wide and safe sidewalks and footpaths, and traffic-calming interventions to reduce vehicular speeds provides needed infrastructure and safety for active mobility, which is critical to improve citizens' uptake. Interventions such as impact fees can make sprawl more expensive, while allowing for transferrable development rights can preserve historic property and existing developments. At the same time, building and environmental regulations coupled with incentive schemes can promote building retrofit, and energy and resource efficiency, while disincentivising demolition.

10.4.2 Procurement

The most direct policy lever at the city's disposal is to use its public procurement powers to transition towards a CE. In Europe, where public procurement accounts for 14 per cent of the European Union's GDP, a 2014 directive on public procurement allowed the incorporation of a life-cycle perspective in pricing criteria and thus integrated the costs of environmental degradation across products' life cycles.[109]

Going beyond financial cost-centred decision-making processes to incorporate the SDGs' economic, social, and environmental considerations gave rise to sustainable public procurement practices which prioritise sustainable supply chain management and waste reduction, while a focus on environmental impact led to the emergence of green public procurement.[110] Such approaches, which are found in Sweden and Finland, among other OECD countries, incorporate life-cycle costing, reduction of waste, and products that have eco-labels and are non-toxic and recyclable, among other measures.[111] Another widely used measure is the replacement by many cities around the world of fossil fuel-based buses with an electric fleet. London introduced criteria for responsible sourcing and recycling in the procurement of materials for the construction of the Olympic Park for the 2012 games.[112]

Despite their advantages, green and sustainable procurement remain conventional approaches for the acquisition of goods as products and for ownership purposes, and as such do not necessarily reduce waste. A more structural shift would be towards the procurement of goods as services under leasing and sharing business models, with manufacturers retaining product ownership. This is at the core of the so-called product-service system (PSS), which is a way to incentivise performance-based management with less onus on the resources themselves.[113] In 2013, Helsinki shifted its procurement of furniture towards rental.[114] Despite the promising idea of focusing on performance and de-emphasising asset ownership, shifting the ownership of a product through PSS is not deemed a guarantee of less resource use per se.[115]

Local governments' ability to drive green and sustainable public procurement appears to be correlated with the size and purchasing power of municipalities. Similarly, agencies with a large public procurement mandate across departments also facilitate the adoption of such approaches.[116] As for smaller municipalities, one option could carry out joint procurement through inter-municipal arrangements to strengthen their collective purchasing power.

10.5 Challenges and Prerequisites to Transition towards a Circular Economy

Transitioning a city towards a CE is a complex endeavour that requires strong leadership, a vision, government coordination, and a long-term time frame. A recent survey of 51 cities and regions in OECD countries found that barely 10 per cent of surveyed sub-national governments viewed themselves as advanced in the transition towards a CE, while the remainder deemed themselves as newcomers (57 per cent), in progress (29 per cent) or not yet in place (4 per cent), despite being overwhelmingly located in high-income countries.[117] This is not to say that those just starting on such transition had not had any advances; several of them had already made inroads in a given area, such as solid waste recycling or water reuse, and were scaling up their transition towards circularity.[118]

The key obstacles identified in the OECD survey are lack of financing (three in four cities), inadequate and incoherent regulation across levels of government (more than half of the cities), lack of vision and political leadership (two in three cities), cultural factors including lack of awareness (two in three cities), and capacity constraints (three in five cities).[119] Additional constraints include lack of familiarity and the fear of the unknown, and the persistence of silo structures and sectoral approaches, which have limited the adoption of a CE model beyond big industries.[120]

Arguably the two key challenges facing cities as they transition towards a CE are financing and implementation constraints (including regulation, capacity, and cultural issues).

10.5.1 Financing

One of the most frequently cited challenges associated with achieving a CE has to do with the lack of financing.[121] For instance, the cost of a waste management system including reuse, recycling, and recovery is substantially higher than a landfilling-centred solution. Indeed, the World Bank underlines that 'affordability considerations limit the scope for implementing advanced, higher cost but more environmentally acceptable technologies which sit higher on the waste hierarchy'.[122] As such, the feasibility of promoting circularity in waste management will depend on the affordability of proposed solutions, the scope for cost recovery, people's willingness to pay, and the availability of subsidies to cover financing gaps.

For this purpose, it's important to devise effective financing plans for the implementation of national or local waste management systems, including cost recovery measures (e.g. introduction of the polluter pays principle and user fees versus reliance on general municipal budgets), coupled with subsidies to cover financing gaps, and incentives for waste reduction and separation at source, such as through charging for the quantity of waste generated.[123]

In low-income countries, waste management costs on average 20 per cent of local government budgets, despite as much as 90 per cent of waste being either openly dumped or burnt.[124] To enable cost recovery, municipalities charge for the service. Many municipalities charge a collection fee, whether a standard amount per household or per capita, as in Ulaanbaatar, Mongolia, where the fee is added to the electricity bill, or a variable amount linked to property type (e.g. residential, commercial, or institutional) or value, as in Bulgaria and Brazil.[125] In a few cases, such as Belgium, municipalities charge according to the volume of waste collected or by type of waste (e.g. charging more for undifferentiated waste), which is intended to incentivise waste reduction and separation, respectively.

Because 'waste management is a net cost activity which has ultimately to be paid for – in one form or another – by residents',[126] and because user charges factor in affordability and mostly fall short of covering service delivery costs, subsidies gain particular importance. With World Bank support, Morocco has introduced a national programme that covers the full investment cost for modernising municipal waste management systems and up to 30 per cent of operating costs for a duration of 5 years, after which local governments should cover the full cost of operation.[127] Estonia uses a combination of EU grants and proceeds from environmental taxes.[128] While such subsidy schemes are costly, the important thing is to incentivise behaviour change and systemic improvement. Morocco's sunset clause of the operating subsidy for municipalities after five years is an incentive to improve cost recovery, while systems such as charging by waste volume or weight, or by waste type, aim to bring about behaviour change.

10.5.2 Implementation

Unlike with businesses, the implementation of a CE within cities is far more complex, for many reasons. First, cities are complex structures with a diverse range of stakeholders, including many public sector entities that do not necessarily coordinate well together, in addition to private, civil society, and community stakeholders. Second, cities do not necessarily have the prerogatives or ability to tackle the key challenges related to circularity, including waste, water, energy, and infrastructure, as some of these areas may not be under a city's control or the challenge may extend beyond a city's jurisdiction to encompass other municipalities or different levels of government.

Williams examined why cities do not fit within the RESOLVE framework, which was developed by the Ellen MacArthur Foundation, is used widely to promote circularity within businesses and industries, and is often being transposed onto cities.[129] The key difference is that cities are complex, dynamic, and adaptive organisms which are centres of both consumption and production, and whose scale and main ingredients – including land (a valuable and finite resource) and infrastructure (typically in sectoral silos and often subject to lock-in effects) – add complexity and thus become more challenging to promote circularity.

Indeed, the implementation of a CE at a large scale – such as that of a city, region, or nation – requires systemic change. This in turn will require important public sector leadership, including through policies, incentives, and regulations. At the same time, to successfully mainstream a CE model, public stewardship will need to be supplemented with important grassroots-level interventions, such as buy-in at the consumer level to enable behaviour change and innovation from businesses and firms to close the material and energy loops. As such, a combination of top-down and bottom-up approaches are important to enable a multifaceted transition towards circularity.[130]

One important example of public leadership is China, which enacted legislation in 2009 that mandates governments at national, provincial, and municipal level to introduce their CE development plans with defined targets.[131] Another example of public leadership is the European Commission, which in 2011 issued a roadmap to achieve resource efficiency (coupled with a scorecard that tracks progress in the areas of materials, water, land, and carbon), and in 2015 introduced an action plan towards the CE.[132] Both approaches are, however, very different. China adopted a top-down approach aiming to transform society and production through regulation and without resorting to market-based instruments, whereas in Europe the approach was more bottom-up in response to demands and activism from non-profit and community groups, and with important incentives to encourage national and local government action.[133]

The role of national governments is critical for the transition towards a CE approach, given the importance of having an enabling regulatory environment and adequate incentives and subsidies to catalyse behaviour change. Regional and local governments also have a critical part to play given their important role in service delivery. At the same time, the extent of decentralisation is an important determinant of the ability of sub-national governments to transition towards a CE model. An important reason that Danish municipalities have achieved significant advances in transitioning towards a CE is their control over water, waste, and energy utilities.[134]

Within cities, the leadership role in terms of planning and coordination varies from one city to the other. In the OECD survey of cities and regions, the two institutions most frequently entrusted with the circular transition were the environment and economic development departments, followed by dedicated structures or the urban planning office.[135] This indicates the range of potential entry points to promote circularity in line with the extent of prominence of the underlying environmental and economic development objectives. The latter are the two facets of the CE's overarching objective, namely 'decoupling environmental pressure from economic growth'.[136] In particular, whereas earlier efforts to promote circularity had been driven mainly by an interest in environmental sustainability, with little mention of the social dimension, the emphasis on economic development and social inclusion objectives has increased over time.[137]

Notwithstanding the critical role of public leadership in catalysing a transition to a CE model, involving the private sector, civil society, and the community is equally important. In particular, the private sector is a key stakeholder in the achievement of the UN SDGs and the 2030 Agenda. A study analysed corporate sustainability reporting of 123 companies in the forestry, food, beverages, mining, and energy sectors and found that CE was systematically present across all sectors, signalling the importance of this agenda to the private sector.[138] Private sector adoption of CE appears, however, to be mostly limited to large companies operating under a regulatory framework of extended producer's responsibility.[139] By contrast, a combination of regulation and incentives – including through PPPs – could accelerate the adoption of a CE.

Payment for ecosystem services (PES) is another great approach to involving the community. In 2020, the city of Freetown, Sierra Leone, initiated a plan through a PES scheme to plant one million trees in the city over three years to offset deforestation and provide sustainable, nature-based solutions to recurrent flooding and soil erosion problems.[140] To implement the plan, Freetown City Council mobilised people in low-income communities to plant the trees and monitor their growth, in return for compensation for their service. This PES process provided a livelihood for people in low-income communities at a time of economic crisis due to the COVID-19 pandemic. It also creates an innovative participatory implementation modality and builds citizen awareness of the importance of environmental sustainability. The city has also created livelihood opportunities in solid waste management for unemployed youths, organising them into a waste collection management association and procuring and distributing tricycles for them to use to collect waste in underserviced neighbourhoods.[141]

Achieving economic growth while reducing waste via closing material and energy loops is done through the development of new business and service delivery models, including through digitalisation and the transition from asset ownership to renting services.[142] A notion that is increasingly gaining ground towards more sustainable consumption and production is that of 'sharing cities', which manifests itself through a range of instruments including energy co-ops, community gardens, product rental, platforms to trade pre-owned goods, shared workspaces, shared accommodation, and shared transport such as rides, cars, and bikes, among others.[143] Technology is clearly an important enabler to support cities in implementing CE strategies. For instance, the sharing of goods, assets, and services within cities was facilitated by technological platforms such as Craigslist, Airbnb, and Uber, among others.[144] However, technological adoption is not guaranteed to achieve development objectives in the absence of institutions and regulations governing the adoption and use of such technologies, protection of property rights, and enforcement of contracts, among other things necessary for success.

10.6 Conclusion

The sustainability crisis our world faces today – including the impact of a changing climate and the loss of nature and biodiversity – calls for a CE approach to minimise waste, close energy and material loops, and regenerate nature and ecosystems. This, however, is much easier said than done. Today, the CE approach is gaining ground predominantly within high-income countries and with very divergent levels of progress, as explained in this chapter, while within low- and middle-income countries the discussion is still very nascent. Indeed, the bulk of published research on circular cities hails from Europe, with a primary focus on waste and wastewater, as well as recycling and recovery at the lower levels of the CE taxonomy.[145]

Introducing a CE approach within a society requires not just vision and boldness, but also comprehensive system change. At the same time, comprehensive system change invariably requires patient and incremental build-up to establish the foundations, strengthen the institutions, and mobilise a whole-of-society approach to change. For instance, getting to a zero-waste model will require building a functional waste management system, including a regulatory framework, viable institutions, effective collection and disposal mechanisms, and appropriate pricing, among other measures. This is typically done gradually in line with the waste hierarchy, towards the end objective of diverting as much waste away from landfills as is feasible within affordability limits. As the service quality and management system get established, it will become increasingly feasible to price waste at the level that can account for negative externalities and incentivise waste reduction, reuse, and recycling, – as well as the use of refuse-derived fuel – to a level that can eventually lead to a zero-waste, no-landfilling scenario. Technology will be able to help leapfrog in some instances, but the reality is that policies, institutions, and regulations, coupled with enforcement of rules, are the key foundations for an effective implementation of the CE, and these take time.

11

Governing the Transition to Circular Economy and Liveable Cities

The Butterfly Potential of the City of Vienna

KARIN HUBER-HEIM, ALEXANDER LASZLO, AND ANNA-VERA DEINHAMMER

11.1 Introduction

A regenerative circular economy (CE) has been described as a concept that mimics living systems. One particular living system that may be helpful in thinking about regenerative liveable cities is the healthy human organism. Like other living systems, our organisms are made up of many subsystems – for example, the circulatory, respiratory, and digestive systems – eleven such subsystems in all. A healthy organism requires each of these systems to work effectively with the others. They are complex, interdependent, dynamic systems that are constantly responding to and adapting with change. Organisms function because materials such as blood and oxygen flow through them, without making this the purpose of life, but rather providing the basics for good living and well-being, with society acting as the backbone – holding the body up and ensuring that the brain's messages get to where they are needed.

We argue that cities are no different: in a healthy city, urban systems such as buildings, mobility, products and services, and food, as well as citizens, need to work effectively for and with each other. And things need to flow – such as materials, capital, knowledge, data, and energy – to ensure the well-being of all. A helpful reframing, consistent with a regenerative CE approach, is to think of cities as living systems that rely on a healthy circulation of resources for the well-being of their citizens. This underscores that each urban system is a set of recurring themes that are integral to the CE. These include but are not limited to the role of design, new business models and means of access, and the use of digital technologies.

To create a liveable environment for all, cities and regions must act as promoters, multipliers, and pioneers of a regenerative CE, sharing responsibility with national governments and stakeholders. They are not only in the position to promote a new economy that thrives within planetary boundaries and act as role models for businesses and citizens, but more importantly need to provide clear information and set targets to organise the transition as promoting a CE culture. These processes are core to building trust in society and key to efforts that seek to 'leave no one behind'. In essence, achieving the goals we have outlined requires the orchestration of multi-layered governance mechanisms that are aligned to balance different dimensions that support a comprehensive and effective transition to a regenerative CE model.

Vienna is a compelling case study for a holistic approach that promotes sustainable practices, CE principles, and collaborative governance. In particular, it demonstrates the transition to a regenerative circular city through implementing CE in its 'Smart Climate City Strategy Vienna',[1] as well as running the transdisciplinary programme 'DoTank Circular City Vienna 2020–2030'.[2] Like a caterpillar that does not yet know what is coming but is attracted by development, the need for transformation is becoming increasingly clear. But just like the transition from a caterpillar to a butterfly, the transformation process will involve a remarkable metamorphosis that encompasses various stages and shows the complicated life cycle of the living system called 'city'.

Similar to a caterpillar, the current phase of the city of Vienna is characterised by rapid growth and an insatiable appetite for the supply of materials and energy. And just as a caterpillar sheds its exoskeleton with each moult and grows ever

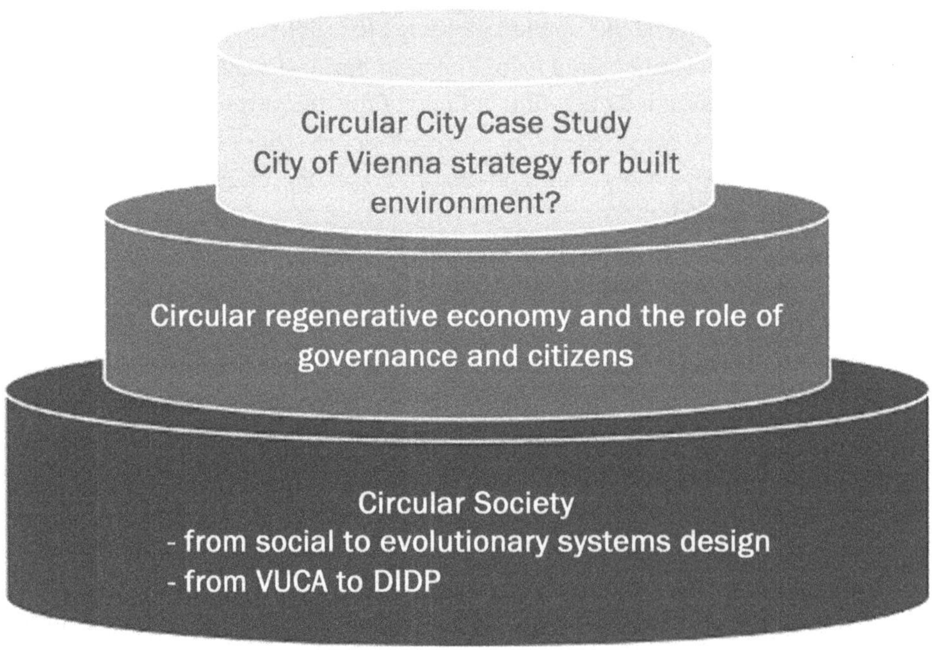

Figure 11.1 Structure of the chapter
Note: VUCA = Volatility, Uncertainty, Complexity, and Ambiguity; DIDP = Diverse, Intricate, Dynamic, Playful

larger, so too have the city's population and built environment grown ever larger in recent decades. Once the caterpillar reaches a certain size, it surrounds itself with a protective shell, the pupa, in which the amazing transformation takes place. This is where the authors start their case study to illustrate what the city of Vienna's strategy for the CE envisages in terms of fundamental reconstruction and subsequent reorganisation – just like how the chrysalis supports the transformation into the complex structures of the adult butterfly. The end of this metamorphic journey is the emergence of the adult butterfly, and just like it, the city's wings need to be expanded and strengthened after hatching into their new urban patterns to enable citizens to live a circular life. Just as with the butterfly, the duration of each stage depends on individual factors, including environmental and climatic conditions, but also economic and political factors.

The authors explore the parallels to the caterpillar evolving into the butterfly in the process of metamorphosis from a linear, exploratory urban system to a regenerative, circular living system, as it too goes beyond mere physical change and is a metaphor for transformation, growth, and rejuvenation for the world of tomorrow (Figure 11.1).

11.2 Circular Society: A Systems View of Circular Change Agency

11.2.1 Life in a VUCA World

Commenting on the emerging paradigm of complexity science almost 40 years ago, Nobel Laureate Ilya Prigogine observed, the danger stems from the recognition that in our universe the assurance of stable and permanent rules has vanished. We now inhabit a world marked by uncertainty and risk – one that no longer inspires unquestioning confidence.[3] Yet, he also articulated a perspective that has since become central to circular living and the circular lifestyle: the recognition that even small fluctuations can evolve and reshape entire systems. In this view, individual actions carry the potential for significant impact and are far from being inconsequential. While the power of individual activity for collective impact may have been recognised years ago, it is finally being acted upon in the spirit of 'inter-being' that flourishes in circular economies.

Research into complex adaptive systems theory applied to social, psychological, and economic systems has shown that human decision-making is far from a rational affair. In his 2008 Nobel Award-winning work, behavioural economist Richard Thaler explains how people tend to be susceptible to messaging that will 'nudge' them to make even difficult decisions that seem to have no obvious benefit at the moment but may be beneficial in the long term. Such realisations increase

- **Situations and contexts appear:**
  - Volatile
  - Uncertain
  - Complex
  - Ambiguous
- **Experiences and encounters appear:**
  - Rapid
  - Unpredictable
  - Paradoxical
  - Tangled
- **Being and identity appears:**
  - Brittle
  - Anxious
  - Non-linear
  - Incomprehensible
- **Flipping VUCA around to bring:**
  - Vision
  - Understanding
  - Clarity
  - Agility
- **Fostering dynamics that are:**
  - Diverse
  - Intricate
  - Dynamic
  - Playful

Figure 11.2 VUCA, RUPT, and BANI vs VUCArev and DIDP

the complexity of decision-making frames, giving rise to the notion that we live in a fundamentally VUCA world: one characterised by dynamics of Volatility, Uncertainty, Complexity, and Ambiguity. While research in the physical sciences continues to explore VUCA patterns and dynamics, the social sciences have recast the same characteristics in more humanistic terms with the acronym RUPT, expressing the lived experience of VUCA as Rapid, Unpredictable, Paradoxical, and Tangled. In either case, both VUCA and RUPT are expressions of the contemporary quandary of coping with the increasingly mercurial dynamics of change in our personal and collective worlds. Indeed, the extent to which this *Weltanschauung* or Worldview has pervaded contemporary concerns is captured by the diversity of expressions of this framing, as captured in Figure 11.2.

Circular cities are designed to help us engage with such situations, and to empower collective action to address them. The initiatives that emerge from the design of such cities herald a new era in the collective self-determination of our species. The particular pressures exerted on humanity by the need to cope with combined and compounded VUCA challenges has resulted in the emergence of entirely new social transaction systems. Clearly, no one person or team can create the needed pathways to viable futures in isolation – we are all in this together.

In essence, a circular lifestyle is concerned with ways to *human better*: how can we, individually and as a species, act in dynamic harmony with all of life and the life-support systems of Earth – especially in the densely packed contexts that urban environments afford? The challenge of addressing this question has become both profound and urgent. The practices, dispositions, and values that favour the emergence of an authentic expression of our full potential to human are varied and multiple – and often ancient. As we engage in the process of ushering in the conditions for the emergence of a truly thrivable planet – listening into the systemic nurturance spaces and seeking to identify the systemic leverage points for the emergence of a *glocal* ecocivilisation (one that is both globally informed and locally relevant) – it will be increasingly important for our species to find ways of taking appropriate action collectively. Indeed, humanity has reached a bridge that can only be crossed in unity.

As part of this sort of 'solarpunk quest' for a thrivable ecocivilisation, a fundamental objective of circular economies is the creation and promotion of relational intelligence applied to systemic innovation. If *connective intelligence* is the capacity to identify and connect with individuals and resources relevant to humaning for thrivability, and *collective intelligence* is the ability to foster synergetic initiatives based on such connective intelligence, then *relational intelligence* is the 'sense-*ability*' required to harness collective intelligence for the greater good. Such evolutionary competence is at the heart of the CE impulse to foster conditions for human societies to manifest our higher potential as a truly planetary species. Authoring this narrative involves taking stock of our evolutionary situation as a species with the power to fundamentally alter the viability of life on Earth – for better or for worse. The emerging narratives of systemic sustainability, of evolutionary interdependence, and of glocal thrivability all depend on our ability to connect with each other in fundamentally human and sacred ways.

Acting as a collective evolutionary guidance system, emerging circular cities such as Vienna foster the ability for us to act as 'response-*able*' agents of evolutionary development – not as human beings with myopic self-centred interests, but as human becomings who are consciously evolving members of an interdependent web of life. This is the evolutionary imperative that circular economies seek to address, extending and augmenting our capacity to act together for a thrivable human presence on Earth and a flourishing future for all life – now and into the future.

11.2.2 From Myopia to Protopia: Strategies and Approaches to Futures Planning

Contemporary approaches to the future tend to fall in one of four categories: they are based on and informed by visions of a utopia, a dystopia, a myopia, or a protopia.[4] This framework offers actionable pathways for systemic innovations that can be realised now or in the nearest future (Figure 11.3). *Utopian* frames are idealistic (and at times overly optimistic) future scenarios: solutions that knowingly cannot be implemented. Even though this scenario can inspire, the inability to realise it often brings frustration rather than action. *Dystopian* frames are reactive

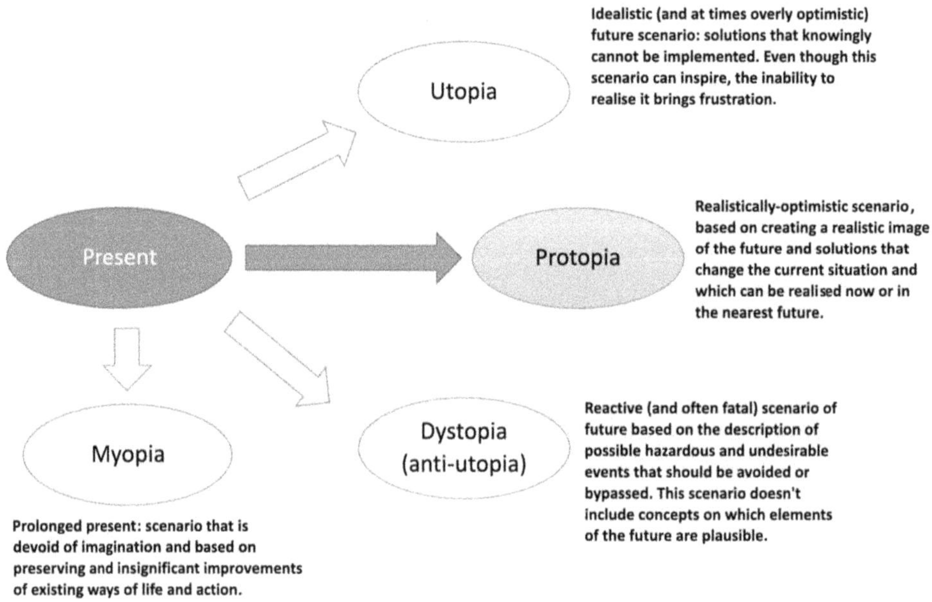

Figure 11.3 Creating a protopian path

(and often fatalistic) scenarios of the future based on the description of possible hazardous and undesirable events that should be avoided or bypassed. This framework doesn't aid in the determination of which elements of the future vision are plausible. *Myopic* frames are simply prolongations of the present: scenarios that are devoid of imagination and seek to preserve and advance the status quo through insignificant improvements of existing ways of life and action. *Protopian* frames are the ones adopted by circular city designers, representing realistically optimistic scenarios based on the creation of desirable, feasible, and realisable images of the future and implementable solutions that change the current situation. This framework offers actionable pathways for systemic innovations that can be realised now or in the nearest future.

Neither hoping for utopian idealistic societal responses to our VUCA challenges or fighting against dystopian fears, practices, or regimes can provide the necessary conditions for the generation of circular societies. The comfortable but false alternative of myopic approaches can only lead to bigger, faster, stronger caterpillars, but it will never provide the conditions necessary for the emergence of butterflies. The needed approach relies on the creation of protopian futures. Protopian vision fosters individual and collective initiatives to creating the future we want to see in the here and now. What is needed now are actionable and navigable pathways towards thrivable circular cities far and wide. For humanity to chart clear paths towards circular futures will require that we learn and lead together through the conscious evolution of our increasingly interconnected lives in an ever more interdependent world. Protopian scenarios serve as systemic nurturance frameworks for the design and curation of circular cities that are evolutionarily viable, actionable, and attainable.

11.2.3 Emerging Trends in Circular City Design: Towards Living Cities and Thrivable Ecosystems

The socio-cultural, relational, attitudinal, and moral-psychological aspects of a healthy and authentic community in urban settings constitutes the research, development, and innovation focus of circular city design. Studies are emerging in this area that point to a concept of *living cities* as successful manifestations of CE designs. These studies explore how to foster an interdependent ecosystem of circular cities across the globe.[5]

Contemporary efforts in this regard include the creation of Integral City Meshworks, which organised the Elab 2012 with an action-based inquiry into the intelligences that constitute an integral city.[6] More recently, it has found expression in such landmark works as 'Systemic Innovation for Thrivable Cities'[7] and related research on the shift 'From Sustainability to Thrivability: Transforming Systems with Purpose'.[8] One general manifestation of the broader living cities initiative is captured by the emerging ecosystem called Living Cities Earth.

Such initiatives demonstrate how the transition towards a regenerative circular society necessitates moving beyond traditional social systems design to a more dynamic and adaptive approach. One such approach is known as evolutionary systems design (ESD). This recognises the interconnectivity of various social, economic, and environmental factors, emphasising collaboration, innovation, and feedback loops to facilitate sustainable and regenerative social systems. As a relatively recent contribution to the field of the social systems sciences, ESD responds to a need for a future-creating design praxis that embraces not only human interests and lifespans, but those on ecosystemic and evolutionary planes as well (Figure 11.4).[9] The split between macro- and micro-scale conceptual frameworks in contemplation of human developmental concerns continues to provide a difference of perspective within the systems sciences that tends to inspire either anthropocentric change efforts or evolutionary interpretive frameworks for them, but little by way of evolutionary strategies for the design of healthy and sustainable modes of being and becoming on a day-to-day basis in partnership with the life-support systems of planet Earth.

As a species, our actions and interventions on this planet have been largely driven by chance and, at best, '20/20 hindsight'. However, as Margaret Mead noted, we are at a point where for the first time in human history, we are able to explain what is happening while it is happening.[10] ESD builds on this relatively

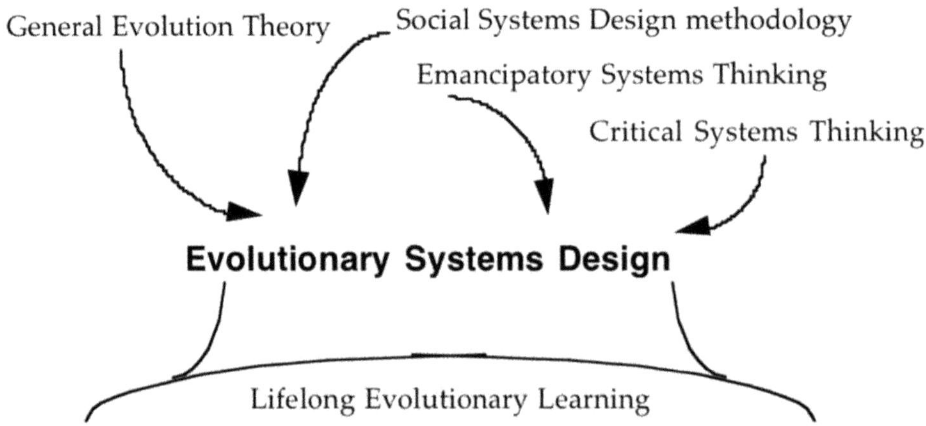

Figure 11.4 Epistemological foundations of ESD

new meta-reflective competence by serving as an instrument for the evolution of consciousness and for conscious evolution. It suggests that with the new understanding of evolutionary dynamics and effective approaches to the participatory design of circular economies and living cities, our species can stop drifting upon the currents of change and begin to adjust its sails in view of sustainable and even thrivable evolutionary futures. 'As evolution becomes history, it can become conscious. As Jonas Salk put it: conscious evolution can emerge from the evolution of consciousness – and from the consciousness of evolution'.[11] This is the understanding upon which ESD has been conceived.

The ESD orientation to circular design is essentially possibilistic. It assumes that human beings have the choice consciously to participate in the co-creation of the future. And yet it seeks neither to predict nor to 'socially engineer' the future. Rather, it seeks to create the conditions for the emergence of circular and evolutionary futures.

> In systems such as contemporary society, evolution is always a promise and devolution always a threat. No system comes with a guarantee of ongoing evolution. The challenge is real. To ignore it is to play dice with all we have. To accept it is not to play God – it is to become an instrument of whatever divine purpose infuses the universe.[12]

The aphorism that captures the spirit of ESD is one of flow: *we cannot direct the wind, but we can adjust the sails*. Learning to sail the currents of evolution – not just to 'go with the flow' but to become active participants in the journey – this is at the heart of the ESD for circular design.

As an evolutionary and circular approach to change, ESD includes and transcends regeneration since it creates conditions for *evolutionary emergence*, identifying distinct phases in the culture of urban development as it has evolved over the years. These can be charted in terms of the worldviews related to nature and the living systems which comprise cities. These positions have emphasised the following objectives at different times in urban development:

- *Extract*: Deplete–Deforest Degrade (1760–1987)
- *Sustain*: Reduce–Reuse–Recycle (1987–2010)
- *Regenerate*: Rethink–Restore–Replenish (2010–2020)
- *Evolve*: Transform–Transmute–Transcend (2020+)

It is the last of these stages that captures the efforts and interests of circular cities such as Vienna. That is, to create conditions that invite the emergence of new ways of being and interbeing, understanding the city as a living whole, a living supra-organism in and of itself. When curated and cared for in this way, the city emerges as an ecosystem of thrivability that engenders qualities of care, life, empathy, relationships, interdependence, interbeing, vitality, and aliveness. These characteristics allow the city to evolve in ways that express ever greater coherence, synergy, and happiness both within itself and in evolutionary relation to its living bioregion.

11.3 Circular Living: Nurturing Cities as Living Organisms of Sustainability

Circular living describes the ability of emergent visionary frameworks to harmonise CE and regenerative principles within urban governance. The concept represents a paradigm shift in urban development, envisioning cities as dynamic, self-sustaining organisms embedded within their ecological and social contexts.[13]

This section explores the integration of CE and regenerative principles into urban governance frameworks, aiming to facilitate the transition towards circular living through collaborative partnerships and adaptive management. The role of transition governance in orchestrating this transformation is discussed, emphasising collaborative efforts and systemic thinking. Conceptualising cities as living entities that continuously regenerate and optimise resource flows according to regenerative circular principles offers a holistic approach to sustainable urban development.

Ever-increasing urbanisation calls for innovative approaches to urban development that can reconcile environmental sustainability, economic prosperity, and societal well-being. Circular living emerges as a transformative concept, viewing cities as dynamic, interconnected ecosystems operating akin to living organisms.

11.3.1 The Metabolism of the City: A Metaphorical Framework

Circular living draws inspiration from the metabolism of a living organism. This concept encompasses the flow of materials and energy within a city, emphasising resource optimisation, waste reduction, and closed-loop systems. Additionally, circular living involves fostering sustainable lifestyles and behaviours among city residents to support the CE.

Cities, like living organisms, have a metabolic cycle where resources flow in, are utilised, and are eventually returned to the ecosystem. The term 'metabolism' is borrowed from biology, where it refers to the set of chemical processes that occur within a living organism to maintain life. In the context of social metabolism, the concept is extended to describe the flow of materials, energy, and information within human societies and their interaction with the environment. It draws from the concept of 'urban metabolism', which refers to the study of material and energy flows in urban areas, similar to how a biological organism processes nutrients and energy. This field of research examines how cities acquire, use, and dispose of resources, and how these processes contribute to environmental impacts and sustainability. Yet there is a strong analogy to biological systems that draws on the parallel between human societies and biological organisms and their effect on societal transitions and similarities in terms of resource consumption, waste generation, and energy exchange, and the scaling relationships between various urban characteristics and their impact on resource consumption.[14]

Society's need for materials and energy to construct, maintain, and use its material assets – buildings, infrastructure, machines, human and animal life – is the starting point for 'metabolism'. This concept can be seen as a functional counterpart to biological metabolism and is referred to as 'social metabolism'. Social metabolism research combines biophysical resource and social structural perspectives.[15] The concept of social metabolism originates from the field of ecological economics and systems theory. It was first introduced by the German biochemist and systems ecologist Georgescu-Roegen in the 1970s and was later expanded upon by other scholars in the realm of sustainability studies. Like living organisms, cities require resources for growth, maintenance, and functioning, and they generate waste products that need to be managed like other complex, self-organising systems that exhibit similarities to biological organisms.

Circular living envisions a city's metabolism that mimics nature's cycles, utilising resources efficiently and regenerating ecosystems. Materials, energy, and people circulate within the city's systems structures, reducing wastefulness and fostering sustainable patterns of consumption and production. It serves the authors as a framework to enhance our understanding of urban dynamics, sustainability, and the capacity for regeneration.

11.3.2 Circular Economy Principles

The ability to lead a circular life in the city is based on the principles of the CE, which is regenerative by nature and aims to gradually decouple growth from the consumption of limited resources and raw materials. It is based upon designing out waste and pollution, keeping products and materials in use, and regenerating natural or living systems.[16]

These principles guide the transformation towards sustainable consumption and production patterns within a circular city, focusing on closing material loops, minimising waste, and promoting resource efficiency, but also on encouraging product design for durability, repairability, and recyclability, thus promoting cradle-to-cradle cycles. Waste should become a resource by promoting activities such as recycling, upcycling, and remanufacturing. Circular by design means that products are designed to have a long life, be repairable and upgradeable, and at the end of life be disassembled and largely reused or recycled. Remaining parts that cannot be reused or recycled are designed to be biodegradable and, in general, products should be manufactured in energy- and resource-efficient processes using secondary raw materials and reusable parts of other products. The aim is to ensure that biogenic products and raw materials are integrated as seamlessly as possible into the natural life cycle. The principles of the CE are seen as a challenge to linear models and a stimulus for innovation across sectors.[17]

Faced with the challenges of climate change, loss of biodiversity, and increasing scarcity of raw materials, the existing linear economy 'take–make–use–waste' approach is becoming increasingly unstable, unprofitable, and inefficient under current and future conditions. A CE is seen as a promising approach and is being discussed by international and national representatives from politics, business, and society as a systemic change for such a transformation. The European Green Deal uses the CE as a key lever to achieve the EU's climate goals by 2050, and thus also aims to empower consumers.

In December 2022, Austria introduced a national CE strategy that has attracted international attention for its ambitious resource consumption targets.[18]

These are urgently needed, as Austria, with the fifth-largest material footprint in the EU, currently consumes 33 tonnes of resources per capita per year – 19 tonnes more than the EU average and about five times more than what is considered sustainable.[19]

As the first metropolitan area in Austria, the city of Vienna has introduced a transition strategy towards a CE as part of the strategy paper 'Vienna 2030 – Economy & Innovation' and the framework 'Smart City Climate Strategy Vienna' and has committed itself to the goal of making Vienna a 'circular city' by 2030. According to the strategy paper, such a circular city 'focuses on resource conservation, reuse and recycling through CE for the benefit of its citizens. The aim is to create wealth, increase livability [sic] and improve the resilience of the city and its citizens. At the same time, a Circular City aims to decouple value creation from

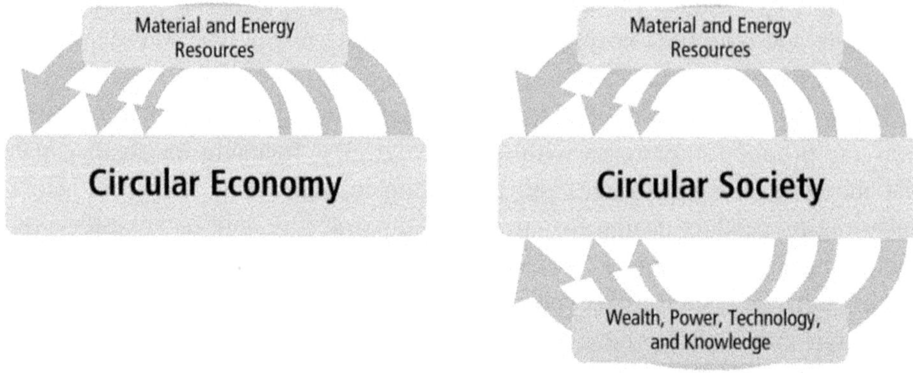

Figure 11.5 Conceptual differentiation between circular economy and circular society
(Credit: Adapted from Martin Calisto Friant *et al.*[20] Reproduced with permission.)

the consumption of finite resources'. To this end, an inter-municipal 'hub', the 'DoTank Circular City Vienna 2020–2030', has been established.[21]

As the counterpart of an economy is society, an important factor is the transition from a disposable society to a circular society, which relies on the acceptance of more sustainable lifestyles for the transformation by citizens (Figure 11.5). This term is gaining more attention recently in academic as well as government and corporate sectors. Like many other modern cities, Vienna is a complex adaptive system with dependencies and interactions between various stakeholders, components, and subsystems that we need to analyse in order to understand their dynamics.[22] A CE must therefore be embedded in social structures that promote human well-being for all within the biophysical limits of our planet.

Enterprises and organisations from the manufacturing and service sectors in the city of Vienna are strongly challenged to play their role as innovation drivers and multipliers of such a new circular innovation system for a modern, regenerative economy, while citizens must be able to acquire competences for the transition to cross-sectoral value cycles. This will require knowledge and skills, from new business models such as sharing, repairing, remanufacturing, or recycling of products to the necessary data-based financing solutions or return logistics.[23]

In terms of the city's economic potential, this will open new business areas that can develop into an important intra-European location advantage for the city, its economy, and its citizens. However, the challenges are many and varied, ranging from systemic and strategic organisational change, innovative companies, funding, corporate governance, tax barriers, or standards to the development of the necessary skills of existing and especially future employees and customers, to the use of digital applications and skills to transform supply chains and return logistics into value webs and thrivable ecosystems.

Addressing and developing transition strategies and skills at the level of policy-makers, business leaders, managers, and workers in a wide range of sectors in traditional industries is as important as the emergence of innovative circular business models in the start-up sector. Significant research and innovation efforts as well as skills development at all levels are needed to redesign economic processes towards a more circular, energy- and resource-efficient economy by reassessing existing business models, processes, risks, and logistics chains.[24]

To enable future decision-makers to make well-informed decisions on research, economic, and innovation policies, the education sector must promote and integrate systemic circular thinking into regular courses of study. Individual and organisational resilience is particularly needed in times of transition and contributes significantly to the successful implementation of existing knowledge and data-based information.

11.3.3 Regenerative Principles

In general, regenerative social-ecological systems – regions, cities, communities as well as economies, or businesses – can be defined as those that sustain positive, reinforcing cycles of well-being.

Something regenerative has the capacity to exist or to emerge again and again. Regenerative principles aim to restore and replenish natural resources and ecosystems. These principles go beyond mere sustainability and focus on actively enhancing the environment's health and resilience through circular practices, thus going beyond the concept of sustainability, as its practices aim to keep the system in operation with no degradation, while restoration practices use management strategies to restore the system to improved productivity and health.[25]

Incorporating regenerative principles elevates the concept of CE beyond mere resource efficiency. Regeneration encompasses the revitalisation and rejuvenation of systems, whether ecological or otherwise, with the aim of reinstating health, resilience, and desirable outcomes. A crucial aspect of regeneration lies in augmenting a system's inherent capacity to effectively restore and renew itself, a recurring and pivotal attribute. To distil, regeneration is fundamentally concerned with leaving both the natural world and society in a state that is more robust, healthier, and more resilient than its initial state. It emerges as the vanguard of sustainability, embracing a trajectory that extends beyond mere preservation. Its practices rejuvenate natural systems, promoting symbiotic relationships between urban areas and their surrounding ecosystems.

Coincidentally, just as sustainability has evolved into an imperative for businesses over the past 15 years, regeneration has emerged as a burgeoning imperative – offering even more substantial advantages than its predecessor, given the science-based facts of having taken our planet to the brink of mass extinction. We now have plenty of evidence that degenerative linear systems, while yielding short-term benefits, erode and undermine nature and society in the long run. Sustaining the existing status quo is not appropriate given the current and projected status of environment and society. Hence, multiple influential organisations, such as the World Business Council for Sustainable Development, the Capital Institute, the Doughnut Economics Action Lab, and Forum for the Future are looking at what regenerative businesses and economies might look like, and entire sectors are beginning to explore how they can enable the shift to a regenerative dynamic economy and society.

Regeneration entails a multitude of pivotal facets, spanning from the revival of natural systems to the rejuvenation of relationships with vital stakeholders in society. This approach entails reimagining a more harmonious balance between material and non-material pursuits while cultivating leadership capable of systemic thinking and prioritising mutually beneficial outcomes for all stakeholders. Regenerative principles therefore embody an evolutionary form of sustainability that seeks more than to uphold and sustain, but also to reinstate, rejuvenate, heal, and nurture. The formula to be considered in every aspect of systems design is to align the criteria of restoration, renewal, and resilience towards a regenerative trajectory.

11.4 Transition Governance

Effective governance is critical for driving the transition towards circular living and a circular city. Research on transition governance frameworks for detecting the societal potential for system's change and for orienting the societal system towards transitions is a multidisciplinary field, and findings vary based on specific contexts, research methodologies, and objectives.

In general, transition governance explores the mechanisms, strategies, and approaches necessary to facilitate and guide societal transitions towards more sustainable and resilient systems. It involves setting a clear vision, fostering stakeholder engagement, and implementing policies and frameworks that support circular initiatives.[26]

Transitioning towards a regenerative CE and regenerative lifestyles for citizens demands robust governance frameworks that promote collaboration, innovation, and adaptive management. It needs multi-stakeholder engagement and the fostering of partnerships between governments, businesses, communities, and academia. Collaborative decision-making processes facilitate the co-creation of policies and strategies that align with regenerative circular principles to foster and enable circular living in the city. To be successful, the transition requires the involvement of all actors in society and their capability to network and create appropriate patterns of cooperation and exchange.[27]

The facilitation of linkages and dialogue by implementing effective multi-level governance to align priorities and incentives across sectors, levels of government, and stakeholders plays a vital role in the process. Pioneering municipalities and city authorities need to promote systems thinking among decision-makers to achieve policy coherence by integrating segmented policies to adopt a functional approach that transcends administrative boundaries and promotes rural–urban linkages and partnerships. Systemic intermediaries – 'transition brokers', according to Jacqueline Cramer's work – can play a vital role in regional governance by enhancing processes of change, building alliances, helping create the necessary preconditions, and developing impactful initiatives from a neutral standpoint. Based on Cramer's research, there is a clear division of labour between transition brokers vis-à-vis other key actors in a multi-stakeholder setting, within which the local government is included.[28]

In pursuing the overarching goal of transforming urban life, it is of paramount importance to establish the necessary governance parameters that encompass a variety of key dimensions. A particularly crucial aspect in this regard concerns the careful examination and delineation of the legal frameworks that need to be readjusted to effectively support the transition to an overall regenerative CE framework. At the same time, the meaningful mobilisation of financial resources, allocated in such a way that the funds are efficiently directed towards the intended development path, is an imperative requirement. Moreover, the adaptation of the available workforce and technologies to meet the emerging challenges becomes a fundamental prerequisite for the realisation of this transformation process.

Related to this, it is essential to stimulate economic progress through strategic initiatives that include the dynamic reshaping of innovative spaces, state-sponsored procurement projects, and the promotion of synergies in cooperation within industrial sectors. Given the intricate interplay between public and private interests, the promotion of collaborative interfaces has a central role to play as a hub for fostering collaboration between non-profit public institutions and businesses.

To understand the above dynamics, it is crucial to establish an information framework that is firmly anchored in empirically robust data systems. This construct is of paramount importance, as it serves as the linchpin for enabling stringent metrics that allow for informed assessment of the wide-ranging impact and consequent effectiveness of policy interventions.[29]

11.5 Towards a Circular City: Methods, Processes, and Tools

A circular city brings the postulated paradigm shift from the well-known take–make–waste model of linear economies that characterises much of our materialised world by upshifting our consciousness and habits of being based on circular mindsets, heart-sets, and skill sets. The physical structure of the city determines not only the climate adaptivity of a city, but moreover the way denizens behave, move, and live within the built environment. Therefore, following the design dictum that 'form follows function', attention to how the built environment of the city serves and promotes the liveability and thrivability of its denizens is of paramount importance.

The emerging paradigm of circular cities promotes an upshift in thinking, doing, and being by dramatically extending the lifespan of its existing built environment in value and usage. This is the balancing act between designing and constructing for eternity, but in parallel developing concepts for the eventuality of eternity not happening due to urban optimisation, profound societal changes in lifestyle, or remarkable technological evolution. Self-evidently, material loops are closed, and all players connected to the circular city are thriving for doing the same in their individual parts of the circular living space provided: they preserve the value and utility of circulating products, components, materials, nutrients as long as possible 'as they are'. A circular city seeks to improve resource access for everyone – lowering its emissions, protecting, and enhancing biodiversity – and strives to reduce social inequalities, as demanded by the Sustainable Development Goals.[30]

11.5.1 Harvesting Circular Construction Material: Urban Mining versus Urban Material Stock

As previously described, our built environment generates a huge material footprint. Cities only cover 2 per cent of the world's land surface, but activities within their boundaries consume over 75 per cent of the planet's material resources.[31] Against this background, integral engineering science, among others, is developing processes and technical–operational options for producing secondary materials. Producing means in this case harvesting already applied construction elements, building products, or construction materials from our built environment.

Urban mining implies the extraction of secondary materials with similar effort to traditional mining. In in the long run, urban mining will always be part of our value chain, replacing naturally exploitable sites (e.g. copper mines). In a circular city, the built environment will be transformed into an urban material stock, requiring that building materials, products, and/or elements can be removed for reuse with minimal (energy) input.

Given the lack of focus on reusability or recyclability in construction in the past, most of the contemporary built environment consists of inseparable combinations of materials and structures and thus, is neither designed nor constructed for deconstruction or reuse.

The anthropogenic stockpile is currently more suitable for urban mining with the consequence that materials and construction elements can only be used for downcycling or – even worse – landfill. Under the current regulatory framework, urban mining is more likely being applied. The vision of an urban building stock will unfold when the legal foundations are laid in the sense of switching from a prohibitive to an enabling legislative environment. This change of approach requires courage, ambition, and pace on policy level, and a certain degree of maturity in society concerning self-responsibility.

The following subsections propose a common thread about 'by what' – introducing the Quadruple Helix approach as a method for innovation and transformation – 'whereby' – using the incubator neighbourhood transformer as an example. We close the chapter by tackling the 'how' – with a brief introduction to the Circular City Funding Guide,[32] one action under the *Urban Agenda Partnership for Circular Economy* that has been developed by the European Investment Advisory Hub.

11.5.2 The DNA of the Transformation to a Circular City Is a Quadruple Helix

The fundamental preconditions for climate protection are decided at city level because cities are responsible for around 75 per cent of global greenhouse gas emissions.[33] Thus, it is becoming ever more widely understood that climate protection can only succeed in the context of a just transition to a CE.

In Austria, citizens commonly refer to the local municipality as the 'commune'. It is an outdated term, but there is an understandable reason for its persistent existence. Another definition of a commune is the binding cohabitation of unrelated individuals – in other words, a freely chosen living community where the interplay between individuals is nurtured and encouraged in the absence of family ties. At the same time, all participants are constantly renegotiating their creative space within this community of purpose.

The Quadruple Helix approach is a concept that was introduced to a wider audience by a recognised article of Fraunhofer IAO, Centre for Responsible Research and Innovation in 2019. According to the research team, the collaboration of academia, industry, government, and society is necessary to ensure that innovative solutions are relevant, feasible, and sustainable.[34]

The existence of the quadruple or fourfold helix in human DNA was first observed at the University of Cambridge in 2013 and will lead to breakthroughs in the fight against major diseases. We are following the exploration of the human genome intellectually in an attempt to get closer. Our DNA structure has been commonly thought of as a double helix, two strands wrapped around each other, for the last 60 years. Similarly, we assume our society is divided into two strands. Those who make rules – 'those up there' – and those who more or less follow or question them – 'at the bottom'.

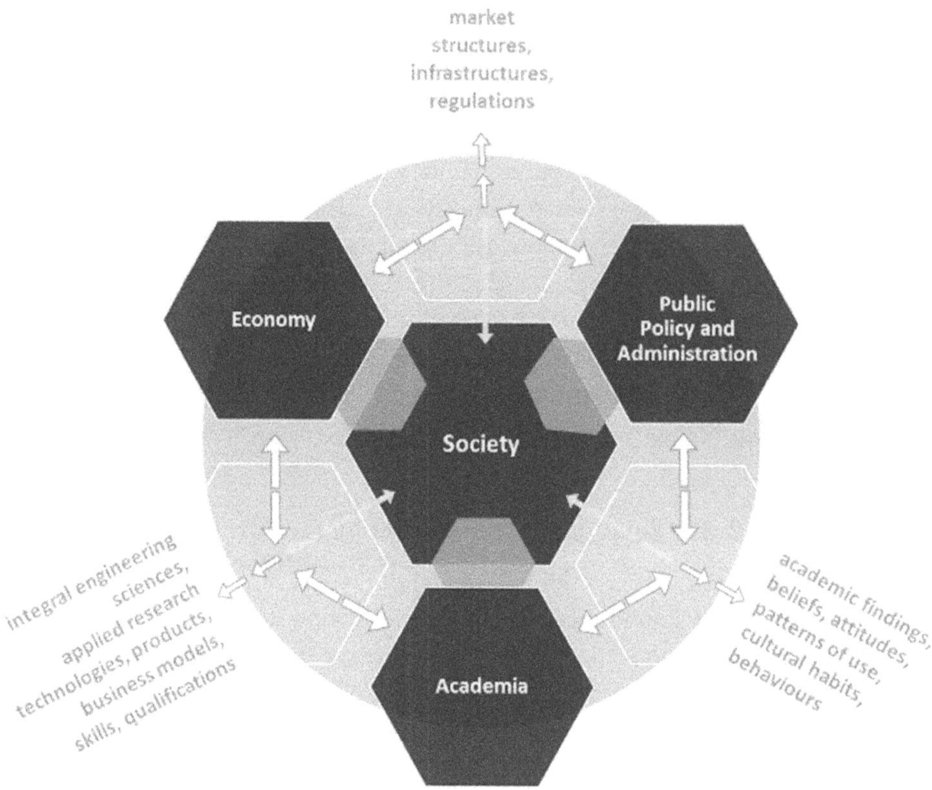

Figure 11.6 Quadruple Helix approach to socio-technical innovation in the circular economy

If we recognise the commune as an organism, which also underlies the DNA mechanism of action, the significance of the Quadruple Helix approach emerges. We can think of climate change, biodiversity loss, and over-consumption of primary resources as serious diseases to which we must adapt and which we must stop by actively protecting the climate and reducing resource use. We can do this through the concerted elaboration of our perspectives in an accompanied manner and the bringing together of these perspectives in recurrent autocatalytic and cross-catalytic loops. The process is visualised in Figure 11.6.

The four strands collaborating tolerantly in this process are business, research, politics, and administration, and certainly civil society. Of course, it is not possible to always discuss all aspects in a grassroots approach with all stakeholders. But that's not necessary if we identify possible contributors from the other strands of the Quadruple Helix as we develop content or concepts for transformation and prioritise the focus groups as part of a knowledge web.[35]

Aspects of research and development should, on the one hand, be integrated into cultural–social habits and, on the other hand, into economic and regulatory capabilities for implementation. Even if we make the transformation somehow happen by solely updating the regulatory frameworks or constantly adding particles for pseudo-novelties just for demonstrating action, a transformed built environment as well as economy cannot function under outdated frameworks.

Using innovation and development as a showcase, we open up the space of possibilities in accordance with the communal DNA. Holistic and in-depth negotiation of relevant topics between affected actors from business, science, politics, and administration – transparent for society at all times – ensures the efficiency required for an understandable, systemic, and thus rapid paradigm shift.

However, transitioning to a CE requires significant changes in the way we produce and consume. This can create disruption and uncertainty, particularly for those who are accustomed to the current linear model of production and consumption. Additionally, in the case of very liveable cities such as Vienna, there is currently no need for transformation. The quote 'never change a winning team' starts circling in many brains – especially in the brains of people who are not part of the sustainability and regenerative bubble and of course many policymakers or politicians.

A good portion of circular measures, such as renovation, waste reduction, and recycling, may require upfront investments that logically lead to short-term costs for individuals and businesses. This could be seen as a burden, particularly for those with limited financial resources when they don't see themselves embedded in a solidarity-framework and do not think of themselves as part of a commune. Therefore, we must put the Quadruple Helix approach into practice if we want the public to follow the path of transitioning to a CE and successfully participate in this upshift. In this context, courageous political decisions will become feasible. Awareness-raising efforts will end in a deeper understanding of the necessity to act, so elected officials will not be punished at the ballot box.[36] By adopting these strategies, residents of the city can be nudged to avoid 'not-in-my-backyard' thinking and become motivated to join the New European Bauhaus initiative of the European Commission.

11.5.3 Cross-Sectoral Collaboration

Whereas the initially described Quadruple Helix approach defines which parts of society should work together on which occasions and why, cross-sectoral collaboration can be seen as the tool which perfectly matches initiatives with each other. The circular city thrives on cross-sectoral collaboration, where diverse industries and sectors come together to develop integrated solutions. This collaboration promotes the efficient use of resources, reduces duplication, and fosters innovation.

It is particularly significant in the case of the built environment to look beyond the processes for effective collaboration towards physical outcomes achievable through site developments within the context of impact. Communes with a high quality of life are characterised by the interplay of urban planning considerations and their implementation in property planning. Ideally, the effects are multiplied by a selection of locally sensible, cross-silo measures in both private and public areas.

If, for example, a municipality redesigns a street space by planting trees, the optimal effect will only occur if adjacent buildings do not counteract this microclimatic improvement. Possibly coordinating the timelines of related projects (i.e. the growth phase of newly planted trees could be aligned with the renewal cycle of the adjoining facades), vertical greening solution would cover with its lifespan the period needed for the tree to develop its complete microclimatic effect. From a circular point of view, in this case the secondary structure of the shell would have to be designed for this change from the very beginning in order to ensure that as few materials as possible must be replaced. These should then have reached the end of their life anyway or be reused nearby.

Likewise, merely legitimising actions by saying 'because it is not forbidden' does not promote the common good. Similarly, it should not lead to suspicion if someone wants to make money. Yes, it is exhausting to negotiate the balance between the expectations of the individual and the needs of the collective, but the fact that neither the 'public hand' nor the 'invisible hand of the market' will be able to play the role of *deux ex machina* must be acknowledged. Everyone must take their share of responsibility for the ecological, economic, and social effects of their activities.

Currently, there is a limited understanding and implementation of this kind of urban development approach within the Viennese municipality. Still, the common five-step model of the policy and roadmap development process is standardly applied: (1) agenda setting, (2) formulation, (3) adoption, (4) implementation, and (5) evaluation.[37]

Every stage of the process has some nodes of participation; however, the administration is not yet ready to cede some of its process, outcome, and negotiation power to the remaining strands of the Quadruple Helix. Up to a point, this patronising approach is comprehensible, as it has given the city an unprecedented track record of raising and sustaining the quality of life to the highest level. A good portion of citizens have also adjusted to this: taking responsibility and do-it-yourself attitudes prevail over complaining about the city administration acting according to 'confidential rules' in the status quo.

To convince citizens to foster circularity and accept cross-sectoral collaboration – which also entails decision dependencies to a certain degree – it is crucial to embrace all perspectives and engage in a continuous dialogue with them. Several parallel strategies can be adopted to motivate citizens towards embracing CE solutions in urban planning, architecture, and everyday life. Therefore, for a while, change agents inside and outside the municipality tried to introduce the 'Paradox of the Red Queen' as a new, additional interpretative paradigm for a modern, transformative municipality. Shortly put, this paradigm says that a successful system has to adapt itself in an increasing number of narrow cycles to ensure its functionality: in this country you have to run as fast as you can if you want to stay in the same spot.[38]

11.5.4 Incubator Neighbourhood Transformer

One practical example of an application of cross-sectoral collaboration is the incubator neighbourhood transformer, jointly developed in 2022 by Green4Cities and ParaMind Brainstorming Software. Although the idea was discussed very positively by municipalities all over Austria, those especially involved in grassroots activities were the most supportive. Unfortunately, as it was not yet time for *medias res*; all the decision-makers at the executive level decided against the idea, one after the other, like a row of dominoes. The concept continues to circulate in Vienna, particularly in architectural circles, and is therefore briefly described as follows.

Incubator neighbourhood transformers are hubs that foster experimentation, innovation, and knowledge-sharing within the circular city. These transformative spaces serve as laboratories for implementing circular solutions and prototyping regenerative practices.

Innovation techniques and methods are methodological developments that include the definition of the process towards the transdisciplinary choice of applicable key performance indicators. This leads to a suitable implementation of potentially high-impact climate mitigation measures in the fields of action nature-based solutions, energy, and mobility. Simultaneously, it also involves development of solution pathways enabling sustainable decision-making when trade-offs arise. A master plan for those cross-siloed climate measures for whole city quarters and their corresponding cost estimation will be developed. In line with the requirements of the European Green Deal, the transition to a CE necessarily also provides the general scope for this project.

Governance innovation includes the design of co-creative neighbourhood organisations as locally set Special Purpose Vehicles (SPVs) to connect private stakeholder groups in collaboration with partners representing the public sector. In this manner, the interdependencies between innovative financing, social inclusiveness, and the impact measures of the master plan are guaranteed. Additionally, this approach ensures operating in accordance with the common good economy.

Financial innovation focuses on blended finance (e.g. revolving funds, private public partnerships, crowd funding, or green bonds), with special focus on Europe's innovative and unique financial instrument – the so-called Environmental

Impact Bonds operated by the suggested SPVs. Philanthropists, as well as impact investors and representatives of the public hand, are brought together under this umbrella. This holds the potential of unleashing the combined power between private money as well as the efficient and responsive use of public money.

11.6 Summary and Conclusions

The exploration of circularity presented in this chapter provides a holistic perspective for envisioning and creating a future that is sustainable, regenerative, and in harmony with the planet's ecosystems. As we navigate the complexities of a VUCA world, the authors establish the urgency of collective action and innovation in response to the challenges we face. The introduction of the concept of interbeing emphasises the interconnectedness of all life forms and ecosystems and serves as a foundation for circular action for change. Protopian thinking, as highlighted in Section 11.2, provides actionable pathways towards circular cities and societies, and promotes conscious participation in shaping a desirable future. Evolutionary systems design emphasises the role of collaboration, innovation, and adaptability in managing change.

Based on these principles, the concept of circular living is applied to urban governance frameworks. Integrating CE and regenerative principles into urban governance is shown to be a powerful approach to achieving sustainability and resilience. The metaphor of a city's metabolism illustrates the potential of circular living to optimise resource use and reduce waste, guided by CE principles. Regeneration, as an extension of these principles, aims to actively improve the health and resilience of urban systems, fostering a symbiotic relationship between cities and their surrounding ecosystems. The emphasis on transitional governance, systemic intermediaries, and collaboration highlights the importance of a holistic approach in driving the transition to circular living.

Turning to the practical application of circularity in urban contexts, the authors point to Vienna as a prime example. The concept of a circular city challenges the conventional linear economy and promotes circular mindsets, heart-sets, and skill sets. Strategies such as urban mining and the transformation of the built environment into a material stock highlight the need to close material loops and minimise waste. The Quadruple Helix approach – involving academia, industry, government, and society – is emerging as a collaborative means to foster innovation and drive circular transformation. The neighbourhood transformer incubator illustrates how experimentation, governance innovation, and cross-sector collaboration can contribute to realising the circular city vision. Further research is emerging on a variety of these focus areas that holds great promise for regenerative circular city design to become much more mainstream in the near future.

Together, these considerations weave a narrative of conscious evolution towards circular societies and liveable cities. The principles of circularity and regeneration, coupled with innovative governance models and collaborative efforts, offer a blueprint for addressing the challenges of the present and creating a thriving future. The transition to a circular way of life is not just a change in practice; it is a profound upshift in mindset and approach. It recognises the interdependence of human well-being and the health of our planet, emphasising harmony and symbiosis rather than extraction and depletion. Navigating our world's uncertainties, these perspectives present a vision of cities and societies evolving in resonance with nature, fostering connectedness, vitality, and resilience.

12

The Role of Education in Developing Liveable Cities with Functioning Circular Economies

ANABEL TERNÈS

12.1 Introduction

More and more people around the world are living in cities. This brings new and great challenges every day. Today's youth have the opportunity to actively influence the future and to help shape it themselves as adults in just a few years. For this, it is necessary to deal with the topic, acquire knowledge and develop visions in order to make them a reality later on with motivation and drive.

Circular economy (CE) enables a sustainable further development of society, as it protects and preserves both the environment and resources for the next generations. The basic principle of our education system is to enable people to develop holistically and completely. CE as a concept is fully in line with this principle. In this context, awareness and understanding of CE in the context of education require interdisciplinary teaching, which above all imparts a socially and ecologically appropriate attitude, as well as practical and not only theoretical knowledge.[1]

Education as the foundation of our society is responsible for social, economic, and political growth and, more generally, further development. School education plays a central role in this, as it shapes and supports young people in forming values, enhancing early childhood well-being, developing transferable learning, overcoming problems, and increasing resilience as they grow up. There are numerous topics that could be integrated into school curricula to enhance sustainable education and awareness. Subjects such as the 17 Sustainable Development Goals (SDGs), environment protection, waste reduction, and resource orientation can equip students with the necessary knowledge to contribute to a more sustainable world.

Additionally, concepts like smart cities, digitisation, and climate change education would provide the foundation for addressing global challenges like CO_2 reduction. Organisations like UNESCO and the OECD can further support engagement in areas such as politics, sustainable development, and urban life. Through education, students can be prepared to take on responsibilities in society, with media, further education, and non-governmental organisations (NGOs) playing vital roles in shaping future leaders.

12.1.1 The UN and UNESCO Framework Definition: SDGs and 'Education for Sustainable Development'

In September 2015, the United Nations General Assembly adopted the SDGs. These outline an ambitious agenda for humanity and our planet. The following are among the 17 goals formulated:

- Quality education with access to education for all and equal advancement opportunities for girls and boys
- Sustainable cities and communities
- Responsible consumption and production patterns
- Reduced poverty and hunger
- Improved health
- Enabling of equality
- Clean water for all and free access to drinking water
- Affordable and clean energy
- Protecting our planet Earth, including climate action.

As real progress is only realistic if children and young people around the world receive quality education, education plays a key role in the SDGs.

The UN 2030 Agenda for Sustainable Development is a commitment of all states that have signed the resolution. At the same time, the Agenda represents an action plan for people, the environment, and prosperity. The 17 formulated goals of the 2030 Agenda are integrated and indivisible and take into account the important three dimensions of sustainable development: environmental, social, and economic.[2]

In addition, the UNESCO World Programme of Action addresses five fields of action for the topic of 'Education for Sustainable Development':

1) Policy support in the areas of education and sustainable development
2) Holistic transformation of learning and teaching environments for the purpose of integrating sustainability principles into educational programmes
3) Development of teachers' and multipliers' competences to achieve better results in the field of education for sustainable development
4) Extensive involvement and mobilisation of youth in the form of practical measures for Education for Sustainable Development, such as project work, workshops, or collaborative group work
5) Promoting sustainable development at the local level. This means an expansion of Education for Sustainable Development programmes and networks at the level of municipalities, cities, and regions.[3]

One problem that is certainly very challenging in this context is the set of long-term objectives established over a decade and the periods, usually lasting only four years, that have the task of realising these objectives.

12.2 The Importance of the Circular Economy and Its Advantages

The predominant economic system in the world is the linear economy. A more accurate description is the throwaway economy. Raw materials are obtained as cheaply as possible where they are most easily accessible. A lot of energy is used for this. The materials used for a product are disposed of as waste after their useful life and are not returned to the cycle. There is no reuse. Part of the linear economy is the concept of planned obsolescence: manufacturers deliberately plan and bring about the ageing of the product and thus bring it to the end of the product life cycle. Planned obsolescence is incompatible with sustainability and the economical use of limited available resources.

In the European Union alone, more than 2.5 billion tonnes of waste are produced every year. The mountains of waste are growing; raw materials are becoming scarcer and more expensive; the environment is becoming increasingly poisoned; and the climate is changing adversely. The goal is therefore to move away from the linear economy, which is an unsustainable economic system. Waste management legislation must be comprehensively revised in order to move towards a CE.[4]

12.2.1 What Exactly Is a Circular Economy?

CE describes a complete and self-contained system of production and consumption. The primary goal is to keep existing materials and products in circulation for as long as possible and at the highest possible level of refinement. This is done by sharing, renting, reusing, refurbishing, repairing, recycling, or upcycling the products and materials. This makes it possible to extend the life cycle of products to the maximum and reduce waste to a minimum. Once a product has reached the end of its life, all materials and resources are kept in the economic cycle as long as possible and used productively again and again.

Why do we need the system transformation from a linear economy to a CE? Raw materials are becoming increasingly scarce, but demand is rising steadily as the world population grows and the living standards of many people rise. At the same time, many materials are only available in limited quantities. Not all countries have the same amount of raw materials, making resource-poor countries disadvantaged and dependent. The extraction and use of raw materials affects the climate and pollutes the environment. As a result, global energy consumption is constantly increasing, as are CO_2 emissions.[5]

The CE makes it possible to reduce energy demand and CO_2 emissions through the intelligent use of raw materials. According to the European Parliament's elaborations, it is feasible to achieve savings of €600 billion per year through reuse, waste prevention, ecological design, and comparable other measures. This is equivalent to 8 per cent of the annual turnover of all companies operating in the European Economic Area. More importantly, it could reduce annual greenhouse gas emissions by 2–4 per cent. The potential for a number of other benefits exists:

- Pressure on the environment as a whole is significantly reduced.
- The security of supply of raw materials is significantly improved.
- Competitiveness can be increased.
- Transformation requires innovation.
- The employment rate in the EU can be improved, with an estimated 580,000 additional jobs.

For consumers, the CE means that products can be used for longer. This saves costs and leads to a better quality of life.[6]

12.3 What We Need for This

Human life is directly and completely dependent on the environment in which we exist. Therefore, it is necessary to internalise the idea of sustainability in our children and young people. This means that a comprehensive and age-appropriate educational investment is required at the respective educational level that establishes a new environmental awareness.

Specific and age-appropriate material is necessary for this, from educational offers for children and young people to higher education.[7] Several institutions have already done pioneering work in this field and, with their elaborated educational offers, invite students to deal with sustainable and future-oriented CE as well as environmentally friendly mobility for a liveable city and environment within the framework of their lessons. In this chapter, an overview of existing initiatives is given and selected educational material is presented. The focus is on educational modules for young, but also older, people with which a new environmental awareness can be brought about, for example:

Consistently conserving all resources used through reflective purchasing decisions, reuse and recycling, and promoting upcycling; addressing various industrial sectors that are particularly important in terms of the CE, such as the construction industry, the automotive industry, aviation, the consumer goods industry, the food industry, and the clothing industry

- Reducing the use of plastics and plastic to a minimum, especially with regard to the use of everyday and consumer goods
- Avoiding waste avoidance and consistently separating waste

- Saving energy and incorporatin its economical use into consumer behaviour: in the use of electrical appliances, mobility, heating, air conditioning, hot water, food purchases, and food preparation
- Using and recycling food instead of disposing of it
- Recognising water as a precious resource, using it sparingly and protecting it as a resource.

The approaches and concepts of these educational materials play a major role in successfully conveying the understanding, knowledge, skills, and motivation for the development of the CE. A promising approach is to introduce children to the seven concepts of the CE: reduce, reuse, recycle, respect, repair, reflect, and reject. In the follow-up step, they are then empowered to explore for themselves how these principles can be applied to everyday life.

Only when young people have recognised and understand the need for a CE can they become experts in the CE in the future – experts who are able to apply CE solutions in everyday life as well as at work, and perhaps even to develop new solutions for the city of the future that will still be liveable tomorrow.[8]

Around the world, there are some impressive examples of sustainable and people-oriented urban development that incorporates a CE as a central element. Examples include Turku in Finland or Changchun in China. In many places, our cities are far from the ideal of an urban environment worth living in. This must be changed.[9]

12.4 Moving from the Instructional to the Participatory Approach

It is necessary to transform the education system from the classical instructional to a participatory approach. The discussion about sustainable consumption and production is always at the forefront. A strong understanding of the impact of our consumption on the whole world is necessary to help young people make the right, because sustainable, choices later in their lives.[10]

By making children and young people aware of the problems through concrete examples, we enable them to reflect and make or at least influence correct consumption decisions themselves. From an early age, they learn to understand how they can contribute to sustainability and the circular system.[11] The examples should be as creative as possible and promote the children's understanding of what possibilities they themselves have to contribute to the benefit of the community. Creativity and sharing in conversation enable the experience of joy as well as curiosity and promote teamwork. Examples could look like this:

- Plastic is not biodegradable and remains in the environment for hundreds of years. Each child reports on the places in the environment where they have already found plastic waste. In a subsequent discussion, the children suggest how plastic waste can be avoided in itself and in our environment and how to make it so that the unavoidable waste goes where it belongs.

- Composite materials and multi-layered plastic are problematic because in practice they are hardly ever recycled. The children are given the task of examining their own school supplies for composite materials. The group discusses what alternatives there are to the problematic items and how to deal with the multi-layered plastic.
- Materials that secrete microplastics enter the food chain and thus affect the entire animal world and us humans. The aim is to achieve an understanding among the children of how to find out which products contain microplastics and why the particles are so dangerous.

  Only those who separate and recycle their own waste contribute to a clean society and environment. The children tell how much waste is produced at home every day and whether it is separated and recycled. The children are allowed to calculate how much rubbish is produced in 1 year or in 10 years by one family and eventually by all the inhabitants of the city. Two calculations are made for comparison: one if the waste is separated and another if this is not done.
- The choice of transport in everyday life makes a difference. The comparison looks at the resources required and the CO_2 emissions for the daily journey to school by car, public transport, or bicycle and on foot, for one day, one month, and one year.

In this way, children and young people can become members of our society who act sustainably and convince their fellow citizens of the importance of this attitude.[12]

12.5 Investing in Education and Teachers

With regard to the CE, a profound revision of the curriculum is necessary. In addition, there is a need to significantly build the capacity of teachers and support staff: Teachers in schools and universities have a key role in educating our youth and in using innovative pedagogical skills to impart understanding, awareness, and knowledge. We need both to sustainably educate a CE-practising society.

The pedagogical approach should include methods such as peer-to-peer education programmes as well as projects with intensive group collaboration. By encouraging students to rethink and critically question existing systems, and by using interdisciplinary learning techniques, students can acquire creative and mediating skills step by step.

The general requirement for education policy is to become adaptable to the dynamic changes in the economy and the labour market in order to continuously develop the skills of pupils and students. This is because students need the best possible skills to be successful in future economic and market scenarios. In order to accomplish this further qualification of students, major investments in education will be needed in the future. It is highly relevant for both students and teachers to develop a global perspective with a local or regional focus and knowledge.

For a holistic development of the individual towards ecological and sustainable action and for the social and economic growth of our society, it is essential to put together and implement this bundle of explained educational measures.[13]

12.6 Ensuring a Mature and Vigilant Society of the Future

In business and politics, the increasingly strong phenomenon of greenwashing has been observed for years. Greenwashing systematically uses public relations and marketing methods with the aim of giving a company, institution, or product a responsible and environmentally friendly image in the public eye even though there is no adequate and sufficient basis for this image.

We need education for our young generation that provides for a reasonable as well as reflective and objective–critical attitude, and that imparts the necessary expertise to be able to conduct a discourse at eye level. Only a mature and vigilant society is in a position to recognise greenwashing as such, to make it public, and to object to it.

For example, in the field of electricity generation, a sustainably functioning CE can never take place on the basis of nuclear power and fossil natural gas. With nuclear power there is the residual risk of a radiation accident and the unsolved problem of the necessary final storage of highly radioactive nuclear waste. Both problems are incompatible with a sustainable and environmentally friendly energy and CE. The burning of fossil natural gas for electricity generation is also incompatible with a sustainable and environmentally friendly energy policy, as the use of fossil natural gas contradicts the circular flow principle.

Nevertheless, the European Commission is vehemently trying to greenwash this form of energy as green and sustainable electricity generation under the title Green Deal.

It is of fundamental importance for a sustainable future of humanity that individual members of society are able to distinguish honest and factually correct information, technologies, products, and decisions from false or embellished ones. The role of education is elementary in this respect. As the popular scientists Oberhummer, Puntigam, and Gruber state in their book title, ‘he who knows nothing must believe everything’.[14]

12.7 Status Report 2021 on Education for Sustainable Development in Germany

According to the report submitted once per legislative period, five German institutions cooperate with UNESCO on specific fields of action:

- The Federal Ministry of Education and Research provides political support and coordination for the German partners.
- The Education for Sustainable Development (ESD) Expert Net of Engagement Global contributes its expertise in the areas of youth empowerment and mobilisation.
- The Free and Hanseatic City of Hamburg co-chairs the network in promoting sustainable development at the local level.
- The UNESCO Chair Higher Education for Sustainable Development at the University of Lüneburg and the company rootAbility promote the holistic transformation of teaching and learning environments with the help of their international partner network.[15]

In the period from 2017 to 2019, 244 awards were presented throughout Germany to institutions that have made exemplary efforts in the field of ESD. These include:

- 7 early childhood education actors (kindergartens)
- 32 schools
- 17 actors in vocational education
- 32 universities
- 107 actors in non-formal and informal learning
- 27 enterprises
- 22 municipalities.

In total, 105 awards, or 43 per cent of all awards, reached the highest level as so-called 'ESD Lighthouses'.[16]

12.8 Specific Activities to Promote the Circular Economy

The Federal Ministry of Justice and Consumer Protection has set an initiative for the shift towards the CE with the project 'Sustainable Consumption 2030 – Narratives for Transformation'. The Institute for Prospective Analysis carried out the project, which describes which measures and activities are necessary to realise sustainable consumption in the sense of a CE by the year 2030. In implementing the project, emphasis was placed on drawing a large coherent overall picture.

Many of the solutions proposed for the transformation to a CE focus on the aspects of market access and the price and availability of products and materials. However, education in and awareness of sustainable development, as well as the promotion of public discourse on prosperity and sustainability, are also essential components of the proposed solutions presented. In the education system, there is great potential to positively influence both awareness and the shaping of public discourse beyond the core area: educated children and young people with an image of values that stands for sustainable development and careful use of nature and resources in terms of the environment can bring about positive change in the family as well as among friends and acquaintances and also lead the way as role models in small ways; for example, by consciously deciding to walk, cycle, or take public transport to school, or by making sure that there are no disposable dishes or packaging when eating at school, and that the food itself is made from sustainable ingredients.[17]

The project report particularly emphasises that the transformation to a CE is ultimately about fundamentally realigning the relationship between people and nature. Education is a central and indispensable element for this cultural change.

In order to be able to implement this repeatedly emphasised potential in the field of education, an ambitious and comprehensive investment in our education system is required: on the one hand, for the training and further education of teachers, on the other hand, to provide significantly more teachers and caregivers as well as additional capacities in childcare facilities and schools. Politicians are called upon to act now, as the necessary measures will take time to become effective.

A number of initiatives show how the skills, knowledge, and understanding of the CE can be developed in schools. Only with motivated young people who become CE experts in the future will it be possible to use solutions and technologies in everyday life and work that ensure that our limited resources are kept in circulation.[18]

The Cologne/Bonn regional group of Scientists for Future (S4F), a non-partisan and interdisciplinary grouping of scientists committed to a sustainable future, has developed a vision for the city of the future in the concrete form of Vision Cologne 2030: Future for All, Germany.[19] A large number of scientists contributed to the elaboration: Kathrin Rothenberg-Elder for the schools and Robert Grimm, Andrea Kamphuis, and Natalie Laibach for the CE should be mentioned by name here. The paper is remarkable for its holistic approach and concrete conception of a variety of urgent problems of today. As Germany's fourth largest city, Cologne has the opportunity to become a model city for many other urban regions in Germany and beyond through Vision Cologne 2030.

The vision focuses on climate change, which is forcing our society to act quickly, and on the great loss of biodiversity. The S4F emphasise that an energy turnaround, that is, the complete coverage of energy needs from renewable energies, is essential for decarbonisation.

Rather, additional system transformations in the sense of a turnaround are required in the following areas:

- Transport
- Resources
- Agriculture and food
- Urban life.

Vision Cologne 2030 formulates the current state, the target vision, and the identified problems and hurdles on the way to the goal for the following topics:

- School
- Circular economy
- Urban planning
- Buildings
- Transport
- Airport.

Common to all topics is the fact that education, among other things, plays a key role in successful implementation. Not least because today's children and young people will be adults in 2030.[20]

12.9 Values Education Takes Place in Childhood and Youth

Many of the measures described for the individual thematic fields directly benefit the population of Cologne. However, incomprehension or resistance is to be expected from all those organisations and people who must make investments, whose property is affected, or who must change their usual processes. Acceptance will only be achieved if the positive effects and the necessity of local action for climate protection are communicated comprehensively and convincingly.

The school system has a very important role to play here, as value education takes place primarily among children and young people, whereas it is much more difficult to establish environmentally related values and norms subsequently among adults. Successful value education for the sustainable protection of the environment, climate, biodiversity, and resources can make a significant contribution to broad as well as strong acceptance and support in our society.

12.9.1 The Future Vision for Cologne's Schools

Two main fields of activity have been defined for the schools of Cologne:

1. Value education and climate-sensitive behaviour are taught to children and young people throughout their schooling, starting in primary school.

2. Climate neutrality of the Cologne schools is to be achieved through their own actions and economic activities. Wherever possible, the pupils should be involved in the activities to achieve climate neutrality and take responsibility themselves.

As already explained, values that determine thinking and acting are primarily formed in childhood and adolescence. Since the children and young people of today are the adults of 2030, promptly implemented educational measures in schools have great significance and potential: they influence the actions of the young adults of tomorrow and also reach all strata of the population.[21]

A comprehensive initiative for teacher training is essential for achieving the goals, on the one hand, to convey the technical content and context for the areas of environment, climate protection, CE, sustainability, biodiversity, renewable energies, mobility concepts, and so on. On the other hand, it is necessary to open new pedagogical concepts and forms of teaching to teachers, complemented by prepared teaching materials. It is about much more than imparting knowledge; it is about supporting, empowering, and motivating young people. Skills worth striving for include:

- A value system that encourages children to behave in an environmentally friendly and CO_2-saving way and motivates young people to critically review routines and develop new sustainable routines, this making environmentally friendly and sustainable behaviour the norm
- Independent, differentiated, as well as reflected thinking and acting
- Systemic thinking that includes the global as well as the local perspective and that explores and recognises complex issues
- A positive attitude and the will to contribute to, shape, and bring about positive change, ideally helping youth and young adults to become ambassadors of sustainable development
- Responsible action and perception of self-efficacy
- Critical questioning and vigilance, because our society needs critical members who recognise dangerous trends such as greenwashing or planned obsolescence
- An understanding that long-term consequences of our actions are to be taken just as seriously as short-term and obvious needs, along with a sensorium for making complex interrelationships and insidious processes tangible. Climate change shows us very clearly how difficult this is.[22]

Thanks to education in schools, it is possible to broadly anchor already known standards of sustainable behaviour in the next generation. Some routines or actions that can have a role-model effect or a positive impulse can be implemented directly by or with the pupils. These include, for example:

- Encouraging environmentally friendly travel to school and home – if the pupils also calculate in class the directly saved CO_2 and the saved energy per pupil and trip as well as for the whole school year, then the pupils quickly get a feeling for what 1 kilogram of CO_2 or 1 kilowatt-hour means and are able to compare different forms of mobility with each other

- Switching to recycled paper or not using paper for certain tasks, for example if the class has laptops and a digital learning platform
- Doing away with disposable tableware and costly packaging material when buying meals from the school buffet, canteen, or shop
- Serving sustainable meals in school canteens – if this cannot be avoided in a transitional phase, in exceptional cases an offer is clearly marked as 'non-sustainable'; it is important to provide specific information as to why this food is not sustainable
- Implementing environmentally friendly renovation and refurbishment of school buildings, including greening as much as possible and the implementation of photovoltaic projects where possible and reasonable due to roof areas and shapes
- Nurturing the greatly important long-term sense of time within a culture of sustainability – projects such as the '10,000-year clock' project of the Long Now Foundation can make a positive contribution here: several prototypes of a clock have been developed that is supposed to function for 10,000 years.

All the goals and measures described above require considerable additional resources in terms of staff in kindergartens and schools. A political will and decision are therefore necessary to enable a significant additional investment in education.

As long as staff resources remain as strained as they are at present, it is an obvious approach to establish isolated solutions at particular schools. When implementing individual projects at schools, it is important to document accordingly those solutions that work best in terms of best practice. This makes it possible to multiply successful projects and thus turn individual school projects into sustainable state-wide or nationwide measures.

12.10 Retraining and Further Training Are Necessary for Climate Protection Measures

The ambitious goal of managing the energy supply entirely from renewable sources by 2030 requires a large number of skilled workers who can also implement the necessary measures, from consultation to conception to execution. Currently, there are far too few skilled workers available. Therefore, the City of Cologne needs to launch a 'Climate Protection Professionals Offensive' to cover the demand. In the field of education and training, it is necessary to promote retraining; to advertise, support, and promote vocational schools and training companies; and to expand their capacity.

CE means that waste is no longer a concept in the city of the future. Instead, there are only recyclables of various kinds. One thing is clear, however: in order to strengthen economic activity in the sense of a CE, new training opportunities are needed: on the one hand, in the area of new technologies needed for the CE, and on the other hand, in product design, so that industrial companies design their products in such a way that they are easy to repair, can be used for a long time, and are as biodegradable as possible.

The concrete task in the education system is, among other things, to convey to children and young people the complexity regarding the effects of our actions and consumption behaviour on the environment. It is also essential to communicate the key points of the legal framework so that young people are aware of the sometimes challenging framework conditions: the legal framework for a comprehensive changeover to a municipal CE is partly determined at federal and EU level. Thus, the municipal scope for action is clearly limited. By dealing with different problems and approaches to solutions, young people realise that it is necessary to take a supra-regional or global perspective.

Educational initiatives for children and young people on the environmental consequences of purchasing decisions raise awareness, promote a change in values, and can encourage reflective consumer behaviour.

12.10.1 Environmental Education and ESD: Target Group-Oriented and Impact-Oriented!

In the project initiated by the Federal Environment Agency, nine participation workshops, among other things, were conducted in order to develop effective and target-group-oriented educational offers.

Children and young people were defined as target groups. The following questions were discussed with the target groups:

- What do children and young people understand by the terms nature, environment, and sustainability? Are these topics relevant to them in everyday life?
- What experiences do children and young people already have with education in the areas of environment and sustainability? What would the target group like to see in the way of further topics? Does the target group have specific wishes regarding methods?
- How should educational programmes be designed in order to motivate children and young people to adopt a sustainable lifestyle despite the low visibility of environmentally friendly lifestyles and in view of global environmental problems?
- How should environmental education address social differences in the classroom, community, or society? How to address the fact that wealthy people who

see themselves as environmentally conscious have a significantly larger ecological footprint compared to those who have less income?

The workshops were held using different methods and were limited to the duration of one hour at the pre-school level:

- Based on the design thinking method
- Based on the method of a future workshop
- With the method 'Philosophising with Children'.

12.10.2 Wishes for Educational Offers

The following interesting results could be elaborated with the help of the educational workshops:

- Methods: In the primary school sector, there is a need for additional methods such as working in nature, using the garden, carrying out projects in the forest, building a school garden, using art and music as forms of engagement, and using digital media to teach. Most of the methods mentioned have in common that students want more 'action' and life-world relevance in the classroom.
- Motivated teachers who use creative learning methods and a concrete practical approach to convey content and deal with problems are in great demand.
- The individual support of each child should be expanded.
- The role of economics and politics should be dealt with in more detail.
- Teamwork and self-efficacy as well as dialogue with other children are to be strengthened.
- More experimentation, learning from practice and independent research using new media are also mentioned. In particular, experiments with sustainable energies meet with interest and are actively demanded.
- Watching the news together enables the children to better orientate and classify what they have seen and heard.
- The inclusion of the emotional level links environmental knowledge and children's and young people's own feelings

Some major problems could be identified in the course of the workshops conducted. These include:

- The importance of environmental issues in the lives of young people is often low.
- Environmental problems are often perceived as threatening. Many young people doubt that they can be solved politically.
- There is often strong doubt as to whether their own behavioural changes have any benefit at all.[23]

In order to counter these comprehensible problems in the best possible way, the Federal Environment Agency has made a number of recommendations for action in its study. Among others, these are:

- Create positive connections and impressions through a motivating solution orientation, taking into account the real-life and political dimensions. The real-life dimension mainly concerns the area of economic and consumption patterns. With regard to the political dimension, it makes sense to deal with environmental policy success stories such as the Renewable Energy Sources Act or the Montreal Protocol to reduce global chlorofluorocarbon emissions.
- Provide orientation towards the living environment and everyday life of children and young people to ensure that environmental policy contexts and problems are not perceived as abstract and remote from life.
- Deal with structures of power, problems, and actors in environmental policy and address the meaningfulness of individual behavioural change.
- Provide participation orientation in the sense of participatory learning and conveying self-efficacy.

With the help of interdisciplinary networking in the projects and the contents dealt with, interdisciplinary topics can be comprehensively worked on, and the children and young people can better understand the consistency and complexity of sustainable development.

12.11 Study on the Implementation of the SDGs in the German Education System and Other Systems

Commissioned by the German Council for Sustainable Development, the University of Bremen conducted a study on the implementation of the SDGs in the German education system. Among other things, this study contains some examples of good practice in the German education sector, which will be briefly presented here:

- Chat der Welten: In this binational school project between a German and a Colombian school, the students dealt with the 17 SDGs and practically considered what this could mean for them personally, for the school, and for their city. The tenor of the students from the project was: 'You learned that you should not only think about yourself'.
- Virtual Academy Sustainability: The virtual academy coordinated by the University of Bremen enables everyone to learn about sustainability by offering courses.
- Challenges of the UN 2030 Agenda and the Sustainable Development Goals: Conducted by the university group Weitblick and the University of Erfurt, SDG

10 could be identified as one of the biggest challenges. SDG 10 aims to reduce inequality within and between countries.

- BildungsCent e.V.: Located in the education sector of non-formal and informal learning, this Berlin-based civil society organisation works with 5,000 schools nationwide. The aim is to inspire the schools, which is done with diverse impulses, forward-looking programmes, and networking with extracurricular partners. This creates good as well as effective practice and enthusiasm for a new culture of teaching and learning.
- Sustainability in Nutrition: What is special about this online video course is that nutrition is looked at from very different angles. The five dimensions considered are environment, economy, society, health, and culture.
- SDG Summer Academy: The summer academy held in a youth centre in Berlin was held under the motto 'Peace, Justice, and Inclusion for All!'
- Klimahaus Bremerhaven 8° Ost: The Klimahaus has taken on climate change and committed to the SDGs. It challenges the visitor: 'Take the fate of the Earth into your own hands in the WORLD FUTURE LAB!'
- Global learning at the VHS and the 2030 Agenda: The VHS is one of the best-known providers of continuing education at the national level and has the vision 'Education for Everyone. Worldwide. Lifelong'.

12.11.1 Finland

Finland is a global pioneer in making principles of sustainability and CE an integral part of the education system. The Finnish Innovation Fund Sitra, which is working towards a successful Finland of tomorrow and promoting sustainable business, has recognised that education is a fundamental and significant element in creating a new CE society. The Finnish education system is aware of the need to create a new kind of expertise and to facilitate successful cooperation between separate disciplines. The aim of the effort is to change attitudes, mindsets, and working methods. Since 2017, they started educational initiatives for students to enable them to study the CE. This led to the development of study modules and communication materials from 2017 to 2019. The elaborated educational materials on CE cover primary school, high school, and vocational school.

12.11.2 Italy

In Italy, the Minister of Education, Lorenzo Fioramonti, has made sustainability and the climate crisis a central theme in schools. This made Italy the first country to introduce the school subject 'Climate Change and Sustainable Development' in the curriculum from summer 2020. The subject is taught once a week from 1st to 13th grade and focuses on the following, depending on age:

- Children between the ages of 6 and 11 engage with stories about different cultures and their relationship to the environment.
- From the age of 12, students acquire a technical understanding of climate change.
- Pupils between the ages of 16 and 18 in the final years of secondary school deal with the UN 2030 Agenda for Sustainable Development.

The climate crisis and sustainable development should also be addressed in other subjects such as mathematics, physics, and geography. In geography lessons in particular, students should focus on the impact of human activities on our planet.

Employees of the Italian Ministry of Education have the task of developing the corresponding curricula and initiating up-to-date further training for teachers. The curricula are reviewed by external experts.

To date, however, the German Federal Ministry of Education has rejected the introduction of climate protection as a school subject.[24]

12.11.3 Tucson, Arizona, USA

In Tucson, a special programme has been introduced in the schools for 10–13-year-olds to learn essential and worth knowing things about waste and recycling. Through the lessons, funded by Tucson City Environmental Services, students learn how each individual can make a difference through their waste management. This initiative is a first small step in the right direction to address Tucson's massive waste problem.

12.11.4 Netherlands

In 2018, the Clean2Antarctica project was initiated. Numerous schools participated by having students collect and sort plastics. This was eventually used to build the Solar Voyager vehicle, which will travel to the South Pole. The aim of the project is to show children that it's a waste to waste.

12.11.5 SmartPlaCE@schools: EU Programme Involving Belgium, Germany, Estonia, and Italy

SmartPlaCE@schools is a games platform for sensible educational games around CE developed within an EU programme in 2019 and 2020. Scientists developed creative teaching materials for secondary schools on the topic based on gamification methods as part of the project. The content covers both an introduction and an in-depth study of concepts and business models of the CE. The materials are based on secondary school curricula and were developed in cooperation with teachers from Belgium, Germany, Estonia, and Italy.

The aim of the project is to help young people understand the complexity and interrelationships between raw materials and environmental sustainability. Further, the young people should be empowered to discuss issues and ultimately be motivated to take responsibility. In addition, the platform will highlight opportunities for a professional career in science and technology.[25]

The German partners include the 'Wuppertal Institute for Climate, Environment, Energy GmbH' (Wuppertal Institute) and the 'bvse Verbände Sekundärrohstoffe und Entsorgung e.V., Germany'.

12.11.6 Austria

The Federal Ministry of Education, Science, and Research has established the subject area of ESD as an educational concern. In this context, educational concerns are to be understood as guiding ideas and recommendations of the Ministry, but do not include curricula and only a rudimentary implementation of teaching materials.

ESD aims to raise awareness of the complexity of problems and to contribute to the teaching of sustainable development, including its concrete implementation. This is intended to promote critical reflection, systemic and future-oriented thinking, and action for sustainable development. Reference is also made to the great importance of cross-curricular references for the education of holistic thinking, taking into account the ecological, economic, and social dimensions.

Some foundations for education for sustainability already exist in Austria:

- Political education and human rights education
- Environmental and health education
- Global learning
- Social learning
- Gender equality.

The Austrian Ministry of Education references the educational goals defined by UNESCO or the UN, in particular the World Programme of Action 'Education for Sustainable Development' adopted by the UN in 2015 as part of the 2030 Agenda. In order to achieve children's engagement with the 17 global goals for sustainable development adopted in Agenda 2030, teaching materials for primary school, suggestions for 5th–9th grade, and a folder for upper secondary school were developed.[26]

12.12 Conclusion

Education for the CE must begin as early as kindergarten. In this early phase of life, children exploring society and engaging with their peers and the process for internalising the attitude necessary for a CE can be initiated with a good chance of success. Education on the topics of the CE and sustainability is embedded across all levels – from primary and secondary school to higher education. This integrated approach is essential to ensure that the CE becomes a fundamental part of everyone's education and lifestyle from an early age. Children thus learn step by step about materials, products, and waste prevention in daily life. They gain an understanding of how companies operate and become alert to distinguish greenwashing from genuinely sustainable offerings. Ultimately, young people acquire both personal skills and knowledge and the principle of collective action for the shift towards a CE.

A comprehensively improved curriculum must take into account the challenges of our world, be adaptable, and have the goal of empowering sovereign young people to one day find a vocation in their lives and address their personal challenge to make our planet a better place and help our society to make a successfully and sustainably functioning CE a reality.

Any systemic change requires a serious and major investment in our education system and thus also requires comprehensive policy reforms. In building a necessary new economic system based on sustainability and CE, already today and even more in the future, those actors of the young generation who think in an interdisciplinary way and act in the spirit of sustainability will play a crucial role.

13

Circular Business Models and Synergies in Circular Economy Liveable Cities

ANDREA ORSAG

13.1 Introduction to the Roles of Leadership, Imagination, and Curiosity in Circular Cities

Circular cities, also known as circular economy cities or circular urban systems, are urban environments designed and organised around the principles of the circular economy (CE). In the context of cities, circularity refers to the application of these principles to urban planning, infrastructure, and resource management. Creating a circular city requires a comprehensive and coordinated effort that involves multiple stakeholders, including government authorities, businesses, communities, and citizens. A clear vision and commitment from city leaders to transition towards a CE are essential. This commitment should be supported by policies, regulations, and long-term strategies to guide the city's circular development. It's not only about new business models. Leadership, imagination, and curiosity play crucial roles in driving the transition to a CE.

13.1.1 Leadership

Leadership is essential in championing the CE and driving change at various levels, including government, businesses, and communities. Leaders who understand the importance of sustainability and circularity can set ambitious goals, develop strategies, and mobilise resources to create an enabling environment for circular practices. They can influence policy decisions, establish supportive regulations, and promote collaboration among stakeholders. Effective leadership is vital in inspiring others to embrace circular principles and make sustainable choices.

Examples include:

The **Ellen MacArthur Foundation**, led by Ellen MacArthur, has been a driving force in promoting the CE globally. Through its leadership and advocacy, the foundation has mobilised businesses, governments, and academia to embrace circularity, driving the adoption of circular principles in various sectors.

Interface, a global carpet manufacturer, has shown leadership in the CE through its Mission Zero commitment. Under the leadership of the late Ray Anderson, Interface set ambitious goals to eliminate its negative environmental impact by 2020. In 1973 Ray Anderson saw a carpet tile in Europe and recognised its future potential in modern offices. He introduced the concept to America and started a commercial flooring revolution that would spread around the world. The company has made significant progress in reducing waste, implementing renewable energy sources, and developing recycling programmes for its products. Some of the accomplishments include:

- Seventy-six per cent of energy used at owned manufacturing sites is renewable.
- Market-based greenhouse gas (GHG) emissions at carpet manufacturing sites have been reduced by 96 per cent.
- Waste sent to landfills from carpet manufacturing is down by 81 per cent since 1996.[1]

13.1.2 Imagination

Imagination enables seeing what the city where all thrive looks like and what is needed to get there. It fuels innovation and enables the envisioning of new possibilities. In the context of the CE, imagination is crucial for developing creative solutions to challenges related to resource scarcity, waste generation, and unsustainable consumption. Imaginative thinking allows individuals and organisations to explore alternative business models, design products and services with circularity in mind, and reimagine systems and processes to minimise environmental impacts. It enables the transformation of linear thinking into circular thinking, envisioning a future where resources are used more efficiently and waste is designed out.

The importance of imagination is demonstrated through examples such as:

Cradle to Cradle® design framework: The Cradle to Cradle® design framework, developed by William McDonough and Michael Braungart, encourages designers and businesses to imagine products and systems that are restorative and regenerative by design. It promotes the idea of creating products that can be easily disassembled and recycled, fostering a circular approach to production and consumption.[2]

The Ocean Cleanup: Boyan Slat, the founder of The Ocean Cleanup, demonstrated imagination by envisioning a system to remove plastic waste from the oceans. Through innovative technologies and designs, The Ocean Cleanup developed floating devices that capture and collect plastic debris, offering a potential solution to the global ocean plastic pollution problem. The organisation has an ambitious goal to remove 90 per cent of floating ocean plastic by 2040. To date, 4,763,826 kilogrammes of trash have been removed from waterways by their advanced technologies.[3]

13.1.3 Curiosity

Curiosity drives the desire to explore, learn, and understand. In the CE, curiosity plays a significant role in questioning conventional practices, seeking alternative approaches, and uncovering new insights. Curiosity drives individuals and organisations to examine the life cycles of products and materials, explore innovative technologies and processes, and identify opportunities for circularity. It fosters a mindset of continuous learning and adaptation, encouraging the exploration of new ideas, experimentation, and the sharing of knowledge. Curiosity drives the search for solutions that have a positive environmental and social impact.

Curiosity and CE are outlined in the examples such as:

Patagonia's Worn Wear programme: Worn Wear encourages customers to repair and reuse their clothing rather than buying new items. The programme was born out of curiosity about how to extend the lifespan of clothing and reduce waste, fostering a culture of curiosity and challenging the notion of constant consumption. The programme enables owners through platform do-it-yourself (DIY) guides to repair their gear and clothes themselves, and holds various events where people can learn mending and repair techniques; the programme also offers repairs of Patagonia clothes and on-location services. Between 2016 and 2018, countless well-loved and worn-out pieces of Patagonia gear were given a second chance in Europe – saved from landfill by Patagonia expert fixers. Repaired and restored, these items were made available to the public at pop-up stores in London, Berlin, and Milan. Since there has been a clear insatiable appetite of the customers for real alternatives to buying new, a permanent Worn Wear space selling pre-loved and patched up gear was made available to customers visiting, for example, the Berlin store. In Amsterdam, Patagonia works with the United Repair Centre, combining their quest for circularity with their responsibility to make a positive social impact. Items sent to a repair centre provide training and employment opportunities to young adults and newcomers with a refugee background. This means Patagonia products purchased through the Worn Wear programme not only save good gear from landfill – they're making a positive social impact too.[4]

Circular Economy at Philips Lighting: Philips Lighting, now known as Signify, has shown curiosity by exploring CE principles in its lighting products. They developed a subscription-based lighting service called 'Light as a Service' (LaaS), which allows customers to pay for the use of light rather than purchasing the physical lighting products. This curiosity-led approach encourages the company to think beyond traditional business models and explore new avenues for reducing waste through product design and increasing resource efficiency. LaaS as a business model was implemented at well-known locations such as Airport Schiphol in Amsterdam and Notre Dame Cathedral in Paris.[5]

The examples above highlight how leadership, imagination, and curiosity have played instrumental roles in driving the CE. They demonstrate how visionary leaders, creative thinking, and a willingness to explore new possibilities can lead to innovative solutions and transformative change in various industries and sectors. They showcase the role of visionary leaders, creative thinking, and a mindset of exploration in developing sustainable solutions, challenging the status quo, and shaping a more circular future. Leadership, imagination, and curiosity can propel the CE in cities forward by fostering a culture of innovation, resilience, and collaboration. They inspire individuals and organisations to embrace sustainability, challenge existing norms, and strive for a future where resources are used efficiently, waste is minimised, and environmental impacts are reduced. And as the following examples demonstrate, cities fully embrace them to drive the transformation towards circularity.

13.2 The City of Amsterdam, The Netherlands

Amsterdam is considered a CE front runner and is recognised as one of the leading cities worldwide in embracing CE principles. In 2023, it scored as the 13th most liveable city according to Monocle's annual Quality of Life survey, Monocle calling it a pioneer in sustainable living.

13.2.1 The Circular Strategy

To foster circularity, Amsterdam has implemented a range of initiatives, strategies, and policies that promote sustainability, resource efficiency, and waste reduction.

It wants to be a thriving and equitable city, ensuring a good life for everyone within the Earth's natural boundaries. As stated by the deputy mayor Marieke van Doorninck, 'We want to be a city in which prosperity and wellbeing for everyone come first. Therefore, we want to be a completely circular city by 2050'.[6]

This vision was accompanied in March 2020 by the launch of the Amsterdam Circular Strategy 2020–2025, which serves as a roadmap for the city's transition to a CE. It outlines specific goals and actions in areas such as waste management, circular procurement, sustainable construction, and circular business support. With this strategy, the City of Amsterdam set the course towards a circular city by 2050. To start with, the city aims to halve the use of new raw materials by 2030. The City of Amsterdam has adopted the objective of the Paris Agreement from 2015, in which the global leaders agreed to limit global warming to 2.0 degrees Celsius, preferably 1.5 degrees. By 2030, the City of Amsterdam wants to reduce CO_2 emissions by 55 per cent compared to 1990. And this reduction will be further increased to 95 per cent by 2050.[7]

CE can provide tremendous climate, social, and economic benefits. That's also why also the Amsterdam coalition agreement among current political coalition parties has given the CE a prominent role.[8]

In a CE, the value of raw materials is preserved as much as possible throughout a product's life, from design to disposal. A ladder of circularity that has been designed for the Amsterdam Circular Strategy showcases which processing options are preferable to others. The ladder moves from the most preferable options at the top to the least preferable options at the bottom.

The three options at the top (refuse, rethink, reduce) relate to the changing use and design of the product, and also to the business models around it. Examples are avoiding plastic cups at a coffee machine, renting and sharing cars, and producing the same products with fewer raw materials. The next four options (reuse, repair, refurbish, remanufacture) relate to the use phase of the product. These are aimed at prolonging the life cycle as much as possible. Second-hand stores and repair centres play a role here. The bottom three options (repurpose, recycle, recover) cover the end of the product's life: components can be repurposed, have their materials recycled and, as a last option, be incinerated with energy recovery.

The CE is sometimes presented as a doughnut. In this concept, doughnut represents a compass for human prosperity in the 21st century, with the aim of meeting the needs of all people within the means of the living planet. Amsterdam was the very first capital city that decided to implement, designed, and put in place a doughnut model.[9] This model was developed with the help of renowned British economist Kate Raworth, working at University of Oxford and the University of Cambridge. In her influential book *Doughnut Economics*, she shows that the current economy does not contribute to broad prosperity.[10]

The model describes how societies and businesses can contribute to economic development while still respecting the limits of the planet and our society. In the circular model, she combines economic, social, and ecological principles. The Amsterdam Doughnut Model shows that there is a lower limit to prosperity in order to be able to offer a socially equitable existence to the inhabitants of a city. People need income to live, so economic activity is essential. If we do not satisfy this, problems such as hunger, scarcity, and inequality will occur. These boundaries form the inside of the doughnut. However, there is also an upper limit to prosperity: the boundaries of our planet. We cannot emit unlimited CO_2 or deplete the oceans. Crossing these planetary boundaries leads to problems such as climate change, loss of biodiversity, ocean acidification, and freshwater shortages. These boundaries form the outside of the doughnut.

In its Circular Strategy 2020–2025, the City of Amsterdam decided to focus on the following three value chains:

1. Food and organic waste streams
2. Consumer goods
3. Built environment.

Those three value chains have been selected because of their economic significance to the city, their impact on ecology and climate, and the opportunities for Amsterdam to exert influence.

13.2.1.1 Food and Organic Waste Streams

Amsterdam aims to fight food waste in households, but also in hotels and restaurants. Organic waste streams can often be reused. For example, fat used for deep frying can be collected and converted into biodiesel for city buses or used as a substitute for plastic in refineries to make high-quality products. The city aims to increase the consumption of regionally produced and plant-based food. This value chain – which is closely linked to the Amsterdam Food Strategy[11] – was chosen because food supply in the city has a major ecological impact. In order to properly process the waste stream and preserve the valuable and increasingly scarce fertilisers, the city needs to keep control at the urban level and work together with the region. This way, Amsterdam can stimulate the economy, close the nutrient cycles, and lower the city's GHG emissions. There are three main ambitions:

a) Short food chains, providing a robust sustainable food system
b) Healthy and sustainable food for the people of Amsterdam
c) High-quality processing of organic waste streams.[12]

13.2.1.2 Consumer Goods

This value chain mainly concerns electronics, textiles, and furniture. These goods can often be repaired by professionals. The City of Amsterdam is committed to preserving value by processing those waste streams more intelligently. Amsterdam has chosen consumer goods because they contribute to the depletion of rare raw materials – their production causes pollution and often occurs under poor working conditions – and because they have a big impact on climate change. There is much to be gained in this value chain: at the front by sharing and trading, and at the back through good collection and reuse. Amsterdam has set three main ambitions for this waste stream:

a) Setting the right example by reducing its own municipality consumption
b) Using what we have more sparingly
c) Making the most of discarded products.

By 2030, the city aims to implement 100 per cent circular procurement and to reduce its overall consumption by 20 per cent. This starts with consumables and the furnishing of the city's own premises and, where possible, the city's public real estate.

By 2030, the environmental footprint of the textiles, electronics, and furniture sold and used in Amsterdam will be reduced. To achieve this, the city worked with businesses, local initiatives, and knowledge institutions in order to establish an efficient and accessible infrastructure of sharing platforms, second-hand shops, online marketplaces, and repair services by 2023. In addition, the city runs various campaigns to encourage the citizens to change their consumption habits and reduce what they consume.

The city envisions that from 2025 onwards, products that can no longer be repaired must be upcycled, that is, processed into products with the maximum possible value. With the help of public–private partnerships, by 2025 Amsterdam wants to be able to collect and separate textiles, electronics, furniture, and plastics so that they can be reused, repaired, or otherwise upcycled.[13]

13.2.1.3 Built Environment

Not only can the buildings be constructed circularly, for example, by using new and scrap wood and by taking changing functions into account, sustainable materials should be used in public spaces – from roads and bridges to playgrounds. Amsterdam believes it can design the city in a climate-adaptive manner so that residents breathe cleaner air and are less affected by rising temperatures and increasing rainfall. In addition, the city is seizing the opportunity that lies in the renovation task of being gas-free by 2040. This value chain was chosen because Amsterdam as a city decides on the organisation of public space and on what will be built where. In addition, the city itself is a major user of buildings. There is a lot of potential for better handling of raw materials and building materials, which is why there is a lot to be gained here. The following three ambitions are outlined:

a) The transition to circular development through a joint effort involving the municipality, private sector (including developers and construction companies), knowledge institutions, and local communities
b) The city setting the right example by formulating circular criteria
c) A circular approach to the existing city.

Since 2022 onwards, all new urban development (including urban transformation) and public space designs in Amsterdam are based on circular criteria. This requires collaboration with the people of Amsterdam, the market, and other public authorities. The joint challenge is to reduce the use of primary raw materials in the built environment so that the city can meet the 2030 target.

From 2023, the City of Amsterdam will implement circular and socially responsible criteria in the development of buildings and public spaces, among other things through its procurement and tender policies. This applies to all stages of the useful life of a structure: from construction and management all the way to the end of its functional life.

From 2025, 50 per cent of all renovations and building maintenance activities in Amsterdam will have to follow the principles of circular construction. This will apply to the existing social and private housing buildings, public real estate, schools, utility buildings, and public spaces above as well as below ground.[14]

13.2.2 Reflections on the Strategy

The City of Amsterdam understands well that the transition to a CE is challenging and far-reaching. 'Learning by doing' is a motto the city has been following. To enable the transition towards circularity, the city has been since 2020 developing relevant policy, designing criteria needed to get it there, and setting up practical pilot projects that can be monitored, further improved, and, ideally, scaled.

Fortunately, Amsterdam's circular strategy is not a standalone vision. The Dutch government and the European Union also have circular ambitions. The city works with the central government and with Europe on policy choices to make the world cleaner and society more equitable. There are several tools that would significantly support transition to a CE, such as a shift from taxation on labour to taxation on raw materials and energy. This change is an important precondition for creating a CE. The City of Amsterdam is now working with the seven city districts and with many local initiatives, market parties, knowledge institutions, and residents.

To evaluate the progress since the intentions set in 2020, in 2022 the City of Amsterdam published a report on lessons learnt and recommendations. After thorough research, the city estimates that 63 per cent of Amsterdam's total CO_2 emissions are caused by products and materials that are consumed in the city but produced elsewhere. In order to measure the progress and see whether the outlined goals and actions are on track, the city has developed a monitor.[15]

Amsterdam Monitor charts the extent to which Amsterdam's economy has become circular and identifies areas in which more needs to be done. The monitor will enable the city to measure whether the goals of halving the use of primary raw materials by 2030 and becoming 100 per cent circular by 2050 are feasible.

Key results of Amsterdam's 2023 findings include:

- If the environmental costs were included in the price, materials would have to be on average 42 per cent more expensive.

- CO_2 emissions within Amsterdam have been falling, yet no significant progress has been made in reducing the city's overall climate footprint.
- CO_2 emissions are just one of the many environmental impacts caused by materials use, and these impacts vary from one product group to another.
- Amsterdam's materials use is not falling rapidly enough to meet the target of a 50 per cent reduction by 2030.
- Too little information is available to accurately measure the circularity of material flows.[16]

13.2.3 The Hidden Costs of Material Use

Based on the latest deep-dive research by the City of Amsterdam, in 2020, approximately €13.4 billion was spent on materials consumption in the city. This amount includes the total sum of the price of materials, labour, and other costs incurred during the extraction and production of materials for the products the city uses. Environmental (or eco-) costs have yet to be incorporated into this expenditure total. These are the costs that would have to be incurred to prevent damage to the environment caused by the extraction, production, and transportation of the materials in order to stay within the planet's boundaries. Material consumption in 2020 was accompanied by €5.6 billion in eco-costs.[17]

These are costs that would be incurred if production were carried out sustainably – but they are currently not included in pricing. As a result, the actual environmental damage leads to higher hidden costs that are borne by current inhabitants, others elsewhere, and future generations. If these environmental costs were to be incurred and factored into the price, on average they would make all materials about 42 per cent more expensive. This does not yet include the social costs, namely the costs that would have to be incurred to make extraction and production fair and humane.[18]

Materials are consumed by households, the public sector, companies that need materials in order to conduct their business operations, as well as companies that provide services (e.g. building contractors). This does not include industry. Households and other consumers (through service companies) are responsible for the largest material consumption through their spending. Households spent €5.4 billion on materials in 2020, primarily on clothing and food. Service companies spent €4.7 billion on materials in 2020, mainly on construction materials. The public sector and business investments were responsible for €3.4 billion in spending, largely on industrial machinery and transport equipment. While a significant amount of money is spent on these product groups, items in this category are expensive. The cost per kilogram is high, and this spend therefore represents a relatively small amount of mass. This is accompanied by relatively low environmental costs

(€0.6 billion). The remainder of the environmental costs (€5 billion) is split almost evenly between service companies and households.[19]

Besides the comprehensive Circular Strategy, some of additional key reasons why Amsterdam is considered a CE front runner include:

- *Multi-stakeholder collaboration*: Amsterdam actively collaborates with various stakeholders, including businesses, research institutions, NGOs, and citizens, to drive CE initiatives. This collaborative approach fosters innovation, knowledge-sharing, and collective action towards circularity.
- *Circular business ecosystem*: Amsterdam has nurtured a thriving circular business ecosystem, with numerous start-ups and established companies focusing on circular solutions. The city supports circular entrepreneurs through funding opportunities, incubators, and networking events.
- *Waste management and recycling*: Amsterdam has implemented efficient waste management practices, including waste separation and recycling programmes. The city has achieved impressive recycling rates and actively promotes resource recovery from waste materials.
- *Circular procurement*: Amsterdam is at the forefront of circular procurement practices. The city government encourages suppliers to offer circular products and services, emphasising sustainability criteria in public procurement decisions.
- *Circular construction*: Amsterdam promotes circular principles in the construction sector, encouraging the use of sustainable materials, circular design, and building deconstruction and reuse.
- *Public awareness and education*: Amsterdam actively engages its residents in CE principles through public awareness campaigns, educational programmes, and circular events. The city promotes responsible consumption and waste reduction.
- *Innovation and research*: Amsterdam invests in circular innovation and research through initiatives like the Amsterdam circular financing programme, supporting early-stage start-ups in and around Amsterdam with co-financing opportunities and an investor readiness.
- *International recognition*: Amsterdam's CE efforts have gained international recognition, with the city being invited to share its experiences and best practices at global conferences and events.

Transitioning to a CE will benefit Amsterdam in areas including employment, research, public health, and reducing CO_2 emissions. Given all these benefits, Amsterdam's city government wants to go circular as quickly as possible. The city foresees that building 70,000 new circular homes before 2040 would contribute €85 million to the economy annually, create 700 new jobs, and reduce CO_2 emissions by 500,000 tonnes per year.[20]

13.2.4 Examples of Circular Economy Initiatives in Amsterdam

There are countless examples of CE initiatives across the City of Amsterdam. The highlighted examples represent just a fraction of all the projects scattered across the city.

13.2.4.1 De Ceuvel: Amsterdam's Circular Living Lab

De Ceuvel is a sustainable workplace and cultural hub built on a former shipyard. The site incorporates various circular principles, such as using reclaimed materials for construction, implementing innovative wastewater treatment systems, and promoting renewable energy sources. The area is also used for urban farming, creating a closed-loop system where waste from the on-site businesses is used as fertiliser for the crops.

De Ceuvel is a blueprint for circular experimentation, showcasing urban, closed-loop thinking in action. Since its conception in 2012, the project has generated significant national and international interest and income to the area. Before the COVID-19 pandemic, the site was receiving over 35,000 visitors each year, attracting everyone from young students to utilities and locals from an older generation. Examples of sustainable technologies in De Ceuvel include:

- *Buiksloterham (BSH)*: De Ceuvel is situated in the old industrial area Buiksloterham and is one of the pioneers in the transformation of this polluted zone into a sustainable residential area. The Circulair Buiksloterham project focuses on integrating circular principles into urban planning, construction, and energy systems. It includes initiatives such as renewable energy generation, circular waste management, and the development of circular buildings and infrastructure. Metabolic (a group of organisations based in Amsterdam and working to drive systems change and build a sustainable economy), together with the Municipality of Amsterdam, several real-estate developers, water company Waternet, and many others involved in BSH, have signed the Manifest Circulair Buiksloterham. As a consequence of this covenant, many sustainable projects are being realised in the area around De Ceuvel, among which are many DIY buildings, sustainable living on the water in Schoonschip ('clean boats'), PEK Ecostroom, and Waternet's bio-refinery. To take the example of water, based on new sanitation in Cityplot Buiksloterham, houses are provided with a double sewage system. Separate drainage for black- and greywater facilitates reuse of water, and resources can be recovered by a brand-new floating installation. Buiksloterham is on its way to becoming Europe's most sustainable neighbourhood.
- *Compost toilets*: Due to the pollution of the De Ceuvel site, it was impossible to dig in order to lay a sewage system. Instead, each boat on De Ceuvel is equipped with a compost toilet. Waste is collected and pre-composts in the toilets before it

is brought to a tumbling composter for further composting. While conventional flushing toilets produce wastewater discharged to the sewer, dry toilets do not use water for flushing and produce solid compost.

- *Heat exchange*: Each office boat has a heat pump and an air-to-air heat exchange ventilation system. As warm air leaves the boat, over 60 per cent of the heat is captured and circulated back inside.
- *Solar energy*: De Ceuvel is equipped with over 150 photovoltaic panels that generate energy from the sun. The panels are installed on the majority of the office boats and produce around 36,000 kilowatt-hours of power yearly.
- *Aquaponic greenhouse*: The greenhouse is the key to recycling nutrients at De Ceuvel. The greenhouse at De Ceuvel produces vegetables and herbs for Cafe de Ceuvel using a closed-loop aquaponics system combining fish and vegetable production. The fish excretes are broken down into nutrients for the plants, and the plants provide a natural filter for the water the fish live in. Aquaponics is thus based on the natural symbiosis between plant and water life.[21]

13.2.4.2 Plastic Whale

Plastic Whale is a company that collects plastic waste from Amsterdam's canals and uses it to create sustainable products. They organise boat tours where participants help collect plastic bottles, which are then transformed into furniture and other products. This initiative not only reduces plastic waste but also raises awareness about the importance of recycling and responsible consumption. Plastic Whale also organises clean-ups after big popular events in Amsterdam, such as the Kingsday (the birthday of the Dutch king in April) or Pride Plastic Fishing (plastic fishing taking place the day after the main Pride event, typically taking place in August). In an average year with 15,000 people on the water, the organisation fishes out about 50,000 PET bottles. In 2022, more than 25,000 PET bottles were collected from nature, and the furniture company Vepa made more than 10,000 pieces out of the plastic trash. Nowadays, plastic fishing with Plastic Whale is also possible in Rotterdam, and events have been organised in 10 different countries.[22]

13.2.4.3 Amsterdam Rainproof

Amsterdam Rainproof is an initiative that aims to make the city more resilient to climate change by managing rainwater in a circular manner. The project promotes the installation of green roofs, rain gardens, and permeable pavements to capture and reuse rainwater, reducing strain on the city's drainage system. It also encourages the use of rainwater harvesting systems for irrigation and non-potable water applications.

The Amsterdam Rooftop Revolution encourages the greening of rooftops in Amsterdam to manage rainwater, reduce the urban heat island effect, and enhance biodiversity. The Rooftop Revolution programme offers guidance and support for individuals and organisations interested in implementing green roofs, creating sustainable urban landscapes, and contributing to a circular water management system.

As an example, the Jan Bommerhuis, also known as 'Floor', located on Wibautstraat in Amsterdam, has been transformed into 162 homes with a new top floor that will be replaced by three floors. A park roof will be constructed by De Dakdokters (the roof doctors) on the 1,600-square-metre roof of the new floor.

The park roof turns the roof into a water storage facility that is controlled. This means that during a rain shower the roof can store water and drain it off when the weather is drier. The stored water ensures that the green roof receives enough water during dry days. The roof will partly consist of roof terraces that the residents can use. The special thing about the design of De Dakdokters is that the parts of the roof on which the terrace is located also store water because the roof system is extended over the entire roof surface.[23]

13.2.4.4 Amsterdam Waste-to-Energy Plant

Amsterdam's waste-to-energy plant, called AEB, is an innovative facility that converts non-recyclable waste into electricity and heat. The plant uses advanced technology to maximise energy recovery from waste while minimising environmental impact. It contributes to Amsterdam's CE by reducing landfill waste and generating renewable energy. Once the plant has extracted as many raw materials as possible from the waste, a residual flow is then used to generate energy. This is done in six incineration lines, four in the Afval Energie Centrale and two in the more modern Hoog Rendement Centrale. With what remains of 1 tonne of waste, the plant generates approximately 628 kilowatt-hours of electricity and 208 kilowatt-hours of heat. This is then supplied to the electricity grid and used to heat approximately 30,000 houses in the north of Amsterdam.[24]

13.2.4.5 Amsterdam Smart City

Amsterdam Smart City is a collaborative platform that brings together businesses, citizens, and local authorities to develop smart and sustainable solutions. The platform encourages the implementation of CE principles in various areas, including energy, mobility, waste management, and digital innovation. Examples include smart grid systems, electric vehicle sharing programmes, and smart waste collection and recycling initiatives. Amsterdam Smart City is part of the Amsterdam Economic Board, the organisation that works on the future of the Amsterdam Metropolitan Area.[25]

13.2.4.6 Hub in the Dutch Circular Textile Valley

Clothing has an enormous environmental footprint. Cotton cultivation and textile production are among the most polluting industries, and the vast majority of textiles that are collected are recycled into low-grade products. The Amsterdam

Metropolitan Area acts as a magnet for businesses and initiatives in the clothing industry, so the city is working hard to promote the area as a hub in the Dutch Circular Textile Valley. In this initiative, knowledge of sustainable and social textile manufacturing is exchanged with other textile regions around the world, which will contribute to the creation of a global ecosystem for circular textiles.

13.2.4.7 Textile (Life) Cycling: Reflow Project Pilot in Amsterdam

Reflow is an EU H2020 funded project that seeks to understand and transform urban material flows and to co-create and test regenerative solutions at the business, governance, and citizen levels in order to create a resilient CE. Textiles has been a critical and polluting industry since the Industrial Revolution – each year, 14,000 tonnes of textiles are thrown away in Amsterdam alone. The goal of Amsterdam's pilot was to increase the recycling percentage of home textiles through redesigning diverse methods for collection with citizens, while providing feedstock for the recycling industries.[26]

The 'EU Strategy for Sustainable and Circular Textiles' to guide the sector's competitiveness, sustainability, and resilience – based on the 'Circular Economy Action Plan' of the European Green deal – sets the scene and scope for action. At a regional level, the Amsterdam Economic Board, in collaboration with the Municipality of Amsterdam and the Amsterdam Metropolitan Area (MRA) Bureau, in line with their sustainability goals for 2020, 2030, and 2050, have developed the 'Green Deals Circular Textiles' agreement. Specific initiatives include a repair shared service centre, a circular fashion innovation lab, integration of circular principles in textile research and education, circular procurement of work clothing (including protective clothing for healthcare), and awareness campaigns for end users. Within the project's lifetime, this has led to a strategic framework, 'Roadmap on Circular Textiles', to serve as a governance guideline and as such to have a lasting effect on the long-term strategic course on circular textiles within the MRA. One of the outcomes of the project was a publication of the Amsterdam Reflow Booklet. By empowering Amsterdam citizens with new knowledge and skills, the pilot programme aims to improve the way textiles are discarded, reused, and brought back into the material flow. The purpose of this publication is to assemble knowledge and educate stakeholders at every stage of the textile industry's cycle. Several additional ideas on how to engage citizens and achieve the ambitious goals of the projects have been identified and are currently being tested.[27]

13.2.5 Conclusion for Amsterdam Examples

In conclusion, Amsterdam's proactive approach, leadership, and commitment to circularity have earned it a reputation as a front runner in the CE movement. The city serves as a role model for other urban areas looking to embrace sustainability and circularity to create more resilient, resource-efficient, and environmentally friendly cities.

13.3 The City of Paris, France

Paris, the capital city of France, has been at the forefront of implementing CE practices. The city has implemented several policy frameworks and supportive initiatives to foster CE practices.

13.3.1 The Roadmap

Paris was among the pioneering cities in defining a vision towards a CE, and already in 2017 it had adopted its First Roadmap for CE. This roadmap outlines specific goals and actions for various sectors, including construction, mobility, and waste management. The roadmap focuses on key areas such as eco-design, recycling infrastructure, and the creation of circular value chains.[28] The Second Roadmap was adopted in November 2018 to include new themes: exemplary administration; culture, events, sustainable consumption, and education. As part of its strategy, Paris opened 15 reuse centres, saving approximately 3,000 tonnes of waste from landfill and incineration each year. It also built public spaces using recycled material, set up a circular business district, promoted deconstruction instead of demolition, and much more.[29]

Furthermore, Paris has established partnerships with businesses, research institutions, and NGOs to facilitate knowledge-sharing, capacity building, and financial support for CE initiatives. The Paris region has already achieved interesting milestones, including 30 per cent of its procurement contracts having included a circular and environmental provision in 2021. It is committed to reuse of products and packaging, the transformation of consumption habits, community empowerment and recycling, and other initiatives. Key actions by 2030 include:

- Reducing food waste by 60 per cent and increasing by 5 times the share of local products on the plates of Paris Region residents.
- Making the 2024 Paris Olympic and Paralympic Games socially and environmentally responsible; 25 per cent of contracts dedicated to the Games were awarded to companies in the social and solidarity economy. At the time, they represented 17 per cent of the first €300 million of orders placed for the construction of Olympic venues.
- Recovering and reusing 85 per cent of construction waste materials by 2030 according to the regional waste recycling and recovery plan.

- Encouraging residents to get involved in projects that aim to improve their daily lives, particularly in the areas of cleanliness, prevention, and waste management; every citizen living, working, or studying in Paris Region was able to participate in the vote and define the projects to be funded (€500 million allocated until 2024) to boost local public investment in the environment sector.[30]

13.3.2 Examples of Circular Economy Initiatives in Paris

CE business models in Paris include sharing economy models such as Vélib' (bike-sharing). Vélib' operates more than 20,000 bikes, and several million rides are made each month; 40 per cent of its fleet is electric. This initiative demonstrates the potential in reducing private vehicle ownership, improving mobility, and minimising environmental impacts.[31]

Furthermore, shared bikes contribute to the '15-Minute City' concept. To create a greener and more climate-resilient future for its residents, under mayoral direction, Paris implemented this urbanism concept under the notion that all essential activities within the city that need to be carried out by citizens could be done within a 15-minute radius by public transportation, foot, or bicycle. A core principle to the 15-Minute City involved planning and redeveloping complete, dense, and walkable communities that had nearby public and active transportation, multifunctional spaces, and mixed-use development.[32]

Paris serves as a leading example of a city embracing CE principles through innovative business models, supportive policy frameworks, and collaborative partnerships. The adoption of CE practices in Paris has resulted in resource efficiency, waste reduction, and the creation of new economic opportunities.

13.4 The City of Prague, Czechia

The city of Prague, renowned for its rich cultural heritage and vibrant economy, has also embraced the CE concept. The city has been actively promoting and implementing various business models to achieve the SDGs.

13.4.1 City Scan

In 2019, the city had a circle city scan called 'Circular Prague' done. This deep-dive analysis provides a visual roadmap identifying the strategies that are best positioned to kick-start the Czech capital's transition towards a CE. The report has highlighted the potential to promote circular lifestyles in reuse hubs using public procurement, boost the construction through circular procurement, and utilise the city's food waste as biomethane to power the city's waste collection fleet. The report also provided tangible steps to take these projects from concept to reality and kick-start Prague's circular transition.[33]

With its 'Circular Prague 2030' strategy launched in 2022, the Czech capital seeks to reduce the consumption of primary raw materials, GHG emissions, and waste production. The strategy comprises 76 actions within 37 projects, and it is structured into 7 thematic areas: building construction; water management; waste management; agriculture and land management and food production; public procurement; support for entrepreneurship, innovation and awareness-raising; and management and implementation. To achieve its goals, the strategy will focus on four key areas: agriculture and food, waste management, water management, and construction.

Taking food as an example, the initial circle scan identified food waste as a major waste with big potential. In Prague, households consume more than 950,000 tonnes of food each year, whereas around 10 per cent of the domestic waste ends up being burned for energy. In an ideal circular city, material flows would be collected separately to retain their value at the highest level and for as long as possible, such as the food waste being returned to the soil as organic fertiliser or converted to biogas.[34]

13.4.2 Examples of Circular Economy Initiatives in Prague

To use its food waste as a resource, Prague has set the ambitious goal of separating 70 per cent of municipal waste at the source by 2035, with the current separation rates standing at 31 per cent. This action is being piloted in three districts, and the city plans to scale it up to all districts by 2026. The currently collected food waste is converted into biogas and used to power waste management trucks. With the instalment of a large bioCNG (compressed natural gas) plant planned, the city hopes to see the entire fleet of waste management trucks powered by household food waste in the future, utilising waste as a resource and cutting GHG emissions (the trucks release 58 per cent fewer pollutants into the atmosphere than diesel-fuelled trucks). In 2023 Czechia's largest CNG retailer Bonett has opened its 10th CNG filling station in Prague.[35]

Increasing inflation rates in 2022 saw consumer prices in Czechia rise across the different consumer goods, including apparel, furniture, and toys. Reuse shops and services that help consumers save while supporting the CE have become increasingly popular in response. Once such concept, 'No Neke' opened its doors in the Czech capital in 2022. Every item inside the store is second-hand, and the items range from fashion brands to electronic gadgets. No Neke calls itself the country's first circular shop and aims to sell only top-quality goods that are built to last. In addition to its environmental mission, No Neke is a pilot project that evaluates how popular reused goods are with the public, and whether it is a good business model.

The first case study results brought interesting insights in consumer behaviours and thinking, such as while the majority of people buy second-hand to save money, one-third are also motivated through the ecological aspect. Twenty-six per cent of people claimed to never shop second-hand, for various reasons; however, after visiting the No Neke store, 96 per cent of them changed their mind and 75 per cent said they would come back.[36]

The city of Prague has made significant strides in embracing the CE concept and implementing various business models across different sectors.

13.5 The City of Helsinki, Finland

Helsinki has emerged as a leading city in promoting and implementing CE practices. In June 2023 the city hosted the World Circular Economy Forum, one of the leading annual CE events in the world.

13.5.1 The Roadmap

Helsinki's Roadmap for Circular and Sharing Economy was approved in May 2020. The roadmap sets goals for circularity in four central focus areas (construction, procurement, green waste, and the sharing economy and new business opportunities) and includes 31 concrete actions.[37]

13.5.2 Examples of Circular Economy Initiatives in Helsinki

A great example of the city's circular initiatives is the CE cluster programme, aiming to promote CE innovations and business. A large proportion of construction companies operate in the Helsinki metropolitan area or at least in the wider metropolitan area. As the material flows in the area are vast and the different functions are located quite close to each other, material transportation costs remain reasonable. Moreover, a significant number of companies and organisations who develop and provide new CE solutions are based in the area.

Participants in the CE cluster programme are working together to improve the reuse and availability of building materials and building components. One of the first measures was developing the concept and operating model for a platform ecosystem of material flows using the Vattuniemi pilot site. The plan is to demolish 16 dilapidated properties previously mainly used as offices. The properties are owned by private companies. The aim is to use as much of the demolition material in construction as possible, preferably as it is. This will result in tremendous amounts of materials. According to estimates there will be 170,000 tonnes of concrete alone, which equals roughly 3,400 lorry loads.

The pilot project will look at how a circular construction economy is affected by anticipation of the demolition surveys and then make use of the learnings to develop a platform ecosystem of material flows aimed at directing both demolition companies and the reusers of rescued materials towards more circular construction.

The aim is to promote business operations that follow the CE model, and data have been immensely useful: information about the demolished materials is compiled on a shared digital platform.[38]

Helsinki has established itself as a global leader in promoting CE practices, including sharing economy models, product-as-a-service models, and remanufacturing and repair models. The factors contributing to their success include collaboration, innovation, supportive policies, and digitalisation.

13.6 The City of Copenhagen, Denmark

Copenhagen's city leadership has set ambitious sustainability goals, including the aim to become a carbon-neutral city by 2025.

13.6.1 Copenhagen's Climate Plan

The city has implemented policies to support circular practices, such as encouraging renewable energy adoption, promoting sustainable transportation, and developing circular waste management systems. Copenhagen's Climate Plan (CPH 2025) demonstrates leadership by setting a clear path to become carbon neutral by 2025. The plan includes initiatives to promote CE practices, such as waste management, energy efficiency, and sustainable transportation solutions.[39]

13.6.2 Examples of Circular Economy Initiatives in Copenhagen

A good example is Amager Resource Center (ARC), also known as Amager Hill or Copenhill, which was designed by Bjake Ingels and opened in 2017. The ARC is a combined heat and power waste-to-energy plant in Copenhagen that showcases imagination by combining waste treatment with energy generation. The plant uses advanced technologies to incinerate waste and convert it into heat and electricity. It delivers electricity and district heating to approximately 150,000 households. It is claimed to be the greenest incineration plant in the world. The facility's design – with an 85-metre-tall sloped roof that doubles as a year-round artificial ski slope, hiking slope, and climbing wall – demonstrates how cities can creatively address waste management and energy needs in a circular manner.[40]

13.7 Other Examples of Cities Utilising Circular Economy

There are several other European cities as well as global cities that have been diligently working on embedding circular business models into their strategies and roadmap, with the goal to create a liveable environment for all their citizens.

13.7.1 City of Glasgow, Scotland

In 2019, the Glasgow Chamber of Commerce launched the Circular Glasgow Network, a platform facilitating collaboration across 175 companies from diverse sectors. After five years of accumulated knowledge, practice, and experimentation, in 2020 Glasgow City Council presented the Circular Economy Route Map for Glasgow.[41]

13.7.2 City of Ljubljana, Slovenia

Ljubljana, the capital city of Slovenia, has embraced the concept of a CE and positioned itself as a 'City of Circular Economy'. The city has implemented various initiatives, including waste separation and recycling programmes, sustainable public transportation, and urban gardening projects.[42]

13.7.3 City of Yokohama, Japan

Yokohama has been a leader in promoting a CE through the Yokohama 3R Dream Project that started over a decade ago. The project focuses on reducing waste generation, promoting resource recycling, and encouraging sustainable consumption and production practices. Circular Yokohama is an online platform to accelerate the CE in Yokohama City, aiming to solve various local issues, create new job opportunities and achieve a thriving community by shedding light on goods, services, and personal skills that have been overlooked in a conventional linear economy.[43]

13.7.4 City of Sydney, Australia

The City of Sydney has set ambitious targets to become a zero-waste city. Based on the Green Economy Study 2018 figures, the city's local green economy had 16,000 workers (2.5 per cent to 3.0 per cent of employment) – half of these focused on managing and supporting the green economy, such as jobs in environmental law, advocacy, and research and development, adding AUD $2.4 billion of gross value to the local economy.[44]

13.8 Conclusion

Circular cities are seen as a response to the challenges posed by traditional linear economic models, which often lead to resource depletion, environmental pollution, and inefficient use of materials. With more people living in cities than ever before and urbanisation continuing to rise, the transition towards creating more liveable environments for all is inevitable.

By adopting CE principles, cities can transition towards more sustainable and resilient urban systems that benefit both the environment and the well-being of their inhabitants.

The examples mentioned in this chapter are just a small showcase of how cities around the world are taking leadership roles in promoting the CE. Through innovative projects, policy frameworks, and collaborative approaches, these cities are driving sustainability, resource efficiency, and waste reduction while fostering imagination and curiosity to explore new possibilities for a circular future.

14

Best Practices and Ways Forward for Cities to Become Circular and Liveable

ROBERT C. BREARS

14.1 Introduction

As cities continue to be the epicentres of global economic activity, innovation, and cultural vibrancy, they also grapple with complex challenges ranging from rapid urbanisation and environmental degradation to social inequality. These issues strain natural resources and undermine the overall liveability of urban environments. Against this backdrop, a transformative approach is gaining traction: the concept of circular economy cities. These cities aim to decouple economic growth from environmental exploitation, redefine waste as a resource, and foster a high quality of life for their inhabitants. They leverage their unique position to implement the 5R approach – reduce, reuse, recycle, restore, and recover – across various sectors, including food, water, energy, and infrastructure. Yet the journey towards circularity isn't solely a technical or economic challenge; it involves overcoming cultural, governance, and financial barriers while synergising efforts across multiple sectors. This chapter delves into best practices and actionable strategies that are crucial for cities aspiring to become both circular and liveable, offering interdisciplinary insights for practitioners, researchers, and policymakers.

The chapter is structured to offer a comprehensive understanding of the best practices that can help cities transition to a circular and liveable model. Each section is dedicated to a specific domain – be it urban food and agriculture, water management, infrastructure and transport, built environment, energy, or resource recovery. Each chapter of this book, authored by subject matter experts, has presented a thorough review of policies, technologies at different stages of development, and case studies that have shown successful implementation of circular principles.

These best practices listed in this chapter serve as valuable lessons learned and provide a roadmap for cities at varying stages of development and climatic conditions. Whether it's the innovative approach of urban mining, the participatory governance models involving academia, industry, and community, or educational initiatives that empower the next generation, each best practice is highlighted for its unique contribution to the circularity agenda.

Moreover, while each chapter focuses on a specific sector, the overarching theme is one of 'circular integration', emphasising that circular principles must be uniformly applied across all functions of a city to achieve true sustainability and liveability. This integrated perspective is essential for understanding how efforts in one sector can have a ripple effect, contributing to circularity in other sectors.

To offer a holistic view, the book also delves into the role of nature-based solutions, human health and well-being initiatives, urban resilience, circular business models, governance, and financing mechanisms that contribute to the evolution of circular, liveable cities.

The culmination of these insights and best practices leads to the 'Ways Forward' section of this chapter. This part synthesises the highlighted practices from each sector to offer a unified, actionable strategy for cities. It aims to serve as a manual for city planners, policymakers, and community leaders, offering them a well-rounded understanding of how to navigate the intricate path towards creating circular economy and liveable cities.

14.2 Best Practices

Navigating the complex landscape of sustainability, this section outlines pivotal best practices that are essential for transforming cities into circular and liveable ecosystems.

14.2.1 Circular Economy and Liveable Cities

Implement Energy Efficiency Financing for Building Retrofits: Establish a financing scheme that offers loans for energy efficiency retrofits in both residential and non-residential buildings. Partner with financial institutions to facilitate the loans, which should cover the cost of equipment, installation, and professional fees. Have clear criteria for qualification, such as a minimum sustainability certification that the building must meet and maintain throughout the loan period.

- *Promote On-Site Water Reuse Through Grant Programmes*: Create a grant programme that incentivises water users to collect, treat, and utilise alternate water sources like rainwater, stormwater, and greywater for non-potable uses such as toilet flushing and irrigation. Offer different grant amounts based on the volume of water the project is expected to save annually. Fund activities like the installation of water collection and treatment systems.
- *Establish a Comprehensive Electronic Waste Collection and Disposal Programme*: Implement a city-wide programme that facilitates the collection

and safe disposal of electronic waste. This can be done through regular garbage pickup, specialised drop-off depots, or community events. Introduce a mobile app or online tool to help residents understand how to properly sort and dispose of different types of waste, including e-waste.

- *Launch a Stormwater Harvesting Fund*: Develop a fund that co-finances community projects aimed at harvesting stormwater for irrigation of public spaces. The fund can support various projects that capture and treat stormwater run-off for use in parks and sports grounds. Include educational components, such as rain gardens, to help clean and filter the stormwater.
- *Resource Recovery from Wastewater*: Integrate technologies into sewage treatment plants that allow for the conversion of waste into valuable resources. For instance, turn sewage sludge into sewage gas for energy generation. Additionally, consider methods for nutrient recovery, such as extracting phosphorus, to create products that can be sold to the horticulture and agriculture sectors.

14.2.2 Urban Agriculture

- *Adopt a Multi-Tiered Recycled Water Programme*: Develop a recycled water programme that caters to the varying needs of your community. Offer different qualities or classes of recycled water to meet specific customer requirements. For example, the highest-quality water can be used for industrial processes or the irrigation of food crops, while lower-quality water can be used for activities like irrigation of non-food crops or washing down hard surfaces. The pricing per unit volume can decrease with water quality to make it more affordable and encourage its use.
- *Create Community Farms Using Recycled Resources*: Utilise vacant land and recycled water to establish community farms. These farms can serve multiple purposes: they can be a source of local food, provide educational opportunities, and even generate renewable energy. Establishing such a farm in partnership with educational institutions and community organisations can create a hub for sustainable agriculture and community development.
- *Implement Incentive Programmes for Greywater Recycling*: Encourage the use of greywater systems by providing rebates and discounts on greywater recycling kits. Offer residents training and consultation services to help them properly install and maintain these systems. For larger systems that require building permits, consider offering financial incentives to offset the cost.
- *Develop Rooftop Urban Agriculture*: Convert unused rooftop spaces into urban farms. Not only does this practice support local food production, but it also aids in stormwater management. Securing grants for green infrastructure can make these projects financially feasible. Such initiatives can also pave the way for further integration of green spaces in urban areas.

- *Introduce Nutrient Recovery Facilities*: Incorporate advanced technologies in wastewater treatment facilities to recover nutrients like phosphorus and nitrogen. Transform these into slow-release, environmentally friendly fertilisers that can be distributed or sold. This approach not only prevents damage to wastewater treatment equipment but also provides an additional revenue stream.
- *Offer Environmentally Friendly Soil Amendments*: Develop and offer different varieties of environmentally friendly soil amendments made from the by-products of wastewater treatment. These can range from wet, high-nutrient biosolids to dry, easy-to-handle soil-like products. Make these products available in bulk and through various retail channels to increase accessibility and use.

14.2.3 Urban Water Management

- *Employ a Portfolio Approach in Demand Management*: Recognise that relying solely on pricing mechanisms to control water demand is fraught with economic, political, and behavioural challenges. Instead, use a mix of demand management instruments such as regulations, market-based incentives, and informational campaigns. This portfolio approach allows for a more robust and adaptable strategy that can more effectively meet specific water conservation targets.
- *Conduct Cost–Benefit Analysis for Each Instrument*: Before adding a particular instrument to the demand management portfolio, conduct a thorough cost–benefit analysis. This helps ensure that the chosen instruments not only align with the overall water conservation strategy but are also financially sustainable. Account for hidden costs such as advertising, monitoring, and enforcement, which are commonly associated with non-price water conservation programmes.
- *Balance Revenue and Conservation Goals*: Be mindful of the revenue impacts when implementing non-price conservation programmes. While these can effectively reduce demand, they may also lead to revenue declines, affecting the financial sustainability of water supply services. Understand the elasticity of water demand to assess how pricing changes will affect overall revenues and adjust strategies accordingly.
- *Address Political Sensitivities around Pricing*: Understand that pricing changes, particularly increases, are politically sensitive and can face public opposition. Therefore, when utilising price as a demand management instrument, be transparent about its environmental justifications. This can help alleviate public scepticism and resistance.
- *Leverage Long-Term Behavioural Change*: Recognise that short-term behaviour modifications, often spurred by initial pricing changes, tend to revert over the long term. To foster lasting changes, integrate educational initiatives and permanent water-saving devices into your demand management strategy.

- *Assess and Adjust Strategy Effectiveness*: Given that pricing often works in conjunction with other demand management instruments, it can be challenging to assess the effectiveness of pricing alone. Utilise comprehensive monitoring tools and metrics to evaluate the impact of your overall strategy. Be prepared to adapt and make adjustments to ensure continued alignment with water conservation goals.

14.2.4 Sustainable Infrastructure and Transport

- *Integrated Urban Planning for Vibrant Streets and Neighbourhoods*: Prioritise the integration of transport systems, community building, and urban planning to boost various goals such as economic growth, public health, and sustainability. A city that successfully aligns these elements creates a positive ripple effect that contributes to making it more circular and liveable.
- *Redesign Streets for Multi-Modal Use*: Reconsider the allocation of street space to include more than just vehicles. By redesigning streets to accommodate pedestrians, bicycles, and public transport, cities can foster a safer and more inclusive urban environment. Examples include widening sidewalks, adding bike lanes, and lowering speed limits to create spaces that are conducive to walking and other activities.
- *Transparent Monitoring and Evaluation*: For any initiative aimed at redesigning streets or promoting walkable neighbourhoods, incorporate a comprehensive monitoring and evaluation system. Transparent tracking allows for the full story of successes and failures to be told, offering valuable insights that can inform future urban planning efforts.
- *Citizen Participation in Decision-Making*: Encourage active citizen involvement in the decision-making processes surrounding urban and transport planning. Public input not only legitimises planning efforts but can also lead to innovative solutions that may not have been considered otherwise. Utilise public consultations, surveys, and participatory design sessions as part of the planning process.
- *Short-Term Initiatives Leading to Long-Term Change*: Engage with community-based initiatives like street parties, pop-up parks, and art installations. These short-term projects often act as testing grounds for more permanent changes and can be pivotal in transforming the urban fabric over the long term.
- *Adaptability in Mobility Systems*: Understand that reducing space for motorised vehicles or implementing local bans doesn't necessarily collapse the transport system. Instead, such changes often lead to adaptations that result in a more sustainable and resilient mobility ecosystem. Be prepared for an initial period of adjustment and have mechanisms in place to monitor and adapt to these changes.
- *Promote Vibrancy through Green and Cultural Spaces*: Increasing the vibrancy of a street or neighbourhood isn't solely about moving people efficiently.

Incorporating greenery, public art, and cultural landmarks can make an area more attractive, promoting foot traffic and community engagement, which in turn enhances liveability and sustainability.

14.2.5 Sustainable Built Environment

- *Opt for Building Renovation over Demolition*: One sustainable practice for urban planning is the reconversion of abandoned or underused structures. Instead of demolishing buildings and contributing to waste, reconceiving them for contemporary uses saves resources and maintains the historical and cultural fabric of the area. This approach embodies the principle of circularity by extending the life cycle of existing structures.
- *Promote Material Reuse in Construction*: A valuable practice for resource management is salvaging materials from obsolete structures for new construction projects. This practice not only minimises waste but also reduces the demand for new resources, thereby saving energy. Material reuse encourages the use of local materials and craftsmanship, adding unique aesthetic value to new constructions.
- *Invest in Green Infrastructures*: Focusing on the development of green infrastructures like parks, vertical gardens, and green roofs can significantly improve urban environments. These features not only help in cooling down the urban atmosphere but also support biodiversity and offer community spaces that contribute to mental and physical well-being.
- *Implement Integrated Waste Management Systems*: Viewing waste as a resource rather than a by-product to be disposed of can revolutionise urban sustainability. Strategies like composting organic waste or repurposing plastic waste into urban furniture can transform waste management systems and substantially reduce landfill waste.
- *Foster Local Circular Economies*: Encouraging localised production and consumption can reduce transportation-related costs and emissions. By sourcing and manufacturing goods within the community, cities can become more resilient and sustainable, aligning with the principles of a circular economy.
- *Prioritise Adaptive Urban Design*: Urban areas should be designed with flexibility to adapt to changing needs over time. For example, creating spaces that can transition from car parks to pedestrian zones or community gardens allows the urban fabric to evolve without the need for resource-intensive alterations.
- *Engage the Community in Urban Development*: The active participation of local communities in decision-making can significantly impact the success of urban projects. Including residents in planning through workshops or participatory platforms ensures that projects are relevant to the community's needs and are more likely to succeed.

- *Incorporate Circular Education and Training*: Awareness-building and educational programmes about circular economy principles can empower both residents and policymakers. Providing the necessary knowledge and tools for understanding and implementing circularity is critical for developing sustainable, liveable cities.

14.2.6 Dynamic Water Resource Management for Regenerative Cities

- *Integrate Water Management into Urban Planning*: Achieving water self-sufficiency necessitates a comprehensive understanding of the urban water cycle. Planners should consider different types of water – rain, surface, ground, drinking, and waste – in terms of demand, usage, and quality. Both retrofit projects and new urban developments should incorporate water management at every stage of design and planning, focusing on reducing water use and promoting water reuse and recycling systems.
- *Develop a Water-Resilient Strategy Backed by Strong Governance*: Building a water-resilient city requires a well-articulated strategy that aligns with other climate-related goals, such as flood risk reduction and heat stress management. Strong governance and political commitment are essential to generate the necessary funds and build capacity. A collective understanding of the issue, a consensus on solutions, and an acknowledged sense of urgency, especially after experiencing climatic extremes, are pivotal for effective governance.
- *Implement Diverse Solutions for Resilience*: For robust and flexible climate-resilient water management, cities should implement a balanced mix of grey infrastructure, hybrid solutions, and nature-based approaches. These might include wetland restoration, rainwater harvesting, and preserving flood plains, which not only enhance water availability and quality but also mitigate the risks from water-related disasters. A diverse array of solutions supports both climate change mitigation and adaptation outcomes.
- *Foster a Culture of Water Stewardship*: Historically, many cultures have valued water, but modern urban planning has often overlooked its importance. For successful transition towards water-resilient cities, a change in public behaviour and awareness is vital. Cities should engage with their communities to instil a sense of value for water, fostering a culture of sustainable water use and long-term stewardship.
- *Opt for Synergy in Addressing Multiple Climate-Related Issues*: The protection of freshwater resources should be synergised with other climate action plans. This approach allows cities to address multiple challenges – like heat stress regulation and flood risk reduction – in an interconnected manner. Combining efforts can result in more comprehensive and effective strategies that are beneficial on multiple fronts.

- *Allocate Sufficient Funding and Resources*: One of the common challenges in making cities water-resilient is the lack of adequate funding and resources. Adequate financial planning, possibly through public–private partnerships or grants, can play a crucial role in implementing ambitious water management plans. Cities should consider long-term investment in water resilience as an integral part of their broader sustainability and liveability goals.

14.2.7 Renewable Energy and Energy Efficiency

- *Adopt a Comprehensive Roadmap and Action Plan*: To effectively transition into a circular and liveable city, a detailed roadmap and action plan are essential. These strategic documents should align with national or regional circular economy goals and include interim targets. Rigorous monitoring tools should continuously evaluate the social and ecological impacts of the transition. Prioritise interventions in key value chains that contribute the most to emissions, such as waste streams, consumer goods, and building materials.
- *Involve Stakeholders in Planning and Execution*: A successful circular economy involves participation from multiple stakeholders, including citizens, entrepreneurs, and project developers. By involving local stakeholders in planning and executing circular initiatives, cities can create a sense of ownership over projects, improving their chances of success and scalability.
- *Provide Financial Incentives and Risk Mitigation*: To encourage the adoption of circular practices, cities should offer financial incentives. This could include creating favourable conditions for circular businesses through grant programmes, tax incentives, or other funding mechanisms. By actively demanding circular solutions and providing funding, cities can mitigate the financial risks associated with the transition to a circular economy.
- *Incorporate Circularity Criteria in Procurement Processes*: Cities themselves can lead by example by integrating circularity criteria into their procurement processes. This not only encourages suppliers to adopt circular practices but also signals to the broader community the city's commitment to a circular economy.
- *Implement Integrated Strategies across Policy Domains*: It is essential to approach circularity from an integrated perspective, encompassing various policy domains that the city actively influences. Focus should not only be on waste prevention and recycling but also on circular design principles for city infrastructure and products, fostering behavioural change, and encouraging circular business models.

Transition to Renewable, Supply-Driven Energy Systems: As cities are major consumers of energy, transitioning to renewable, supply-driven systems is crucial for both sustainability and circularity. While this transition is resource-intensive initially, long-term benefits include greater efficiency and a significant reduction in emissions. Public–private partnerships can accelerate the shift by investing in new technologies and systems that support a circular approach to energy use.

14.2.8 Urban Nature-Based Solutions

- *Implement Financial Incentives for Sustainable Infrastructure*: Offer financial incentives like subsidies and rebates to a wide range of stakeholders for implementing green infrastructure such as rain barrels, permeable surfaces, and green roofs. This encourages broad-based adoption of sustainable practices, enhances climate resilience, and improves urban water management. Clear guidelines on subsidy eligibility and application processes are essential for the programmes' success.
- *Grants for Aesthetic and Sustainable Urban Upgrades*: Provide grants to property owners for improving exposed party walls with green elements, energy-producing systems, or other features enhancing natural light and ventilation. Such initiatives beautify the urban fabric while promoting sustainability and energy efficiency.
- *Promote Community Gardening through Funding*: Establish grant programmes to support community groups and schools in creating and maintaining community gardens. This fosters community bonding, promotes local food production, and raises environmental awareness.
- *Large-Scale Permeable Paving for Stormwater Management*: Invest in extensive permeable paving projects to manage stormwater effectively, reduce flooding, and control sewer overflows. Collaboration with experts and substantial investment are required, but the long-term benefits in urban sustainability are considerable.
- *Rebate Programmes for Rain Garden and Cistern Installation*: Introduce rebate programmes to motivate homeowners to install rain gardens and cisterns on their properties. This mitigates the strain on municipal sewer systems and encourages a culture of sustainability.
- *Invest in Green Stormwater Infrastructure*: Develop green infrastructure solutions like bioswales or vegetated tree pits for stormwater management. Such installations require regular maintenance and public education to ensure long-term success and awareness.
- *Transform Unused Spaces into Green Areas*: Collaborate across city departments to identify and transform unused or underutilised areas into functional green spaces. Such initiatives improve air quality, manage stormwater, and provide potential habitats for urban wildlife.

- *Wetland Restoration and Water Reuse for Urban Revitalisation*: Invest in the restoration of urban wetlands and implement water reuse systems. These projects serve as educational platforms and recreational areas while enhancing urban biodiversity and ecological health.
- *Urban Forest Strategy for Green Cover*: Establish a comprehensive urban forest strategy that involves protecting existing trees and planting new ones, particularly in areas lacking greenery. Citizen engagement through tree-planting programmes can foster community participation and environmental stewardship.
- *Green Corridors for Heat Mitigation*: Identify and transform suitable areas into green corridors filled with native and climate-resilient plants. This approach mitigates the urban heat island effect and could involve public–private partnerships for funding and maintenance.

14.2.9 Human Health and Well-being

- *Prioritise Environmental Justice*: Recognise the importance of addressing environmental justice when planning city development and resource management. Addressing environmental injustice not only ensures that the benefits of a sustainable lifestyle are accessible to all residents regardless of socio-economic status, ethnicity, or location, but also fosters social harmony. Policies should aim for equitable access to clean air, water, and other environmental resources, particularly for vulnerable populations.
- *Adopt Circular Economy Models*: Implement a circular economy model that focuses on waste reduction, recycling, and reusing materials. Such an approach helps in managing end-of-life materials more sustainably and fosters an ecosystem that minimises waste. This not only aids in reducing environmental impact but also creates new employment opportunities and contributes to overall well-being.
- *Emphasise Zero-Waste Initiatives*: Develop zero-waste policies that go beyond simple waste management practices. These policies should be comprehensive, including aspects such as waste sorting, recycling, composting, and initiatives to encourage businesses and households to minimise waste. This leads to a cleaner environment and better health outcomes for the community.
- *Leverage Innovative Models for Sustainable Development*: Utilise successful models that integrate sustainability into the city's core functioning. This can be done by designing and implementing plans that simultaneously address environmental, economic, and social factors. For example, models that focus on reducing waste can drastically diminish landfill use and pollution, thus creating a more liveable environment for residents.
- *Invest in Employment Through Sustainability*: Prioritise job creation through the implementation of sustainable practices. The circular economy not only

promotes environmental wellness but also provides the opportunity for increased employment in new, green sectors. This two-pronged benefit enriches the community both economically and environmentally.

- *Promote Health and Well-Being Through Environment*: Invest in green spaces, cleaner technology, and pollution controls to boost the health and well-being of the populace. Encourage active modes of transportation like cycling and walking through proper urban planning. A cleaner, greener city will result in healthier citizens, thereby improving overall quality of life.
- *Engage Communities in Environmental Practices*: Foster community involvement in sustainable initiatives. Providing platforms for citizen input in planning and execution phases increases a sense of ownership and responsibility among residents. Community education and involvement can be powerful tools in achieving sustainability goals.
- *Implement Policies That Are Inclusive*: Create policies that are inclusive and do not discriminate based on socio-economic status, race, or ethnicity. The benefits of a circular, sustainable city should be accessible to all, and measures should be in place to ensure that marginalised communities are not left behind in the push for sustainability.
- *Measure and Report*: Consistently measure the impact of implemented policies and practices using robust metrics. Transparency in reporting these impacts can go a long way in gaining public trust and in refining approaches for better performance.
- *Seek Interdepartmental Collaboration*: To ensure the successful implementation of a circular and liveable city, foster cooperation among various departments such as urban planning, waste management, and social services. Interdepartmental collaboration allows for a more holistic approach to creating a sustainable environment.

14.2.10 City Resilience and Sustainability

- *Embrace a Whole-of-Society Approach*: Acknowledge that introducing a circular economy involves a comprehensive system change. This is not just about technological solutions but encompasses legal frameworks, governance structures, and public engagement. Efforts should be made to mobilise a whole-of-society approach to facilitate this change, engaging local communities, businesses, and policymakers.
- *Incremental Build-Up Is Key*: Understand that systemic change is gradual. It starts with laying the foundational elements such as a functional waste management system. In the beginning, focus should be on the basic tiers of waste hierarchy – collection, sorting, and disposal. Once these are established, it becomes easier to aim for higher-order objectives like zero waste and complete circularity.

- *Strengthen Regulatory Frameworks*: Develop robust laws and regulations that support a circular economy. Regulatory frameworks should cover various aspects like waste management, water treatment, and materials recycling. These laws should be aimed at minimising waste and making the most of available resources.
- *Invest in Institutional Strengthening*: A strong institutional base is essential for sustaining any circular economy model. This includes not just governmental bodies but also organisations that can work towards waste reduction, recycling, and other circular initiatives. The more robust the institutions, the more effective the implementation.
- *Prioritise Affordability and Accessibility*: Any effort towards circularity should take into account the affordability constraints, especially in low- and middle-income regions. It is important that circular economy solutions are inclusive and can be adopted widely, irrespective of the socio-economic status of the citizens.
- *Account for Negative Externalities:* As waste management and circular economy systems mature, it is crucial to price waste and resources in a way that accounts for negative externalities. This will act as an incentive for reducing waste and encouraging more sustainable practices among individuals and corporations.
- *Leverage Technology Wisely*: While technology can offer shortcuts to achieving some circular economy goals, it is not a silver bullet. Technology should be used to supplement, not replace, fundamental changes in policies, institutions, and societal behaviours.
- *Implement a Waste Hierarchy*: Implement a structured approach to waste management that starts with the most basic levels of waste management, such as collection and disposal, and gradually moves towards more advanced stages like recycling, reusing, and finally leading to zero waste.
- *Enforce Rules and Regulations*: It is not enough to just have rules – effective enforcement mechanisms are also necessary. This requires a well-trained workforce, appropriate penalties for non-compliance, and ongoing monitoring systems to ensure that circular economy principles are being followed.
- *Measure, Evaluate, and Adapt*: Always keep track of progress using quantifiable metrics. This allows for periodic assessment and helps in adapting strategies based on what is working and what needs improvement. It also fosters transparency, which is crucial for public engagement and trust.

14.2.11 Circular Business Models

- *Commitment and Vision from Leadership*: A circular city's transition begins with a strong vision and commitment from city leaders. These leaders should be backed by long-term strategies, policies, and regulations focused on creating a circular economy. While new business models are crucial, leadership, imagination, and curiosity also play significant roles in this transformation.

- *Stakeholder Collaboration*: Developing a circular city is not an isolated effort; it requires a multi-stakeholder approach. Government authorities, businesses, communities, and citizens must come together to share insights, resources, and responsibilities. Coordinated, collaborative efforts are key to driving a city towards circularity.
- *Move Beyond Traditional Economic Models*: Transitioning to a circular economy is also a response to the shortcomings of traditional linear economic models, which lead to resource depletion and environmental pollution. Adopting circular economy principles allows for a more sustainable and resilient urban environment.
- *Efficient Waste Management*: Proper waste management, including clean incineration plants, is vital. Smart design considerations should also be made to ensure that these facilities are not just efficient but also allow citizens to interact with their environment in a positive way, thereby contributing to well-being.
- *Engage Citizens in Sustainable Practices*: Citizen engagement is key to extending the lifespan of products and reducing waste. Activities such as repair, reuse, and recycling should be encouraged through public awareness campaigns, workshops, and incentives.
- *Adopt the '15-Minute City' Concept or Similar Urban Designs*: An efficient and accessible urban design can be a cornerstone of circular cities. The concept, where all essential services are accessible within a 15-minute walk or bike ride from any point in the city, promotes local living and reduces the need for long commutes and their associated emissions.
- *Innovative Projects and Frameworks*: Leverage innovative projects that set the stage for a circular economy. These could range from pilot projects to fully fledged policy frameworks aimed at promoting sustainability, resource efficiency, and waste reduction.
- *Foster Imagination and Curiosity*: While policies and regulations are necessary, fostering a culture of imagination and curiosity can lead to the exploration of new possibilities for a circular future. This can be encouraged through educational programmes, community events, and other public engagement initiatives.
- *Policy Frameworks for Circular Development*: Regulatory backing is necessary to ensure the success and sustainability of circular initiatives. These frameworks should cover a wide range of areas, including urban planning, resource management, waste management, and more.
- *Ongoing Monitoring and Improvement*: The journey to a circular city is ongoing. Continual monitoring, review, and improvement of circular initiatives should be a standard practice, guided by data-driven insights and community feedback.

14.2.12 Governing the Transition to Circular Economy Liveable Cities

- *Holistic Approach to Sustainability and Circular Economy*: A city aiming to become circular needs to take a comprehensive approach. This involves incorporating circular economy principles into broader sustainability and climate strategies. The city governance should take a proactive role in promoting sustainable practices through various initiatives and programmes, establishing a foundation upon which circular practices can be built.
- *Transformation as a Multi-Stage Process*: Just as transformation in nature involves several stages and a complex life cycle, the transition to a circular city will be a gradual process. It will require rethinking traditional, linear models and adopting circular mindsets, heart-sets, and skill sets. This transformation will necessitate various strategies and phases, illustrating the complicated dynamics of urban development.
- *Impact of Physical Structure*: The design and structure of the city itself are crucial elements that influence both climate adaptability and resident behaviour. Strategies like urban mining and considering the built environment as a material stock are vital in closing material loops and minimising waste.
- *Collaborative Governance Using the Quadruple Helix Approach*: Collaboration is essential for innovation in circular cities. A model involving academia, industry, government, and society – often called the Quadruple Helix approach – can provide a collaborative platform to foster innovation and drive transformation. Such approaches can be instrumental in realising the vision of a circular city.
- *Experimentation and Governance Innovation*: It's essential to allow room for experimentation in the transformation process. Incubators and other initiatives focused on cross-sector collaboration can serve as a fertile ground for governance innovation. These platforms can help in testing new strategies and refining existing ones, thereby speeding up the transition to a circular model.
- *Emerging Research and Forward Thinking*: The journey to a circular city is an ongoing one and should be informed by ongoing research in various focus areas related to sustainability, circular economy, and urban design. Keeping abreast of current studies and projections can help a city adapt its strategies for maximum impact and future readiness.
- *Public and Community Engagement*: Engaging the public and community stakeholders is critical for the success of a circular city. Public understanding and participation in circular practices, like recycling or urban agriculture, can make the initiatives more robust and widely accepted. Public engagement methods can range from awareness campaigns to participatory decision-making processes.

14.2.13 Role of Education

- *Integrate Education for Sustainable Development*: A key component of building a circular and liveable city is education that goes beyond the conventional curriculum. Educational programmes focused on sustainable development should be integrated into existing educational systems to help create a more informed and vigilant society. This prepares the younger generation to recognise and challenge misleading claims about environmental sustainability, commonly known as greenwashing.
- *Skill Development for Climate Initiatives*: Addressing the climate crisis requires specialised skills. As part of a city's sustainability initiatives, vocational training programmes should be promoted to meet the growing demand for skilled workers in fields like renewable energy management. These training programmes need to be well supported and adequately funded to ensure their effectiveness.
- *Expand Training Capacity*: To facilitate a circular economy, there needs to be an expansion of training opportunities in new technologies and product design. This is particularly important for sectors that are undergoing rapid changes due to sustainability needs. The expanded training capacity should cater to both new students and professionals looking to retrain in these emerging fields.
- *Education on Consumption Behaviour and Environmental Impact*: Building a circular and liveable city isn't just about infrastructure and policies; it's also about changing individual behaviours. Education should impart knowledge on the complex interplay between human actions, consumption patterns, and their impacts on the environment. This will help children and young adults make more responsible choices that align with circular economy principles.
- *Local Context and Participatory Learning*: Education for sustainable development should be context-sensitive, drawing upon the local environment to make learning more relatable and effective. Adopting participatory learning approaches can encourage students to engage in their local communities, allowing them to feel more empowered and capable of effecting change.
- *Address Structures of Power and Inclusion*: Educational initiatives should not only focus on knowledge and skills but also examine and address the structures of power that affect sustainable development and circular economies. This means including diverse perspectives and focusing on inclusivity and equitable opportunities for all.
- *Positive Reinforcement and Self-Efficacy*: Effective education instils a sense of self-efficacy among learners. Programmes should aim to create positive associations with sustainable behaviours and practices, empowering individuals to feel that their actions can make a meaningful difference in achieving a more circular and liveable city.

14.3 Ways Forward

Creating a circular economy and liveable cities is a multidimensional challenge requiring a combination of innovative strategies, strong policy frameworks, and active community participation. As cities around the world grapple with issues of waste management, resource scarcity, and social inequality, the concept of a circular economy presents a transformative approach to urban planning and development. This section outlines some concrete ways forward, drawing from best practices in education, policy, and governance, to create more circular and liveable urban spaces.

14.3.1 Building Comprehensive Regulatory Frameworks

One of the most pressing tasks is the development of comprehensive regulatory frameworks that promote circular practices. Regulations can range from incentivising waste reduction and recycling to implementing more stringent rules for urban construction, ensuring that materials are either recyclable or biodegradable. Zoning laws can also be revised to encourage or mandate the use of green building materials and renewable energy sources. But the success of these regulations does not solely rest on the law; effective enforcement mechanisms must be put in place to ensure compliance.

14.3.2 Technology and Data Utilisation

The role of technology cannot be understated. Smart cities can leverage data analytics, the Internet of Things, and other emerging technologies to monitor waste management systems, energy consumption, and transportation logistics. The data collected can provide valuable insights into the urban metabolism, showing how resources flow through the city and where the opportunities for improvement lie. Apps could be developed to help residents track their waste output or navigate to the nearest recycling centre, among other utilities.

14.3.3 Engaging Multiple Stakeholders

The Quadruple Helix model of innovation – involving academia, industry, government, and civil society – has shown promise in fostering a more circular approach to urban planning. By creating platforms where these stakeholders can collaborate, cities can tap into a rich vein of ideas, expertise, and resources. This approach accelerates the sharing of best practices and the development of pilot projects, offering a faster track to circularity.

14.3.4 Education and Skill Development

Equally critical is the role of education in shaping a city's move towards circularity and liveability. Incorporating education for sustainable development can cultivate a society that is aware of, and resistant to, greenwashing tactics. Specialised training programmes should be developed to meet the demand for new skills required for circular economies, like waste management and renewable energy technology. Beyond formal education, public awareness campaigns can also play a crucial role in informing citizens about their consumption choices and their impact on the environment.

14.3.5 Social Equity and Environmental Justice

Incorporating environmental justice considerations into the planning and execution of circular economy strategies is vital. It ensures that the benefits of a more sustainable and efficient system are equitably distributed among all segments of the population, irrespective of socio-economic status. This becomes especially crucial when considering waste management systems. Policies must be in place to ensure that waste sites and treatment facilities are not disproportionately located in disadvantaged communities.

14.3.6 Grassroots Participation

Community-led initiatives can often fill the gaps left by large-scale governmental projects. Citizen participation can range from localised waste management efforts to community gardens and repair cafes that promote the reuse of goods. The success of these grassroots initiatives often depends on their inclusivity and their ability to engage with the community on a level that larger organisations might not be able to achieve.

14.3.7 Public–Private Partnerships

Investment is a significant hurdle for many cities aiming to transition to circular models. Public–private partnerships can offer a solution, providing the capital and expertise needed to get complex projects off the ground. These collaborations can take multiple forms, from a simple allocation of tasks and responsibilities to more complex, long-term commitments that involve shared risks and rewards.

14.4 The Road Ahead

The path towards creating circular and liveable cities is fraught with challenges, but the multifaceted approach outlined here offers a realistic and comprehensive strategy. Policy frameworks need to be adaptive and robust; technology must be leveraged intelligently; and, most importantly, the human element of change must not be underestimated. Through education and community participation, we can hope to instil a sense of collective responsibility and agency, fostering a population that is not only aware of the necessity for change but is also empowered to act upon it. The transition to circularity is not a single leap but a series of incremental steps. Every stakeholder, from policymakers and industry leaders to ordinary citizens, has a role to play in this transformative journey towards a more sustainable and equitable future.

Notes

1 An Overview of Circular Economy and Liveable Cities

1. OECD, "Global Material Resources Outlook to 2060: Economic Drivers and Environmental Consequences," (2018), www.oecd.org/en/publications/global-material-resources-outlook-to-2060_9789264307452-en.html.
2. International Resource Panel, "The Weight of Cities: Resource Requirements of Future Urbanization," (2018), www.resourcepanel.org/reports/weight-cities.
3. R. C. Brears, *Natural Resource Management and the Circular Economy* (Cham: Springer International Publishing, 2018), https://books.google.co.nz/books?id=SphMDwAAQBAJ.
4. International Resource Panel, "The Weight of Cities."
5. Anna Petit-Boix and Sina Leipold, "Circular Economy in Cities: Reviewing How Environmental Research Aligns with Local Practices," *Journal of Cleaner Production* 195 (2018), https://doi.org/10.1016/j.jclepro.2018.05.281; Antonia Gravagnuolo, Mariarosaria Angrisano, and Luigi Fusco Girard, "Circular Economy Strategies in Eight Historic Port Cities: Criteria and Indicators towards a Circular City Assessment Framework," *Sustainability* 11, no. 13 (2019), https://doi.org/10.3390/su11133512; Carla Ferreira, Zahra Kalantari, and Paulo Pereira, "Liveable Cities: Current Environmental Challenges and Paths to Urban Sustainability," *Journal of Environmental Management* 277 (2021), https://doi.org/10.1016/j.jenvman.2020.111458; Martin Knuijt, "Liveable Green Cities: Integrating Climate Adaptive Solutions and Circular Economy into the Built Environment," in *Designing Sustainable Cities*, ed. Rob Roggema (Cham: Springer International Publishing, 2020), 87–99; Ellen Macarthur Foundation, "Cities in the Circular Economy: An Initial Exploration," (2017), https://emf.thirdlight.com/file/24/MC1eXz-MW2hx60MCEvuM6Pt5sI/Cities%20in%20the%20circular%20economy%3A%20An%20initial%20exploration.pdf.
6. Robert C. Brears, "Circular Economy Cities," in *The Palgrave Encyclopedia of Urban and Regional Futures* (Cham: Springer International Publishing, 2020), 1–6.
7. Brears, "Circular Economy Cities"; Brears, *Natural Resource Management and the Circular Economy*.
8. Ellen Macarthur Foundation, "What Is a Circular Economy," (2023), https://ellenmacarthurfoundation.org/topics/circular-economy-introduction/overview.
9. Ellen Macarthur Foundation, "Cities in the Circular Economy"; R. C. Brears, *Developing the Circular Water Economy* (Cham: Palgrave Macmillan, 2020).
10. Rebecca L. H. Chiu, "Liveable Cities/Urban Liveability," in *The Wiley Blackwell Encyclopedia of Urban and Regional Studies* (Hoboken, NJ: Wiley, 2019), 1–7.
11. Ellen Macarthur Foundation, "Cities in the Circular Economy"; Brears, *Natural Resource Management and the Circular Economy*; R. C. Brears, *Blue and Green Cities: The Role of Blue–Green Infrastructure in Managing Urban Water Resources* (Cham: Palgrave Macmillan, 2018); R. C. Brears, *Nature-Based Solutions to 21st Century Challenges* (Oxfordshire: Routledge, 2020), https://books.google.co.nz/books?id=0zgKzQEACAAJ.

12. Brears, "Circular Economy Cities"; Robert C. Brears, "Building Circular Economy Cities," in *The Palgrave Handbook of Climate Resilient Societies*, ed. Robert C. Brears (Cham: Springer International Publishing, 2020), 1–23; Brears, *Natural Resource Management and the Circular Economy*; Brears, *Developing the Circular Water Economy*.
13. Sofia Ritzén and Gunilla Ölundh Sandström, "Barriers to the Circular Economy: Integration of Perspectives and Domains," *Procedia CIRP* 64 (2017), /https://doi.org/10.1016/j.procir.2017.03.005.
14. European Commission, "Circular Economy: Definition, Importance and Benefits," 2023, www.europarl.europa.eu/news/en/headlines/economy/20151201STO05603/circular-economy-definition-importance-and-benefits; Ellen Macarthur Foundation, "Cities in the Circular Economy"; Ellen Macarthur Foundation, "The Nature Imperative: How the Circular Economy Tackles Biodiversity Loss," (2021), https://cmf.thirdlight.com/file/24/FM9nvqPFM.IixvIFMZ6iFC9A.NLF/The%20Nature%20Imperative%3A%20How%20the%20circular%20economy%20tackles%20biodiversity%20loss.pdf; OECD, "Circular Economy – Waste and Materials," (2019), www.oecd.org/en/publications/environment-at-a-glance-indicators_ac4b8b89-en.html.
15. Ritzén and Sandström, "Barriers to the Circular Economy"; Bjoern Jaeger and Arvind Upadhyay, "Understanding Barriers to Circular Economy: Cases from the Manufacturing Industry," *Journal of Enterprise Information Management* 33, no. 4 (2020), https://doi.org/10.1108/JEIM-02-2019-0047; Acceleratio, "Barriers & Drivers towards a Circular Economy," (2015), https://circulareconomy.europa.eu/platform/sites/default/files/e00e8643951aef8adde612123e824493.pdf; Deloitte, *Breaking the Barriers to the Circular Economy* (2017), https://circulareconomy.europa.eu/platform/sites/default/files/171106_white_paper_breaking_the_barriers_to_the_circular_economy_white_paper_vweb-14021.pdf.
16. Ellen Macarthur Foundation, "Circular Economy in Cities: Policy Levers," (2023), https://ellenmacarthurfoundation.org/policy-levers; Armin Razmjoo *et al.*, "Effective Policies to Overcome Barriers in the Development of Smart Cities," *Energy Research & Social Science* 79 (2021), https://doi.org/10.1016/j.erss.2021.102175; Ellen Macarthur Foundation, "The Circular Economy in Cities: Resources Suite," 2023, https://ellenmacarthurfoundation.org/circular-economy-in-cities#:~:text=It%20is%20based%20on%20three%20principles%2C%20driven%20by,can%20work%20to%20enable%20a%20circular%20economy%20transition; Brears, *Natural Resource Management and the Circular Economy*; Brears, *Developing the Circular Water Economy*.
17. "Building Retrofit Energy Efficiency Financing (BREEF) Scheme," (2023), www1.bca.gov.sg/buildsg/sustainability/green-mark-incentive-schemes/building-retrofit-energy-efficiency-financing-breef-scheme.
18. SFPUC, "Onsite Water Reuse Grant Program Rules," (2022), www.sfpuc.org/sites/default/files/documents/OWR_Grant_Program_Rules_and_App_June_2022.pdf#:~:text=The%20San%20Francisco%20Public%20Utilities%20Commission%20%28SFPUC%29%20Onsite,as%20toilet%20flushing%2C%20irrigation%2C%20and%20cooling%20tower%20makeup.
19. "Electronic Waste," (2023), www.toronto.ca/services-payments/recycling-organics-garbage/electronic-waste/#:~:text=The%20City%20of%20Toronto%20collects%20unwanted%20electronics%20for,or%20Community%20Environment%20Day%20or%20donated%20for%20reuse.
20. Robert C. Brears, "Stormwater Harvesting to Ensure Water Security," Mark and Focus, (2021), https://medium.com/mark-and-focus/stormwater-harvesting-to-ensure-water-security-9c45df311001.
21. Brears, "Circular Economy Cities."

2 Circular Urban Agriculture

1. Ivanka Puigdueta *et al.*, "Urban Agriculture May Change Food Consumption towards Low Carbon Diets," *Global Food Security* 28 (2021), https://doi.org/https://doi.org/10.1016/j.gfs.2021.100507; Robert McDougall, Paul Kristiansen, and Romina Rader, "Small-Scale Urban Agriculture Results in High Yields but Requires Judicious Management of Inputs to Achieve Sustainability," *Proceedings of the National Academy of Sciences* 116, no. 1 (2019), https://doi.org/10.1073/pnas.1809707115.

2. Carlos Tapia *et al.*, "Monitoring the Contribution of Urban Agriculture to Urban Sustainability: An Indicator-Based Framework," *Sustainable Cities and Society* 74 (2021), https://doi.org/https://doi.org/10.1016/j.scs.2021.103130; Ioannis Manikas, George Malindretos, and Konstadinos Abeliotis, "Sustainable Cities through Alternative Urban Farming: The Case of Floriculture," *Journal of International Food & Agribusiness Marketing* 32, no. 3 (2020), https://doi.org/10.1080/08974438.2019.1599762; S. L. G. Skar *et al.*, "Urban Agriculture as a Keystone Contribution towards Securing Sustainable and Healthy Development for Cities in the Future," *Blue-Green Systems* 2, no. 1 (2019), https://doi.org/10.2166/bgs.2019.931.
3. Michele D'Ostuni and Leonardo Zaffi, "Nurturing Cities: Pathways towards a Circular Urban Agriculture," (paper presented at the World Heritage and Design for Health conference, Napoli-Capri, 2021), www.researchgate.net/publication/353851009_Nurturing_cities_pathways_towards_a_circular_urban_agriculture.
4. K. Hodgson, M. C. Campbell, and M. Bailkey, *Urban Agriculture: Growing Healthy, Sustainable Places* (Washington DC: American Planning Advisory Service, 2011), 14.
5. Manikas, Malindretos, and Abeliotis, "Sustainable Cities through Alternative Urban Farming"; Urban Green Train, "Introduction into Urban Agriculture Concept and Types," (2023), https://ruaf.org/assets/2019/11/Module-1-Introduction-into-urban-agriculture-concept-and-types.pdf.
6. ChangeLab Solutions, "Seeding the City: Land Use Policies to Promote Urban Agriculture," (2012), www.changelabsolutions.org/sites/default/files/Urban_Ag_SeedingTheCity_FINAL_%28CLS_20120530%29_20111021_0.pdf; AITC, "Urban Agriculture," (2023), https://aitc-canada.ca/Portals/0/adam/snapAG/jRa_KWrZBkq7gB2j9Ogz8A/Link/Urban%20Agriculture%20Final.pdf; Urban Green Train, "Urban Agriculture Types/Production Systems and Short Food Chains," (2023), https://ruaf.org/assets/2019/11/Module-3-Urban-Agriculture-types-production-systems-and-short-food-chains.pdf; "10 Types of Urban Farming to Practice," (2021), https://help.synnefa.io/articles/2021/11/19/10-types-of-urban-farming-to-practice.
7. Johannes Langemeyer *et al.*, "Urban Agriculture – A Necessary Pathway towards Urban resilience and Global Sustainability?" *Landscape and Urban Planning* 210 (1 June 2021), https://doi.org/https://doi.org/10.1016/j.landurbplan.2021.104055; Maria Contesse, Bas J. M. van Vliet, and Jennifer Lenhart, "Is Urban Agriculture Urban Green Space? A Comparison of Policy Arrangements for Urban Green Space and Urban Agriculture in Santiago de Chile," *Land Use Policy* 71 (2018), https://doi.org/https://doi.org/10.1016/j.landusepol.2017.11.006; D. L. Evans *et al.*, "Ecosystem Service Delivery by Urban Agriculture and Green Infrastructure – a Systematic Review," *Ecosystem Services* 54 (2022), https://doi.org/10.1016/j.ecoser.2022.101405; Rachel Surls *et al.*, "Gearing Up to Support Urban Farming in California Preliminary Results of a Needs Assessment," *Renewable Agriculture and Food Systems* 30, no. 1 (2015), https://doi.org/10.1017/S1742170514000052; Zachary Piso *et al.*, "Types of Urban Agricultural Stakeholders and Their Understandings of Governance," *Ecology and Society* 24, no. 2 (2019), www.jstor.org/stable/26796944.
8. R. C. Brears, *Regional Water Security* (Hoboken, NJ: Wiley, 2021); "Water Use and Reuse for Urban Agriculture," (2023), https://cdn.who.int/media/docs/default-source/wash-documents/food-for-the-cities.pdf?sfvrsn=c998fe5_8; Pacific Institute, "Sustainable Water Management for Urban Agriculture: Planting Justice, Oakland," (2013), https://pacinst.org/wp-content/uploads/2013/02/sustainable_water_management_for_urban_agriculture3.pdf.
9. Muhammad M. Khan *et al.*, "Towards Sustainable Application of Wastewater in Agriculture: A Review on Reusability and Risk Assessment," *Agronomy* 12, no. 6 (2022), https://doi.org/10.3390/agronomy12061397.
10. R. C. Brears, *Water Resources Management: Innovative and Green Solutions* (Berlin: De Gruyter, 2021); Brears, *Regional Water Security*.
11. US EPA, "How Wastewater Treatment Works … The Basics," (1998), www3.epa.gov/npdes/pubs/bastre.pdf.
12. Shirly Tentile Magwaza *et al.*, "Hydroponic Technology as Decentralised System for Domestic Wastewater Treatment and Vegetable Production in Urban Agriculture: A Review," *Science of The Total Environment* 698 (2020), https://doi.org/10.1016/j.scitotenv.2019.134154; IDRC, "Wastewater Use in Urban Agriculture: Assessing Current Research and Options for National and Local Governments," (2004).

13. IDRC, "Treatment and Use of Wastewater in Urban Agriculture," (2019), https://ruaf.org/assets/2019/11/Guideline-6-Treatment-and-use-of-waste-water-in-Urban-Agriculture.pdf; IDRC, "Wastewater Use in Urban Agriculture."
14. Brears, *Developing the Circular Water Economy*; "Recycled Water," (2023), https://urbanutilities.com.au/business/business-services/recycled-water.
15. R. C. Brears, "Circular Economy and the Water–Food Nexus," Mark and Focus, (2022), https://medium.com/mark-and-focus/circular-economy-and-the-water-food-nexus-df284b72a375.
16. Brears, *Water Resources Management*.
17. Pacific Institute, "Sustainable Water Management for Urban Agriculture."
18. Pacific Institute, "Sustainable Water Management for Urban Agriculture."
19. "Graywater: Laundry to Landscape Rebate," (2023), https://sfpuc.org/learning/conserve-water/graywater-laundry-landscape-rebate.
20. "Brooklyn Grange Opens Largest Rooftop Farm in the City with Funding from DEP's Green Infrastructure Grant Program," (2019), www.nyc.gov/site/dep/news/19-065/brooklyn-grange-opens-largest-rooftop-farm-the-city-funding-dep-s-green-infrastructure#/0.
21. Rosanne C. Wielemaker, Jan Weijma, and Grietje Zeeman, "Harvest to Harvest: Recovering Nutrients with New Sanitation Systems for Reuse in Urban Agriculture," *Resources, Conservation and Recycling* 128 (2018), https://doi.org/10.1016/j.resconrec.2016.09.015.
22. Martí Rufí-Salís *et al.*, "Can Wastewater Feed Cities? Determining the Feasibility and Environmental Burdens of Struvite Recovery and Reuse for Urban Regions," *Science of The Total Environment* 737 (2020), https://doi.org/10.1016/j.scitotenv.2020.139783.
23. Rufí-Salís *et al.*, "Can Wastewater Ffeed Cities?"
24. Odiney Alvarez-Campos and Gregory K. Evanylo, "Biosolids Improve Urban Soil Properties and Vegetable Production in Urban Agriculture," *Urban Agriculture & Regional Food Systems* 4, no. 1 (2019), https://doi.org/10.2134/urbanag2019.04.0002; Sally Brown *et al.*, "Municipal Biosolids – A Resource for Sustainable Communities," *Current Opinion in Environmental Science & Health* 14 (2020), https://doi.org/10.1016/j.coesh.2020.02.007; Virginia Biosolids Council, "Biosolids Use for Urban Landscapes," (2019), www.virginiabiosolids.com/wp-content/uploads/2019/04/VBC_Urban-Landscapes.pdf; "Beneficial Reuse of Municipal Biosolids in Agriculture," (2017), https://extension.uga.edu/publications/detail.html?number=SB27.
25. "Nutrient Recovery Facility," (2023), www.saskatoon.ca/services-residents/power-water-sewer/wastewater/wastewater-treatment-plant/nutrient-recovery-facility.
26. "Valuing Every Drop of Water," Mark and Focus, (2019), https://medium.com/mark-and-focus/valuing-every-drop-of-water-7d6552c3650c; "About Bloom," 2023, https://bloomsoil.com/about-bloom-soil-amendment/.

3 Urban Water Demand Management

1. China Water, Department for International Development, and Mott MacDonald, "Water Demand Management – an International Perspective" (2010), https://assets.publishing.service.gov.uk/media/57aaf21940f0b608ab000066/OV2-Demand_management_Mar_2010rev10FINAL.pdf.
2. Chunyang He *et al.*, "Future Global Urban Water Scarcity and Potential Solutions," *Nature Communications* 12, no. 1 (2021), https://doi.org/10.1038/s41467-021-25026-3.
3. UN-Water, "Water Security and the Global Water Agenda," (2013): 1, www.unwater.org/publications/water-security-global-water-agenda/.
4. "Securing Water, Sustaining Growth," (2015), www.gwp.org/Global/About%20GWP/Publications/The%20Global%20Dialogue/SECURING%20WATER%20SUSTAINING%20GROWTH.PDF.
5. UNESCO, *Managing Water under Uncertainty and Risk* (2012), http://unesdoc.unesco.org/images/0021/002156/215644e.pdf.
6. IPCC, "The Fifth Assessment Report (AR5) of the Intergovernmental Panel on Climate Change," (2014). www.ipcc.ch/assessment-report/ar5/; UN-Water, "UN-Water Policy Brief on Climate Change and Water," (2019), www.unwater.org/publications/un-water-policy-brief-on-climate-change-and-water/; UN-Water, "Water and Climate Change," 2020, www

.unwater.org/water-facts/climate-change/; EEA, "Climate Impacts on Water Resources," 2018, www.eea.europa.eu/archived/archived-content-water-topic/water-resources/climate-impacts-on-water-resources; United Nations Department of Economic and Social Affairs, "World Population Prospects 2019: Highlights," (2019), www.un.org/development/desa/pd/news/world-population-prospects-2019-0; Alberto Boretti and Lorenzo Rosa, "Reassessing the Projections of the World Water Development Report," *NPJ Clean Water* 2, no. 1 (2019), https://doi.org/10.1038/s41545-019-0039-9; United Nations Department of Economic and Social Affairs, "World Urbanization Prospects: The 2018 Revision," (2019), www.un.org/en/desa/2018-revision-world-urbanization-prospects; "Urbanisation," (2020), https://iwa-network.org/urbanisation/; Dustin Garrick *et al.*, "Rural Water for Thirsty Cities: A Systematic Review of Water Reallocation from Rural to Urban Regions," *Environmental Research Letters* 14, no. 4 (2019), https://doi.org/10.1088/1748-9326/ab0db7; The Nature Conservancy, "Beyond the Source: The Environmental, Economic and Community Benefits of Source Water Protection," (2017), www.nature.org/content/dam/tnc/nature/en/documents/Beyond_The_Source_Full_Report_FinalV4.pdf; OECD, "Global Material Resources Outlook to 2060: Economic Drivers and Environmental Consequences," (2019), www.oecd.org/environment/waste/highlights-global-material-resources-outlook-to-2060.pdf; UN-Water, "Water and Jobs," (2016), https://unesdoc.unesco.org/ark:/48223/pf0000244040/PDF/244040eng.pdf.multi; IEA, "WEO-2016 Special Report: Water–Energy Nexus," (2016), www.iea.org/reports/world-energy-outlook-2016; FAO, "The State of the World's Land and Water Resources for Food and Agriculture: Managing Systems at Risk," (2011), www.fao.org/3/i1688e/i1688e.pdf; FAO, "Towards a Water and Food Secure Future: Critical Perspectives for Policy-Makers," (2015), www.fao.org/3/a-i4560e.pdf.

7. He *et al.*, "Future Global Urban Water Scarcity and Potential Solutions."
8. He *et al.*, "Future Global Urban Water Scarcity and Potential Solutions."
9. R. C. Brears, *Urban Water Security* (Hoboken, NJ: John Wiley & Sons, 2016).
10. Global Water Partnership, "Water Demand Management (WDM) – The Mediterranean Experience," technical focus paper (2012): 22–24, www.pseau.org/outils/ouvrages/plan_bleu_gwp_water_demand_management_the_mediterranean_experience_2012.pdf; H. Savenije and P. van der Zaag, "Water as an Economic Good and Demand Management: Paradigms with Pitfalls," *Water International* 27, no. 1 (2002): 100.
11. Global Water Partnership, "Water Demand Management (WDM) – The Mediterranean Experience": 39.
12. Global Water Partnership, "Water Demand Management (WDM) – The Mediterranean Experience": 20.
13. Shiroma Maheepala *et al.*, "Towards the Adoption of Integrated Urban Water Management Approach for Planning," *Proceedings of the Water Environment Federation* 2010, no. 9 (2010); Francois Molle and Jeremy Berkoff, "Cities vs. Agriculture: A Review of Intersectoral Water Re-allocation" (paper presented at the Natural Resources Forum, 2009); Robert Gifford, Christine Kormos, and Amanda McIntyre, "Behavioral Dimensions of climate Change: Drivers, Responses, Barriers, and Interventions," *Wiley Interdisciplinary Reviews: Climate Change* 2, no. 6 (2011).
14. Brears, *Urban Water Security*.
15. OECD, "Addressing the Social Consequences of Tariffs for Water Supply and Sanitation," (2020), www.oecd.org/en/publications/addressing-the-social-consequences-of-tariffs-for-water-supply-and-sanitation_afede7d6-en.html; World Bank, "Doing More with Less – Smarter Subsidies for Water Supply and Sanitation," (2019), www.worldbank.org/en/topic/water/publication/smarter-subsidies-for-water-supply-and-sanitation; Celine Nauges and Dale Whittington, "Evaluating the Performance of Alternative Municipal Water Tariff Designs: Quantifying the Tradeoffs between Equity, Economic Efficiency, and Cost Recovery," *World Development* 91 (22017), https://doi.org/10.1016/j.worlddev.2016.10.014.
16. Lei Gao *et al.*, "Opportunity for Peri-Urban Perth Groundwater Trade," *Journal of Hydrology* 496 (2013), https://doi.org/10.1016/j.jhydrol.2013.05.009; Andrew B. Ayres, Kyle C. Meng, and Andrew J. Plantinga, "Do Environmental Markets Improve on Open Access? Evidence from California Groundwater Rights," *Journal of Political Economy* 129, no. 10 (2021), https://doi.org/10.1086/715075.

17. Mario Schmack *et al.*, "Urban Water Trading – Hybrid Water Systems and Niche Opportunities in the Urban Water Market – a Literature Review," *Environmental Technology Reviews* 8, no. 1 (2019), https://doi.org/10.1080/21622515.2019.1647292.
18. Australian Government Productivity Commission, "Water Trading and Markets," (2020), www.pc.gov.au/inquiries/completed/water-reform-2020/report/water-reform-2020-supportingb.pdf.
19. Brears, *Urban Water Security*; Brears, *Water Resources Management: Innovative and Green Solutions*; Kirsten Davies *et al.*, "Water-Saving Impacts of Smart Meter technology: An Empirical 5 Year, Whole-of-Community Study in Sydney, Australia," *Water Resources Research* 50, no. 9 (2014), https://doi.org/10.1002/2014WR015812; Andrea Cominola *et al.*, "Long-Term Water Conservation Is Fostered by Smart Meter-Based Feedback and Digital User Engagement," *NPJ Clean Water* 4, no. 1 (2021), https://doi.org/10.1038/s41545-021-00119-0.
20. "Smart Water Meter Project Approved," (2021), www.thenews.com.pk/print/917092-smart-water-meter-project-approved.
21. S. N. Ghosh, *Environmental Hydrology and Hydraulics: Eco-technological Practices for Sustainable Development* (CRC Press, 2016), https://books.google.co.nz/books?id=jj7NBQAAQBAJ; Mahmud Güngör, Ufuk Yarar, and Mahmut Firat, "Reduction of Water Losses by Rehabilitation of Water Distribution Network," *Environmental Monitoring and Assessment* 189, no. 10 (2017), https://doi.org/10.1007/s10661-017-6219-5; Luigi Berardi *et al.*, "Active Leakage Control with WDNetXL," *Procedia Engineering* 154 (2016), https://doi.org/10.1016/j.proeng.2016.07.420; Brears, *Water Resources Management: Innovative and Green Solutions*; "Testing Smart Water Tech Down Under," (2020), https://medium.com/mark-and-focus/testing-smart-water-tech-down-under-d08688f7609a.
22. Robert C. Brears, "How Can Cities Reduce Water–Energy Nexus Pressures?" *World Bank*, (2016), https://blogs.worldbank.org/water/how-can-cities-reduce-water-energy-nexus-pressures.
23. World Bank, "Doing More with Less – Smarter Subsidies for Water Supply and Sanitation."
24. World Bank, "Doing More with Less – Smarter Subsidies for Water Supply and Sanitation."
25. Water Supply & Sanitation Collaborative Council, "Public Funding for Sanitation. The Many Faces of Sanitation Subsidies," (2009). https://sswm.info/sites/default/files/reference_attachments/EVANS%20et%20al%202009%20Public%20Funding%20for%20Sanitation%20Subsidies.pdf; World Bank, "Doing More with Less – Smarter Subsidies for Water Supply and Sanitation."
26. Brears, *Urban Water Security*.
27. Brears, *Regional Water Security*; Brears, *Nature-based Solutions to 21st Century Challenges*.
28. "Source Water Protection," (2020), www.epa.gov/sourcewaterprotection; American Rivers, The Forest Guild, and Mountain Conservation Trust of Georgia, "Forests to Faucets: Protecting Upstream Forests for Clean Water Downstream," (2013), https://americanrivers.org/wp-content/uploads/2016/05/AmericanRivers_forests-to-faucets-report.pdf; G. Tracy Mehan III and Adam T. Carpenter, "Bringing Agriculture and Drinking Water Utilities Together for Source Water Protection," *Journal – AWWA* 111, no. 8 (2019), https://doi.org/10.1002/awwa.1340; Monica B. Emelko *et al.*, "Implications of Land Disturbance on Drinking Water Treatability in a Changing Climate: Demonstrating the Need for 'Source Water Supply and Protection' Strategies," *Water Research* 45, no. 2 (2011), https://doi.org/10.1016/j.watres.2010.08.051.
29. The Nature Conservancy, "Estimating the Water Supply Benefits from Forest Restoration in the Northern Sierra Nevada," (2015), www.researchgate.net/publication/305767082_Estimating_the_Water_Supply_Benefits_from_Forest_Restoration_in_the_Northern_Sierra_Nevada.
30. Brears, *Water Resources Management: Innovative and Green Solutions*.
31. Nicole Nel *et al.*, "Supplementary household water sources to augment potable municipal supply in South Africa," *Water SA* 43 (11/06 2017), https://doi.org/10.4314/wsa.v43i4.03.
32. Brears, *Regional Water Security*.
33. Brears, *Urban Water Security*.
34. Rabab I. El-Nwsany, Ibrahim Maarouf, and Waled Abd el-Aal, "Water Management as a Vital Factor for a Sustainable School," *Alexandria Engineering Journal* 58, no. 1 (2019), https://doi.org/10.1016/j.aej.2018.12.012; Omar Amahmid *et al.*, "Water Education in School Curricula: Impact on Children Knowledge, Attitudes and Behaviours towards Water Use,"

International Research in Geographical and Environmental Education 28, no. 3 (2019), https://doi.org/10.1080/10382046.2018.1513446; Waterwise, "Investigating the Impact of Water Efficiency Educational Programmes in Schools: A Scoping Study," (2012), www.waterwise.org.uk/wp-content/uploads/2018/02/Investigating-the-impact-of-water-efficiency-educational-programmes-in-schools_final.pdf.

35. Waterwise, "H2eco Behavioural Research (Phase 10)," (2019), www.waterwise.org.uk/knowledge-base/h2eco-behavioural-research-phase-10/; Robert C. Brears, "Urban Water Security in Asia-Pacific: Promoting Demand Management Strategies," (2014), https://refubium.fu-berlin.de/bitstream/handle/fub188/18349/pp414-urban-water-security-asiapacific.pdf?sequence=1&isAllowed=y; Isaac B. Addo, Martin C. Thoms, and Melissa Parsons, "The Influence of Water-Conservation Messages on reducing Household Water Use," *Applied Water Science* 9, no. 5 (2019), https://doi.org/10.1007/s13201-019-1002-0; "Raising Public Awareness," (2020), www.gwp.org/en/learn/iwrm-toolbox/Management-Instruments/Promoting_Social_Change/Raising_public_awareness/; Georgia Environmental Protection Division Watershed Protection Branch, (2007), www1.gadnr.org/cws/Documents/Conservation_Education.pdf; El-Nwsany, Maarouf, and Abd el-Aal, "Water Management as a Vital Factor for a Sustainable School"; Damian C. Adams *et al.*, "The Influence of Water Attitudes, Perceptions, and Learning Preferences on Water-Conserving Actions," *Natural Sciences Education* 42, no. 1 (2013), https://doi.org/10.4195/nse.2012.0027; Fransiscus Xaverius Prins *et al.*, "Water Scarcity and Alternative Water Sources in South Africa: Can Information Provision Shift Perceptions?" *Urban Water Journal* (2022), https://doi.org/10.1080/1573062X.2022.2026984.
36. Policy Research Institute, *Economic Instruments for Water Demand Management in an Integrated Water Resources Management Framework: Synthesis Report* (Government of Canada, 2005), 11, http://publications.gc.ca/site/eng/269935/publication.html; Martin Patchen, "What Shapes Public Reactions to Climate Change? Overview of Research and Policy Implications," *Analyses of Social Issues and Public Policy* 10, no. 1 (2010): 62.
37. Georgia Environmental Protection Division Watershed Protection Branch, "Water Conservation Education Programs EPD Guidance Document," (2007): 8, www1.gadnr.org/cws/Documents/Conservation_Education.pdf; Patchen, "What Shapes Public Reactions to Climate Change? Overview of Research and Policy Implications," 62.
38. Linda Steg and Charles Vlek, "Encouraging Pro-environmental Behaviour: An Integrative Review and Research Agenda," *Journal of Environmental Psychology* 29, no. 3 (2009): 313; OECD, "Behavioural Economics and Environmental Policy Design," (2012), www.oecd.org/en/publications/behavioural-economics-and-environmental-incentives_5k8zwbhqs1xn-en.html; Ricardo Correia and Catarina Roseta-Palma, "Behavioural Economics in Water Management," (2012): 19, www.isecoeco.org/conferences/isee2012-versao3/pdf/742.pdf.
39. Brears, "Urban Water Security in Asia-Pacific: Promoting Demand Management Strategies"; D. A. Kelly, "Labelling and water conservation: A European perspective on a global challenge," *Building Services Engineering Research & Technology* 36, no. 6 (2015), https://doi.org/10.1177/0143624415571758.
40. R. C. Brears, *The Green Economy and the Water–Energy–Food Nexus* (London: Palgrave Macmillan UK, 2017), https://books.google.co.nz/books?id=m9IxDwAAQBAJ.
41. CAP-NET, "Economics in Sustainable Water Management: Training Manual and Facilitators' Guide," (2008): 55, www.ircwash.org/resources/economics-sustainable-water-management-training-manual-and-facilitators-guide.
42. Policy Research Institute, *Economic Instruments for Water Demand Management in an Integrated Water Resources Management Framework*, 25.
43. S. M. Olmstead and R. N. Stavins, "Managing Water Demand: Price vs. Non-Price Conservation Programs," *Pioneer Institute White Paper* 39 (2007): 27.
44. CAP-NET, "Economics in Sustainable Water Managemente," 45; OECD, *Environmental Outlook to 2050: The Consequences of Inaction* (OECD Publishing, 2012), 238, http://books.google.co.nz/books?id=sLldM0i0HwgC.
45. Policy Research Institute, *Economic Instruments for Water Demand Management in an Integrated Water Resources Management Framework*, 36.
46. Olmstead and Stavins, "Managing Water Demand: Price vs. Non-Price Conservation Programs," 27 and 30.

4 Vibrant Streets

1. Gerike *et al.*, "Cross-Site Assessment of Case Study Design Packages. Deliverable D5.5, MORE project (Multimodal Optimisation of Roadspace in Europe)," (2018) www.roadspace.eu/results.
2. Sevtsuk, "Street Commerce. Creating Vibrant Urban Sidewalks," (2020).
3. Jordan and Ivey, "Complete Streets: Promises and Proof," *Journal of Urban Planning and Development*, 2 (2021); Hui *et al.*, "Measuring the Completeness of Complete Streets," *Transport Reviews*, 1 (2018); Litman, "Evaluating Complete Streets," (2015), www.researchgate.net/publication/352031437_Complete_Streets_Promises_and_Proof.
4. Appleyard and Appleyard, "Livable streets 2.0" (2021); Dumbaugh and King "Engineering Livable Streets: A Thematic Review of Advancements in Urban Street Design," *Journal of Planning Literature*, 4 (2018).
5. Wang *et al.*, "Research on Traffic Design of Urban Vital Streets," *Sustainability*, 11 (2022).
6. Aslan, "Praxitopia: How Shopping Makes a Street Vibrant," (2021); North, "Design for Vibrant Streets: Proposed Framework for a Small Area in Newmarket," (2012). https://hdl.handle.net/10652/2067; Sevtsuk, "Street Commerce. Creating Vibrant Urban Sidewalks," (2020).
7. Gascon *et al.*, "What Explains Public Transport Use? Evidence from Seven European Cities," *Transport Policy* (2020); Gascon *et al.*, "Correlates of Walking for Travel in Seven European Cities: The PASTA Project," *Environmental Health Perspectives*, 9 (2019).
8. Mehta, "The Street. A Quintessential Social Public Space," (2014).
9. Ewing and Handy, "Measuring the Unmeasurable: Urban Design Qualities Related to Walkability," *Journal of Urban Design*, 1 (2009).
10. Ewing *et al.*, "Measuring Urban Design" (2013); Su *et al.*, "Rhythm of the Streets: A Street Classification Framework Based on Street Activity Patterns," *EPJ Data Science*, 1 (2022).
11. Mehta, "The Street. A Quintessential Social Public Space," (2014); Hahm *et al.*, "The Effect of Built Environments on the Walking and Shopping Behaviors of Pedestrians; A Study with GPS Experiment in Sinchon Retail District in Seoul, South Korea," *Cities* (2019).
12. European Commission, "EU Transport in Figures: Statistical Pocketbook 2022," (2022), https://transport.ec.europa.eu/facts-funding/studies-data/eu-transport-figures-statistical-pocketbook/statistical-pocketbook-2022_en.
13. Ewing and Cervero, "Travel and the Built Environment," *Journal of the American Planning Association*, 3 (2010); Götschi *et al.*, "Towards a Comprehensive Conceptual Framework of Active Travel Behavior: A Review and Synthesis of Published Frameworks," *Curr Envir Health Rpt*, 3 (2017); Lai and Kontokosta, "Quantifying Place: Analyzing the Drivers of Pedestrian Activity in Dense Urban Environments," *Landscape and Urban Planning* (2018); Toralles, "Relationships Between Walkable Urban Environments and the Creative and Knowledge Economies," *IRSPSD International*, 1 (2023).
14. Ewing *et al.*, "Validating Urban Design Measures," TRB 92nd Annual Meeting Compendium of Papers (2013); Ewing *et al.*, "Streetscape Features Related to Pedestrian Activity," *Journal of Planning Education and Research*, 1 (2016).
15. Ewing and Cervero, "Travel and the Built Environment"; Lai and Kontokosta, "Quantifying Place."
16. Ewing *et al.*, "Validating Urban Design Measures."
17. Ewing *et al.*, "Streetscape Features Related to Pedestrian Activity."
18. Ewing *et al.*, "Measuring Urban Design" (2013); Kim *et al.*, "Spatially-Varying Effects of Built Environment Determinants on Walking," *Transportation Research* Part A*: Policy and Practice* (2019).
19. Ewing and Cervero, "Travel and the Built Environment"; Berrigan *et al.*, "Associations between Street Connectivity and Active Transportation," *International Journal of Health Geographics* (2010).
20. Ewing *et al.*, "Streetscape Features Related to Pedestrian Activity."
21. Ewing and Cervero "Travel and the Built Environment"; Vale *et al.*, "Active Accessibility: A Review of Operational Measures of Walking and Cycling Accessibility," *JTLU* (2013).
22. Ewing *et al.*, "Validating Urban Design Measures"; Ewing *et al.*, "Streetscape Features Related to Pedestrian Activity."
23. Cambra *et al.*, "On the Correlation of Pedestrian Flows to Urban Environment Measures: A Space Syntax and Walkability Analysis Comparison Case," 11th Space Syntax Forum (2017), www

.researchgate.net/publication/319956237_ON_THE_CORRELATION_OF_PEDESTRIAN_FLOWS_TO_URBAN_ENVIRONMENT_MEASURES_A_Space_Syntax_and_Walkability_Analysis_comparison_case; Moura *et al.*, "Measuring Walkability for Distinct Pedestrian Groups with a Participatory Assessment Method: A Case Study in Lisbon," *Landscape and Urban Planning* (2017).

24. Ewing *et al.*, "Streetscape Features Related to Pedestrian Activity."
25. Ewing and Handy, "Measuring the Unmeasurable."
26. Ewing and Handy, "Measuring the Unmeasurable"; Ewing *et al.*, "Validating Urban Design Measures."
27. Ameli *et al.*, "Do Better Urban Design Qualities Lead to More Walking in Salt Lake City, Utah?" *Journal of Urban Design*, 3 (2015); Hamidi and Moazzeni, "Examining the Relationship between Urban Design Qualities and Walking Behavior: Empirical Evidence from Dallas, TX," *Sustainability*, 10 (2019).
28. Ameli *et al.*, "Do Better Urban Design Qualities Lead to More Walking in Salt Lake City, Utah?"
29. Ewing *et al.*, "Streetscape Features Related to Pedestrian Activity."
30. Kang, "The Effects of Spatial Accessibility and Centrality to Land Use on Walking in Seoul, Korea," *Cities* (2015).
31. Kim *et al.*, "Spatially-Varying Effects of Built Environment Determinants on Walking."
32. Lai and Kontokosta, "Quantifying Place."
33. Mehta, "The Street. A Quintessential Social Public Space"; Mehta and Bosson, "Revisiting Lively Streets: Social Interactions in Public Space," *Journal of Planning Education and Research*, 2 (2021); Mehta, "Lively Streets," *Journal of Planning Education and Research*, 2 (2007); Su *et al.*, "Rhythm of the Streets"; Njeru and Kinoshita, "Stay Activities on Carfree Neighborhood Shopping Streets," *E-BPJ*, 9 (2018); Hall and Ram, "Measuring the Relationship between Tourism and Walkability? Walk Score and English Tourist Attractions," *Journal of Sustainable Tourism*, 2 (2019).
34. Hall and Ram, "Measuring the Relationship between Tourism and Walkability?"; Njeru and Kinoshita, "Stay Activities on Carfree Neighborhood Shopping Streets."
35. Mehta, "The Street. A Quintessential Social Public Space"; Mehta and Bosson, "Revisiting Lively Streets"; Mehta, "Look Closely and You Will See, Listen Carefully and You Will Hear: Urban Design and Social Interaction on Streets," *Journal of Urban Design*, 1 (2009).
36. Mehta and Bosson, "Revisiting Lively Streets."
37. Mehta and Bosson, "Revisiting Lively Streets"; Mehta, "Lively Streets."
38. Mehta, "Lively Streets."
39. Gehl, "Cities for People," (2010).
40. Gehl "Cities for People."
41. Gehl and Svarre, "How to Study Public Life," (2013).
42. Gerike *et al.*, "Aktive Mobilität: Mehr Lebensqualität in Ballungsräumen," 226/2020 (2020). www.umweltbundesamt.de/publikationen/aktive-mobilitaet-mehr-lebensqualitaet-in.
43. Buehler *et al.*, "Reducing Car Dependence in the Heart of Europe: Lessons from Germany, Austria, and Switzerland," *Transport Reviews*, 1 (2017); Gascon *et al.*, "Correlates of Walking for Travel in Seven European Cities"; Gascon *et al.*, "What Explains Public Transport Use?"
44. Liao *et al.*, "Empirical Analysis of Walkability Using Data from the Netherlands," *Transportation Research* Part D*: Transport and Environment* (2020).
45. Gascon *et al.*, "Correlates of Walking for Travel in Seven European Cities."
46. Wang *et al.*, "Objective Environmental Exposures Correlate Differently with Recreational and Transportation Walking: A Cross-Sectional National Study in the Netherlands," *Environmental Research (*2021); Wasfi *et al.*, "Place Matters: A Longitudinal Analysis Measuring the Association between Neighbourhood Walkability and Walking by Age Group and Population Center Size in Canada," *PloS one*, 12 (2017); Gascon *et al.*, "What Explains Public Transport Use?"
47. Gascon *et al.*, "Correlates of Walking for Travel in Seven European Cities."
48. Wang *et al.*, "Objective Environmental Exposures"; Wasfi *et al.*, "Place Matters."
49. Brüchert *et al.*, "Walking for Transport among Older Adults: A Cross-Sectional Study on the Role of the Built Environment in Less Densely Populated Areas in Northern Germany," *International Journal of Environmental Research and Public Health*, 24 (2020).

50. Wang *et al.*, "Objective Environmental Exposures."
51. Gascon *et al.*, "Correlates of Walking for Travel in Seven European Cities."
52. Gascon *et al.*, "What Explains Public Transport Use?"
53. Gascon *et al.*, "Correlates of Walking for Travel in Seven European Cities"; Wang *et al.*, "Objective Environmental Exposures."
54. Gascon *et al.*, "What Explains Public Transport Use?"
55. Gascon *et al.*, "Correlates of Walking for Travel in Seven European Cities."
56. Wasfi *et al.*, "Place Matters."
57. Moudon *et al.*, "Attributes of Environments Supporting Walking," *American Journal of Health Promotion: AJHP*, 5 (2007); Wasfi *et al.*, "Place Matters."
58. Kroesen *et al.*, "Do Attitudes Cause Behavior or Vice Versa? An Alternative Conceptualization of the Attitude–Behavior Relationship in Travel Behavior Modeling," *Transportation Research* Part A*: Policy and Practice* (2017).
59. Wang and Wen, "The Relationship between the Neighborhood Built Environment and Active Transportation among Adults: A Systematic Literature Review," *Urban Science*, 3 (2017); Gascon *et al.*, "What Explains Public Transport Use?"; Agarwal *et al.*, "Public Transit," (2019).
60. Wang and Wen, "The Relationship between the Neighborhood Built Environment and Active Transportation among Adults."
61. Gascon *et al.*, "Correlates of Walking for Travel in Seven European Cities"; Knuiman *et al.*, "A Longitudinal Analysis of the Influence of the Neighborhood Built Environment on Walking for Transportation: The RESIDE Study," *American Journal of Epidemiology*, 5 (2014).
62. Gascon *et al.*, "What Explains Public Transport Use?"
63. Wang and Wen, "The Relationship between the Neighborhood Built Environment and Active Transportation among Adults"; Agarwal *et al.* "Public Transit."
64. Christiansen *et al.*, "International Comparisons of the Associations between Objective Measures of the Built Environment and Transport-Related Walking and Cycling: IPEN Adult Study," *Journal of Transport & Health*, 4 (2016); Wang *et al.*, "Objective Environmental Exposures."
65. Christiansen *et al.* "International Comparisons."
66. Koszowski *et al.*, "Perceived Importance of Context-Specific Built-Environment Factors of Walking: A New Perspective for Prioritizing Policy Measures for Promoting Walking," *International Journal of Sustainable Transportation.* (in publication).
67. Gehl "Cities for People."
68. Agarwal *et al.*, "Public Transit."
69. Buehler *et al.*, "Reducing Car Dependence in the Heart of Europe: Lessons from Germany, Austria, and Switzerland"; Wittwer *et al.*, "Peak-Car Phenomenon Revisited for Urban Areas: Microdata Analysis of Household Travel Surveys from Five European Capital Cities," *Transportation Research Record*, 3 (2019).
70. Mehta, "Lively Streets"; Mehta, "Look Closely and You Will See, Listen Carefully and You Will Hear"; Mehta, "The Street. A Quintessential Social Public Space"; Mehta and Bosson, "Revisiting Lively Streets."
71. Gehl, "Cities for People"; Gehl and Svarre, "How to Study Public Life."
72. United Nations, "Transforming Our World: The 2030 Agenda for Sustainable Development," (2015), https://sdgs.un.org/.
73. WCED, "Report of the World Commission on Environment and Development: Our Common Future," (1987), www.un-documents.net/wced-ocf.htm.
74. Gerike *et al.* "From Sustainable Urban Transport to Responsible Urban Mobility: Function, Form, Fairness, Forever," (2022).
75. United Nations, "Transforming Our World: The 2030 Agenda for Sustainable Development."
76. Gerike *et al.*, "From Sustainable Urban Transport to Responsible Urban Mobility: Function, Form, Fairness, Forever," (2022); Velasco Arevalo and Gerike, "Sustainability Evaluation Methods for Public Transport with a Focus on Latin American Cities: A Literature Review," *International Journal of Sustainable Transportation* (2023).
77. Nieuwenhuijsen, "Urban and Transport Planning Pathways to Carbon Neutral, Liveable and Healthy Cities; A Review of the Current Evidence," *Environment International* (2020).

78. Carson *et al.*, "Neighborhood Walkability, Neighborhood Social Health, and Self-Selection among US Adults," *Health & Place* (2023).
79. Frehlich *et al.*, "The Neighbourhood Built Environment and Health-Related Fitness: A Narrative Systematic Review," *The International Journal of Behavioral Nutrition and Physical Activity*, 1 (2022).
80. Mouratidis, "Urban Planning and Quality of Life: A Review of Pathways Linking the Built Environment to Subjective Well-being," *Cities* (2021).
81. van den Berg *et al.*, "The Relationship between Walkability and Place Attachment and the Mediating Role of Neighborhood-Based Social Interaction," *Journal of Planning Education and Research* (2022).
82. Rashidfarokhi and Danivska, "Managing Crises 'Together': How Can the Built Environment Contribute to Social Resilience?" *Building Research & Information*, 7 (2023).
83. Browning *et al.*, "Where Greenspace Matters Most: A Systematic Review of Urbanicity, Greenspace, and Physical Health," *Landscape and Urban Planning* (2022).
84. Elmqvist *et al.*, "Benefits of Restoring Ecosystem Services in Urban Areas," *Current Opinion in Environmental Sustainability* (2015).
85. Nieuwenhuijsen, "Urban and Transport Planning Pathways to Carbon Neutral, Liveable and Healthy Cities; A Review of the Current Evidence."
86. Buehler *et al.*, "Reducing Car Dependence in the Heart of Europe: Lessons from Germany, Austria, and Switzerland."
87. City of Kassel, "Friedrich-Ebert-Street 2009–2019" (2020), https://mittendrin-kassel.de/wp-content/uploads/2020/09/Monitoringbericht_2020_Aktiver_Kernbereich_FES_Web.pdf.pdf; DVR and TH Köln, "Goethestreet, Germaniastreet in the City of Kassel – An Example for Successful Urban Street Design," (2022), www.dvr.de/themen/infrastruktur/beispielsammlung-gute-strassen-in-stadt-und-dorf.
88. Mayor of London, "Walking Action Plan," (2018), https://content.tfl.gov.uk/mts-walking-action-plan.pdf; Mayor of London, "Mayor's Transport Strategy," (2018), www.london.gov.uk/sites/default/files/mayors-transport-strategy-2018.pdf.
89. Aumann *et al.*, "Driving Towards Car-Independent Neighborhoods in Europe: A Typology and Systematic Literature Review," *UP*, 3 (2023).
90. City of Zurich, "The Limmatquai Before and After Redesign," (2009), https://ub-swasearch.ub.unibas.ch/de/detail/swasearch_9957586700105504.
91. Lydon and Garcia, "Tactical Urbanism," (2015).

5 Sustainable Built Environment in Circular Economy Liveable Cities

1. Joanna Williams, "Circular Cities: Challenges to Implementing Looping Actions," *Sustainability* 11, no. 2 (2019): 423.
2. Constantinos Cartalis, "Toward Resilient Cities – a Review of Definitions, Challenges and Prospects," *Advances in Building Energy Research* 8, no. 2 (2014): 259–66.
3. Elena Simina Lakatos *et al.*, "Conceptualizing Core Aspects on Circular Economy in Cities," *Sustainability* 13, no. 14 (2021): 7549.
4. "Circular Economy: Definition, Importance and Benefits: News: European Parliament," (2023), www.europarl.europa.eu/news/en/headlines/economy/20151201STO05603/circular-economy-definition-importance-and-benefits.
5. Ellen MacArthur, "Towards the Circular Economy," *Journal of Industrial Ecology* 2, no. 1 (2013): 23–44.
6. Eric Hannon, Marianne Kuhlmann, and Benjamin Thaidigsmann, "Developing Products for a Circular Economy," McKinsey & Company, (2016): 2020.
7. "World Urbanization Prospects," (2018), OECD iLibrary, https://population.un.org/wup/.
8. David W. Pearce and R. Kerry Turner, *Economics of Natural Resources and the Environment* (Baltimore, MD: Johns Hopkins University Press, 1989).
9. Santosh Nandi *et al.*, "Conceptualising Circular Economy Performance with Non-Traditional Valuation Methods: Lessons for a Post-Pandemic Recovery," *International Journal of Logistics Research and Applications* 26, no. 6 (2023): 662–82.

10. Williams, "Circular Cities: Challenges to Implementing Looping Actions"; MacArthur, "Towards the Circular Economy."
11. Lakatos *et al.*, "Conceptualizing Core Aspects on Circular Economy in Cities."
12. "Resilient Societies and Liveable Cities," Ramboll Group, www.ramboll.com/resilient-societies-and-liveability.
13. McKinsey & Company, "Urban World: The Global Consumers to Watch," (2016), www.mckinsey.com/global-themes/urbanization/urban-world-the-global-consumers-to-watch/~/media/57C6AD7F7F1B44A6BD2E24F0777B4CD6.ashx.
14. Benedek József, "Urban Policy and Urbanisation in the Transition Romania," *Romanian Review of Regional Studies* 1 (2006): 1.
15. Ellen MacArthur, Klaus Zumwinkel, and Martin R. Stuchtey, "Growth Within: A Circular Economy Vision for a Competitive Europe," Ellen MacArthur Foundation (2015).
16. Charles J. Kibert, "Policy Instruments for Sustainable Built Environment," *Journal of Land Use and Environmental Law* 17 (2001): 379.
17. Thomas Lützkendorf, Wei Fan, and David Lorenz, "Engaging Financial Stakeholders: Opportunities for a Sustainable Built Environment," *Building Research & Information* 39, no. 5 (2011): 483–503.
18. Elena Simina Lakatos *et al.*, "Creating Livable Cities through Sustainable Built Environments in the Circular Economy," *Innovative Economics and Management* 10, no. 2 (2023): 260–70.
19. József, "Urban Policy and Urbanisation in the Transition Romania."
20. Sharon Prendeville, Emma Cherim, and Nancy Bocken, "Circular Cities: Mapping Six Cities in Transition," *Environmental Innovation and Societal Transitions* 26 (2018): 171–94, https://doi.org/10.1016/j.eist.2017.03.002.
21. Philip J. Vergragt *et al.*, "Transitions to Sustainable Consumption and Production in Cities," *Journal of Cleaner Production* 134 (2016): 1–12.
22. Kibert, "Policy Instruments for Sustainable Built Environment."
23. Nandi *et al.*, "Conceptualising Circular Economy Performance with Non-Traditional Valuation Methods."
24. McKinsey & Company, "Urban World: The Global Consumers to Watch."
25. Joakim Krook, Niclas Svensson, and Mats Eklund, "Landfill Mining: A Critical Review of Two Decades of Research," *Waste Management* 32, no. 3 (2012): 513–20.
26. Sandra Leville and Matthew Taylor, "Stop Exporting Plastic Waste to China to Boost Recycling at Home, Say Experts," (2017), www.theguardian.com/environment/2017/jun/29/stop-exporting-plastic-waste-to-china-to-boost-recycling-at-home-say-experts.
27. Joanna Williams, "Circular Cities," *Urban Studies* 56, no. 13 (2019): 2746–62.
28. Mark J. McDonnell, Amy K. Hahs, and Jürgen H. Breuste (eds), *Ecology of Cities and Towns: A Comparative Approach* (Cambridge University Press, 2009).
29. David Orr, *Environmental Literacy: Education as if the Earth Mattered* (Human Scale Education, 1994).
30. Natalie Rosales, "How Can an Ecological Perspective Be Used to Enrich Cities Planning and Management?" *urbe. Revista Brasileira de Gestão Urbana* 9 (2017): 314–26.
31. Nandi *et al.*, "Conceptualising Circular Economy Performance with Non-Traditional Valuation Methods."
32. Eleni Iacovidou and Phil Purnell, "Mining the Physical Infrastructure: Opportunities, Barriers and Interventions in Promoting Structural Components Reuse," *Science of the Total Environment* 557 (2016): 791–807.
33. K. C. Seto, B. Güneralp, and L. R. Hutyra, "Global Forecasts of Urban Expansion to 2030 and Direct Impacts on Biodiversity and Carbon Pools," *Proceedings of the National Academy of Sciences* 109, no. 40 (2012). 16083–8.
34. Julie Marin, and Bruno De Meulder, "Interpreting Circularity. Circular City Representations Concealing Transition Drivers," *Sustainability* 10, no. 5 (2018): 1310.
35. Paolo Neirotti *et al.*, "Current Trends in Smart City Initiatives: Some Stylised Facts," *Cities* 38 (2014): 25–36.
36. Antonio Barragán-Escandón, Julio Terrados-Cepeda, and Esteban Zalamea-León, "The Role of Renewable Energy in the Promotion of Circular Urban Metabolism," *Sustainability* 9, no. 12 (2017): 2341.

37. MacArthur, "Towards the Circular Economy."
38. MacArthur, "Towards the Circular Economy."
39. Kibert, "Policy Instruments for Sustainable Built Environment."
40. Jo Williams, "Circular Cities: Planning for Circular Development in European Cities," *European Planning Studies* 31, no. 1 (2023): 14–35.
41. Kibert, "Policy Instruments for Sustainable Built Environment."
42. Kibert, "Policy Instruments for Sustainable Built Environment."
43. Kibert, "Policy Instruments for Sustainable Built Environment."
44. Kibert, "Policy Instruments for Sustainable Built Environment."
45. Petit-Boix and Leipold, "Circular Economy in Cities."
46. Enel Group, "Cities of Tomorrow," (2018), www.enel.com/content/dam/enel-com/documenti/media/cities-of-tomorrow_en.pdf.

6 Dynamic Water Resource Management for Regenerative Cities

1. UN-HABITAT, "Slum Almanac 2015–2016," (2016), https://unhabitat.org/slum-almanac-2015-2016-0.
2. T. Wong and R. Brown, "Transitioning to Water Sensitive Cities: Ensuring Resilience through a New Hydro-Social Contract," 11th International Conference on Urban Drainage, Edinburgh, Scotland, UK (2008).
3. R. Brown, B. Rogers, and L. Werbeloff, "Moving toward Water Sensitive Cities: A Guidance Manual for Strategists and Policy Makers," (2016), https://watersensitivecities.org.au/wp-content/uploads/2016/05/TMR_A4-1_MovingTowardWSC.pdf.
4. T. H. Wong and R. R. Brown, "The Water Sensitive City: Principles for Practice," *Water Science & Technology* 60, no. 3 (2009), https://doi.org/10.2166/wst.2009.436.
5. Nanco Dolman and Fola Ogunyoye, "How Water Challenges Can Shape Tomorrow's Cities – Discussion Contribution," *ICE Proceedings Civil Engineering* 172 (2019), https://doi.org/10.1680/jcien.2019.172.1.13.
6. Nanco Dolman and Fola Ogunyoye, "How Water Challenges Can Shape Tomorrow's Cities," *Proceedings of the Institution of Civil Engineers – Civil Engineering* 171 (2018), https://doi.org/10.1680/jcien.17.00052.
7. FAO, "The Water–Energy–Food Nexus. A New Approach in Support of Food Security and Sustainable Agriculture," (2014), www.fao.org/land-water/water/watergovernance/waterfoodenergynexus/en/.
8. A. T. Jones and W. Finley, "Recent Development in Salinity Gradient Power" (paper presented at the Oceans 2003: Celebrating the Past … Teaming Toward the Future (IEEE Cat. No.03CH37492), 22–26 September 2003).
9. EEA, "Green Infrastructure (GI) – Enhancing Europe's Natural Capital," (2013), www.eea.europa.eu/policy-documents/green-infrastructure-gi-2014-enhancing.
10. I. M. Voskamp and F. H. M. Van de Ven, "Planning Support System for Climate Adaptation: Composing Effective Sets of Blue–Green Measures to Reduce Urban Vulnerability to Extreme Weather Events," *Building and Environment* 83 (2015), https://doi.org/10.1016/j.buildenv.2014.07.018.
11. Zahra Ghofrani, Victor Sposito, and Robert Faggian, "A Comprehensive Review of Blue–Green Infrastructure Concepts," *International Journal of Environment and Sustainability* 6 (2017), www.semanticscholar.org/paper/A-Comprehensive-Review-of-Blue-Green-Infrastructure-Ghofrani-Sposito/4052eb537c5edad387f889e247a1fade83bdf0be.
12. P. Newton *et al.*, *Decarbonising the Built Environment: Charting the Transition* (Singapore: Springer Nature Singapore, 2019). https://books.google.co.nz/books?id=c22cDwAAQBAJ.
13. Claudia Agudelo-Vera, "Dynamic Water Resource Management for Achieving Self-Sufficiency of Cities of Tomorrow," *BMC Public Health* (2012), https://repository.tudelft.nl/record/uuid:817c33c6-f716-44ca-bb17-80d20ef2100e.
14. R. E. de Graaf, "Innovations in Urban Water Management to Reduce the Vulnerability of Cities" (Delft University of Technology, 2009).

15. Zheng Wang *et al.*, "Analysis of the Water Demand–Supply Gap and Scarcity Index in Lower Amu Darya River Basin, Central Asia," *International Journal of Environmental Research and Public Health* 19, no. 2 (2022), https://doi.org/10.3390/ijerph19020743.
16. European Commission, "Report on the Review of the European Water Scarcity and Drought Policy," (2012), https://climate-adapt.eea.europa.eu/en/metadata/publications/report-on-the-review-of-the-european-water-scarcity-and-drought-policy.
17. Malin Falkenmark, Jan Lundqvist, and Carl Widstrand, "Macro-Scale Water Scarcity Requires Micro-Scale Approaches," *Natural Resources Forum* 13, no. 4 (1989), https://doi .org/10.1111/j.1477-8947.1989.tb00348.x.
18. D. W. Seckler and I. W. M. Institute, *World Water Demand and Supply, 1990 to 2025: Scenarios and Issues* (International Water Management Institute, 1998). https://books.google.co.nz/books?id=DIVFSmeL2OkC; J. Alcamo, T. Henrichs, and T. Rösch, "World Water in 2025 – Global Modelling and Scenario Analysis for the World Commission on Water for the 21st Century," (2000), www.env-edu.gr/Documents/World%20Water%20in%202025.pdf.
19. C. A. Sullivan, J. R. Meigh, and A. M. Giacomello, "The Water Poverty Index: Development and Application at the Community Scale," *Natural Resources Forum* 27, no. 3 (2003), https://doi.org/10.1111/1477-8947.00054.
20. UN, "Comprehensive Assessment of the Freshwater Resources of the World: Report of the Secretary-General," (1997), https://digitallibrary.un.org/record/231336?ln=en&v=pdf; Taikan Oki and Shinjiro Kanae, "Global Hydrological Cycles and World Water Resources," *Science* 313, no. 5790 (2006), https://doi.org/10.1126/science.1128845; H. H. G. Savenije, "Water Scarcity Indicators; the Deception of the Numbers," *Physics and Chemistry of the Earth*, Part B*: Hydrology, Oceans and Atmosphere* 25, no. 3 (2000), https://doi.org/10.1016/S1464-1909(00)00004-6; Zhao Zeng, Junguo Liu, and Hubert H. G. Savenije, "A Simple Approach to Assess Water Scarcity Integrating Water Quantity and Quality," *Ecological Indicators* 34 (2013), https://doi.org/10.1016/j.ecolind.2013.06.012; María Pedro-Monzonís *et al.*, "A Review of Water Scarcity and Drought Indexes in Water Resources Planning and Management," *Journal of Hydrology* 527 (2015), https://doi.org/10.1016/j.jhydrol.2015.05.003; Weijing Ma, Christian Opp, and Dewei Yang, "Spatiotemporal Supply–Demand Characteristics and Economic Benefits of Crop Water Footprint in the Semi-Arid Region," *Science of The Total Environment* 738 (2020), https://doi.org/10.1016/j.scitotenv.2020.139502.
21. Ying Guo and Yanjun Shen, "Agricultural Water Supply/Demand Changes under Projected Future Climate Change in the Arid Region of Northwestern China," *Journal of Hydrology* 540 (22016), https://doi.org/10.1016/j.jhydrol.2016.06.033.
22. Ministry of Transport *et al.*, *A Different Approach to Water: Water Management Policy in the 21st Century: Cabinet's Position* (The Hague: Ministry of Transport, Public Works and Water Management, 2000), https://books.google.co.nz/books?id=6J940AEACAAJ.
23. Nanco Dolman and R. J. Brolsma, "Groenblauwe Maatregelen en Nature-Based Solutions voor de Waterrobuuste en Klimaatbestendige Stad (Water Governance 01/2023 – Kwaliteit van Bestuur)," (2023).
24. Dolman and Ogunyoye, "How Water Challenges Can Shape Tomorrow's Cities"; Xiu-Juan Qiao *et al.*, "Governance Factors of Sustainable Stormwater Management: A Study of Case Cities in China and Sweden," *Journal of Environmental Management* 248 (2019), https://doi .org/10.1016/j.jenvman.2019.07.020.
25. Wong and Brown, "Transitioning to Water Sensitive Cities."; ADB, "Asian Water Development Outlook 2016: Strengthening Water Security in Asia and the Pacific," (2016), www.adb.org/sites/default/files/publication/189411/awdo-2016.pdf.
26. Dolman and Ogunyoye, "How Water Challenges Can Shape Tomorrow's Cities."
27. R. de Graaf and F. Hooimeijer, *Urban Water in Japan* (London: Taylor & Francis, 2008), https://books.google.co.nz/books?id=Fl0yjHGXQEgC.
28. "Aqueduct Projected Water Stress Country Rankings," (2015), www.wri.org/data/aqueduct-projected-water-stress-country-rankings.
29. PUB, "Our Water, Our Future," (2016), www.jkgeography.com/uploads/1/0/8/4/108433405/singapore_-_our_water_our_future.pdf.
30. PUB, "Our Water, Our Future."

31. "Singapore's Water Loop," (2024), www.pub.gov.sg/public/waterloop.
32. Qiao *et al.*, "Governance Factors of Sustainable Stormwater Management."
33. West 8 and RHDHV, *Solicitation for Concept Design Schemes of Public Space of the Ecological Flood Control Levee around the Starting Area in Xiong'an New District (Hebei Province, China), Vol. 8* (Rotterdam, the Netherlands: West 8, 2018).
34. West 8 and RHDHV, *Solicitation for Concept Design Schemes of Public Space.*
35. "The Sponge Revolution," (2021), www.thewirechina.com/2021/07/18/the-sponge-revolution/.
36. Deltares, *Low River Discharge of the Meuse – A Meuse River Basin Water Management Modelling Study Using RIBASIM* (Rotterdam, the Netherlands: RIWA Meuse publication, 2022).
37. Municipality of Rotterdam, "Rotterdam Weather Wise Program," (2019), https://rotterdamsweerwoord.nl/content/uploads/2023/06/RWW_Programmakader-2030_ENG.pdf.
38. Municipality of Rotterdam, *Implementation Agenda Weather Wise 2023–2026* (Rotterdam, the Netherlands, 2023).
39. Florian Boer, Eric-Jan Pleijster, and Nanco Dolman, *Rotterdam, from a Port City to a Port Archipelago + Sponge Water City – Redesigning Deltas Design Study* (Delft, the Netherlands: Delft University of Technology, 2022), http://dx.doi.org/10.13140/RG.2.2.28597.76002.
40. De Urbanisten, *Redesigning Deltas Design Study "Rotterdam, from a Port City to a Port Archipelago + Sponge Water City,"* Delft University of Technology (Delft, the Netherlands, 2022).
41. De Urbanisten, *Redesigning Deltas Design Study "Rotterdam, from a Port City to a Port Archipelago + Sponge Water City."*
42. M. Hillen and N. Dolman, "Towards Water Adaptive Cities" (World Engineers Summit on Climate Change (WES), Singapore, 2015).
43. Nanco Dolman, "Integration of Water Management and Urban Design for Climate Resilient Cities," (2021).
44. UN-Water/WWAP (World Water Assessment Programme), "Nature-Based Solutions for Water," (2018), www.unwater.org/publications/world-water-development-report-2018.
45. S. P. Tjallingii, *Ecological Conditions: Strategies and Structures in Environmental Planning* (Wageningen: DLO Institute for Forestry and Nature Research (IBN-DLO), 1996), https://books.google.co.nz/books?id=ul7bAAAACAAJ.

7 Renewable Energy and Energy Efficiency in Circular Economy Liveable Cities

1. European Commission, *The European Green Deal* (COM(2019) 640 final) (Brussels: European Commission, 2019), https://eur-lex.europa.eu/legal-content/EN/TXT/?uri=CELEX%3A52019DC0640.
2. K. Bolger and A. Doyon, "Circular Cities: Exploring Local Government Strategies to Facilitate a Circular Economy," *European Planning Studies* 27:11 (2019): 2184–2205, https://doi.org/10.1080/09654313.2019.1642854.
3. Williams, "Circular Cities."
4. T. Santonen *et al.*, "Cities as Living Labs: Increasing the Impact of Investment in the Circular Economy for Sustainable Cities," (2017), www.theseus.fi/handle/10024/138868; A. Gravagnuolo, A. Mariarosaria, and F. G. Luigi, "Circular Economy Strategies in Eight Historic Port Cities: Criteria and Indicators Towards a Circular City Assessment Framework," *Sustainability*, 11, no. 13 (2019): 3512, https://doi.org/10.3390/su11133512.
5. P. Ghisellini, C. Cialani, and S. Ulgiati, A Review on Circular Economy: The Expected Transition to a Balanced Interplay of Environmental and Economic Systems, *Journal of Cleaner Production* 114 (2016): 11–32, https://doi.org/10.1016/j.jclepro.2015.09.007; A. Murray, K. Skene, and K. Haynes, "The Circular Economy: An Interdisciplinary Exploration of the Concept and Application in a Global Context," *Journal of Business Ethics* 140 (2017): 369–80, https://doi.org/10.1007/s10551-015-2693-2.
6. T. Shevchenko *et al.*, "Consumer Behavior in the Circular Economy: Developing a Product-Centric Framework," *Journal of Cleaner Production* 384, (2023), https://doi.org/10.1016/j.jclepro.2022.135568.

7. Murray, Skene, and Haynes, "The Circular Economy."
8. European Commission, "A New Circular Economy Action Plan for a Cleaner and More Competitive Europe," COM/2020/98 final (2020).
9. World Health Organization Regional Office for Europe, "Circular Economy and Health: Opportunities and Risks," (2018), https://apps.who.int/iris/handle/10665/342218.
10. Carrara *et al.*, *Supply Chain Analysis and Material Demand Forecast in Strategic Technologies and Sectors in the EU – A Foresight Study*, JRC132889 (Luxembourg: Publications Office of the European Union 2023), https://doi.org.10.2760/334074.
11. J. Potting *et al.*, "Circular Economy: Measuring Innovation in Product Chains," The Hague: PBL Netherlands Environmental Assessment Agency (2017), www.pbl.nl/sites/default/files/downloads/pbl-2016-circular-economy-measuring-innovation-in-product-chains-2544.pdf.
12. Bolger and Doyon, "Circular Cities."
13. Williams, "Circular Cities."
14. United Nations Department of Economic and Social Affairs, "World Populations Prospects: Summary of Results," (2022), www.un.org/development/desa/pd/sites/www.un.org.development.desa.pd/files/wpp2022_summary_of_results.pdf.
15. Petit-Boix and Leipold, "Circular Economy in Cities."
16. Prendeville, Cherim, and Bocken, "Circular Cities: Mapping Six Cities in Transition."
17. Circle Economy, "Circular Amsterdam: A Vision and Action Agenda for the City and Metropolitan Area," (2016), www.circle-economy.com/resources/developing-a-roadmap-for-the-first-circular-city-amsterdam.
18. City of Amsterdam, "Circular Innovation Programme 2016–2018" (in Dutch) (2016), www.circle-economy.com/resources/developing-a-roadmap-for-the-first-circular-city-amsterdam.
19. K. Raworth, *Doughnut Economics: Seven Ways to Think Like a Twenty-First-Century Economist* (White River Junction, VT: Chelsea Green Publishing, 2017).
20. M. Kottari, "Amsterdam's Pathway to Climate Neutrality: Creating an Enabling Environment," in R. Brears (ed.), *The Palgrave Encyclopedia of Urban and Regional Futures* (Cham: Palgrave Macmillan, 2021), https://doi.org/10.1007/978-3-030-51812-7_209-1.
21. City of Amsterdam, "Amsterdam Circular 2020–2025 Strategy," (2020), https://assets.amsterdam.nl/publish/pages/867635/amsterdam-circular-2020-2025_strategy.pdf.
22. City of Amsterdam, "Amsterdam Circular Monitor," (2020b), https://onderzoek.amsterdam.nl/publicatie/the-circular-economy-monitor-an-outline.
23. Kottari, "Amsterdam's Pathway to Climate Neutrality."
24. Potting *et al.*, "Circular Economy: Measuring Innovation in Product Chains."
25. IEA, "Empowering Cities for a Net Zero Future," (2021), www.iea.org/reports/empowering-cities-for-a-net-zero-future.
26. R. Mishra *et al.*, "Circular Economy Principles in Community Energy Initiatives through Stakeholder Perspectives," *Sustainable Production and Consumption* 33 (2022): 256–70, https://doi.org/10.1016/j.spc.2022.07.001.
27. European Commission, "A New Circular Economy Action Plan for a Cleaner and More Competitive Europe."
28. "Urban Innovative Actions (UIA)," (n.d.), Leidal Intermunicipal Association, https://uia-initiative.eu/en/uia-cities/leiedal-intermunicipal-association.
29. T. Meister *et al.*, "How Municipalities Support Energy Cooperatives: Survey Results from Germany and Switzerland," *Energy, Sustainability and Society* 10 (2020):18, https://doi.org/10.1186/s13705-020-00248-3.
30. C. Wortmann *et al.*, "Analysis of Electric Moped Scooter Sharing in Berlin: A Technical, Economic and Environmental Perspective," *World Electric Vehicle Journal* 12, no. 3 (2021): 96, https://doi.org/10.3390/wevj12030096.
31. Nora Schelte *et al.*, "Life Cycle Assessment on Electric Moped Scooter Sharing," *Sustainability* 13, no. 15 (2021): 8297, https://doi.org/10.3390/su13158297.
32. T. Joensuu, H. Edelman, and A Saari, "Circular Economy Practices in the Built Environment," *Journal of Cleaner Production* 276 (2020), https://doi.org/10.1016/j.jclepro.2020.124215.
33. F. Krausmann *et al.*, "Global Socioeconomic Material Stocks Rise 23-Fold over the 20th Century and Require Half of Annual Resource Use," *PNAS* 114, no.8 (2017), https://doi.org/10.1073/pnas.1613773114.

34. K. Hara *et al.*, "Energy Intensity Trends and Scenarios for China's Industrial Sectors: A Regional Case Study," *Sustainability Science* 6 (2011): 123–34, https://doi.org/10.1007/s11625-010-0125-x.
35. M. R. Esa, A. Halog, and L. Rigamonti, "Developing Strategies for Managing Construction and Demolition Wastes in Malaysia Based on the Concept of Circular Economy," *Journal of Material Cycles and Waste Management* 19 (2017): 1144–54, https://doi.org/10.1007/s10163-016-0516-x.
36. Esa, Halog, and Rigamonti, "Developing Strategies for Managing Construction and Demolition Wastes in Malaysia."
37. B. C. Renger, J. L. Birkeland, and D. J. Midmore, "Net-Positive Building Carbon Sequestration," *Building Research and Information* 43, no. 1 (2015): 11–24, https://doi.org/10.1080/09613218.2015.961001.
38. A. Barragán-Escandón, J. Terrados-Cepeda, and E. Zalamea-León, "The Role of Renewable Energy in the Promotion of Circular Urban Metabolism," *Sustainability* 9 (2017): 2341, https://doi.org/10.3390/su9122341.
39. C.-L. Lin *et al.*, "Assessing the Anthropogenic Carbon Emission of Wooden Construction: An LCA Study," *Building Research & Information*,51, no. 2 (2023): 138–57, https://doi.org/10.1080/09613218.2022.2087171.
40. D. Zhou, C. Y. Zhao, and Y. Tian, "Review on Thermal Energy Storage with Phase Change Materials (PCMs) in Building Applications," *Applied Energy* 92 (2012): 593–605, https://doi.org/10.1016/j.apenergy.2011.08.025.
41. Joensuu, Edelman, and Saari, "Circular Economy Practices in the Built Environment."
42. European Court of Auditors (ECA), "Transition to Circular Economy behind Schedule in EU Countries: Special Report," (2023), www.eca.europa.eu/ECAPublications/SR-2023-17/SR-2023-17_EN.pdf.
43. Joensuu, Edelman, and Saari, "Circular Economy Practices in the Built Environment."

8 Urban Nature-Based Solutions to Create Circular and Liveable Cities

1. Brears, *Nature-Based Solutions to 21st Century Challenges*; Brears, *Blue and Green Cities: The Role of Blue–Green Infrastructure in Managing Urban Water Resources*.
2. Brears, *Nature-Based Solutions to 21st Century Challenges*.
3. BRANZ, "BU533 Green Roofs – An Overview," (2011). www.branz.co.nz/pubs/bulletins/bu533/; "Green Roof Types," (2023), https://greenrooftechnology.com/green-roof-finder/green-roof-types/; Muhammad Shafique, Xiaowei Luo, and Jian Zuo, "Photovoltaic-Green roofs: A Review of Benefits, Limitations, and Trends," *Solar Energy* 202 (2020), https://doi.org/10.1016/j.solener.2020.02.101; "Blue Green Roofs," (2023), https://greenrooftechnology.com/green-roof-finder/blue_green-roofs/.
4. "Apply for a Climate Adaptation Subsidy (for Rainwater Harvesting)," (2023), www.denhaag.nl/en/subsidies/apply-for-a-climate-adaptation-subsidy-for-rainwater-harvesting-.htm.
5. Adel Samy El Menshawy, Abdelaziz Farouk Mohamed, and Nayera Mahmoud Fathy, "A Comparative Study on Green Wall Construction Systems, Case Study: South Valley Campus of AASTMT," *Case Studies in Construction Materials* 16 (2022), https://doi.org/10.1016/j.cscm.2021.e00808; "The Amazing Benefits of Green Walls, Roofs and Facades," (2023), https://citygreen.com/benefits-of-green-roofs-walls-and-facades/; Elena Montacchini *et al.*, "Green Walls as Nature-Based Solutions for Urban and Building Resilience: A Case Study," (2019), www.sustainablemediterraneanconstruction.eu/en/rivista/2019-09/2019-09-132/.
6. "Subsidies for Heritage Work, Party Walls and Green Rooftops," (2023), https://ajuntament.barcelona.cat/ciutatpatrimoni/en/news/subsidies-for-heritage-work-party-walls-and-green-rooftops-1279009.
7. Ines Cabral *et al.*, "Urban Gardens as Multifunctional Nature-Based Solutions for Societal Goals in a Changing Climate," in *Nature-Based Solutions to Climate Change Adaptation in Urban Areas: Linkages between Science, Policy and Practice*, ed. Nadja Kabisch *et al.* (Cham: Springer International Publishing, 2017); "How to Organize a Community Garden," (2023),

https://content.ces.ncsu.edu/how-to-organize-a-community-garden#:~:text=Types%20of%20Community%20Gardens%201%20Plot%20Gardens%20%28divide,Entrepreneurial%20Market%20Gardens%20%28sell%20produce%29%205%20Therapeutic%20Gardens.

8. "Cultivating Community Gardens Grants Guidelines," (2023), www.brisbane.qld.gov.au/community-and-safety/grants-awards-and-sponsorships/environment-and-sustainability-grants/cultivating-community-gardens-grants/guidelines.
9. "Evaluating the Potential Benefits of Permeable Pavement on the Quantity and Quality of Stormwater Runoff," (2019), www.usgs.gov/centers/upper-midwest-water-science-center/science/evaluating-potential-benefits-permeable-pavement; "Permeable Pavement: The Pros and Cons You Need to Know," (2023), https://greenblue.com/na/permeable-pavement-the-pros-and-cons-you-need-to-know/.
10. "Case Study: City of Atlanta Permeable Paver Retrofit," (2023), www.belgardcommercial.com/case_studies/case_study_city_of_atlanta_permeable_paver_retrofit#.
11. Christchurch City Council, "Rain Garden Design, Construction and Maintenance Manual," (2016), https://ccc.govt.nz/assets/Documents/Environment/Water/Rain-garden-design-construction-and-maintenance-manual.pdf; US EPA, "Stormwater Best Management Practice Bioretention (Rain Gardens)," (2021), www.epa.gov/system/files/documents/2021-11/bmp-bioretention-rain-gardens.pdf.
12. "Be RainWise," (2023), https://kingcounty.gov/services/environment/wastewater/cso/rainwise.aspx.
13. "Rain Gardens and Bioswales," (2023), https://extension.usu.edu/laep/research/nontraditional; "Bioswale vs Rain Garden," (2022), https://engineeringtraininginstitute.com/bioswale-vs-rain-garden/; "Bioswales," (2023), www.crd.bc.ca/education/stormwater-wastewater-septic/green-stormwater-infrastructure/bioswales; Sujit A. Ekka *et al.*, "Next Generation Swale Design for Stormwater Runoff Treatment: A Comprehensive Approach," *Journal of Environmental Management* 279 (2021), https://doi.org/10.1016/j.jenvman.2020.111756.
14. "DEP Unveils New Green Infrastructure Installations in Brooklyn," (2011), www.nyc.gov/html/dep/html/press_releases/11-99pr.shtml#:~:text=The%20bioswales%20are%20part%20of%20the%20NYC%20Green,stormwater%20runoff%20before%20it%20enters%20the%20sewer%20system.
15. Brears, *Nature-Based Solutions to 21st Century Challenges.*
16. "Green Infrastructure," (2023), www.nycgovparks.org/greening/green-infrastructure.
17. Brears, *Nature-Based Solutions to 21st Century Challenges.*
18. "Green Streets Projects," (2023), www.toronto.ca/services-payments/streets-parking-transportation/enhancing-our-streets-and-public-realm/green-streets/green-streets-projects/.
19. Brears, *Blue and Green Cities: The Role of Blue–Green Infrastructure in Managing Urban Water Resources.*
20. "Sydney Park Wetlands: Major Works, Creation and History," (2023), www.cityofsydney.nsw.gov.au/improving-streets-public-spaces/sydney-park-wetlands-major-works-creation-and-history.
21. Brears, *Nature-Based Solutions to 21st Century Challenges.*
22. "Vancouver's Urban Forest," (2023), https://vancouver.ca/parks-recreation-culture/urban-forest-strategy.aspx#redirect.
23. Brears, *Nature-Based Solutions to 21st Century Challenges.*
24. "Medellín Shows How Nature-Based Solutions Can Keep People and Planet Cool," (2019), www.unep.org/news-and-stories/story/medellin-shows-how-nature-based-solutions-can-keep-people-and-planet-cool.

9 Environmental Justice, Circular Economies, and Green Living

1. L. Sun, J. Du, and Y. Li, "A New Method for Dividing the Scopes and Priorities of Air Pollution Control Based on Environmental Justice," *Environmental Science and Pollution Research* 28, no. 10 (2021), 12859, https://doi.org/10.1007/s11356-020-11160-w.
2. Harold Rickenbacker, Fred Brown, and Melissa Bilec, "Creating Environmental Consciousness in Underserved Communities: Implementation and Outcomes of Community-Based

Environmental Justice and Air Pollution Research," *Sustainable Cities and Society* 47 (2019), https://doi.org/10.1016/j.scs.2019.101473.

3. Rickenbacker, Brown, and Bilec, "Creating Environmental Consciousness in Underserved Communities."
4. Rickenbacker, Brown, and Bilec, "Creating Environmental Consciousness in Underserved Communities."
5. Sara Grineski, Bob Bolin, and Christopher Boone, "Criteria Air Pollution and Marginalized Populations: Environmental Inequity in Metropolitan Phoenix, Arizona," *Social Science Quarterly* 88, no. 2 (2007), https://doi.org/10.1111/j.1540-6237.2007.00470.x.
6. A. L. DeMarco *et al.*, "Air Pollution-Related Health Impacts on Individuals Experiencing Homelessness: Environmental Justice and Health Vulnerability in Salt Lake County, Utah," *International Journal of Environmental Research and Public Health* 17, no. 22 (2020), https://doi.org/10.3390/ijerph17228413.
7. Thomas Verbeek, "Unequal Residential Exposure to Air Pollution and Noise: A Geospatial Environmental Justice Analysis for Ghent, Belgium," *SSM – Population Health* 7 (2019), https://doi.org/10.1016/j.ssmph.2018.100340.
8. Henry W. Wyes, "Hazardous Waste: Its Impact on Human Health in Europe," *Toxicology and Industrial Health* 13, no. 2–3 (1997), https://doi.org/10.1177/074823379701300202.
9. Mikael Höök and Xu Tang, "Depletion of Fossil Fuels and Anthropogenic Climate Change – A Review," *Energy Policy* 52 (2013), https://doi.org/10.1016/j.enpol.2012.10.046.
10. Höök and Tang, "Depletion of Fossil Fuels and Anthropogenic Climate Change – A Review."
11. "Fossil Fuels: The Dirty Facts," (2022), www.nrdc.org/stories/fossil-fuels-dirty-facts#sec-whatis.
12. EESI, "Fossil Fuels," (2024), www.eesi.org/topics/fossil-fuels/description#:~:text=Fossil%20fuels—including%20coal%2C%20oil,were%20compressed%20and%20heated%20underground.
13. "Fossil Fuels: The Dirty Facts."
14. Our World in Data, "Fossil Fuels," (2024), https://ourworldindata.org/fossil-fuels#citation.
15. "Fossil," (2024), www.energy.gov/fossil.
16. "Fossil Fuels: The Dirty Facts."
17. "Fossil Fuels: The Dirty Facts."
18. Sun, Du, and Li, "A New Method for Dividing the Scopes and Priorities of Air Pollution Control Based on Environmental Justice."
19. D. Warner North, "Introduction to Special Issue on Air Pollution Health Risks," *Risk Analysis* 36, no. 9 (2016), https://doi.org/10.1111/risa.12707.
20. P. Hunter, "The Health Toll of Air Pollution: Despite Global Efforts to Clean Up the Air, Outdoor and Indoor Air Pollution Still Have a Drastic Negative Effect on Public Health," *EMBO Reports* 21, no. 8 (2020), https://doi.org/10.15252/embr.202051183.
21. North, "Introduction to Special Issue on Air Pollution Health Risks"; F. Forastiere *et al.*, "Health Impact Assessment of Waste Management Facilities in Three European Countries," *Environmental Health* 10 (2011), https://doi.org/10.1186/1476-069x-10-53; Our World in Data, "Fossil Fuels"; J. Jason West *et al.*, "What We Breathe Impacts Our Health: Improving Understanding of the Link between Air Pollution and Health," *Environmental Science & Technology* 50, no. 10 (2016), https://doi.org/10.1021/acs.est.5b03827.
22. DeMarco *et al.*, "Air Pollution-Related Health Impacts on Individuals Experiencing Homelessness."
23. Hunter, "The Health Toll of Air Pollution"; West *et al.*, "What We Breathe Impacts Our Health."
24. Hunter, "The Health Toll of Air Pollution"; Sun, Du, and Li, "A New Method for Dividing the Scopes and Priorities of Air Pollution Control Based on Environmental Justice."
25. M. L. Miranda *et al.*, "Making the Environmental Justice Grade: The Relative Burden of Air Pollution Exposure in the United States," *International Journal of Environmental Research and Public Health* 8, no. 6 (2011), https://doi.org/10.3390/ijerph8061755; X. Morelli *et al.*, "Which Decreases in Air Pollution Should be Targeted to Bring Health and Economic Benefits and Improve Environmental Justice?" *Environment International* 129 (2019), https://doi.org/10.1016/j.envint.2019.04.077; Verbeek, "Unequal Residential Exposure to Air Pollution and Noise."

26. Miranda *et al.*, "Making the Environmental Justice Grade."
27. North, "Introduction to Special Issue on Air Pollution Health Risks."
28. West *et al.*, "What We Breathe Impacts Our Health."
29. J. Zhao, L. Gladson, and K. Cromar, "A Novel Environmental Justice Indicator for Managing Local Air Pollution," *International Journal of Environmental Research and Public Health* 15, no. 6 (2018), https://doi.org/10.3390/ijerph15061260.
30. Clair Bullock, Kerry Ard, and Grace Saalman, "Measuring the Relationship between State Environmental Justice Action and Air Pollution Inequality, 1990–2009," *Review of Policy Research* 35, no. 3 (2018), https://doi.org/10.1111/ropr.12292.
31. Bullock, Ard, and Saalman, "Measuring the Relationship between State Environmental Justice Action and Air Pollution Inequality, 1990–2009."
32. D. A. Sarigiannis, "Assessing the Empact of Hazardous Waste on Children's Health: The Exposome Paradigm," *Environmental Research* 158 (2017), https://doi.org/10.1016/j.envres.2017.06.031.
33. Anna K. Harding and Marsha L. Greer, "The Health Impact of Hazardous Waste Sites on Minority Communities: Implications for Public Health and Environmental Health Professionals," *Journal of Environmental Health* 55, no. 7 (1993), www.jstor.org/stable/44535497.
34. L. Fazzo *et al.*, "Hazardous Waste and Health Impact: A Systematic Review of the Scientific Literature," *Environmental Health* 16, no. 1 (2017), https://doi.org/10.1186/s12940-017-0311-8.
35. Harding and Greer, "The Health Impact of Hazardous Waste Sites on Minority Communities."
36. Forastiere *et al.*, "Health Impact Assessment of Waste Management Facilities in Three European Countries"; P. Elliott *et al.*, "Risk of Adverse Birth Outcomes in Populations Living Near Landfill Sites," *BMJ* 323, no. 7309 (2001), https://doi.org/10.1136/bmj.323.7309.363.
37. Barry L. Johnson, "Hazardous Waste: Human Health Effects," *Toxicology and Industrial Health* 13, no. 2–3 (1997), https://doi.org/10.1177/074823379701300203.
38. Rickenbacker, Brown, and Bilec, "Creating Environmental Consciousness in Underserved Communities."
39. Magdi R. I. Soliman *et al.*, "Hazardous Wastes, Hazardous Materials and Environmental Health Inequity," *Toxicology and Industrial Health* 9, no. 5 (1993), https://doi.org/10.1177/074823379300900511.
40. Harding and Greer, "The Health Impact of Hazardous Waste Sites on Minority Communities."
41. Dieter Helm, "The Future of Fossil Fuels – Is It the End?" *Oxford Review of Economic Policy* 32, no. 2 (2016), www.jstor.org/stable/26363162.
42. Hunter, "The Health Toll of Air Pollution."
43. "Fossil Fuels: The Dirty Facts."
44. "Fossil Fuels: The Dirty Facts."
45. "Fossil Fuels: The Dirty Facts."
46. Höök and Tang, "Depletion of Fossil Fuels and Anthropogenic Climate Change – A Review."
47. John Kotcher, Edward Maibach, and Wen-Tsing Choi, "Fossil Fuels Are Harming Our Brains: Identifying Key Messages about the Health Effects of Air Pollution from Fossil Fuels," *BMC Public Health* 19, no. 1 (2019), https://doi.org/10.1186/s12889-019-7373-1.
48. EESI, "Fossil Fuels."
49. "Fossil Fuels: The Dirty Facts."
50. DeMarco *et al.*, "Air Pollution-Related Health Impacts on Individuals Experiencing Homelessness."
51. North, "Introduction to Special Issue on Air Pollution Health Risks."
52. Kotcher, Maibach, and Choi, "Fossil Fuels Are Harming Our Brains."
53. C. M. Anderson *et al.*, "Climate Change Mitigation, Air Pollution, and Environmental Justice in California," *Environmental Science and Technology* 52, no. 18 (2018), https://doi.org/10.1021/acs.est.8b00908.
54. Anna Rita Germani, Piergiuseppe Morone, and Giuseppina Testa, "Environmental Justice and Air Pollution: A Case Study on Italian Provinces," *Ecological Economics* 106 (2014), https://doi.org/10.1016/j.ecolecon.2014.07.010.
55. Zhao, Gladson, and Cromar, "A Novel Environmental Justice Indicator for Managing Local Air Pollution."

56. Martin Geissdoerfer *et al.*, "The Circular Economy – A New Sustainability Paradigm?" *Journal of Cleaner Production* 143 (2017), https://doi.org/10.1016/j.jclepro.2016.12.048.
57. Geissdoerfer *et al.*, "The Circular Economy – A New Sustainability Paradigm?"
58. Geissdoerfer *et al.*, "The Circular Economy – A New Sustainability Paradigm?"
59. Jouni Korhonen, Antero Honkasalo, and Jyri Seppälä, "Circular Economy: The Concept and Its Limitations," *Ecological Economics* 143 (2018), https://doi.org/10.1016/j.ecolecon.2017.06.041.
60. Korhonen, Honkasalo, and Seppälä, "Circular Economy: The Concept and Its Limitations."
61. Julian Kirchherr *et al.*, "Barriers to the Circular Economy: Evidence from the European Union (EU)," *Ecological Economics* 150 (2018), https://doi.org/10.1016/j.ecolecon.2018.04.028.
62. Geissdoerfer *et al.*, "The Circular Economy – A New Sustainability Paradigm?"
63. Kirchherr *et al.*, "Barriers to the Circular Economy: Evidence from the European Union (EU)."
64. Yuliya Kalmykova, Madumita Sadagopan, and Leonardo Rosado, "Circular Economy – From Review of Theories and Practices to Development of Implementation Tools," *Resources, Conservation and Recycling* 135 (2018), https://doi.org/10.1016/j.resconrec.2017.10.034.
65. Purva Mhatre *et al.*, "A Systematic Literature Review on the Circular Economy Initiatives in the European Union," *Sustainable Production and Consumption* 26 (2021), https://doi.org/10.1016/j.spc.2020.09.008.
66. J. Williams, *Circular Cities: A Revolution in Urban Sustainability* (London: Taylor & Francis, 2021). https://books.google.co.nz/books?id=JcMfEAAAQBAJ.
67. A. A. Rashid, "Doughnut Economics: A Roadmap for a Thriving Sustainable City," (2020). www.academia.edu/44910863/DOUGHNUT_ECONOMICS_A_ROADMAP_FOR_A_THRIVING_SUSTAINABLE_CITY.
68. WHO, "Circular Economy and Health: Opportunities and Risks," (2018), https://apps.who.int/iris/bitstream/handle/10665/342218/9789289053341-eng.pdf?sequence=1.
69. WHO, "Circular Economy and Health: Opportunities and Risks."
70. Montira J. Pongsiri *et al.*, "The Need for a Systems Approach to Planetary Health," *The Lancet Planetary Health* 1, no. 7 (2017), https://doi.org/10.1016/S2542-5196(17)30116-X.
71. "Policy: Circular Economy," (2024), www.amsterdam.nl/en/policy/sustainability/circular-economy/.
72. L. Aleksandrowicz *et al.*, "The Impacts of Dietary Change on Greenhouse Gas Emissions, Land Use, Water Use, and Health: A Systematic Review," *PLoS One* 11, no. 11 (2016), https://doi.org/10.1371/journal.pone.0165797.
73. Circle Economy, "The Amsterdam City Doughnut: A Tool for Transformative Action," (2020). www.circle-economy.com/resources/the-amsterdam-city-doughnut-a-tool-for-transformative-action.
74. Pongsiri *et al.*, "The Need for a Systems Approach to Planetary Health."
75. Wojciech Kębłowski, Deborah Lambert, and David Bassens, "Circular Economy and the City: An Urban Political Economy Agenda," *Culture and Organization* 26, no. 2 (2020), https://doi.org/10.1080/14759551.2020.1718148.
76. Anna Golebiowska *et al.*, "The Post-Pandemic Development of the Green Circular Economy and the Declarations Made during the UN Climate Change Conference (COP26) as Security Determinant," *European Research Studies Journal* XXIV, no. 4B (2021).
77. Glasgow City Council, "Circular Economy Route Map for Glasgow," (2020), www.glasgow.gov.uk/article/2392/Circular-Economy.
78. Glasgow City Council, "Resource and Recycling Strategy 2020–2030," (2020), www.glasgow.gov.uk/article/5731/Resource-and-Recycling-Strategy-2020-30.
79. OECD, "The Circular Economy in Glasgow, United Kingdom," (2021), www.oecd-ilibrary.org/urban-rural-and-regional-development/the-circular-economy-in-glasgow-united-kingdom_7717a310-en.
80. Peter Jones and Daphne Comfort, "Winning Hearts and Minds: A Commentary on Circular Cities," *Journal of Public Affairs* 18, no. 4 (2018), https://doi.org/10.1002/pa.1726.
81. OECD, "The Circular Economy in Glasgow, United Kingdom"; Iuliana Mădălina Lică, "Cities Going Circular: Glasgow's Approach to the Circular Economy Model," *Oeconomica* 3, no. 19 (2019).

10 Circular Economy as a Pathway to City Resilience and Sustainability

1. United Nations Department for Economic and Social Affairs (UN DESA), "World Urbanization Prospects 2018."
2. World Bank and International Monetary Fund, *Global Monitoring Report 2013: Rural–Urban Dynamics and the Millennium Development Goals* (Washington, DC: World Bank and IMF, 2013), https://documents.worldbank.org//en/publication/documents-reports/documentdetail/720451468171242999.
3. United Nations Environment Program, (UNEP), *City-Level Decoupling: Urban Resource Flows and the Governance of Infrastructure Transitions* (Nairobi, Kenya: UNEP, 2013). www.unep.org/resources/report/city-level-decoupling-urban-resource-flows-and-governance-infrastructure.
4. Silpa Kaza *et al.*, *What a Waste 2.0: A Global Snapshot of Solid Waste Management to 2050. Urban Development* (Washington, DC: World Bank, 2018), https://openknowledge.worldbank.org/handle/10986/30317.
5. United Nations Framework Convention on Climate Change (UNFCCC), *Nationally Determined Contributions under the Paris Agreement Synthesis Report by the Secretariat* (New York: UNFCCC, 2021), https://unfccc.int/sites/default/files/resource/cma2021_08E.pdf.
6. UNFCCC and Antonio Guterres, "Cities Are Where the Climate Battle Will Be Largely Won or Lost," *UN Climate Change News*, 11 October 2019, https://unfccc.int/news/guterres-cities-are-where-the-climate-battle-will-largely-be-won-or-lost.
7. Ellen MacArthur Foundation, "Growth Within: A Circular Economy Vision for a Competitive Europe"; OECD, *Policy Guidance on Resource Efficiency* (Paris: OECD Publishing, 2016), http://dx.doi.org/10.1787/9789264257344-en.
8. Jouni Korhonen, Antero Honkasalo, and Jyri Seppälä, "Circular Economy: The Concept and Its Limitations," *Ecological Economics* 143, no. 1 (2018), https://doi.org/10.1016/j.ecolecon.2017.06.041.
9. Murillo Vetroni Barros *et al.*, "Circular Economy as a Driver to Sustainable Businesses," *Cleaner Environmental Systems* 2, no. 2 (2020), https://doi.org/10.1016/j.cesys.2020.100006.
10. Kieran Campbell-Johnston *et al.*, "City Level Circular Transitions: Barriers and Limits in Amsterdam, Utrecht and the Hague," *Journal of Cleaner Production* 235 (2019), https://doi.org/10.1016/j.jclepro.2019.06.106.
11. Julian Kirchherr, Denise Reike, and Marko Hekkert, "Conceptualizing the Circular Economy: An Analysis of 114 Definitions," *Resources, Conservation and Recycling* 127, no. 0921–3449 (2017), 224.
12. Kirchherr, Reike, and Hekkert, "Conceptualizing the Circular Economy: An Analysis of 114 Definitions."
13. Korhonen *et al.*, "Circular Economy: The Concept and Its Limitations."
14. MacArthur, "Towards the Circular Economy"; Ellen MacArthur Foundation *Towards the Circular Economy Vol. 1* (London, UK: Ellen MacArthur Foundation, 2013), www.ellenmacarthurfoundation.org/towards-the-circular-economy-vol-1-an-economic-and-business-rationale-for-an.
15. Piyush Dhawan and Janpeter Beckmann, *Circular Economy Guidebook for Cities.* (Wuppertal, Germany: The Collaborating Centre on Sustainable Consumption and Production (CSCP), 2019) www.cscp.org/publications/ce-guidebook-cities/.
16. Kirchherr, Reike, and Hekkert, "Conceptualizing the Circular Economy: An Analysis of 114 Definitions."
17. Judith Rodin, *The Resilience Dividend: Managing Disruption, Avoiding Disaster, and Growing Stronger in an Unpredictable World* (London: Profile Books, 2015); World Bank Group, *Investing in Urban Resilience: Protecting and Promoting Development in a Changing World* (Washington, DC: World Bank Group, 2016), https://openknowledge.worldbank.org/handle/10986/25219.
18. Michael Spence, Patricia Clarke Annez, and Robert M. Buckley, *Planning, Connecting, and Financing Cities – Now: Priorities for City Leaders* (Washington, DC: World Bank, 2013), https://openknowledge.worldbank.org/handle/10986/12238.

19. World Bank and International Monetary Fund, *Global Monitoring Report 2013: Rural–Urban Dynamics and the Millennium Development Goals.*
20. Peter Ellis and Mark Roberts, *Leveraging Urbanization in South Asia: Managing Spatial Transformation for Prosperity and Livability* (Washington, DC: World Bank, 2015), https://doi.org/10.1596/978-1-4648-0662-9.
21. Thomas Budde Christensen, "Towards a Circular Economy in Cities: Exploring Local Modes of Governance in the Transition towards a Circular Economy in Construction and Textile Recycling," *Journal of Cleaner Production*, (2021), https://doi.org/10.1016/j.jclepro.2021.127058.
22. Kaza *et al.*, *What a Waste 2.0: A Global Snapshot of Solid Waste Management to 2050.*
23. United Cities and Local Governments (UCLG), "Towards the Localization of the SDGs," *Local and Regional Governments' Report Towards the 2019 HLPF, 3rd Report, Global Task Force of Local and Regional Governments* (Barcelona: United Cities and Local Governments (UCLG), 2019), www.uclg.org/sites/default/files/towards_the_localization_of_the_sdgs_0.pdf.
24. Prendeville, Cherim, and Bocken, "Circular Cities: Mapping Six Cities in Transition."
25. European Commission, "Closing the Loop – An EU Action Plan for the Circular Economy," *Communication from the Commission to the European Parliament, The Council, The European Economic and Social Committee and the Committee to the Regions* COM/2015/0614 final (Brussels: European Commission, 2015), https://eur-lex.europa.eu/legal-content/EN/TXT/?uri=CELEX:52015DC0614.
26. For a discussion on closing the energy and material loops, see Patrizia Ghisellini and Sergio Ulgiati, "Managing the Transition to the Circular Economy," in *Handbook of the Circular Economy*, ed. Migueal Brandão, David Lazarevic, and Göran Finnveden (Cheltenham and Camberley, UK: Edward Elgar Publishing Ltd, 2020).
27. Campbell-Johnston *et al.*, "City Level Circular Transitions: Barriers and Limits in Amsterdam, Utrecht and the Hague."
28. Dhawan and Beckmann, *Circular Economy Guidebook for Cities.*
29. Dhawan and Beckmann, *Circular Economy Guidebook for Cities.*
30. Bin Guo *et al.*, "Comparative Assessment of Circular Economy Development in China's Four Megacities: The Case of Beijing, Chongqing, Shanghai and Urumqi," *Journal of Cleaner Production* 162 (2017), https://doi.org/10.1016/j.jclepro.2017.06.061.
31. Guo *et al.*, "Comparative Assessment of Circular Economy Development in China's Four Megacities."
32. Kaza *et al.*, *What a Waste 2.0: A Global Snapshot of Solid Waste Management to 2050.*
33. Navarro Ferronato *et al.*, "Introduction of the Circular Economy within Developing Regions: A Comparative Analysis of Advantages and Opportunities for Waste Valorization," *Journal of Environmental Management* 230 (2019), https://doi.org/10.1016/j.jenvman.2018.09.095.
34. Ghisellini and Ulgiati, "Managing the Transition to the Circular Economy."
35. OECD, "The Circular Economy in Cities and Regions," *OECD Urban Studies* (Washington, DC: OECD, 2020), https://doi.org/10.1787/10ac6ae4-en.
36. World Bank, *Bridging the Gap in Solid Waste Management* (Washington, DC: World Bank, 2021a), https://openknowledge.worldbank.org/handle/10986/35703.
37. OECD, *Policy Guidance on Resource Efficiency* (Washington, DC: OECD, 2016).
38. OECD, *Policy Guidance on Resource Efficiency* (Washington, DC: OECD, 2016).
39. Kaza *et al.*, *What a Waste 2.0: A Global Snapshot of Solid Waste Management to 2050.*
40. World Bank, *Bridging the Gap in Solid Waste Management.*
41. World Bank, *Bridging the Gap in Solid Waste Management.*
42. World Bank, *Kitakyushu Model Subsector: Interplay between Solid Waste and Urban Flood Risk* (Washington, DC: World Bank, 2017), https://openknowledge.worldbank.org/handle/10986/30950.
43. Sameh Wahba, Silpa Kaza, and Kremena Ionkova, "A New Phenomenon – Realizing Economic Growth While Cutting Waste. HOW?" *Sustainable Cities Blog*, 12 November 2019, https://blogs.worldbank.org/sustainablecities/new-phenomenon-realizing-economic-growth-while-cutting-waste-how.
44. Wahba, Kaza, and Ionkova, "A New Phenomenon – Realizing Economic Growth While Cutting Waste. HOW?"
45. World Bank, *Kitakyushu Model Subsector: Interplay between Solid Waste and Urban Flood Risk.*

46. World Bank, *Kitakyushu Model Subsector: Interplay between Solid Waste and Urban Flood Risk.*
47. Wahba, Kaza, and Ionkova, "A New Phenomenon – Realizing Economic Growth While Cutting Waste. HOW?"
48. Wahba, Kaza, and Ionkova, "A New Phenomenon – Realizing Economic Growth While Cutting Waste. HOW?"
49. Wahba, Kaza, and Ionkova, "A New Phenomenon – Realizing Economic Growth While Cutting Waste. HOW?"
50. Kathleen Bolger and Andréanne Doyon, "Circular Cities: Exploring Local Government Strategies to Facilitate a Circular Economy," *European Planning Studies* 27, no. 11 (2019), https://doi.org/10.1080/09654313.2019.1642854.
51. World Bank, "Improving Waste Management and Resource Efficiency: The Ningbo Experience," *Results Briefs*, 27 April 2021, www.worldbank.org/en/results/2021/04/27/improving-waste-management-and-resource-efficiency-the-ningbo-experience.
52. World Bank, "Improving Waste Management and Resource Efficiency: The Ningbo Experience."
53. World Bank, "Improving Waste Management and Resource Efficiency: The Ningbo Experience."
54. World Bank, "Improving Waste Management and Resource Efficiency: The Ningbo Experience."
55. World Bank, "Improving Waste Management and Resource Efficiency: The Ningbo Experience."
56. World Bank, *Results-Based Financing for Municipal Solid Waste*, Urban Development Series (Washington, DC: World Bank, 2014), https://documents1.worldbank.org/curated/en/237191468330923040/pdf/918610v20WP0FM0BE0CATALOGED0BY0WED0.pdf.
57. World Bank, *Results-Based Financing for Municipal Solid Waste.*
58. Christensen, "Towards a Circular Economy in Cities."
59. Christensen, "Towards a Circular Economy in Cities."
60. Christensen, "Towards a Circular Economy in Cities."
61. Mathilde Bouvier and Sonia Dias, "Waste Pickers in Brazil: A Statistical Profile," *Statistical Brief No. 29*, November 2021, Women in Informal Employment: Globalizing and Organizing (WIEGO), www.wiego.org/sites/default/files/publications/file/WIEGO_Statistical_Brief_N29_Brazil_WPs.pdf.
62. Bouvier and Dias, "Waste Pickers in Brazil: A Statistical Profile."
63. Bouvier and Dias, "Waste Pickers in Brazil: A Statistical Profile."
64. Bouvier and Dias, "Waste Pickers in Brazil: A Statistical Profile."
65. Sonia Dias *et al.*, *Impacts of the COVID-19 Pandemic on Inclusive Recycling in Brazil* (Manchester, UK: Women in Informal Employment: Globalizing and Organizing (WIEGO), 2020), www.wiego.org/sites/default/files/publications/file/Impacts%20of%20the%20COVID-19%20Pandemic%20on%20Inclusive%20Recycling%20in%20Brazil%20for%20web%20%281%29.pdf
66. Kaza *et al.*, *What a Waste 2.0: A Global Snapshot of Solid Waste Management to 2050.*
67. Kaza *et al.*, *What a Waste 2.0: A Global Snapshot of Solid Waste Management to 2050.*
68. World Bank, *Bridging the Gap in Solid Waste Management.*
69. World Bank, *Bridging the Gap in Solid Waste Management.*
70. World Bank, *Bridging the Gap in Solid Waste Management.*
71. Kaza *et al.*, *What a Waste 2.0: A Global Snapshot of Solid Waste Management to 2050.*
72. World Bank, *Bridging the Gap in Solid Waste Management.*
73. World Bank, *High and Dry: Climate Change, Water, and the Economy* (Washington, DC: World Bank, 2016b), https://openknowledge.worldbank.org/handle/10986/23665.
74. Chunyang He *et al.*, "Future Global Urban Water Scarcity and Potential Solutions."
75. Chunyang He *et al.*, "Future Global Urban Water Scarcity and Potential Solutions."
76. Chunyang He *et al.*, "Future Global Urban Water Scarcity and Potential Solutions."
77. Thomas G. LaVanchy, Michael W. Kerwin, and James K. Adamson, "Beyond 'Day Zero': Insights and Lessons from Cape Town (South Africa)," *Hydrogeology Journal* 27, no. 5 (2019), http://dx.doi.org/10.1007/s10040-019-01979-0.
78. LaVanchy, Kerwin, and Adamson, "Beyond 'Day Zero': Insights and Lessons from Cape Town (South Africa)."
79. Marianne Milano *et al.*, "Water Supply Basins of São Paulo Metropolitan Region: Hydro-Climatic Characteristics of the 2013–2015 Water Crisis," *Water* 10, no. 11 (2018), https://doi.org/10.3390/w10111517.

80. Milano *et al.*, "Water Supply Basins of São Paulo Metropolitan Region."
81. Yong Jiang, Chris Zevenbergen, and Yongchi Ma, "Urban Pluvial Flooding and Stormwater Management: A Contemporary Review of China's Challenges and 'Sponge Cities' Strategy," *Environmental Science & Policy* 80 (2018), https://doi.org/10.1016/j.envsci.2017.11.016.
82. Jiang, Zevenbergen, and Ma, "Urban Pluvial Flooding and Stormwater Management."
83. Jiang, Zevenbergen, and Ma, "Urban Pluvial Flooding and Stormwater Management."
84. Jiang, Zevenbergen, and Ma, "Urban Pluvial Flooding and Stormwater Management."
85. Jiang, Zevenbergen, and Ma, "Urban Pluvial Flooding and Stormwater Management."
86. Rui Wang, Hong Wu, and Robert Chiles, "Ecosystem Benefits Provision of Green Stormwater Infrastructure in Chinese Sponge Cities," *Environmental Management* 69, no. 3 (2022), https://doi.org/10.1007/s00267-021-01565-9.
87. Nancy Andrea Ramírez-Agudelo, Joan de Pablo, and Elisabet Roca, "Exploring Alternative Practices in Urban Water Management through the Lens of Circular Economy – A Case Study in the Barcelona Metropolitan Area," *Journal of Cleaner Production* 329 (2021), https://doi.org/10.1016/j.jclepro.2021.129565.
88. Ramírez-Agudelo, de Pablo, and Roca, "Exploring Alternative Practices in Urban Water Management through the Lens of Circular Economy."
89. Zhonghua Gou and Xiaohuan Xie, "Evolving Green Building: Triple Bottom Line or Regenerative Design?" *Journal of Cleaner Production* 153 (2017), https://doi.org/10.1016/j.jclepro.2016.02.077.
90. Gou and Xie, "Evolving Green Building: Triple Bottom Line or Regenerative Design?"
91. Cecilia Tortajada and Pierre van Rensburg, "Drink More Recycled Wastewater," *Nature* 577, no. 7788 (2019), https://doi.org/10.1038/d41586-019-03913-6.
92. Monica Crippa *et al.*, "Global Anthropogenic Emissions in Urban Areas: Patterns, Trends, and Challenges," *Environmental Research Letters* 16, no 7 (2021), https://doi.org/10.1088/1748-9326/ac00e2. Urban areas here are defined in accordance with the degree of urbanisation approach, which was developed by the European Commission in collaboration with a range of stakeholders and was endorsed by the United Nations Statistical Commission for comparison purposes; see United Nations, *Report of the 51st Session of the United Nations Statistical Commission* (3–6 March 2020). E/2020/24–E/CN.3/2020/34 (New York: United Nations, 2020), https://unstats.un.org/unsd/statcom/51st-session/documents/.
93. World Bank, *The World Bank Annual Report 2013: End Extreme Poverty, Promote Shared Prosperity (Vol. 1 of 3): Main Report (English)* (Washington, DC: World Bank, 2013), http://documents.worldbank.org/curated/en/947341468338396810.
94. Joensuu, Edelman, and Saari, "Circular Economy Practice in the Built Environment."
95. Coalition for Urban Transitions. "Climate Emergency, Urban Opportunity: How National Governments Can Secure Economic Prosperity and Avert Climate Catastrophe by Transforming Cities," Coalition for Urban Transitions, (2019), https://urbantransitions.global/wp-content/uploads/2019/09/Climate-Emergency-Urban-Opportunity-report.pdf.
96. Coalition for Urban Transitions, "Climate Emergency, Urban Opportunity."
97. Coalition for Urban Transitions, "Climate Emergency, Urban Opportunity."
98. Nathalie Whittle, "Welcome to the 15 Minute City," *Financial Times*, 17 July 2020, www.ft.com/content/c1a53744-90d5-4560-9e3f-17ce06aba69a.
99. Edward Glaeser, "The 15-Minute City Is a Dead End – Cities Must Be Places of Opportunity for Everyone," *LSE Blogs*, 28 May 2021, https://blogs.lse.ac.uk/covid19/2021/05/28/the-15-minute-city-is-a-dead-end-cities-must-be-places-of-opportunity-for-everyone/.
100. Sameh N. Wahba, "Can Cities Bounce Back Better from COVID-19? Reflections from Emerging Post-Pandemic Recovery Plans and Trade-Offs," *Environment & Urbanization*, 34, no. 2 (2022), https://doi.org/10.1177/09562478221102867.
101. Rana Amirtahmasebi *et al.*, *Regenerating Urban Land: A Practitioners Guide to Leverage Private Investment* (Washington, DC: World Bank, 2016), https://openknowledge.worldbank.org/handle/10986/24377.
102. Joensuu, Edelman, and Saari, "Circular Economy Practice in the Built Environment."
103. Joensuu, Edelman, and Saari, "Circular Economy Practice in the Built Environment"; Lukman Akanbi *et al.*, "Reusability Analytics Tool for End-of-Life Assessment of Building Materials

in a Circular Economy," *World Journal of Science, Technology and Sustainable Development* 16, no. 1 (2019), https://doi.org/10.1108/wjstsd-05-2018-0041.
104. Gou and Xie, "Evolving Green Building: Triple Bottom Line or Regenerative Design?"
105. Eleni Polychroniadou, "Unlocking the Green Building Market for Banks with EDGE," *EDGE Buildings*, 13 April 2021, https://edgebuildings.com/unlocking-the-green-building-market-for-banks-with-edge/.
106. Guo and Xie, "Evolving Green Building: Triple Bottom Line or Regenerative Design?"
107. Guo and Xie, "Evolving Green Building: Triple Bottom Line or Regenerative Design?"
108. Alain Bertaud and Harry W. Richardson, "Transit and Density: Atlanta, the United States and Western Europe," in *Urban Sprawl in Western Europe and the United States, Urban Planning and Environment*, ed Chang-Hee Christine Bae and Harry W. Richardson (Milton Park, Oxfordshire, UK: Routledge, 2016).
109. Katriina Alhola *et al.*, "Exploiting the Potential of Public Procurement: Opportunities for Circular Economy," *Journal of Industrial Ecology* 23, no. 1 (2018), https://doi.org/10.1111/jiec.12770.
110. Alhola *et al.*, "Exploiting the Potential of Public Procurement: Opportunities for Circular Economy."
111. Alhola *et al.*, "Exploiting the Potential of Public Procurement: Opportunities for Circular Economy."
112. Alhola *et al.*, "Exploiting the Potential of Public Procurement: Opportunities for Circular Economy."
113. Louise Laumann Kjaer *et al.*, "Product/Service-Systems for a Circular Economy: The Route to Decoupling Economic Growth from Resource Consumption?" *Journal of Industrial Ecology* 23, no. 1 (2019), https://doi.org/10.1111/jiec.12747.
114. Alhola *et al.*, "Exploiting the Potential of Public Procurement: Opportunities for Circular Economy."
115. Alhola *et al.*, "Exploiting the Potential of Public Procurement: Opportunities for Circular Economy."
116. Leonidas Milios, "Advancing to a Circular Economy: Three Essential Ingredients for a Comprehensive Policy Mix," *Sustainability Science* 13, no. 3 (2017), https://doi.org/10.1007/s11625-017-0502-9.
117. OECD, "The Circular Economy in Cities and Regions." The 51 cities and regions surveyed were from The Netherlands, Belgium, USA, Spain, Denmark, New Zealand, United Kingdom, Portugal, Finland, Japan, Slovenia, Colombia, Australia, Italy, Canada, Germany, France, Chile, Latvia, Norway, and Sweden. Only Amsterdam, Kitakyushu, Paris, London, and the Flanders region in Belgium viewed themselves as advanced.
118. OECD, "The Circular Economy in Cities and Regions."
119. OECD, "The Circular Economy in Cities and Regions."
120. Walter R. Stahel, "The Circular Economy," *Nature* 531, no.7595 (2016), http://dx.doi.org/10.1038/531435a.
121. OECD, "The Circular Economy in Cities and Regions."
122. World Bank, *Bridging the Gap in Solid Waste Management*, p. 40.
123. World Bank, *Bridging the Gap in Solid Waste Management*.
124. Kaza *et al.*, *What a Waste 2.0: A Global Snapshot of Solid Waste Management to 2050*.
125. World Bank, *Bridging the Gap in Solid Waste Management*.
126. World Bank, *Bridging the Gap in Solid Waste Management*, p. 29.
127. World Bank, *Bridging the Gap in Solid Waste Management*.
128. World Bank, *Bridging the Gap in Solid Waste Management*.
129. Joanna Williams, "Circular Cities"; the RESOLVE framework comprises six steps: Regenerate (use of renewable energy and materials), Share (to maximise utilisation of products), Optimise (remove waste from production), Loop (closing material loops via reuse, recycling, recovery, and remanufacturing), Virtualise (dematerialising resource use), and Exchange (using materials and services with lower resource consumption).
130. Prendeville, Cherim, and Bocken, "Circular Cities: Mapping Six Cities in Transition"; Joensuu, Edelman, and Saari, "Circular Economy Practice in the Built Environment."

131. Guo *et al.*, "Evolving Green Building: Triple Bottom Line or Regenerative Design?"
132. European Commission, "Closing the Loop – An EU Action Plan for the Circular Economy."
133. Ghisellini and Ulgiati, "Managing the Transition to the Circular Economy."
134. Heidi Simone Kristensen, Mette Alberg Mosgaard, and Arne Remmen, "Circular Public Procurement Practices in Danish Municipalities," *Journal of Cleaner Production* 281 (2021), https://doi.org/10.1016/j.jclepro.2020.124962.
135. OECD, "The Circular Economy in Cities and Regions."
136. Ghisellini and Ulgiati, "Managing the Transition to the Circular Economy," p. 11.
137. Kirchherr, Reike, and Hekkert, "Conceptualizing the Circular Economy: An Analysis of 114 Definitions"; Prendeville, Cherim, and Bocken, "Circular Cities: Mapping Six Cities in Transition."
138. Dalia D'Amato, Jaana Korhonen, and Anne Toppinen, "Circular, Green, and Bio Economy: How Do Companies in Land-Use Intensive Sectors Align with Sustainability Concepts?" *Ecological Economics* 158 (2019), https://doi.org/10.1016/j.ecolecon.2018.12.026.
139. Ghisellini and Ulgiati, "Managing the Transition to the Circular Economy."
140. Tiguist Fisseha *et al.*, "#FreetownTheTreeTown Campaign: Using Digital Tools to Encourage Tree Cultivation in Cities," *Global Environment Facility, GEF.org*, 5 August 2021, www.thegef.org/blog/freetownthetreetown-campaign-using-digital-tools-encourage-tree-cultivation-cities.
141. Abdul Rashid Thomas, "Waste Collection Management Association Launched in Freetown," *The Sierra Leone Telegraph*, 26 January 2022, www.thesierraleonetelegraph.com/waste-collection-management-association-launched-in-freetown.
142. OECD, "The Circular Economy in Cities and Regions."
143. Boyd Cohen and Pablo Muñoz, "Sharing Cities and Sustainable Consumption and Production: Towards an Integrated Framework," *Journal of Cleaner Production* 134 (2016), https://doi.org/10.1016/j.jclepro.2015.07.133.
144. Cohen and Muñoz, "Sharing Cities and Sustainable Consumption and Production: Towards an Integrated Framework."
145. Fedra Vanhuyse, Neal R. Haddaway, and Maryna Henrysson, "Circular Cities: An Evidence Map of Research between 2010 and 2020," *Discover Sustainability* 2, no. 1 (2021), https://link.springer.com/content/pdf/10.1007/s43621-021-00059-2.pdf.

11 Governing the Transition to Circular Economy and Liveable Cities

1. City of Vienna, "Vienna Smart Climate City Strategy," (2022), https://smartcity.wien.gv.at/wp-content/uploads/sites/3/2022/05/scwr_klima_2022_web-EN.pdf.
2. City of Vienna, "DoTank Circular City Wien 2020–2030," (2020), https://enviaments.accio.gencat.cat/ACC1O/cat/docs/enviaments/docs/Project9-Barca.pdf.
3. I. Stengers I. and I. Prigogine, *Order Out of Chaos: Man's New Dialogue with Nature* (Brussels, Belgium: Verso, 2018), https://books.google.co.nz/books?id=Cm_nDwAAQBAJ.
4. "Protopia," 2024, https://kk.org/thetechnium/protopia/.
5. M. Demchenko *et al.*, "From Sustainable to Thrivable Urban Development: Conceptual Frameworks for Designing a Socio-Cultural, Relational, and Educational Ecosystem of Cities," in *Urban Planning and Design for Megacities in the Global South: Strategies for Smart and Sustainable Urban Development*, ed. Mohammed Firoz C. *et al.* (Cham: Springer Nature, 2023).
6. M. Hamilton and B. Sanders, "A Radically Optimistic Inquiry into Operating System 2.0," (The Integral City 2.0 Online Conference, Online, 2012).
7. Alexander Laszlo *et al.*, "Systemic Innovation for Thrivable Cities," in *The Palgrave Encyclopedia of Urban and Regional Futures*, ed. Robert C. Brears (Cham: Springer International Publishing, 2020).
8. Alexander Laszlo, Karin Huber-Heim, and Stefan Blachfellner, "From Sustainability to Thrivability: Transforming Systems with Purpose," in *The Kyoto Post-COVID Manifesto For Global Economics: Confronting Our Shattered Society*, ed. Stephen Hill, Tadashi Yagi, and Stomu Yamash'ta (Singapore: Springer Nature Singapore, 2022).

9. Alexander Laszlo, "Evolutionary Systems Design," *Journal of Organisational Transformation & Social Change* 1, no. 1 (2004), https://doi.org/10.1386/jots.1.1.29/0.
10. A. A. Montuori, *Evolutionary Competence: Creating the Future* (Leiden, the Netherlands: Brill, 1989), https://books.google.co.nz/books?id=3eUyAAAAIAAJ.
11. E. Laszlo, *Evolution: The General Theory* (Cresskill, NJ: Hampton, 1996).
12. Laszlo, *Evolution: The General Theory.*
13. Laszlo *et al.*, "Systemic Innovation for Thrivable Cities."
14. Marina Fischer-Kowalski and Walter Hüttler, "Society's Metabolism," *Journal of Industrial Ecology* 2, no. 4 (1998), https://doi.org/10.1162/jiec.1998.2.4.107.
15. B. Plank *et al.*, "We Want It All. But Do We Need It All? Material Stocks of Societies and Their Interrelation with Economic Growth and Wellbeing," (The 14th Biennial International Conference on EcoBalance, Online, 2021).
16. Ellen MacArthur Foundation, *Towards the Circular Economy Vol. 1.*
17. Ellen MacArthur Foundation, *Towards the Circular Economy Vol. 1.*
18. Federal Ministry Republic of Austria Climate Action, Energy, Mobility, and Innovation and Technology, "The Austrian Circular Economy Strategy," (2022). www.bmk.gv.at/en/topics/climate-environment/waste-resource-management/ces.html.
19. EEA, "Circular Economy in Europe – Developing the Knowledge Base," (2015), www.eea.europa.eu/publications/circular-economy-in-europe; Nikolai Jacobi *et al.*, "Providing an Economy-Wide Monitoring Framework for the Circular Economy in Austria: Status Quo and Challenges," *Resources, Conservation and Recycling* 137 (2018), https://doi.org/10.1016/j.resconrec.2018.05.022.
20. Martin Calisto Friant, Walter J. V. Vermeulen, and Roberta Salomone, "A Typology of Circular Economy Discourses: Navigating the Diverse Visions of a Contested Paradigm," *Resources, Conservation and Recycling* 161 (2020), https://doi.org/10.1016/j.resconrec.2020.104917.
21. City of Vienna, "VIENNA 2030 – Economy & Innovation," (2024). www.wien.gv.at/english/business-media/vienna-2030.html; City of Vienna, "Vienna Smart Climate City Strategy"; City of Vienna, "DoTank Circular City Wien 2020–2030."
22. Umme Ammara *et al.*, "Smart Cities from the Perspective of Systems," *Systems* 10, no. 3 (2022), https://doi.org/10.3390/systems10030077.
23. Martin Geissdoerfer *et al.*, "Business Models and Supply Chains for the Circular Economy," *Journal of Cleaner Production* 190 (2018), https://doi.org/10.1016/j.jclepro.2018.04.159.
24. Geissdoerfer *et al.*, "Business Models and Supply Chains for the Circular Economy."
25. Sam J. Buckton *et al.*, "The Regenerative Lens: A Conceptual Framework for Regenerative Social-Ecological Systems," *One Earth* 6, no. 7 (2023), https://doi.org/10.1016/j.oneear.2023.06.006.
26. N. Frantzeskaki and D. Loorbach, "Transitions Governance: Towards a New Governance Paradigm," (13th Annual Conference of the International Research Society for Public Management (IRSPM XIII), Copenhagen, Denmark, 2009).
27. Ghisellini, Cialani, and Ulgiati, "A Review on Circular Economy: The Expected Transition to a Balanced Interplay of Environmental and Economic Systems."
28. Jacqueline M. Cramer, "The Function of Transition Brokers in the Regional Governance of Implementing Circular Economy – A Comparative Case Study of Six Dutch Regions," *Sustainability* 12, no. 12 (2020), https://doi.org/10.3390/su12125015.
29. Frantzeskaki and Loorbach, "Short Transitions Governance: Towards a New Governance Paradigm"; Asterios Papageorgiou *et al.*, "Mapping and Assessing Indicator-Based Frameworks for Monitoring Circular Economy Development at the City-Level," *Sustainable Cities and Society* 75 (2021), https://doi.org/10.1016/j.scs.2021.103378.
30. ICLEI, "Circular City Actions Framework: Bringing the Circular Economy to Every City," (2021). https://circulars.iclei.org/wp-content/uploads/2021/10/Circular-City-Action-Framework_V2.pdf.
31. "This Chart Shows the Impact Rising Urbanization Will Have on the World," 2022, www.weforum.org/agenda/2022/04/global-urbanization-material-consumption/.
32. "Circular City Funding Guide," (n.d.), www.circularcityfundingguide.eu.
33. "Cities and Climate Change," 2024, www.unep.org/explore-topics/resource-efficiency/what-we-do/cities-and-climate-change#:~:text=At%20the%20same%20time%2C%20cities,contributors%20(IPCC%2C%202022).

34. Florian Schütz, Marie Lena Heidingsfelder, and Martina Schraudner, "Co-Shaping the Future in Quadruple Helix Innovation Systems: Uncovering Public Preferences toward Participatory Research and Innovation," *She Ji: The Journal of Design, Economics, and Innovation* 5, no. 2 (2019), https://doi.org/10.1016/j.sheji.2019.04.002.
35. Elias G. Carayannis and David F. J. Campbell, "'Mode 3' and 'Quadruple Helix': Toward a 21st Century Fractal Innovation Ecosystem," *International Journal of Technology Management* 46, no. 3–4 (2009), https://doi.org/10.1504/IJTM.2009.023374; Johan Schot and W. Edward Steinmueller, "Three Frames for Innovation Policy: R&D, Systems of Innovation and Transformative Change," *Research Policy* 47, no. 9 (2018), https://doi.org/10.1016/j.respol.2018.08.011.
36. Anna-Vera Deinhammer, "It's Time Cities Came Around to a Circular Economy," *The Parliament*, 20 September 2023, www.theparliamentmagazine.eu/news/article/create-circular-economy-cities.
37. Madeleine W. McNamara and John C. Morris, "Expanding the Utility of Cross-Sectoral Collaboration in Policy Studies: Present and Future," *Policy Studies Yearbook* (2022).
38. Elias L. Khalil, "The Red Queen Paradox: A Proper Name for a Popular Game: Note," *Journal of Institutional and Theoretical Economics (JITE) / Zeitschrift für die gesamte Staatswissenschaft* 153, no. 2 (1997), www.jstor.org/stable/40751982.

12 The Role of Education in Developing Liveable Cities with Functioning Circular Economies

1. Werner Rieß, "Bildung für nachhaltige Entwicklung – Kann durch Unterricht das nachhaltigkeitsrelevante Handeln von Grundschuler/innen gefördert werden?" (Conference: 20. Internationale Tagung der Fachsektion Didaktik der Biologie (FDdB) im VBio und des Forums Fachdidaktik & Schulbiologie, Online, 2015).
2. United Nations, "Ziele für nachhaltige Entwicklung," (2021), www.un.org/depts/german/millennium/SDG%20Bericht%202021.pdf.
3. UNESCO, "Education for Sustainable Development," (2012), https://sustainabledevelopment.un.org/content/documents/926unesco9.pdf.
4. United Nations, "Ziele für nachhaltige Entwicklung."
5. Jörg-Robert Schreiber and Hannes Siege, "Curriculum Framework: Education for Sustainable Development," (2016), www.globaleslernen.de/sites/default/files/files/link-elements/curriculum_framework_education_for_sustainable_development_barrierefrei.pdf.
6. "Kreislaufwirtschaft: Definition und Vorteile," (2023), www.europarl.europa.eu/topics/de/article/20151201STO05603/kreislaufwirtschaft-definition-und-vorteile.
7. Petra Baisch, "Schülervorstellungen zum Stoffkreislauf. Eine Interventionsstudie im Kontext einer Bildung für nachhaltige Entwicklung," (Pädagogischen Hochschule Ludwigsburg, 2009).
8. Schreiber and Siege, "Curriculum Framework Education for Sustainable Development."
9. Volker Ludwig, "Transition to Circular Economy: The Role of Education from Youth to Higher Education," *European Commission*, 30 September 2020, https://epale.ec.europa.eu/en/blog/transition-circular-economy-role-education-youth-higher-education.
10. Daniel Fischer and Gerd Michelsen, "Sustainability and Education," in *Sustainable Development Policy: A European Perspective*, ed. Claudia Kuhnke and Michael von Hauff, (London: Routledge, 2017).
11. Julius Grund and Antje Brock, "Bildung für nachhaltige Entwicklung in Lehr-Lernsettings – Quantitative Studie des nationalen Monitorings – Befragung junger Menschen. Executive Summary," (2018), www.researchgate.net/publication/328957682_Bildung_fur_nachhaltige_Entwicklung_in_Lehr-Lernsettings_-_Quantitative_Studie_des_nationalen_Monitorings_-_Befragung_junger_Menschen_Executive_Summary.
12. United Nations, "Ziele für nachhaltige Entwicklung."
13. Bundesministerium Bildung, "Bildung für Nachhaltige Entwicklung," (2024), www.bmbwf.gv.at/Themen/schule/schulpraxis/ba/bine.html#heading_Bildung_f_r_Nachhaltige_Entwicklung_2.
14. H. Oberhummer, W. Gruber, and M. Puntigam, *Wer nichts weiß, muss alles glauben.* (Salzburg: Ecowin Verlag, 2012).

15. UNESCO, "Sustainable Development Goals (SDGs)," (2024), www.unesco.at/bildung/bildung-2030/bildungsagenda-2030/sdgs.
16. "Bundesregierung Bericht der Bundesregierung zur Bildung für nachhaltige Entwicklung – 19. Legislaturperiode," (2021), https://dip.bundestag.de/vorgang/bericht-der-bundesregierung-zur-bildung-für-nachhaltige-entwicklung-19-legislaturperiode/277029.
17. Alexander Wandl *et al.*, "The Circular Economy Concept in Design Education: Enhancing Understanding and Innovation by Means of Situated Learning," *Urban Planning* 4, no. 3 (2019): *Facilitating Circular Economy in Urban Planning*, https://doi.org/10.17645/up.v4i3.2147.
18. Bundesministerium Bildung, "Bildung für Nachhaltige Entwicklung."
19. Stadt Köln, "Kölner Perspektiven 2030+ (English Summary)," (n.d.). www.stadt-koeln.de/mediaasset/content/pdf15/kp2030/kurzfassung_englisch.pdf.
20. City of Cologne, "Urban strategy 2.0 – The perspectives of Cologne 2030+," (2023), www.stadt-koeln.de/mediaasset/content/pdf15/kp2030/kurzfassung_englisch.pdf.
21. City of Cologne, "Standort Köln – Perspektive 2030," (2016), www.stadt-koeln.de/mediaasset/content/pdf80/standort_köln-perspektive_2030_kurzfassung.pdf.
22. "Vision Köln 2030: Dokumentation unserer Diskussion mit der Kommunalpolitik," (2020), https://koelnbonn.scientists4future.org/2020/06/20/vision-koeln-2030-dokumentation-unserer-diskussion-mit-der-kommunalpolitik/.
23. Anna Carnap, Marie-Therese Arnold, and Inka Bormann, *Bestandsaufnahme zur Verankerung von Bildung für nachhaltige Entwicklung Bildungs- und Lehrplänen* (Berlin: Haus der Kleinen Forscher, 2017).
24. "Klimawandel und nachhaltige Entwicklung werden Schulfach," (2019), www.energiezukunft.eu/klimakrise/klimawandel-und-nachhaltige-entwicklung-werden-schulfach/.
25. "SmartPlaCE@schools: Serious Game Platform for Education on Circular Economy in Highschools," (2019), https://old.eitrawmaterials.eu/project/smartplaceschools/.
26. Bundesministerium Bildung, "Bildung für Nachhaltige Entwicklung."

13 Circular Business Models and Synergies in Circular Economy Liveable Cities

1. "Sustainability Is in Our DNA," (2024), www.interface.com/GB/en-GB/sustainability/sustainability-overview.html.
2. "Cradle to Cradle," (2024), https://mcdonough.com/cradle-to-cradle/.
3. "About," (2024), https://theoceancleanup.com.
4. "Patagonia Care & Repair," (2024), www.ifixit.com/collaborations/patagonia.
5. "Light as a Service," (2024), www.signify.com/global/lighting-services/managed-services/light-as-a-service.
6. City of Amsterdam, "Amsterdam Circular 2020–2025 Strategy."
7. City of Amsterdam, "Amsterdam Circular 2020–2025 Strategy."
8. "Coalitieakkoord 2022–2026," (2022), www.amsterdam.nl/nieuws/coalitieakkoord/.
9. "Amsterdam City Doughnut," (2024), https://doughnuteconomics.org/stories/amsterdam-city-doughnut.
10. K. Raworth, *Doughnut Economics: Seven Ways to Think Like a 21st-Century Economist.*
11. City of Amsterdam, "Policy: Food Strategy," (n.d.), www.amsterdam.nl/en/policy/sustainability/food-strategy/.
12. "Policy: Food Strategy," (2024), www.amsterdam.nl/en/policy/sustainability/food-strategy/.
13. City of Amsterdam, "Amsterdam Circular 2020–2025 Strategy."
14. City of Amsterdam, "Amsterdam Circular 2020–2025 Strategy."
15. City of Amsterdam, "Circular Economy Programme: Lessons and Recommendations 2020–2021," (2022), https://assets.amsterdam.nl/publish/pages/1043702/circular_economy_lessons_and_recommendations_2020-2021.pdf.
16. City of Amsterdam, "Research & Statistics," (2024), https://openresearch.amsterdam/en/page/31753/research-statistics.
17. City of Amsterdam, "Research & Statistics."
18. City of Amsterdam, "Research & Statistics."

19. City of Amsterdam, “Research & Statistics.”
20. City of Amsterdam, “Policy: Circular Economy.”
21. “Home,” (2024), https://deceuvel.nl/nl/.
22. “Come Fishing for Plastic!” (2024), https://plasticwhale.com/plastic-fishing/.
23. “Polderdak Floor Voormalig Jan Bommerhuis,” (2024), https://weerproof.nl/project/polderdak-floor-voormalig-jan-bommerhuis/.
24. AEB Amsterdam, “For a Clean Society, Now and in the Future,” (2024), www.aebamsterdam.com/media/is2je2to/aeb230407_schone-samenleving_online_eng.pdf.
25. “About,” (2024), https://amsterdamsmartcity.com/about.
26. “About REFLOW,” (2024), https://reflowproject.eu/about/.
27. Waag Futurelab, “Amsterdam Reflow Booklet,” (2021), https://waag.org/en/article/amsterdam-reflow-booklet/.
28. Mayor of Paris, “Paris Circular Economy Plan,” (2017), https://cdn.paris.fr/paris/2019/07/24/38de2f4891329bbaf04585ced5fbdf0f.pdf.
29. Oriana Romano, “Never Waste a Good Waste Crisis: Paris and the Circular Economy,” OECD (2023), 17 September, https://oecdstatistics.blog/2023/03/28/never-waste-a-good-waste-crisis-paris-and-the-circular-economy/.
30. “Circular Economy,” (2024), www.chooseparisregion.org/industries/circular-economy.
31. “Home,” (2024), www.velib-metropole.fr/en_GB.
32. REFLOW, “Planning a Circular Paris,” (2022), https://reflowproject.eu/wp-content/uploads/2022/03/PARIS_REFLOW_CaseStudy_final.pdf.
33. Circle Economy, “Circular Prague,” (2019), www.circle-economy.com/resources/circular-prague.
34. Prague Innovation Institute and Circle Economy, “Circulární Praha 2030, Strategie hl.m. Prahy pro prechod na cirulární ekonomiku,” (2022), www.pragueconvention.cz/file/8500/cirkularni-praha-2030-strategie-ce.pdf.
35. “Prague: The Circular European Capital You Haven’t Heard About Yet,” (2021), www.circle-economy.com/blogs/prague-the-circular-european-capital-you-havent-heard-about-yet; “Bonett Opens Its 10th CNG Filling Station in Prague,” (2023), www.bioenergy-news.com/news/bonett-opens-its-10th-cng-filling-station-in-prague/.
36. “První cirkulární store v ČR? No neke!,” (2024), https://no-neke.netlify.app.
37. City of Helsinki, “The City of Helsinki’s Roadmap for Circular and Sharing Economy,” (2020), www.hel.fi/static/kanslia/Julkaisut/the-city-of-helsinkis-roadmap-for-circular-and-sharing-economy.pdf.
38. “Construction Boosts Circular Economy – Demolition in Vattuniemi Shows the Way,” (2024), https://testbed.hel.fi/en/circular-economy/construction-boosts-circular-economy/.
39. City of Copenhagen, “CPH 2025 Climate Plan – Roadmap 2021–2025,” (2020), https://kk.sites.itera.dk/apps/kk_pub2/index.asp?mode=detalje&id=2062.
40. “Visit Amager Bakke,” (2024), https://a-r-c.dk/klima-og-miljo/viden-og-inspiration/visit-arc/.
41. “Circular Economy,” (2020), https://sustainableglasgow.org.uk/circular-economy.
42. “Circular Economy Examples in the City of Ljubljana,” (2024), www.ljubljana.si/en/ljubljana-for-you/environmental-protection/towards-circular-economy/examples-of-circular-economy/.
43. City of Yokohama, “Yokohama 3R Dream!: Yokohama Municipal Solid Waste Management Master Plan,” (2011), www.city.yokohama.lg.jp/city-info/yokohamashi/org/shigen/sonota/hoshin/3r-plan/plan.files/0010_20180906.pdf.
44. City of Sydney, “Building a Strong Green and Circular Economy for Sydney,” (2023), www.cityofsydney.nsw.gov.au/research-reports/green-economy-study.

Bibliography

Acceleratio. "Barriers & Drivers Towards a Circular Economy." (2015). https://circulareconomy.europa.eu/platform/sites/default/files/e00e8643951aef8adde612123e824493.pdf.

Adams, Damian C., Derek Allen, Tatiana Borisova, Diane E. Boellstorff, Michael D. Smolen, and Robert L. Mahler. "The Influence of Water Attitudes, Perceptions, and Learning Preferences on Water-Conserving Actions." [In English]. *Natural Sciences Education* 42, no. 1 (2013): 114–22. http://dx.doi.org/10.4195/nse.2012.0027.

ADB. "Asian Water Development Outlook 2016: Strengthening Water Security in Asia and the Pacific." (2016). www.adb.org/sites/default/files/publication/189411/awdo-2016.pdf.

Addo, Isaac B., Martin C. Thoms, and Melissa Parsons. "The Influence of Water-Conservation Messages on Reducing Household Water Use." *Applied Water Science* 9, no. 5 (2019): 126. https://doi.org/10.1007/s13201-019-1002-0.

AEB Amsterdam. "For a Clean Society, Now and in the Future." (2024). www.aebamsterdam.com/media/is2je2to/aeb230407_schone-samenleving_online_eng.pdf.

Agarwal, O. P., Ajay Kumar, and Samuel Zimmerman. "Public Transit." In *Emerging Paradigms in Urban Mobility*, 77–99. Elsevier, 2019.

Agudelo-Vera, C. M. "Dynamic Water Resource Management for Achieving Self-sufficiency of Cities of Tomorrow [Doctoral dissertation, Wageningen University]." Wageningen University Repository. https://doi.org/10.18174/216692.

AITC. "Urban Agriculture." (2023). https://aitc-canada.ca/Portals/0/adam/snapAG/jRa_KWrZBkq7gB2j9Ogz8A/Link/Urban%20Agriculture%20Final.pdf.

Akanbi, Lukman, Lukumon Oyedele, Juan Manuel Davila Delgado, Muhammad Bilal, Olugbenga Akinade, Anuoluwapo Ajayi, and Naimah Mohammed-Yakub, "Reusability Analytics Tool for End-of-Life Assessment of Building Materials in a Circular Economy." *World Journal of Science, Technology and Sustainable Development* 16, no. 1 (January 7, 2019): 40–55. https://doi.org/10.1108/wjstsd-05-2018-0041.

Alcamo, J., T. Henrichs, and T. Rösch. "World Water in 2025 – Global Modelling and Scenario Analysis for the World Commission on Water for the 21st Century." (2000). www.env-edu.gr/Documents/World%20Water%20in%202025.pdf.

Aleksandrowicz, L., R. Green, E. J. Joy, P. Smith, and A. Haines. "The Impacts of Dietary Change on Greenhouse Gas Emissions, Land Use, Water Use, and Health: A Systematic Review." [In English]. *PLoS One* 11, no. 11 (2016): e0165797. https://doi.org/10.1371/journal.pone.0165797.

Alhola, Katriina, Sven- Olof Ryding, Hanna Salmenperä, and Niels Juul Busch, "Exploiting the Potential of Public Procurement: Opportunities for Circular Economy." *Journal of Industrial Ecology* 23, no. 1 (May 15, 2018): 96–109. https://doi.org/10.1111/jiec.12770.

Alvarez-Campos, Odiney, and Gregory K. Evanylo. "Biosolids Improve Urban Soil Properties and Vegetable Production in Urban Agriculture." *Urban Agriculture & Regional Food Systems* 4, no. 1 (2019): 190002. https://doi.org/10.2134/urbanag2019.04.0002.

Amahmid, Omar, Youssef El Guamri, Mohamed Yazidi, Bouchra Razoki, Khadija Kaid Rassou, Youness Rakibi, Ghizlane Knini, and Touria El Ouardi. "Water Education in School Curricula: Impact on Children Knowledge, Attitudes and Behaviours Towards Water Use." *International Research in Geographical and Environmental Education* 28, no. 3 (2019): 178-93. https://doi.org/10.1080/10382046.2018.1513446.

Ameli, S. Hassan, Shima Hamidi, Andrea Garfinkel-Castro, and Reid Ewing. "Do Better Urban Design Qualities Lead to More Walking in Salt Lake City, Utah?" *Journal of Urban Design* 20, no. 3 (2015): 393–410. https://doi.org/10.1080/13574809.2015.1041894.

American Rivers, The Forest Guild and Mountain Conservation Trust of Georgia. "Forests to Faucets: Protecting Upstream Forests for Clean Water Downstream." (2013). https://americanrivers.org/wp-content/uploads/2016/05/AmericanRivers_forests-to-faucets-report.pdf.

Amirtahmasebi, Rana, Mariana Orloff, Sameh Wahba, and Andrew Altman, *Regenerating Urban Land: A Practitioners Guide to Leverage Private Investment*. Washington, DC: World Bank, 2016. https://openknowledge.worldbank.org/handle/10986/24377.

Ammara, Umme, Khansa Rasheed, Athar Mansoor, Ala Al-Fuqaha, and Junaid Qadir. "Smart Cities from the Perspective of Systems." *Systems* 10, no. 3. (2022). https://doi.org/10.3390/systems10030077.

"About." 2024, accessed September 17, 2024. https://amsterdamsmartcity.com/about.

"Polderdak Floor Voormalig Jan Bommerhuis." 2024, accessed September 17, 2024. https://weerproof.nl/project/polderdak-floor-voormalig-jan-bommerhuis/.

Anderson, C. M., K. A. Kissel, C. B. Field, and K. J. Mach. "Climate Change Mitigation, Air Pollution, and Environmental Justice in California." [In English]. *Environmental Science and Technology* 52, no. 18 (2018): 10829–38. https://doi.org/10.1021/acs.est.8b00908.

Appleyard, Bruce and Donald Appleyard. Livable streets 2.0: Elsevier, 2021.

Aslan, Devrim Umut. *Praxitopia: How Shopping Makes a Street Vibrant*. Lund: Lund University, 2021.

Aumann, Simone, Julia Kinigadner, David Duran-Rodas, and Benjamin Büttner. "Driving towards Car-Independent Neighborhoods in Europe: A Typology and Systematic Literature Review." *UP* 8, no. 3 (2023). https://doi.org/10.17645/up.v8i3.6552.

Golebiowska, Anna, Weronika Jakubczak, Dariusz Prokopowicz, Ryszard Jakubczak. "The Post-Pandemic Development of the Green Circular Economy and the Declarations Made during the Un Climate Change Conference (Cop26) as Security Determinant." *European Research Studies Journal* XXIV, no. 4B (2021): 251–75.

"Visit Amager Bakke." 2024, accessed September 17, 2024. https://a-r-c.dk/klima-og-miljo/viden-og-inspiration/visit-arc/.

Australian Goverment Productivity Commission. "Water Trading and Markets." (2020). www.pc.gov.au/inquiries/completed/water-reform-2020/report/water-reform-2020-supportingb.pdf.

Ayres, Andrew B., Kyle C. Meng, and Andrew J. Plantinga. "Do Environmental Markets Improve on Open Access? Evidence from California Groundwater Rights." *Journal of Political Economy* 129, no. 10 (2021): 2817–60. https://doi.org/10.1086/715075.

Baisch, Petra. "Schülervorstellungen Zum Stoffkreislauf. Eine Interventionsstudie Im Kontext Einer Bildung Für Nachhaltige Entwicklung." Pädagogischen Hochschule Ludwigsburg, 2009.

"Subsidies for Heritage Work, Party Walls and Green Rooftops." 2023, accessed August 15, 2023. https://ajuntament.barcelona.cat/ciutatpatrimoni/en/news/subsidies-for-heritage-work-party-walls-and-green-rooftops-1279009.

"Building Retrofit Energy Efficiency Financing (Breef) Scheme." 2023, accessed September 24, 2023. www1.bca.gov.sg/buildsg/sustainability/green-mark-incentive-schemes/building-retrofit-energy-efficiency-financing-breef-scheme.

"Case Study: City of Atlanta Permeable Paver Retrofit." 2023, accessed August 15, 2023. www.belgardcommercial.com/case_studies/case_study_city_of_atlanta_permeable_paver_retrofit#.

Barragán-Escandón, Antonio, Julio Terrados-Cepeda, and Esteban Zalamea-León. "The Role of Renewable Energy in the Promotion of Circular Urban Metabolism." *Sustainability* 9, no. 12 (2017): 2341.

Barros, Murillo Vetroni et al. "Circular Economy as a Driver to Sustainable Businesses," *Cleaner Environmental Systems* 2, no. 2 (2020). https://doi.org/10.1016/j.cesys.2020.100006.

Berardi, Luigi, Daniele B. Laucelli, Antonietta Simone, Gianfredi Mazzolani, and Orazio Giustolisi. "Active Leakage Control with Wdnetxl." *Procedia Engineering* 154 (2016): 62–70. https://doi.org/10.1016/j.proeng.2016.07.420.

"Bonett Opens Its 10th Cng Filling Station in Prague." 2023, accessed September 17, 2024. www.bioenergy-news.com/news/bonett-opens-its-10th-cng-filling-station-in-prague/.

"About Bloom." 2023, accessed August 21, 2023. https://bloomsoil.com/about-bloom-soil-amendment/.

Bertaud, Alain, and Harry W. Richardson, "Transit and Density: Atlanta, the United States and Western Europe." In *Urban Sprawl in Western Europe and the United States, Urban Planning and Environment*, edited by Chang-Hee Christine Bae and Harry W. Richardson. Milton Park, Oxfordshire, UK: Routledge, 2016.

Berrigan, David, Linda W. Pickle, and Jennifer Dill. "Associations between Street Connectivity and Active Transportation." *International Journal of Health Geographics* 9 (2010): 20. https://doi.org/10.1186/1476-072X-9-20.

Boer, Florian, Eric-Jan Pleijster, and Nanco Dolman. *Rotterdam, from a Port City to a Port Archipelago + Sponge Water City – Redesigning Deltas Design Study*. Delft, the Netherlands: Delft University of Technology, 2022. http://dx.doi.org/10.13140/RG.2.2.28597.76002.

Bolger, Kathleen, and Andreéanne Doyon. "Circular Cities: Exploring Local Government Strategies to Facilitate a Circular Economy." *European Planning Studies* 27, no. 11 (July 17, 2019), 2184–205. https://doi.org/10.1080/09654313.2019.1642854.

Boretti, Alberto, and Lorenzo Rosa. "Reassessing the Projections of the World Water Development Report." *npj Clean Water* 2, no. 1 (2019): 15. https://doi.org/10.1038/s41545-019-0039-9.

Bouvier, Mathilde, and Sonia Dias. "Waste Pickers in Brazil: A Statistical Profile," Statistical Brief No. 29, November 2021, Women in Informal Employment: Globalizing and Organizing (WIEGO). www.wiego.org/sites/default/files/publications/file/WIEGO_Statistical_Brief_N29_Brazil_WPs.pdf.

BRANZ. "Bu533 Green Roofs – An Overview." (2011). www.branz.co.nz/pubs/bulletins/bu533/.

Brears, Robert "How Can Cities Reduce Water-Energy Nexus Pressures?" *World Bank*, 2016. https://blogs.worldbank.org/water/how-can-cities-reduce-water-energy-nexus-pressures.

Brears, R.C. *Blue and Green Cities: The Role of Blue-Green Infrastructure in Managing Urban Water Resources*. Cham, Switzerland: Palgrave Macmillan UK, 2018.

Brears, R.C. "Circular Economy and the Water–Food Nexus." Mark and Focus, 2022. https://medium.com/mark-and-focus/circular-economy-and-the-water-food-nexus-df284b72a375.

Brears, R.C. *Developing the Circular Water Economy*. Cham, Switzerland: Palgrave Macmillan, 2020.

Brears, R.C. *The Green Economy and the Water-Energy-Food Nexus*. London: Palgrave Macmillan UK, 2017. https://books.google.co.nz/books?id=m9IxDwAAQBAJ.

Brears, R.C. *Natural Resource Management and the Circular Economy*. Cham, Switzerland: Springer International Publishing, 2018. https://books.google.co.nz/books?id=SphMDwAAQBAJ.

Brears, R.C. *Nature-Based Solutions to 21st Century Challenges*. Oxfordshire, UK: Routledge, 2020. https://books.google.co.nz/books?id=0zgKzQEACAAJ.

Brears, R.C. *Regional Water Security*. Hoboken, NJ: Wiley, 2021.

"Stormwater Harvesting to Ensure Water Security." Mark and Focus, 2021, accessed September 24, 2023. https://medium.com/mark-and-focus/stormwater-harvesting-to-ensure-water-security-9c45df311001.

Brears, R.C. *Urban Water Security*. Hoboken, NJ: John Wiley & Sons, 2016.

Brears, R.C. "Urban Water Security in Asia-Pacific: Promoting Demand Management Strategies." (2014). https://refubium.fu-berlin.de/bitstream/handle/fub188/18349/pp414-urban-water-security-asiapacific.pdf?sequence=1&isAllowed=y.

"Valuing Every Drop of Water." Mark and Focus, 2019. https://medium.com/mark-and-focus/valuing-every-drop-of-water-7d6552c3650c.

Brears, R.C. *Water Resources Management: Innovative and Green Solutions*. Berlin: De Gruyter, 2021.

Brears, Robert C. "Building Circular Economy Cities." In *The Palgrave Handbook of Climate Resilient Societies*, Volume 1. 1–23. Cham: Springer International Publishing, 2020.

Brears, Robert C. "Circular Economy Cities." In *The Palgrave Encyclopedia of Urban and Regional Futures*, 1–6. Cham: Springer International Publishing, 2020.

"Cultivating Community Gardens Grants Guidelines." 2023, accessed August 15, 2023. www.brisbane.qld.gov.au/community-and-safety/grants-awards-and-sponsorships/environment-and-sustainability-grants/cultivating-community-gardens-grants/guidelines.

Brown, R., Keath, N., and Wong, T. Urban Water Management Transition Framework: Illustrating the transition to water sensitive cities and resilience through a new hydro-social contract. Proceedings of the 11th International Conference on Urban Drainage (ICUD), (2008).

Brown, R., Rogers, B., and Werbeloff, L. "Moving toward Water Sensitive Cities: A Guidance Manual for Strategists and Policy Makers." (2016). https://watersensitivecities.org.au/wp-content/uploads/2016/05/TMR_A4-1_MovingTowardWSC.pdf.

Brown, Sally, James A. Ippolito, Lakhwinder S. Hundal, and Nicholas T. Basta. "Municipal Biosolids – A Resource for Sustainable Communities." *Current Opinion in Environmental Science & Health* 14 (2020): 56–62. https://doi.org/10.1016/j.coesh.2020.02.007.

Browning, Matthew H. E. M., Alessandro Rigolon, Olivia McAnirlin, and Hyunseo Yoon. "Where Greenspace Matters Most: A Systematic Review of Urbanicity, Greenspace, and Physical Health." *Landscape and Urban Planning* 217 (2022): 104233. https://doi.org/10.1016/j.landurbplan.2021.104233.

Brüchert, Tanja, Pia Hasselder, Paula Quentin, and Gabriele Bolte. Walking for "Transport among Older Adults: A Cross-Sectional Study on the Role of the Built Environment in Less Densely Populated Areas in Northern Germany." *International Journal of Environmental Research and Public Health* 17 no. 24 (2020). https://doi.org/10.3390/ijerph17249479.

Buckton, Sam J., Ioan Fazey, Bill Sharpe, Eugyen Suzanne Om, Bob Doherty, Peter Ball, Katherine Denby, et al. "The Regenerative Lens: A Conceptual Framework for Regenerative Social-Ecological Systems." *One Earth* 6, no. 7 (2023): 824–42. https://doi.org/10.1016/j.oneear.2023.06.006.

Buehler, Ralph, John Pucher, Regine Gerike, and Thomas Götschi. "Reducing car dependence in the heart of Europe: lessons from Germany, Austria, and Switzerland." *Transport Reviews* 37 no. 1 (2017): 4–28. https://doi.org/10.1080/01441647.2016.1177799.

Bullock, Clair, Kerry Ard, and Grace Saalman. "Measuring the Relationship between State Environmental Justice Action and Air Pollution Inequality, 1990–2009." *Review of Policy Research* 35, no. 3 (2018): 466–90. https://doi.org/10.1111/ropr.12292.

Bundesministerium Bildung. "Bildung Für Nachhaltige Entwicklung." 2024, accessed September 23, 2024. www.bmbwf.gv.at/Themen/schule/schulpraxis/ba/bine.html #heading_Bildung_f_r_Nachhaltige_Entwicklung_2.

Cabral, Ines, Sandra Costa, Ulrike Weiland, and Aletta Bonn. "Urban Gardens as Multifunctional Nature-Based Solutions for Societal Goals in a Changing Climate." In *Nature-Based Solutions to Climate Change Adaptation in Urban Areas: Linkages between Science, Policy and Practice*, edited by Nadja Kabisch, Horst Korn, Jutta Stadler and Aletta Bonn, 237–53. Cham: Springer International Publishing, 2017.

Calisto Friant, Martin, Walter J. V. Vermeulen, and Roberta Salomone. "A Typology of Circular Economy Discourses: Navigating the Diverse Visions of a Contested Paradigm." *Resources, Conservation and Recycling* 161 (2020): 104917. https://doi.org/10.1016/j.resconrec.2020.104917.

CAP-NET. "Economics in Sustainable Water Management: Training Manual and Facilitators' Guide." (2008). www.ircwash.org/resources/economics-sustainable-water-management-training-manual-and-facilitators-guide.

"Bioswales." 2023, accessed August 15, 2023. www.crd.bc.ca/education/stormwater-wastewater-septic/green-stormwater-infrastructure/bioswales.

Cambra, Paulo, Filipe Moura, and Alexandre B. Gonçalves. On the correlation of pedestrian flows to urban environment measures: A space syntax and walkability analysis comparison case. 11th Space Syntax Forum. Lisbon. (2017). Online verfügbar unter www.researchgate.net/publication/319956237_ON_THE_CORRELATION_OF_PEDESTRIAN_FLOWS_TO_URBAN_ENVIRONMENT_MEASURES_A_Space_Syntax_and_Walkability_Analysis_comparison_case,zuletztgeprüftam21.08.2023.

Campbell-Johnston, Kieran, Joey ten Cate, Maja Elfering-Petrovic, and Joyeeta Gupta. "City Level Circular Transitions: Barriers and Limits in Amsterdam, Utrecht and the Hague." *Journal of Cleaner Production* 235 (October 2019): 1232–39. https://doi.org/10.1016/j.jclepro.2019.06.106.

Carayannis, Elias G., and David F. J. Campbell. "'Mode 3' and 'Quadruple Helix': Toward a 21st Century Fractal Innovation Ecosystem." *International Journal of Technology Management* 46, no. 3–4 (2009): 201–34. https://doi.org/10.1504/IJTM.2009.023374.

Carrara, S., S. Bobba, D. Blagoeva, P. Alves Dias, A. Cavalli, K. Georgitzikis, M. Grohol, A. Itul, T. Kuzov, C. Latunussa, L. Lyons, G. Malano, T. Maury, A. Prior Arce, J. Somers, T. Telsnig, C. Veeh, D. Wittmer, C. Black, D. Pennington, and M. Christou. Supply chain analysis and material demand forecast in strategic technologies and sectors in the EU – A foresight study, Publications Office of the European Union, Luxembourg, JRC132889, (2023). https://doi.org.10.2760/334074.

Carnap, Anna, Marie-Therese Arnold, and Inka Bormann. *Bestandsaufnahme Zur Verankerung Von Bildung Für Nachhaltige Entwicklung Bildungs- Und Lehrplänen.* Berlin: Haus der Kleinen Forscher, 2017.

Carson, Jacob R., Terry L. Conway, Lilian G. Perez, Lawrence D. Frank, Brian E. Saelens, Kelli L. Cain, and James F. Sallis. "Neighborhood walkability, neighborhood social health, and self-selection among U.S. adults." *Health & Place* 82, (2023): 103036. https://doi.org/10.1016/j.healthplace.2023.103036.

Cartalis, Constantinos. "Toward Resilient Cities – A Review of Definitions, Challenges and Prospects." *Advances in Building Energy Research* 8, no. 2 (2014): 259–66.

ChangeLab Solutions. "Seeding the City: Land Use Policies to Promote Urban Agriculture." (2012). www.changelabsolutions.org/sites/default/files/Urban_Ag_SeedingTheCity_FINAL_%28CLS_20120530%29_20111021_0.pdf.

China Water, Department for International Development, and Mott MacDonald,. "Water Demand Management – An International Perspective." (2010). https://assets.publishing.service.gov.uk/media/57aaf21940f0b608ab000066/OV2-Demand_management_Mar_2010rev10FINAL.pdf.

Chiu, Rebecca L. H. "Liveable Cities/Urban Liveability." In *The Wiley Blackwell Encyclopedia of Urban and Regional Studies*, edited by Anthony M. Orum, 1–7. Hoboken, NJ.2019.

"Circular Economy." 2024, accessed September 17, 2024. www.chooseparisregion.org/industries/circular-economy.

Christchurch City Council. "Rain Garden Design, Construction and Maintenance Manual." (2016). https://ccc.govt.nz/assets/Documents/Environment/Water/Rain-garden-design-construction-and-maintenance-manual.pdf.

Christiansen, Lars B., Ester Cerin, Hannah Badland, Jacqueline Kerr, Rachel Davey, Jens Troelsen et al. "International comparisons of the associations between objective measures of the built environment and transport-related walking and cycling: IPEN Adult Study." *Journal of Transport & Health* 3, no. 4 (2016): 467–78. https://doi.org/10.1016/j.jth.2016.02.010.

Circle Economy. "Circular Amsterdam. A vision and action agenda for the city and metropolitan area." (2016). www.circle-economy.com/resources/developing-a-roadmap-for-the-first-circular-city-amsterdam.

"Circular Prague." (2019). www.circle-economy.com/resources/circular-prague.

"The Amsterdam City Doughnut: A Tool for Transformative Action." (2020). www.circle-economy.com/resources/the-amsterdam-city-doughnut-a-tool-for-transformative-action.

"Prague: The Circular European Capital You Haven't Heard About Yet." 2021, accessed September 17, 2024. www.circle-economy.com/blogs/prague-the-circular-european-capital-you-havent-heard-about-yet.

"Circular City Funding Guide." (n.d.). www.circularcityfundingguide.eu.

"Circular Economy: Definition, Importance and Benefits: News: European Parliament." Circular Economy: Definition, Importance and Benefits | News European Parliament, May 24, 2023. www.europarl.europa.eu/news/en/headlines/economy/20151201STO05603/circular-economy-definition-importance-and-benefits.

City of Amsterdam. Policy: Food Strategy. (n.d.). www.amsterdam.nl/en/policy/sustainability/food-strategy/.

"Circular Innovation Programme 2016–2018." (in Dutch) (2016). www.circle-economy.com/resources/developing-a-roadmap-for-the-first-circular-city-amsterdam.

"Amsterdam Circular 2020–2025 Strategy." (2020a). https://assets.amsterdam.nl/publish/pages/1043702/amsterdam-circular-2020-2025-public_version.pdf.

"Amsterdam Circular Monitor." (2020b). https://onderzoek.amsterdam.nl/publicatie/the-circular-economy-monitor-an-outline.

"Circular Economy Programme: Lessons and Recommendations 2020–2021." (2022). https://assets.amsterdam.nl/publish/pages/1043702/circular_economy_lessons_and_recommendations_2020-2021.pdf.

"Coalitieakkoord 2022–2026." 2022, accessed September 16, 2024. www.amsterdam.nl/nieuws/coalitieakkoord/.
"Policy: Circular Economy." 2024, accessed September 12, 2024. www.amsterdam.nl/en/policy/sustainability/circular-economy/.
"Policy: Food Strategy." 2024, accessed September 16, 2024. www.amsterdam.nl/en/policy/sustainability/food-strategy/.
"Research & Statistics." 2024, accessed September 16, 2024. https://openresearch.amsterdam/en/page/31753/research-statistics.
City of Cologne. "Standort Köln – Perspektive 2030." (2016). www.stadt-koeln.de/mediaasset/content/pdf80/standort_köln-perspektive_2030_kurzfassung.pdf.
City of Cologne. "Urban Strategy 2.0 – the Perspectives of Cologne 2030+" (2023). www.stadt-koeln.de/mediaasset/content/pdf15/kp2030/kurzfassung_englisch.pdf.
City of Copenhagen. "Cph 2025 Climate Plan – Roadmap 2021–2025." (2020). https://kk.sites.itera.dk/apps/kk_pub2/index.asp?mode=detalje&id=2062.
"Circular Economy." 2020, accessed September 17, 2024. https://sustainableglasgow.org.uk/circular-economy.
City of Helsinki. "The City of Helsinki's Roadmap for Circular and Sharing Economy." (2020). www.hel.fi/static/kanslia/Julkaisut/the-city-of-helsinkis-roadmap-for-circular-and-sharing-economy.pdf.
"Circular Economy Examples in the City of Ljubljana." 2024, accessed September 17, 2024. www.ljubljana.si/en/ljubljana-for-you/environmental-protection/towards-circular-economy/examples-of-circular-economy/.
"Nutrient Recovery Facility." 2023, accessed August 21, 2023. www.saskatoon.ca/services-residents/power-water-sewer/wastewater/wastewater-treatment-plant/nutrient-recovery-facility.
City of Kassel Friedrich-Ebert-Street 2009-2019. (2020). Online verfügbar unter https://mittendrin-kassel.de/wp-content/uploads/2020/09/Monitoringbericht_2020_Aktiver_Kernbereich_FES_Web.pdf.pdf, zuletzt geprüft am 21.08.2023.
City of Sydney. "Building a Strong Green and Circular Economy for Sydney." (2023). www.cityofsydney.nsw.gov.au/research-reports/green-economy-study.
"Sydney Park Wetlands: Major Works, Creation and History." 2023, accessed August 15, 2023. www.cityofsydney.nsw.gov.au/improving-streets-public spaces/sydney-park-wetlands-major-works-creation-and-history.
"Electronic Waste." 2023, accessed September 24, 2023. www.toronto.ca/services-payments/recycling-organics-garbage/electronic-waste/#:~:text=The%20City%20of%20Toronto%20collects%20unwanted%20electronics%20for,or%20Community%20Environment%20Day%20or%20donated%20for%20reuse.
"Green Streets Projects." 2023, accessed August 15, 2023. www.toronto.ca/services-payments/streets-parking-transportation/enhancing-our-streets-and-public-realm/green-streets/green-streets-projects/.
"Vancouver's Urban Forest." 2023, accessed August 15, 2023. https://vancouver.ca/parks-recreation-culture/urban-forest-strategy.aspx#redirect.
City of Vienna. "DoTank Circular City Wien 2020–2030." (2020). https://enviaments.accio.gencat.cat/ACC1O/cat/docs/enviaments/docs/Project9-Barca.pdf.
City of Vienna. "Vienna 2030 – Economy & Innovation." (2024). www.wien.gv.at/english/business-media/vienna-2030.html.
City of Vienna. "Vienna Smart Climate City Strategy." (2022). https://smartcity.wien.gv.at/wp-content/uploads/sites/3/2022/05/scwr_klima_2022_web-EN.pdf.
City of Yokohama. "Yokohama 3R Dream!: Yokohama Municipal Solid Waste Management Master Plan." (2011). www.city.yokohama.lg.jp/city-info/yokohamashi/org/shigen/sonota/hoshin/3r-plan/plan.files/0010_20180906.pdf.

"The Amazing Benefits of Green Walls, Roofs and Facades." 2023, accessed August 15, 2023. https://citygreen.com/benefits-of-green-roofs-walls-and-facades/.

City of Zurich, Mobilität+Planung The Limmatquai before and after redesign. (2009). Online verfügbar unter https://ub-swasearch.ub.unibas.ch/de/detail/swasearch_9957586700105504, zuletzt geprüft am 21.08.2023.

Coalition for Urban Transitions. "Climate Emergency, Urban Opportunity: How National Governments Can Secure Economic Prosperity and Avert Climate Catastrophe by Transforming Cities." Coalition for Urban Transitions, (2019). https://urbantransitions.global/wp-content/uploads/2019/09/Climate-Emergency-Urban-Opportunity-report.pdf.

Cohen, Boyd, and Pablo Muñoz. "Sharing Cities and Sustainable Consumption and Production: Towards an Integrated Framework." *Journal of Cleaner Production* 134 (October 2016): 87–97. https://doi.org/10.1016/j.jclepro.2015.07.133.

Cominola, Andrea, Matteo Giuliani, Andrea Castelletti, Piero Fraternali, Sergio Luis Herrera Gonzalez, Joan Carles Guardiola Herrero, Jasminko Novak, and Andrea Emilio Rizzoli. "Long-Term Water Conservation Is Fostered by Smart Meter-Based Feedback and Digital User Engagement." *npj Clean Water* 4, no. 1 (2021): 29. https://doi.org/10.1038/s41545-021-00119-0.

Contesse, Maria, Bas J. M. van Vliet, and Jennifer Lenhart. "Is Urban Agriculture Urban Green Space? A Comparison of Policy Arrangements for Urban Green Space and Urban Agriculture in Santiago De Chile." *Land Use Policy* 71 (2018): 566–77. https://doi.org/10.1016/j.landusepol.2017.11.006.

Correia, Ricardo, and Catarina Roseta-Palma. "Behavioural Economics in Water Management." (2012). www.isecoeco.org/conferences/isee2012-versao3/pdf/742.pdf.

Cramer, Jacqueline M. "The Function of Transition Brokers in the Regional Governance of Implementing Circular Economy – A Comparative Case Study of Six Dutch Regions." *Sustainability* 12, no. 12. (2020). https://doi.org/10.3390/su12125015.

Crippa, Monica, Diego Guizzardi, Enrico Pisoni, Efisio Solazzo, Antoine Guion, Marilena Muntean, Aneta Florczyk, Marcello Schiavina, Michele Melchhiorri, and Andres Fuentes Hutfilter. "Global Anthropogenic Emissions in Urban Areas: Patterns, Trends, and Challenges." *Environmental Research Letters* 16, no. (7) (2021): 074033. Published July 6, 16, no 7 (2021). https://doi.org/10.1088/1748-9326/ac00e2.

D'Amato, Dalia, Jaana Korhonen, and Anne Toppinen, "Circular, Green, and Bio Economy: How Do Companies in Land-Use Intensive Sectors Align with Sustainability Concepts?" *Ecological Economics* 158 (April 2019): 116–33. https://doi.org/10.1016/j.ecolecon.2018.12.026.

D'Ostuni, Michele, and Leonardo Zaffi. *Nurturing Cities: Pathways Towards a Circular Urban Agriculture*. Conference: World Heritage and Design for HealthAt: Napoli-Capri. 2021. www.researchgate.net/publication/353851009_Nurturing_cities_pathways_towards_a_circular_urban_agriculture.

Davies, Kirsten, Corinna Doolan, Robin van den Honert, and Rose Shi. "Water-Saving Impacts of Smart Meter Technology: An Empirical 5 Year, Whole-of-Community Study in Sydney, Australia." *Water Resources Research* 50, no. 9 (2014): 7348–58. https://doi.org/10.1002/2014WR015812.

Deinhammer, Anna-Vera. "It's Time Cities Came around to a Circular Economy." The Parliament, accessed September 20, 2023. www.theparliamentmagazine.eu/news/article/create-circular-economy-cities.

"Home." 2024, accessed September 16, 2024. https://deceuvel.nl/nl/.

de Graaf, R.E. "Innovations in Urban Water Management to Reduce the Vulnerability of Cities." Delft University of Technology, 2009. https://repository.tudelft.nl/record/uuid:817c33c6-f716-44ca-bb17-80d20ef2100e.

de Graaf, R., and F. Hooimeijer. *Urban Water in Japan*. 1st edn. London: CRC Press, 2008. https://doi.org/10.1201/9781482266221.

De Urbanisten. *Redesigning Deltas Design Study 'Rotterdam, from a Port City to a Port Archipelago + Sponge Water City*. Delft, Netherlands: Delft University of Technology, 2022.

Deloitte. Breaking the Barriers to the Circular Economy. 2017. https://circulareconomy.europa.eu/platform/sites/default/files/171106_white_paper_breaking_the_barriers_to_the_circular_economy_white_paper_vweb-14021.pdf.

Deltares. *Low River Discharge of the Meuse – A Meuse River Basin Water Management Modelling Study Using Ribasim*. Rotterdam, the Netherlands: RIWA Meuse publication, 2022.

DeMarco, A. L., R. Hardenbrook, J. Rose, and D. L. Mendoza. "Air Pollution-Related Health Impacts on Individuals Experiencing Homelessness: Environmental Justice and Health Vulnerability in Salt Lake County, Utah." [In English]. *International Journal of Environmental Research and Public Health* 17, no. 22 (2020). https://doi.org/10.3390/ijerph17228413.

Demchenko, M., Laszlo, A., Hamilton, M., Srivastav, S., Balasubramanian, R., Voorhoeve, A.M., and Wackers, P. "From Sustainable to Thrivable Urban Development: Conceptual Frameworks for Designing a Socio-Cultural, Relational, and Educational Ecosystem of Cities." In *Urban Planning and Design for Megacities in the Global South: Strategies for Smart and Sustainable Urban Development*, edited by C. Mohammed Firoz, Bharat Dahiya, Lakshmi Priya Rajendran, Lalit Kumar Dashora, and Uday Chatterjee. Cham: Springer Nature, 2023.

"Bundesregierung Bericht Der Bundesregierung Zur Bildung Für Nachhaltige Entwicklung – 19. Legislaturperiode." 2021. https://dip.bundestag.de/vorgang/bericht-der-bundesregierung-zur-bildung-für-nachhaltige-entwicklung-19-legislaturperiode/277029.

Dhawan, Piyush, and Janpeter Beckmann. *Circular Economy Guidebook for Cities*. Wuppertal, Germany: The Collaborating Centre on Sustainable Consumption and Production (CSCP), 2019. www.cscp.org/publications/ce-guidebook-cities/.

Dias, Sonia, Ricardo Abussafy, Juliana Goncalves, and Joao Pedro Martins. *Impacts of the COVID-19 Pandemic on Inclusive Recycling in Brazil*. Manchester, UK: Women in Informal Employment: Globalizing and Organizing (WIEGO), 2020. www.wiego.org/sites/default/files/publications/file/Impacts%20of%20the%20COVID-19%20Pandemic%20on%20Inclusive%20Recycling%20in%20Brazil%20for%20web%20%281%29.pdf.

Dolman, Nanco. "Integration of Water Management and Urban Design for Climate Resilient Cities." In *Climate Resilient Urban Areas. Palgrave Studies in Climate Resilient Societies*, edited by R. de Graaf-van Dinther, 21–43. Cham: Palgrave Macmillan, 2021. https://doi.org/10.1007/978-3-030-57537-3_2.

Dolman, Nanco, and R. J. Brolsma. "Groenblauwe maatregelen en nature based solutions: Voor de waterrobuuste en klimaatbestendige stad." *Water Governance*, 1 (2023): 40–47.

Dolman, Nanco, and Fola Ogunyoye. "How Water Challenges Can Shape Tomorrow's Cities." *Proceedings of the Institution of Civil Engineers – Civil Engineering* 171 (2018): 1–37. https://doi.org/10.1680/jcien.17.00052.

Dolman, Nanco, and Fola Ogunyoye. "How Water Challenges Can Shape Tomorrow's Cities – Discussion Contribution." *ICE Proceedings Civil Engineering* 172 (2019): 13–14. https://doi.org/10.1680/jcien.2019.172.1.13.

"Amsterdam City Doughnut." 2024. https://doughnuteconomics.org/stories/amsterdam-city-doughnut.

Dumbaugh, Eric and Michael King. "Engineering Livable Streets: A Thematic Review of Advancements in Urban Street Design." *Journal of Planning Literature* 33, no. 4 (2018): 451–65. https://doi.org/10.1177/0885412218783471.

DVR, TH Köln Goethestreet. Germaniastreet in the City of Kassel – An Example for Successful Urban Street Design. (2022). Online verfügbar unter www.dvr.de/themen/infrastruktur/beispielsammlung-gute-strassen-in-stadt-und-dorf, zuletzt geprüft am 21.08.2023.

EEA. "Circular Economy in Europe – Developing the Knowledge Base." (2015). www.eea.europa.eu/publications/circular-economy-in-europe.

EEA. "Climate Impacts on Water Resources." 2018, accessed January 15, 2020. www.eea.europa.eu/archived/archived-content-water-topic/water-resources/climate-impacts-on-water-resources.

EEA. "Green Infrastructure (GI) – Enhancing Europe's Natural Capital." (2013). www.eea.europa.eu/policy-documents/green-infrastructure-gi-2014-enhancing.

EESI. "Fossil Fuels." 2024, accessed September 12, 2024. www.eesi.org/topics/fossil-fuels/description#:~:text=Fossil%20fuels—including%20coal%2C%20oil,were%20compressed%20and%20heated%20underground.

Ekka, Sujit A., Hendrik Rujner, Günther Leonhardt, Godecke-Tobias Blecken, Maria Viklander, and William F. Hunt. "Next Generation Swale Design for Stormwater Runoff Treatment: A Comprehensive Approach." *Journal of Environmental Management* 279 (2021): 111756. https://doi.org/10.1016/j.jenvman.2020.111756.

El Menshawy, Adel Samy, Abdelaziz Farouk Mohamed, and Nayera Mahmoud Fathy. "A Comparative Study on Green Wall Construction Systems, Case Study: South Valley Campus of Aastmt." *Case Studies in Construction Materials* 16 (2022): e00808. https://doi.org/10.1016/j.cscm.2021.e00808.

Elmqvist, T., H. Setälä, S. N. Handel, S. van der Ploeg, J. Aronson, J. N. Blignaut et al. "Benefits of restoring ecosystem services in urban areas." *Current Opinion in Environmental Sustainability* 14, (2015): 101–8. https://doi.org/10.1016/j.cosust.2015.05.001.

El-Nwsany, Rabab I., Ibrahim Maarouf, and Waled Abd el-Aal. "Water Management as a Vital Factor for a Sustainable School." *Alexandria Engineering Journal* 58, no. 1 (2019): 303–13. https://doi.org/10.1016/j.aej.2018.12.012.

"About Us." 2024, accessed September 16, 2024. www.ellenmacarthurfoundation.org.

"Circular Economy in Cities: Policy Levers." 2023. https://ellenmacarthurfoundation.org/policy-levers.

"The Circular Economy in Cities: Resources Suite." 2023, accessed September 24, 2023. https://ellenmacarthurfoundation.org/circular-economy-in-cities#:~:text=It%20is%20based%20on%20three%20principles%2C%20driven%20by,can%20work%20to%20enable%20a%20circular%20economy%20transition.

Ellen Macarthur Foundation. "Cities in the Circular Economy: An Initial Exploration." (2017). https://emf.thirdlight.com/file/24/MC1eXz-MW2hx60MCEvuM6Pt5sI/Cities%20in%20the%20circular%20economy%3A%20An%20initial%20exploration.pdf.

Ellen Macarthur Foundation. "The Nature Imperative: How the Circular Economy Tackles Biodiversity Loss." (2021). https://emf.thirdlight.com/file/24/FM9nvqPFM.IixvIFMZ6iFC9A.NLF/The%20Nature%20Imperative%3A%20How%20the%20circular%20economy%20tackles%20biodiversity%20loss.pdf.

Ellen Macarthur Foundation. "Towards the Circular Economy Vol. 1: An Economic and Business Rationale for an Accelerated Transition." (2013). www.ellenmacarthurfoundation.org/towards-the-circular-economy-vol-1-an-economic-and-business-rationale-for-an.

"What Is a Circular Economy." 2023, accessed September 24, 2023. https://ellenmacarthurfoundation.org/topics/circular-economy-introduction/overview.

Elliott, P., D. Briggs, S. Morris, C. de Hoogh, C. Hurt, T. K. Jensen, I. Maitland, et al. "Risk of Adverse Birth Outcomes in Populations Living near Landfill Sites." [In English]. *BMJ* 323, no. 7309 (2001): 363–68. https://doi.org/10.1136/bmj.323.7309.363.

Ellis, Peter, and Mark Roberts. *Leveraging Urbanization in South Asia: Managing Spatial Transformation for Prosperity and Livability*. Washington, DC: World Bank, 2015. https://doi.org/10.1596/978-1-4648-0662-9.

Emelko, Monica B., Uldis Silins, Kevin D. Bladon, and Micheal Stone. "Implications of Land Disturbance on Drinking Water Treatability in a Changing Climate: Demonstrating the Need for "Source Water Supply and Protection" Strategies." *Water Research* 45, no. 2 (2011): 461–72. https://doi.org/10.1016/j.watres.2010.08.051.

"Klimawandel Und Nachhaltige Entwicklung Werden Schulfach." 2019, accessed September 23, 2024. www.energiezukunft.eu/klimakrise/klimawandel-und-nachhaltige-entwicklung-werden-schulfach/.

"Bioswale Vs Rain Garden." 2022, accessed August 15, 2023. https://engineeringtraininginstitute.com/bioswale-vs-rain-garden/.

"Kreislaufwirtschaft: Definition Und Vorteile." 2023, accessed September 23, 2024. www.europarl.europa.eu/topics/de/article/20151201STO05603/kreislaufwirtschaft-definition-und-vorteile.

ENEL Group, Cities of Tomorrow, accessed October 20, 2023. www.enel.com/content/dam/enel-com/documenti/media/cities-of-tomorrow_en.pdf.

Esa, M. R., A. Halog, and L. Rigamonti. "Developing Strategies for Managing Construction and Demolition Wastes in Malaysia Based on the Concept of Circular Economy." *Journal of Material Cycles and Waste Management* 19 (2017): 1144–54. https://doi.org/10.1007/s10163-016-0516-x.

European Commission. "Report on the Review of the European Water Scarcity and Drought Policy." (2012). https://climate-adapt.eea.europa.eu/en/metadata/publications/report-on-the-review-of-the-european-water-scarcity-and-drought-policy.

"A new Circular Economy Action Plan For a cleaner and more competitive Europe." (2020). https://eur-lex.europa.eu/resource.html?uri=cellar:9903b325-6388-11ea-b735-01aa75ed71a1.0017.02/DOC_1&format=PDF.

"The European Green Deal (COM(2019)640final). Brussels: European Commission." (2019). https://eur-lex.europa.eu/legal-content/EN/TXT/?uri=CELEX%3A52019DC0640.

"EU Transport in Figures: Statistical Pocketbook 2022." Brussels. (2022). Online verfügbar unter https://transport.ec.europa.eu/facts-funding/studies-data/eu-transport-figures-statistical-pocketbook/statistical-pocketbook-2022_en, zuletzt geprüft am 21.08.2023.

"Circular Economy: Definition, Importance and Benefits." 2023, accessed September 24, 2023. www.europarl.europa.eu/news/en/headlines/economy/20151201STO05603/circular-economy-definition-importance-and-benefits.

"Closing the Loop – An EU Action Plan for the Circular Economy." Communication from the Commission to the European Parliament, The Council, The European Economic and Social Committee and the Committee to the Regions COM/2015/0614 final (Brussels: European Commission, 2015). https://eur-lex.europa.eu/legal-content/EN/TXT/?uri=CELEX:52015DC0614.

European Court of Auditors (ECA). Transition to Circular Economy behind Schedule in EU Countries, Special Report. (2023). www.eca.europa.eu/ECAPublications/SR-2023-17/SR-2023-17_EN.pdf.

Evans, D. L., N. Falagán, C. A. Hardman, S. Kourmpetli, L. Liu, B. R. Mead, and J. A. C. Davies. "Ecosystem Service Delivery by Urban Agriculture and Green Infrastructure – A Systematic Review." *Ecosystem Services* 54 (2022): 101405. https://doi.org/10.1016/j.ecoser.2022.101405.

Ewing, Reid and Robert Cervero. "Travel and the Built Environment." *Journal of the American Planning Association* 76, no. 3 (2010): 265–94. https://doi.org/10.1080/01944361003766766.

Ewing, Reid and Susan Handy. "Measuring the Unmeasurable: Urban Design Qualities Related to Walkability." *Journal of Urban Design* 14, no. 1 (2009): 65–84. https://doi.org/10.1080/13574800802451155.

Ewing, Reid, Otto Clemente, Kathryn M. Neckerman, Marnie Purciel-Hill, James W. Quinn-Hill, and Andrew Rundle. *Measuring Urban Design*. Washington, DC: Island Press/Center for Resource Economics, 2013.

Ewing, Reid, Mark B. Connors, Jonathan P. Goates, Amir Hajrasouliha, Kathy Neckerman, Arthur C. Nelson, and William Greene. Validating Urban Design Measures. TRB 92nd Annual Meeting Compendium of Papers. (2013). Washington, DC.

Ewing, Reid, Amir Hajrasouliha, Kathryn M. Neckerman, Marnie Purciel-Hill, and William Greene. "Streetscape Features Related to Pedestrian Activity." *Journal of Planning Education and Research* 36, no. 1, (2016): 5–15. https://doi.org/10.1177/0739456X15591585.

Falkenmark, Malin, Jan Lundqvist, and Carl Widstrand. "Macro-Scale Water Scarcity Requires Micro-Scale Approaches." *Natural Resources Forum* 13, no. 4 (1989): 258–67. https://doi.org/10.1111/j.1477-8947.1989.tb00348.x.

FAO. "The State of the World's Land and Water Resources for Food and Agriculture: Managing Systems at Risk." (2011). www.fao.org/3/i1688e/i1688e.pdf.

FAO. "Towards a Water and Food Secure Future: Critical Perspectives for Policy-Makers." (2015). www.fao.org/3/a-i4560e.pdf.

"Water Use and Reuse for Urban Agriculture." 2023, accessed August 21, 2023. https://cdn.who.int/media/docs/default-source/wash-documents/food-for-the-cities.pdf?sfvrsn=c998fe5_8.

FAO. "The Water–Energy–Food Nexus. A New Approach in Support of Food Security and Sustainable Agriculture." (2014). https://openknowledge.fao.org/items/c171bc10-9788-4f3d-878a-a137be150c71.

Fazzo, L., F. Minichilli, M. Santoro, A. Ceccarini, M. Della Seta, F. Bianchi, P. Comba, and M. Martuzzi. "Hazardous Waste and Health Impact: A Systematic Review of the Scientific Literature." *Environmental Health* 16, no. 1 (2017): 107. https://doi.org/10.1186/s12940-017-0311-8.

Federal Ministry Republic of Austria Climate Action, Environment, Energy, Mobility, and Innovation and Technology. "The Austrian Circular Economy Strategy." (2022). www.bmk.gv.at/en/topics/climate-environment/waste-resource-management/ces.html.

Ferreira, Carla, Zahra Kalantari, and Paulo Pereira. "Liveable Cities: Current Environmental Challenges and Paths to Urban Sustainability." *Journal of Environmental Management* 277 (2021): 111458. https://doi.org/10.1016/j.jenvman.2020.111458.

Ferronato, Navarro, Elena Cristina Rada, Marcelo Antonio Gorritty Portillo, Lucian Ionel Cioca, Marco Ragazzi, and Vincenzo Torretta. "Introduction of the Circular Economy within Developing Regions: A Comparative Analysis of Advantages and Opportunities for Waste Valorization." *Journal of Environmental Management* 230 (January 2019): 366–78. https://doi.org/10.1016/j.jenvman.2018.09.095.

Fischer, Daniel, and Michelsen, Gerd. "Sustainability and Education." In *Sustainable Development Policy: A European Perspective*, edited by Claudia Kuhnke and Michael von Hauff, 131–54. London: Routledge, 2017.

Fischer-Kowalski, Marina, and Walter Hüttler. "Society's Metabolism." *Journal of Industrial Ecology* 2, no. 4 (1998): 107–36. https://doi.org/10.1162/jiec.1998.2.4.107.

Fisseha, Tiguist, Akiko Toya, Nuala Margaret Cowan, and Larissa Duma. "#FreetownTheTreeTown Campaign: Using Digital Tools to Encourage Tree Cultivation in Cities," Global Environment Facility, GEF.org, August 5, 2021. www.thegef.org/blog/freetownthetreetown-campaign-using-digital-tools-encourage-tree-cultivation-cities.

Forastiere, F., C. Badaloni, K. de Hoogh, M. K. von Kraus, M. Martuzzi, F. Mitis, L. Palkovicova, et al. "Health Impact Assessment of Waste Management Facilities in Three European Countries." [In eng]. *Environmental Health* 10 (Jun 2 2011): 53. https://doi.org/10.1186/1476-069x-10-53.

Frantzeskaki, N., & Loorbach, D. "Transitions Governance: Towards a New Governance Paradigm." Paper presented at the 13th Annual Conference of the International Research Society for Public Management (IRSPM XIII), Copenhagen, Denmark, 2009.

Frehlich, Levi, Chelsea D. Christie, Paul E. Ronksley, Tanvir C. Turin, Patricia Doyle-Baker, and Gavin R. McCormack. "The neighbourhood built environment and health-related fitness: a narrative systematic review." *The International Journal of Behavioral Nutrition and Physical Activity* 19, no. 1 (2022): 124. https://doi.org/10.1186/s12966-022-01359-0.

Gao, Lei, Jeff Connor, Rebecca Doble, Riasat Ali, and Don McFarlane. "Opportunity for Peri-Urban Perth Groundwater Trade." *Journal of Hydrology* 496 (2013): 89–99. https://doi.org/10.1016/j.jhydrol.2013.05.009.

Garrick, Dustin, Lucia De Stefano, Winston Yu, Isabel Jorgensen, Erin O'Donnell, Laura Turley, Ismael Aguilar-Barajas, et al. "Rural Water for Thirsty Cities: A Systematic Review of Water Reallocation from Rural to Urban Regions." *Environmental Research Letters* 14, no. 4 (2019): 043003. https://doi.org/10.1088/1748-9326/ab0db7.

Gascon, Mircia, Thomas Götschi, Audrey de Nazelle, Esther Gracia, Albert Ambròs, Sandra Márquez et al. "Correlates of Walking for Travel in Seven European Cities: The PASTA Project." *Environmental Health Perspectives* 127, no. 9 (2019): 97003. https://doi.org/10.1289/EHP4603.

Gascon, Mireia, Oriol Marquet, Esther Gràcia-Lavedan, Albert Ambròs, Thomas Götschi, and Audrey de Nazelle et al. "What explains public transport use? Evidence from seven European cities." *Transport Policy* 99, (2020): 362–74. https://doi.org/10.1016/j.tranpol.2020.08.009.

Geissdoerfer, Martin, Sandra Naomi Morioka, Marly Monteiro de Carvalho, and Steve Evans. "Business Models and Supply Chains for the Circular Economy." *Journal of Cleaner Production* 190 (2018): 712–21. https://doi.org/10.1016/j.jclepro.2018.04.159.

Geissdoerfer, Martin, Paulo Savaget, Nancy M. P. Bocken, and Erik Jan Hultink. "The Circular Economy – A New Sustainability Paradigm?" *Journal of Cleaner Production* 143 (2017): 757–68. https://doi.org/10.1016/j.jclepro.2016.12.048.

Gehl, Jan. *Cities for people*. Washington, DC: Island Press, 2010.

Gehl, Jan and Birgitte Svarre. *How to Study Public Life*. Washington, DC: Island Press/Center for Resource Economics, 2013.

Georgia Environmental Protection Division Watershed Protection Branch. (2007). www1.gadnr.org/cws/Documents/Conservation_Education.pdf.

Georgia Environmental Protection Division Watershed Protection Branch. "Water Conservation Education Programs Epd Guidance Document." (2007). www1.gadnr.org/cws/Documents/Conservation_Education.pdf.

Gerike, Regine, Klaus Bogenberger, Kai Nagel, Susann Wagenknecht, Dominik Ziemke, and Travis Waller. From Sustainable Urban Transport to Responsible Urban Mobility: Function, Form, Fairness, Forever. In: *Reference Module in Earth Systems and Environmental Sciences*: Elsevier, 2022.

Gerike, Regine, Caroline Koszowski, Stefan Hubrich, Weert Canzler, and Julia Epp. Aktive Mobilität: Mehr Lebensqualität in Ballungsräumen. Dessau (UBA-Texte, 226/2020). (2020). Online verfügbar unter www.umweltbundesamt.de/publikationen/aktive-mobilitaet-mehr-lebensqualitaet-in, zuletzt geprüft am 21.08.2023.

Gerike, Regine, Caroline Koszowski, Bettina Schröter, Rico Wittwer, Paulo Anciaes, Ellen Hill, and Peter Jones. Cross-site assessment of case study design packages. Deliverable

D5.5, MORE project (Multimodal Optimisation of Roadspace in Europe). (2018). Online verfügbar unter www.roadspace.eu/results, zuletzt geprüft am 21.08.2023.

Germani, Anna Rita, Piergiuseppe Morone, and Giuseppina Testa. "Environmental Justice and Air Pollution: A Case Study on Italian Provinces." *Ecological Economics* 106 (2014): 69–82. https://doi.org/10.1016/j.ecolecon.2014.07.010.

Ghisellini, Patrizia, Catia Cialani, and Sergio Ulgiati. "A Review on Circular Economy: The Expected Transition to a Balanced Interplay of Environmental and Economic Systems." *Journal of Cleaner Production* 114 (2016): 11–32. doi.org/10.1016/j.jclepro.2015.09.007.

Ghofrani, Zahra, Victor Sposito, and Robert Faggian. "A Comprehensive Review of Blue-Green Infrastructure Concepts." *International Journal of Environment and Sustainability* 6 (2017): 15–36. www.semanticscholar.org/paper/A-Comprehensive-Review-of-Blue-Green-Infrastructure-Ghofrani-Sposito/4052eb537c5edad387f889e247a1fade83bdf0be.

Ghosh, S.N. *Environmental Hydrology and Hydraulics: Eco-Technological Practices for Sustainable Development*. CRC Press, 2016. https://books.google.co.nz/books?id=jj7NBQAAQBAJ.

Gifford, Robert, Christine Kormos, and Amanda McIntyre. "Behavioral Dimensions of Climate Change: Drivers, Responses, Barriers, and Interventions." *Wiley Interdisciplinary Reviews: Climate Change* 2, no. 6 (2011): 801–27.

Glaeser, Edward. "The 15-Minute City Is a Dead End – Cities Must Be Places of Opportunity for Everyone." *LSE Blogs*, May 28, 2021. https://blogs.lse.ac.uk/covid19/2021/05/28/the-15-minute-city-is-a-dead-end-cities-must-be-places-of-opportunity-for-everyone/.

Glasgow City Council. *Circular Economy Route Map for Glasgow*, (2020). www.glasgow.gov.uk/article/2392/Circular-Economy.

Glasgow City Council *Resource and Recycling Strategy 2020–2030*, (2020). www.glasgow.gov.uk/article/5731/Resource-and-Recycling-Strategy-2020-30.

Global Water Partnership. "Water Demand Management (WDM) – The Mediterranean Experience." *Technical focus paper*. (2012). www.pseau.org/outils/ouvrages/plan_bleu_gwp_water_demand_management_the_mediterranean_experience_2012.pdf.

Gravagnuolo, A., M. Angrisano, and L. Fusco Girard. "Circular Economy Strategies in Eight Historic Port Cities: Criteria and Indicators towards a Circular City Assessment Framework." *Sustainability*, 11, no. 13 (2019), Article 3512. https://doi.org/10.3390/su11133512.

Grund, Julius and Antje Brock. "Bildung Für Nachhaltige Entwicklung in Lehr-Lernsettings – Quantitative Studie Des Nationalen Monitorings – Befragung Junger Menschen. Executive Summary." (2018). www.researchgate.net/publication/328957682_Bildung_fur_nachhaltige_Entwicklung_in_Lehr-Lernsettings_-_Quantitative_Studie_des_nationalen_Monitorings_-_Befragung_junger_Menschen_Executive_Summary.

Götschi, Thomas, Audrey de Nazelle, Christian Brand, and Regine Gerike. "Towards a Comprehensive Conceptual Framework of Active Travel Behavior: a Review and Synthesis of Published Frameworks." *Current Environmental Health Reports* 4, no. 3 (2017). 286–95. https://doi.org/10.1007/s40572-017-0149-9.

Gou, Zhonghua, and Xiaohuan Xie, "Evolving Green Building: Triple Bottom Line or Regenerative Design?" *Journal of Cleaner Production* 153 (June 2017): 600–607. https://doi.org/10.1016/j.jclepro.2016.02.077.

Guo, Bin, Yong Geng, Jingzheng Ren, Lei Zhu, Yaxuan Liu, and Thomas Sterr. "Comparative Assessment of Circular Economy Development in China's Four Megacities: The Case of Beijing, Chongqing, Shanghai and Urumqi." *Journal of Cleaner Production* 162 (September 2017): 234–46. https://doi.org/10.1016/j.jclepro.2017.06.061.

Gravagnuolo, Antonia, Mariarosaria Angrisano, and Luigi Fusco Girard. "Circular Economy Strategies in Eight Historic Port Cities: Criteria and Indicators Towards a Circular City Assessment Framework." *Sustainability* 11, no. 13. (2019). https://doi.org/10.3390/su11133512.

"Blue Green Roofs." 2023, accessed August 15, 2023. https://greenrooftechnology.com/green-roof-finder/blue_green-roofs/.

"Green Roof Types." 2023, accessed August 15, 2023. https://greenrooftechnology.com/green-roof-finder/green-roof-types/.

"Permeable Pavement: The Pros and Cons You Need to Know." 2023, accessed August 15, 2023. https://greenbluc.com/na/permeable-pavement-the-pros-and-cons-you-need-to-know/.

Grineski, Sara, Bob Bolin, and Christopher Boone. "Criteria Air Pollution and Marginalized Populations: Environmental Inequity in Metropolitan Phoenix, Arizona." *Social Science Quarterly* 88, no. 2 (2007): 535–54. https://doi.org/10.1111/j.1540-6237.2007.00470.x.

Güngör, Mahmud, Ufuk Yarar, and Mahmut Firat. "Reduction of Water Losses by Rehabilitation of Water Distribution Network." *Environmental Monitoring and Assessment* 189, no. 10 (2017): 498. https://doi.org/10.1007/s10661-017-6219-5.

Guo, Ying, and Yanjun Shen. "Agricultural Water Supply/Demand Changes under Projected Future Climate Change in the Arid Region of Northwestern China." *Journal of Hydrology* 540 (2016): 257–73. https://doi.org/10.1016/j.jhydrol.2016.06.033.

"Raising Public Awareness." 2020, accessed March 3, 2020. www.gwp.org/en/learn/iwrm-toolbox/Management-Instruments/Promoting_Social_Change/Raising_public_awareness/.

"Securing Water Sustaining Growth." 2015. www.gwp.org/Global/About%20GWP/Publications/The%20Global%20Dialogue/SECURING%20WATER%20SUSTAINING%20GROWTH.PDF.

Hahm, Yeankyoung, Heeyeun Yoon, and Yunwon Choi. "The effect of built environments on the walking and shopping behaviors of pedestrians; A study with GPS experiment in Sinchon retail district in Seoul, South Korea." *Cities* 89, (2019): 1–13. https://doi.org/10.1016/j.cities.2019.01.020.

Hall, C. Michael, and Yael Ram. "Measuring the relationship between tourism and walkability? Walk Score and English tourist attractions." *Journal of Sustainable Tourism* 27, no. 2 (2019): 223–40. https://doi.org/10.1080/09669582.2017.1404607.

Hamidi, Shima and Somayeh Moazzeni. "Examining the Relationship between Urban Design Qualities and Walking Behavior: Empirical Evidence from Dallas, TX." *Sustainability* 11, no. 10 (2019): 2720. https://doi.org/10.3390/su11102720.

Hamilton M. and B. Sanders. "A Radically Optimistic Inquiry into Operating System 2.0." The Integral City 2.0 Online Conference, Online, 2012.

Hannon, Eric, Marianne Kuhlmann, and Benjamin Thaidigsmann. "Developing Products for a Circular Economy." *McKinsey&Company, Retrieved April* 21 (2016): 2020.

Hara, K., H. Yabar, M. Uwasu et al. "Energy Intensity Trends and Scenarios for China's Industrial Sectors: A Regional Case Study." *Sustainability Science* 6 (2011): 123–34. https://doi.org/10.1007/s11625-010-0125-x.

Harding, Anna K., and Marsha L. Greer. "The Health Impact of Hazardous Waste Sites on Minority Communities: Implications for Public Health and Environmental Health Professionals." *Journal of Environmental Health* 55, no. 7 (1993): 6–10. www.jstor.org/stable/44535497.

He, Chunyang, Zhifeng Liu, Jianguo Wu, Xinhao Pan, Zihang Fang, Jingwei Li, and Brett A. Bryan. "Future Global Urban Water Scarcity and Potential Solutions." *Nature Communications* 12, no. 1 (2021): 4667. https://doi.org/10.1038/s41467-021-25026-3.

Helm, Dieter. "The Future of Fossil Fuels – Is It the End?" *Oxford Review of Economic Policy* 32, no. 2 (2016): 191–205. www.jstor.org/stable/26363162.

Hillen M., and Dolman N. "Towards Water Adaptive Cities." Paper presented at the World Engineers Summit on Climate Change (WES), Singapore, 2015.

Hodgson K., M. C. Campbell, and M. Bailkey. *Urban Agriculture: Growing Healthy, Sustainable Places*. Washington, DC: American Planning Advisory Service, 2011.

Höök, Mikael, and Xu Tang. "Depletion of Fossil Fuels and Anthropogenic Climate Change – a Review." *Energy Policy* 52 (2013): 797–809. https://doi.org/10.1016/j.enpol.2012.10.046.

Hui, Nancy, Shoshanna Saxe, Matthew Roorda, Paul Hess, and Eric J. Miller. "Measuring the completeness of complete streets." *Transport Reviews* 38, no. 1 (2018): 73–95. https://doi.org/10.1080/01441647.2017.1299815.

Hunter, P. "The Health Toll of Air Pollution: Despite Global Efforts to Clean up the Air, Outdoor and Indoor Air Pollution Still Have a Drastic Negative Effect on Public Health." [In eng]. *EMBO Reports* 21, no. 8 (2020): e51183. https://doi.org/10.15252/embr.202051183.

Iacovidou, Eleni, and Phil Purnell. "Mining the Physical Infrastructure: Opportunities, Barriers and Interventions in Promoting Structural Components Reuse." *Science of the Total Environment* 557 (2016): 791–807.

ICLEI. "Circular City Actions Framework. Bringing the Circular Economy to Every City." (2021). https://circulars.iclei.org/wp-content/uploads/2021/10/Circular-City-Action-Framework_V2.pdf.

IDRC. "Treatment and Use of Wastewater in Urban Agriculture." (2019). https://ruaf.org/assets/2019/11/Guideline-6-Treatment-and-use-of-waste-water-in-Urban-Agriculture.pdf.

IDRC. "Wastewater Use in Urban Agriculture: Assessing Current Research and Options for National and Local Governments." (2004). www.ircwash.org/sites/default/files/Redwood-2004-Wastewater.pdf.

IEA. "Weo-2016 Special Report: Water-Energy Nexus." (2016). www.iea.org/reports/world-energy-outlook-2016.

"Empowering Cities for a Net Zero Future." (2021). www.iea.org/reports/empowering-cities-for-a-net-zero-future.

"Sustainability Is in Our DNA." (2024). accessed September 16, 2024. www.interface.com/GB/en-GB/sustainability/sustainability-overview.html.

International Resource Panel. "The Weight of Cities: Resource Requirements of Future Urbanization." (2018). www.resourcepanel.org/reports/weight-cities.

"Urbanisation." 2020, accessed January 15, 2020. https://iwa-network.org/urbanisation/.

IPCC. "The Fifth Assessment Report (Ar5) of the Intergovernmental Panel on Climate Change." (2014). www.ipcc.ch/assessment-report/ar5/.

Jacobi, Nikolai, Willi Haas, Dominik Wiedenhofer, and Andreas Mayer. "Providing an Economy-Wide Monitoring Framework for the Circular Economy in Austria: Status Quo and Challenges." *Resources, Conservation and Recycling* 137 (2018): 156–66. https://doi.org/10.1016/j.resconrec.2018.05.022.

Jaeger, Bjoern, and Arvind Upadhyay. "Understanding Barriers to Circular Economy: Cases from the Manufacturing Industry." *Journal of Enterprise Information Management* 33, no. 4 (2020): 729–45. https://doi.org/10.1108/JEIM-02-2019-0047.

Jiang, Yong, Chris Zevenbergen, and Yongchi Ma. "Urban Pluvial Flooding and Stormwater Management: A Contemporary Review of China's Challenges and 'Sponge Cities' Strategy." *Environmental Science & Policy* 80 (February 2018): 132–43. https://doi.org/10.1016/j.envsci.2017.11.016.

Joensu, T., H. Edelman, and A. Saari. "Circular Economy Practices in the Built Environment." *Journal of Cleaner Production* 276 (2020): 124215. https://doi.org/10.1016/j.jclepro.2020.124215.

Johnson, Barry L. "Hazardous Waste: Human Health Effects." *Toxicology and Industrial Health* 13, no. 2–3 (1997): 121–43. https://doi.org/10.1177/074823379701300203.

Jones, A. T., and W. Finley. "Recent Development in Salinity Gradient Power." Paper presented at the Oceans 2003: Celebrating the Past … Teaming Toward the Future (IEEE Cat. No.03CH37492), September 22–26, 2003.

Jones, Peter, and Daphne Comfort. "Winning Hearts and Minds: A Commentary on Circular Cities." *Journal of Public Affairs* 18, no. 4 (2018). https://doi.org/10.1002/pa.1726.

Jordan, Samuel W. and Stephanie Ivey. "Complete Streets: Promises and Proof." *Journal of Urban Planning and Development* 147, no.2 (2021): Artikel 04021011. https://doi.org/10.1061/(ASCE)UP.1943-5444.0000684.

József, Benedek. "Urban Policy and Urbanisation in the Transition Romania." *Romanian Review of Regional Studies* 1 (2006): 1.

Kalmykova, Yuliya, Madumita Sadagopan, and Leonardo Rosado. "Circular Economy – From Review of Theories and Practices to Development of Implementation Tools." *Resources, Conservation and Recycling* 135 (2018): 190–201. https://doi.org/10.1016/j.resconrec.2017.10.034.

Kang, Chang-Deok "The effects of spatial accessibility and centrality to land use on walking in Seoul, Korea." *Cities* 46, (2015): 94–103. https://doi.org/10.1016/j.cities.2015.05.006.

Kaza, Silpa et al. *What a Waste 2.0: A Global Snapshot of Solid Waste Management to 2050. Urban Development.* Washington, DC: World Bank, 2018. https://openknowledge.worldbank.org/handle/10986/30317.

Kębłowski, Wojciech, Deborah Lambert, and David Bassens. "Circular Economy and the City: An Urban Political Economy Agenda." *Culture and Organization* 26, no. 2 (2020): 142–58. https://doi.org/10.1080/14759551.2020.1718148.

Kelly, D. A. "Labelling and Water Conservation: A European Perspective on a Global Challenge." [In English]. *Building Services Engineering Research & Technology* 36, no. 6 (Nov 2015 2015-11-19 2015): 643–57. https://dx.doi.org/10.1177/0143624415571758.

Khalil, Elias L. "The Red Queen Paradox: A Proper Name for a Popular Game: Note." *Journal of Institutional and Theoretical Economics (JITE) / Zeitschrift für die gesamte Staatswissenschaft* 153, no. 2 (1997): 411–15. www.jstor.org/stable/40751982.

Khan, Muhammad M., Sajjad A. Siddiqi, Aitazaz A. Farooque, Qumer Iqbal, Shabbir A. Shahid, Muhammad T. Akram, Sadik Rahman, Waleed Al-Busaidi, and Imran Khan. "Towards Sustainable Application of Wastewater in Agriculture: A Review on Reusability and Risk Assessment." *Agronomy* 12, no. 6. (2022). https://doi.org/10.3390/agronomy12061397.

"Be Rainwise." 2023, accessed August 15, 2023. https://kingcounty.gov/services/environment/wastewater/cso/rainwise.aspx.

Kibert, Charles J. "Policy Instruments for Sustainable Built Environment." *Journal of Land Use & Environmental Law* 17 (2001): 379.

Kim, Suji, Sungjin Park, and Kitae Jang. "Spatially-varying effects of built environment determinants on walking." *Transportation Research Part A: Policy and Practice* 123, (2019): 188–99. https://doi.org/10.1016/j.tra.2019.02.003.

Kirchherr, Julian, Denise Reike, and Marko Hekkert. "Conceptualizing the Circular Economy: An Analysis of 114 Definitions." *Resources, Conservation and Recycling* 127, no. 0921–3449 (December 2017): 221–32.

Kirchherr, Julian, Laura Piscicelli, Ruben Bour, Erica Kostense-Smit, Jennifer Muller, Anne Huibrechtse-Truijens, and Marko Hekkert. "Barriers to the Circular Economy: Evidence from the European Union (Eu)." *Ecological Economics* 150 (2018): 264–72. https://doi.org/10.1016/j.ecolecon.2018.04.0283.

"Protopia." 2024, accessed September 18, 2024. https://kk.org/thetechnium/protopia/.

Kristensen, Heidi Simone, Mette Alberg Mosgaard, and Arne Remmen. "Circular Public Procurement Practices in Danish Municipalities." *Journal of Cleaner Production* 281 (2021): 124962. https://doi.org/10.1016/j.jclepro.2020.124962.

Kjaer, Louise Laumann, Daniela C. A. Pigosso, Monia Niero, Marie Nynne, and Tim C. McAloone. "Product/Service-Systems for a Circular Economy: The Route to Decoupling Economic Growth from Resource Consumption?" *Journal of Industrial Ecology* 23, no. (1) (2019): 22–35. https://doi.org/10.1111/jiec.12747.

Knuijt, Martin. "Liveable Green Cities: Integrating Climate Adaptive Solutions and Circular Economy into the Built Environment." In Designing Sustainable Cities, edited by Rob Roggema, 87–99. Cham: Springer International Publishing, 2020.

Knuiman, Matthew W., Hayley E. Christian, Mark L. Divitini, Sarah A. Foster, Fiona C. Bull, Hannah M. Badland, and Billie Giles-Corti. "A longitudinal analysis of the influence of the neighborhood built environment on walking for transportation: the RESIDE study." *American Journal of Epidemiology* 180, no. 5 (2014): 453–61. https://doi.org/10.1093/aje/kwu171.

Korhonen, Jouni, Antero Honkasalo, and Jyri Seppälä. "Circular Economy: The Concept and Its Limitations." *Ecological Economics* 143 (2018): 37–46. https://doi.org/10.1016/j.ecolecon.2017.06.041.

Kotcher, John, Edward Maibach, and Wen-Tsing Choi. "Fossil Fuels Are Harming Our Brains: Identifying Key Messages About the Health Effects of Air Pollution from Fossil Fuels." *BMC Public Health* 19, no. 1 (2019): 1079. https://doi.org/10.1186/s12889-019-7373-1.

Kottari, M. "Amsterdam's Pathway to Climate Neutrality: Creating an Enabling Environment." In *The Palgrave Encyclopedia of Urban and Regional Futures*, edited by R. Brears. Cham: Palgrave Macmillan, 2021. https://doi.org/10.1007/978-3-030-51812-7_209-1.

Koszowski, C., R. Wittwer, S. Hubrich, and R. Gerike. Perceived Importance of Context-Specific Built-Environment Factors of Walking: A New Perspective for Prioritizing Policy Measures for Promoting Walking. International Journal of Sustainable Transportation. (in publication).

Kraussman, F., D. Wiedenhofer, C. Lauk, W. Haas, H. Tanikawa, T. Fishman, A. Miatto, H. Schandl, and H. Haberl. "Global Socioeconomic Material Stocks Rise 23-fold over the 20th Century and Require Half of Annual Resource Use." *Proceedings of the National Academy of Sciences of the United States of America* 114, no.8 (2017). https://doi.org/10.1073/pnas.1613773114.

Kroesen, Maarten, Susan Handy, and Caspar Chorus. "Do attitudes cause behavior or vice versa? An alternative conceptualization of the attitude-behavior relationship in travel behavior modeling." *Transportation Research Part A: Policy and Practice* 101, (2017): 190–202. https://doi.org/10.1016/j.tra.2017.05.013.

Krook, Joakim, Niclas Svensson, and Mats Eklund. "Landfill Mining: A Critical Review of Two Decades of Research." *Waste Management* 32, no. 3 (2012): 513–20.

Lakatos, Elena Simina, Geng Yong, Andrea Szilagyi, Dan Sorin Clinci, Lucian Georgescu, Catalina Iticescu, and Lucian-Ionel Cioca. "Conceptualizing Core Aspects on Circular Economy in Cities." *Sustainability* 13, no. 14 (2021): 7549.

Lakatos, Elena Simina, Sorin Dan Clinci, Viktor Koval, and Gheorghe Daniel Lakatos. "Creating Livable Cities through Sustainable Built Environments in the Circular Economy." *Innovative Economics and Management* 10, no. 2 (2023): 260–70.

Lai, Yuan and Constantine E. Kontokosta. "Quantifying place: Analyzing the drivers of pedestrian activity in dense urban environments." *Landscape and Urban Planning* 180, (2018): 166–78. https://doi.org/10.1016/j.landurbplan.2018.08.018.

Langemeyer, Johannes, Cristina Madrid-Lopez, Angelica Mendoza Beltran, and Gara Villalba Mendez. "Urban Agriculture – A Necessary Pathway towards Urban Resilience and Global Sustainability?" *Landscape and Urban Planning* 210 (2021): 104055. https://doi.org/10.1016/j.landurbplan.2021.104055.

Laszlo, Alexander. "Evolutionary Systems Design." *Journal of Organisational Transformation & Social Change* 1, no. 1 (2004): 29–46. https://doi.org/10.1386/jots.1.1.29/0.

Laszlo, Alexander, Karin Huber-Heim, and Stefan Blachfellner. "From Sustainability to Thrivability: Transforming Systems with Purpose." In *The Kyoto Post-Covid Manifesto for Global Economics: Confronting Our Shattered Society*, edited by Stephen Hill, Tadashi Yagi and Stomu Yamash'ta, 305–16. Singapore: Springer Nature Singapore, 2022.

Laszlo, Alexander, Karin Huber-Heim, Stefan Blachfellner, and Pavel Luksha. "Systemic Innovation for Thrivable Cities." In *The Palgrave Encyclopedia of Urban and Regional Futures*, Volume 1, 1–20. Cham: Springer International Publishing, 2020.

Laszlo, E. *Evolution: The General Theory*. Cresskill, NJ: Hampton, 1996.

LaVanchy, Thomas G., Michael W. Kerwin, and James K. Adamson, "Beyond 'Day Zero': Insights and Lessons from Cape Town (South Africa)." *Hydrogeology Journal* 27, no. 5 (June 14, 2019): 1537–40. http://dx.doi.org/10.1007/s10040-019-01979-0.

Leville, Sandra, and Matthew Taylor, "Stop Exporting Plastic Waste to China to Boost Recycling at Home, Say Experts," *The Guardian*, June 29, 2017. www.theguardian.com/environment/2017/jun/29/stop-exporting-plastic-waste-to-china-to-boost-recycling-at-home-say-experts.

Liao, Bojing, Pauline E.W. Kontokosta, P.J.V. van Wesemael, and Theo A. Arentze. "Empirical analysis of walkability using data from the Netherlands." *Transportation Research Part D: Transport and Environment* 85, (2020): 102390. https://doi.org/10.1016/j.trd.2020.102390.

Lică, Iuliana Mădălina. "Cities Going Circular: Glasgow's Approach to the Circular Economy Model." *Oeconomica* 3, no. 19 (2019).

Lin, Ch., W. Chiang, Y. Weng, and H. Wu. "Assessing the Anthropogenic Carbon Emission of Wconstruction: An LCA Study." *Building Research & Information* 51, no. 2 (2023): 138–57. https://doi.org/10.1080/09613218.2022.2087171.

Litman, Todd. Evaluating complete streets. Victoria Transport Policy Institute, 1250 Rudlin Street, Victoria, British Columbia V8V 3R7, Canada. (2015). Online verfügbar unter www.vtpi.org/compstr.pdf, zuletzt geprüft am 21.08.2023.

Ludwig, Volker. "Transition to Circular Economy: The Role of Education from Youth to Higher Education." *European Commission*, September 23, 2020. https://epale.ec.europa.eu/en/blog/transition-circular-economy-role-education-youth-higher-education.

Lützkendorf, Thomas, Wei Fan, and David Lorenz. "Engaging Financial Stakeholders: Opportunities for a Sustainable Built Environment." *Building Research & Information* 39, no. 5 (2011): 483–503.

Lydon, Mike and Anthony Garcia. *Tactical urbanism*. Washington, DC: Island Press, 2015.

Ma, Weijing, Christian Opp, and Dewei Yang. "Spatiotemporal Supply-Demand Characteristics and Economic Benefits of Crop Water Footprint in the Semi-Arid Region." *Science of the Total Environment* 738 (2020): 139502. https://doi.org/10.1016/j.scitotenv.2020.139502.

MacArthur, Ellen, Klaus Zumwinkel, and Martin R. Stuchtey. "Growth Within: A Circular Economy Vision for a Competitive Europe." *Ellen MacArthur Foundation* (2015).

MacArthur, Ellen. “Towards the Circular Economy.” *Journal of Industrial Ecology* 2, no. 1 (2013): 23–44.

Magwaza, Shirly Tentile, Lembe Samukelo Magwaza, Alfred Oduor Odindo, and Asanda Mditshwa. “Hydroponic Technology as Decentralised System for Domestic Wastewater Treatment and Vegetable Production in Urban Agriculture: A Review.” *Science of the Total Environment* 698 (2020): 134154. https://doi.org/10.1016/j.scitotenv.2019.134154.

Maheepala, Shiroma, Jane Blackmore, Clare Diaper, Magnus Moglia, Ashok Sharma, and Steven Kenway. “Towards the Adoption of Integrated Urban Water Management Approach for Planning.” *Proceedings of the Water Environment Federation* 2010, no. 9 (2010): 6734–53.

Manikas, Ioannis, George Malindretos, and Konstadinos Abeliotis. “Sustainable Cities through Alternative Urban Farming: The Case of Floriculture.” *Journal of International Food & Agribusiness Marketing* 32, no. 3 (2020): 295–311. https://doi.org/10.1080/08974438.2019.1599762.

Marin, Julie, and Bruno De Meulder. “Interpreting Circularity. Circular City Representations Concealing Transition Drivers.” *Sustainability* 10, no. 5 (2018): 1310.

Mayor of London Mayor’s Transport Strategy. (2018). Online verfügbar unter www.london.gov.uk/sites/default/files/mayors-transport-strategy-2018.pdf, zuletzt geprüft am 21.08.2023.

Mayor of London Walking Action Plan. (2018). Online verfügbar unter https://content.tfl.gov.uk/mts-walking-action-plan.pdf, zuletzt geprüft am 21.08.2023.

Mayor of Paris. “Paris Circular Economy Plan.” (2017). https://cdn.paris.fr/paris/2019/07/24/38de2f4891329bbaf04585ced5fbdf0f.pdf.

McDonnell, Mark J., Amy K. Hahs, and Jürgen H. Breuste, eds. *Ecology of Cities and Towns: A Comparative Approach*. Cambridge University Press, 2009.

McDougall, R., P. Kristiansen, and R. Rader. “Small-Scale Urban Agriculture Results in High Yields but Requires Judicious Management of Inputs to Achieve Sustainability.” *Proceedings of the National Academy of Sciences of the United States of America* 116, no. 1 (2019): 129–34. https://doi.org/10.1073/pnas.1809707115.

Mckinsey & company. Urban World: The global consumers to watch, accessed July 10, 2023. www.mckinsey.com/global-themes/urbanization/urban-world-the-global-consumers-to-watch/~/media/57C6AD7F7F1B44A6BD2E24F0777B4CD6.ashx.

McNamara, Madeleine W., and John C. Morris. “Expanding the Utility of Cross-Sectoral Collaboration in Policy Studies: Present and Future.” *Policy Studies Yearbook*, 12, no. 1 (2022), 53–70. https://doi.org/10.18278/psy.12.1.3.

Mehan III, G. Tracy, and Adam T. Carpenter. “Bringing Agriculture and Drinking Water Utilities Together for Source Water Protection.” *Journal – AWWA* 111, no. 8 (2019): 34–39. https://doi.org/10.1002/awwa.1340.

Mehta, Vikas. “Lively Streets.” *Journal of Planning Education and Research* 27, no. 2 (2007): 165–87. https://doi.org/10.1177/0739456X07307947.

Mehta, Vikas. “Look Closely and You Will See, Listen Carefully and You Will Hear: Urban Design and Social Interaction on Streets.” *Journal of Urban Design* 14, no. 1 (2009): 29–64. https://doi.org/10.1080/13574800802452658.

Mehta, Vikas. *The street. A quintessential social public space*. London, New York: Routledge Taylor & Francis Group, 2014.

Mehta, Vikas and Jennifer K. Bosson. “Revisiting Lively Streets: Social Interactions in Public Space.” *Journal of Planning Education and Research* 41, no. 2 (2021): 160–72. https://doi.org/10.1177/0739456X18781453.

Meister, T., B. Schmid, I. Seidl et al. “How Municipalities Support Energy Cooperatives: Survey Results from Germany and Switzerland.” *Energy, Sustainability and Society* 10 (2020): 18. https://doi.org/10.1186/s13705-020-00248-3.

Mhatre, Purva, Rohit Panchal, Anju Singh, and Shyam Bibyan. "A Systematic Literature Review on the Circular Economy Initiatives in the European Union." *Sustainable Production and Consumption* 26 (2021): 187–202. https://doi.org/10.1016/j.spc.2020.09.008.

Milano, Marianne, Emmanuel Reynard, Graziele Muniz-Miranda, and Joana Guerrin. "Water Supply Basins of São Paulo Metropolitan Region: Hydro-Climatic Characteristics of the 2013–2015 Water Crisis." *Water* 10, no. 11 (October 25, 2018): 1517. https://doi.org/10.3390/w10111517.

Milios, Leonidas. "Advancing to a Circular Economy: Three Essential Ingredients for a Comprehensive Policy Mix." *Sustainability Science* 13, no. 3 (November 7, 2017): 861–78. https://doi.org/10.1007/s11625-017-0502-9.

Ministry of Transport, Public Works, Water Management. Directorate General for Public Works, Water Management, and Netherlands. Ministerie van Verkeer en Waterstaat. *A Different Approach to Water: Water Management Policy in the 21st Century: Cabinet's Position*. The Hague: Ministry of Transport, Public Works and Water Management, 2000. https://books.google.co.nz/books?id=6J940AEACAAJ.

Mishra, R. et al. "Circular Economy Principles in Community Energy Initiatives through Stakeholder Perspectives." *Sustainable Production and Consumption* 33 (2022): 256–70. https://doi.org/10.1016/j.spc.2022.07.001.

Miranda, M. L., S. E. Edwards, M. H. Keating, and C. J. Paul. "Making the Environmental Justice Grade: The Relative Burden of Air Pollution Exposure in the United States." [In eng]. *International Journal of Environmental Research and Public Health* 8, no. 6 (2011): 1755–71. https://doi.org/10.3390/ijerph8061755.

Molle, Francois, and Jeremy Berkoff. "Cities Vs. Agriculture: A Review of Intersectoral Water Re-Allocation." Paper presented at the Natural Resources Forum, 2009.

Montuori, A. A. *Evolutionary Competence: Creating the Future*. Leiden, the Netherlands: Brill, 1989. https://books.google.co.nz/books?id=3eUyAAAAIAAJ.

Morelli, X., S. Gabet, C. Rieux, H. Bouscasse, S. Mathy, and R. Slama. "Which Decreases in Air Pollution Should Be Targeted to Bring Health and Economic Benefits and Improve Environmental Justice?" [In eng]. *Environment International* 129 (2019): 538–50. https://doi.org/10.1016/j.envint.2019.04.077.

Moudon, Anne Vernez, Chanam Lee, Allen D. Cheadle, Cheza Garvin, Rd, Donna B. Johnson, Thomas L. Schmid, and Robert D. Weathers. "Attributes of environments supporting walking." *American Journal of Health Promotion: AJHP* 21, no. 5 (2007): 448–59. https://doi.org/10.4278/0890-1171-21.5.448.

Moura, Filipe, Paulo Cambra, and Alexandre B. Gonçalves. "Measuring walkability for distinct pedestrian groups with a participatory assessment method: A case study in Lisbon." *Landscape and Urban Planning* 157, (2017): 282–96. https://doi.org/10.1016/j.landurbplan.2016.07.002.

Mouratidis, Kostas. "Urban planning and quality of life: A review of pathways linking the built environment to subjective well-being." *Cities* 115, (2021): 103229. https://doi.org/10.1016/j.cities.2021.103229.

Municipality of Rotterdam. *Implementation Agenda Weather Wise 2023–2026*. (Rotterdam, the Netherlands: 2023).

Municipality of Rotterdam. "Programme Framework Rotterdam WeatherWise." (2019). https://rotterdamsweerwoord.nl/content/uploads/2023/06/RWW_Programmakader-2030_ENG.pdf.

Murray, A., K. Skene, and K. Haynes, "The Circular Economy: An Interdisciplinary Exploration of the Concept and Application in a Global Context," *Journal of Business Ethics* 140 (2017): 369–80. https://doi.org/10.1007/s10551-015-2693-2.

Nandi, Santosh, Aref Aghaei Hervani, Marilyn M. Helms, and Joseph Sarkis. "Conceptualising Circular Economy Performance with Non-traditional Valuation Methods: Lessons for a Post-Pandemic Recovery." *International Journal of Logistics Research and Applications* 26, no. 6 (2023): 662–82.

Nauges, Celine, and Dale Whittington. "Evaluating the Performance of Alternative Municipal Water Tariff Designs: Quantifying the Tradeoffs between Equity, Economic Efficiency, and Cost Recovery." *World Development* 91 (2017): 125–43. https://doi.org/10.1016/j.worlddev.2016.10.014.

"How to Organize a Community Garden." 2023, accessed August 15, 2023. https://content.ces.ncsu.edu/how-to-organize-a-community-garden#:~:text=Types%20of%20Community%20Gardens%201%20Plot%20Gardens%20%28divide,Entrepreneurial%20Market%20Gardens%20%28sell%20produce%29%205%20Therapeutic%20Gardens.

Neirotti, Paolo, Alberto De Marco, Anna Corinna Cagliano, Giulio Mangano, and Francesco Scorrano. "Current Trends in Smart City Initiatives: Some Stylised Facts." *Cities* 38 (2014): 25–36.

Nel, Nicole, Heinz Jacobs, Carlo Loubser, and Kobus Du Plessis. "Supplementary Household Water Sources to Augment Potable Municipal Supply in South Africa." *Water SA* 43 (2017): 553. https://doi.org/10.4314/wsa.v43i4.03.

"DEP Unveils New Green Infrastructure Installations in Brooklyn." 2011, accessed August 15, 2023. www.nyc.gov/html/dep/html/press_releases/11-99pr.shtml#:~:text=The%20bioswales%20are%20part%20of%20the%20NYC%20Green,stormwater%20runoff%20before%20it%20enters%20the%20sewer%20system.

Newton, P., D. Prasad, A. Sproul, and S. White. *Decarbonising the Built Environment: Charting the Transition*. Singapore: Springer Nature Singapore, 2019. https://books.google.co.nz/books?id=c22cDwAAQBAJ.

"První Cirkulární Store V Čr? No Neke!," 2024, accessed September 17, 2024. https://no-neke.netlify.app.

Nieuwenhuijsen, Mark J. "Urban and transport planning pathways to carbon neutral, liveable and healthy cities; A review of the current evidence." *Environment International* 140, (2020): 105661. https://doi.org/10.1016/j.envint.2020.105661.

Njeru, Anthony Murithi and Isami Kinoshita. "Stay Activities on Carfree Neighborhood Shopping Streets." *E-BPJ* 3, no. 9 (2018): 14. https://doi.org/10.21834/e-bpj.v3i9.1527.

North, D. Warner. "Introduction to Special Issue on Air Pollution Health Risks." *Risk Analysis* 36, no. 9 (2016): 1688–92. https://doi.org/10.1111/risa.12707.

North, F. M. Design for vibrant streets: proposed framework for a small area in Newmarket. Unitec Institute of Technology. Auckland, New Zealand. (2012). Online verfügbar unter https://hdl.handle.net/10652/2067, zuletzt geprüft am 21.08.2023.

"Fossil Fuels: The Dirty Facts." 2022, accessed September 12, 2024. www.nrdc.org/stories/fossil-fuels-dirty-facts#sec-whatis.

"Brooklyn Grange Opens Largest Rooftop Farm in the City with Funding from Dep's Green Infrastructure Grant Program." 2019, accessed August 21, 2023. www.nyc.gov/site/dep/news/19-065/brooklyn-grange-opens-largest-rooftop-farm-the-city-funding-dep-s-green-infrastructure#/0.

"Green Infrastructure." 2023, accessed August 15, 2023. www.nycgovparks.org/greening/green-infrastructure.

Oberhummer, H., W. Gruber, and M. Puntigam. *Wer nichts weiß, muss alles glauben*. Salzburg: Ecowin Verlag, 2012.

OECD. *Policy Guidance on Resource Efficiency*. Paris: OECD Publishing, 2016. http://dx.doi.org/10.1787/9789264257344-en.

"The Circular Economy in Cities and Regions," OECD Urban Studies. Washington, DC: OECD, 2020a. https://doi.org/10.1787/10ac6ae4-en.

"Addressing the Social Consequences of Tariffs for Water Supply and Sanitation." (2020b). www.oecd.org/en/publications/addressing-the-social-consequences-of-tariffs-for-water-supply-and-sanitation_afede7d6-en.html.

OECD. "Behavioural Economics and Environmental Policy Design." (2012). www.oecd.org/en/publications/behavioural-economics-and-environmental-incentives_5k8zwbhqs1xn-en.html.

OECD. "Circular Economy – Waste and Materials." (2019). www.oecd.org/environment/environment-at-a-glance/env-2019-2343-en.pdf.

OECD. "The Circular Economy in Glasgow, United Kingdom." (2021). www.oecd-ilibrary.org/urban-rural-and-regional-development/the-circular-economy-in-glasgow-united-kingdom_7717a310-en.

OECD. *Environmental Outlook to 2050 the Consequences of Inaction: The Consequences of Inaction*. OECD Publishing, 2012. http://books.google.co.nz/books?id=sLldM0i0HwgC.

OECD. "Global Material Resources Outlook to 2060: Economic Drivers and Environmental Consequences." (2018). https://espas.secure.europarl.europa.eu/orbis/sites/default/files/generated/document/en/OECD.pdf.

OECD. "Global Material Resources Outlook to 2060: Economic Drivers and Environmental Consequences." (2019). www.oecd.org/environment/waste/highlights-global-material-resources-outlook-to-2060.pdf.

Oki, Taikan, and Shinjiro Kanae. "Global Hydrological Cycles and World Water Resources." *Science* 313, no. 5790 (2006): 1068–72. https://doi.org/10.1126/science.1128845.

Olmstead, S. M., and R. N. Stavins. "Managing Water Demand: Price Vs. Non-Price Conservation Programs." (Pioneer Institute White Paper No. 39). Boston, MA: Pioneer Institute for Public Policy Research, 2007.

Orr, David. *Environmental Literacy: Education as If the Earth Mattered*. Human Scale Education, 1994.

Our World in Data. "Fossil Fuels." 2024, accessed September 12, 2024. https://ourworldindata.org/fossil-fuels#citation.

Pacific Institute. "Sustainable Water Management for Urban Agriculture: Planting Justice, Oakland." (2013). https://pacinst.org/wp-content/uploads/2013/02/sustainable_water_management_for_urban_agriculture3.pdf.

Papageorgiou, Asterios, Maryna Henrysson, Cali Nuur, Rajib Sinha, Cecilia Sundberg, and Fedra Vanhuyse. "Mapping and Assessing Indicator-Based Frameworks for Monitoring Circular Economy Development at the City-Level." *Sustainable Cities and Society* 75 (2021): 103378. https://doi.org/10.1016/j.scs.2021.103378.

"Patagonia Care & Repair." Patagonia, 2024, accessed September 16, 2024. www.ifixit.com/collaborations/patagonia.

Patchen, Martin. "What Shapes Public Reactions to Climate Change? Overview of Research and Policy Implications." *Analyses of Social Issues and Public Policy* 10, no. 1 (2010): 47–68.

Patrizia Ghisellini and Sergio Ulgiati. "Managing the Transition to the Circular Economy." In *Handbook of the Circular Economy*, edited by Migueal Brandão, David Lazarevic, and Göran Finnveden, 491–504. Cheltenham and Camberley, UK: Edward Elgar Publishing Ltd, 2020.

Pearce, David W., and R. Kerry Turner. *Economics of Natural Resources and the Environment*. Johns Hopkins University Press, 1989.

Pedro-Monzonís, María, Abel Solera, Javier Ferrer, Teodoro Estrela, and Javier Paredes-Arquiola. "A Review of Water Scarcity and Drought Indexes in Water Resources Planning and Management." *Journal of Hydrology* 527 (2015): 482–93. https://doi.org/10.1016/j.jhydrol.2015.05.003.

Petit-Boix, Anna, and Sina Leipold. "Circular Economy in Cities: Reviewing How Environmental Research Aligns with Local Practices." *Journal of Cleaner Production* 195 (2018): 1270–81. https://doi.org/10.1016/j.jclepro.2018.05.281.

Piso, Zachary, Lissy Goralnik, Julie C. Libarkin, and Maria Claudia Lopez. "Types of Urban Agricultural Stakeholders and Their Understandings of Governance." *Ecology and Society* 24, no. 2 (2019). www.jstor.org/stable/26796944.

Plank, B, D. Wiedenhofer, J. Streeck, F. Krausmann, D. Virág, and H. Haberl. "We Want It All. But Do We Need It All? Material Stocks of Societies and Their Interrelation with Economic Growth and Wellbeing." Paper presented at the 14th Biennial International Conference on EcoBalance: Materializing Sustainability Visions, Online, 2021.

"Come Fishing for Plastic!," 2024, accessed September 17, 2024. https://plasticwhale.com/plastic-fishing/.

Policy Research Institute. *Economic Instruments for Water Demand Management in an Integrated Water Resources Management Framework: Synthesis Report.* Government of Canada, 2005. http://publications.gc.ca/site/eng/269935/publication.html.

Polychroniadou, Eleni. "Unlocking the Green Building Market for Banks with EDGE." *EDGE Buildings*, April 13, 2021. https://edgebuildings.com/unlocking-the-green-building-market-for-banks-with-edge/.

Pongsiri, Montira J., Franz W. Gatzweiler, Andrea M. Bassi, Andy Haines, and Fanny Demassieux. "The Need for a Systems Approach to Planetary Health." *The Lancet Planetary Health* 1, no. 7 (2017): e257–e59. https://doi.org/10.1016/S2542-5196(17)30116-X.

Potting, J., M. Hekkert, E. Worrell, and A. Hanemaaijer. Circular Economy: Measuring innovation in product chains. PBL Netherlands Environmental Assessment Agency, The Hague, (2017). www.pbl.nl/sites/default/files/downloads/pbl-2016-circular-economy-measuring-innovation-in-product-chains-2544.pdf.

Prague Innovation Institute and Circle Economy. "Circulární Praha 2030, Strategie Hl.M. Prahy Pro Prechod Na Cirulární Ekonomiku." (2022). www.pragueconvention.cz/file/8500/cirkularni-praha-2030-strategie-ce.pdf.

Prendeville, Sharon, Emma Cherim, and Nancy Bocken. "Circular Cities: Mapping Six Cities in Transition." *Environmental Innovation and Societal Transitions* 26 (2018): 171–94.

Prins, Fransiscus Xaverius, Anita Etale, Austin Dziwornu Ablo, and Andrew Thatcher. "Water Scarcity and Alternative Water Sources in South Africa: Can Information Provision Shift Perceptions?" *Urban Water Journal* (2022): 1–12. https://doi.org/10.1080/1573062X.2022.2026984.

PUB. "Our Water, Our Future." (2016). www.jkgeography.com/uploads/1/0/8/4/108433405/singapore_-_our_water_our_future.pdf.

PUB. "Singapore's Water Loop." (2024), accessed September 15, 2024. www.pub.gov.sg/public/waterloop.

Puigdueta, Ivanka, Eduardo Aguilera, José Luis Cruz, Ana Iglesias, and Alberto Sanz-Cobena. "Urban Agriculture May Change Food Consumption Towards Low Carbon Diets." *Global Food Security* 28 (2021): 100507. https://doi.org/10.1016/j.gfs.2021.100507.

Qiao, Xiu-Juan, Li Liu, Anders Kristoffersson, and Thomas B. Randrup. "Governance Factors of Sustainable Stormwater Management: A Study of Case Cities in China and Sweden." *Journal of Environmental Management* 248 (2019): 109249. https://doi.org/10.1016/j.jenvman.2019.07.020.

Ramboll Group. Resilient Societies and Liveable Cities. Architecture, engineering and Consultancy – Ramboll Group, 2023, accessed October 20, 2023. www.ramboll.com/en-us/lets-close-the-gap/resilient-societies.

Ramírez-Agudelo, Nancy Andrea, Joan de Pablo, and Elisabet Roca. "Exploring Alternative Practices in Urban Water Management through the Lens of Circular Economy – A Case Study in the Barcelona Metropolitan Area." *Journal of Cleaner Production* 329 (December 2021): 129565. https://doi.org/10.1016/j.jclepro.2021.129565.

Rashid, A. A., "Doughnut Economics: A Roadmap for a Thriving Sustainable City." (2020). www.academia.edu/44910863/DOUGHNUT_ECONOMICS_A_ROADMAP_FOR_A_THRIVING_SUSTAINABLE_CITY.

"Smartplace@Schools. Serious Game Platform for Education on Circular Economy in Highschools." 2019, accessed September 24, 2024. https://old.eitrawmaterials.eu/project/smartplaceschools/.

Rashidfarokhi, Anahita and Vitalija Danivska. "Managing crises 'together': how can the built environment contribute to social resilience?" *Building Research & Information* 51, no. 7 (2023): 747–63. https://doi.org/10.1080/09613218.2023.2191922.

Raworth, K. *Doughnut Economics: Seven Ways to Think Like a 21st-Century Economist.* White River Junction, VT: Chelsea Green Publishing, 2017. https://books.google.co.nz/books?id=SUYtDgAAQBAJ.

Razmjoo, Armin, Poul Alberg Østergaard, Mouloud Denaï, Meysam Majidi Nezhad, and Seyedali Mirjalili. "Effective Policies to Overcome Barriers in the Development of Smart Cities." *Energy Research & Social Science* 79 (2021): 102175. https://doi.org/10.1016/j.erss.2021.102175.

"About Reflow." 2024, accessed September 17, 2024. https://reflowproject.eu/about/.

REFLOW. "Planning a Circular Paris." (2022). https://reflowproject.eu/wp-content/uploads/2022/03/PARIS_REFLOW_CaseStudy_final.pdf.

Renger, B. C., J. L. Birkeland, and D. J. Midmore. "Net-Positive Building Carbon Sequestration." *Building Research & Information* 43, no. 1 (2015): 11–24. https://doi.org/10.1080/09613218.2015.961001.

Rickenbacker, Harold, Fred Brown, and Melissa Bilec. "Creating Environmental Consciousness in Underserved Communities: Implementation and Outcomes of Community-Based Environmental Justice and Air Pollution Research." *Sustainable Cities and Society* 47 (2019): 101473. https://doi.org/10.1016/j.scs.2019.101473.

Rieß, Werner. "Bildung Für Nachhaltige Entwicklung – Kann Durch Unterricht Das Nachhaltigkeitsrelevante Handeln Von Grundschuler/Innen Gefördert Werden?" Conference: 20. Internationale Tagung der Fachsektion Didaktik der Biologie (FDdB) im VBio und des Forums Fachdidaktik & Schulbiologie, Online, 2015.

Ritzén, Sofia, and Gunilla Ölundh Sandström. "Barriers to the Circular Economy – Integration of Perspectives and Domains." *Procedia CIRP* 64 (2017): 7–12. https://doi.org/10.1016/j.procir.2017.03.005.

Rodin, Judith. *The Resilience Dividend: Managing Disruption, Avoiding Disaster, and Growing Stronger in an Unpredictable World.* London: Profile Books, 2015.

Romano, Oriana, "Never Waste a Good Waste Crisis: Paris and the Circular Economy." *OECD*, September 17, 2023. https://oecdstatistics.blog/2023/03/28/never-waste-a-good-waste-crisis-paris-and-the-circular-economy/.

"Testing Smart Water Tech down Under." 2020, accessed May 12, 2022. https://medium.com/mark-and-focus/testing-smart-water-tech-down-under-d08688f7609a.

Rosales, Natalie. "How Can an Ecological Perspective Be Used to Enrich Cities Planning and Management?" *urbe. Revista Brasileira de Gestão Urbana* 9 (2017): 314–26.

Rufí-Salís, Martí, Nadin Brunnhofer, Anna Petit-Boix, Xavier Gabarrell, Albert Guisasola, and Gara Villalba. "Can Wastewater Feed Cities? Determining the Feasibility and Environmental Burdens of Struvite Recovery and Reuse for Urban Regions." *Science of the Total Environment* 737 (2020): 139783. https://doi.org/10.1016/j.scitotenv.2020.139783.

"Vision Köln 2030: Dokumentation Unserer Diskussion Mit Der Kommunalpolitik." 2020, accessed September 23, 2024. https://koelnbonn.scientists4future.org/2020/06/20/vision-koeln-2030-dokumentation-unserer-diskussion-mit-der-kommunalpolitik/.

Santonen, Teemu, Laura Creazzo, Axelle Griffon, Zsuzsanna Bódi, and Paolo Aversano. Cities as Living Labs: Increasing the Impact of Investment in the Circular Economy for Sustainable Cities, (2017). www.theseus.fi/handle/10024/138868.

Sarigiannis, D. A. "Assessing the Impact of Hazardous Waste on Children's Health: The Exposome Paradigm." [In English]. *Environmental Research* 158 (2017): 531–41. https://doi.org/10.1016/j.envres.2017.06.031.

Savenije, H. H. G. "Water Scarcity Indicators; the Deception of the Numbers." *Physics and Chemistry of the Earth, Part B: Hydrology, Oceans and Atmosphere* 25, no. 3 (2000): 199–204. https://doi.org/10.1016/S1464-1909(00)00004-6.

Savenije, H., and P. van der Zaag. "Water as an Economic Good and Demand Management: Paradigms with Pitfalls." *Water International* 27, no. 1 (2002): 98-104.

Schelte, Nora, Semih Severengiz, Jaron Schünemann, Sebastian Finke, Oskar Bauer, and Matthias Metzen. "Life Cycle Assessment on Electric Moped Scooter Sharing." *Sustainability* 13, no. 15 (2021): 8297. https://doi.org/10.3390/su13158297.

Schmack, Mario, Martin Anda, Stewart Dallas, and Roberta Fornarelli. "Urban Water Trading – Hybrid Water Systems and Niche Opportunities in the Urban Water Market – A Literature Review." *Environmental Technology Reviews* 8, no. 1 (2019): 65-81. https://doi.org/10.1080/21622515.2019.1647292.

Schot, Johan, and W. Edward Steinmueller. "Three Frames for Innovation Policy: R&D, Systems of Innovation and Transformative Change." *Research Policy* 47, no. 9 (2018): 1554-67. https://doi.org/10.1016/j.respol.2018.08.011.

Schreiber, Jörg-Robert and Hannes Siege. "Curriculum Framework: Education for Sustainable Development" (2016). www.globaleslernen.de/sites/default/files/files/link-elements/curriculum_framework_education_for_sustainable_development_barrierefrei.pdf.

Schütz, Florian, Marie Lena Heidingsfelder, and Martina Schraudner. "Co-Shaping the Future in Quadruple Helix Innovation Systems: Uncovering Public Preferences toward Participatory Research and Innovation." *She Ji: The Journal of Design, Economics, and Innovation* 5, no. 2 (2019): 128-46. https://doi.org/10.1016/j.sheji.2019.04.002.

Seckler, D. W., and I. W. M. Institute. *World Water Demand and Supply, 1990 to 2025: Scenarios and Issues*. International Water Management Institute, 1998. https://books.google.co.nz/books?id=DIVFSmeL2OkC.

"Graywater: Laundry to Landscape Rebate." 2023, accessed August 21, 2023. https://sfpuc.org/learning/conserve-water/graywater-laundry-landscape-rebate.

Seto, K. C., B. Güneralp, and L. R. Hutyra. "Global Forecasts of Urban Expansion to 2030 and Direct Impacts on Biodiversity and Carbon Pools." *Proceedings of the National Academy of Sciences* 109, no. 40 (2012): 16083–88.

Sevtsuk, Andres *Street commerce. Creating vibrant urban sidewalks*. Philadelphia: University of Pennsylvania, 2020.

SFPUC. "Onsite Water Reuse Grant Program Rules." (2022). www.sfpuc.org/sites/default/files/documents/OWR_Grant_Program_Rules_and_App_June_2022.pdf#:~:text=The%20San%20Francisco%20Public%20Utilities%20Commission%20%28SFPUC%29%20Onsite,as%20toilet%20flushing%2C%20irrigation%2C%20and%20cooling%20tower%20makeup.

Shafique, Muhammad, Xiaowei Luo, and Jian Zuo. "Photovoltaic-Green Roofs: A Review of Benefits, Limitations, and Trends." *Solar Energy* 202 (2020): 485–97. https://doi.org/10.1016/j.solener.2020.02.101.

"Light as a Service." 2024, accessed September 16, 2024. www.signify.com/global/lighting-services/managed-services/light-as-a-service.

Shevchenko, T., M. Saidani, M. Meisam Ranjbari, J. Kronenberg, Y. Danko, and K. Laitala. "Consumer Behavior in the Circular Economy: Developing a Product-Centric Framework." *Journal of Cleaner Production* 384 (2023): 135568. https://doi.org/10.1016/j.jclepro.2022.135568.

Skar, S. L. G., R. Pineda-Martos, A. Timpe, B. Pölling, K. Bohn, M. Külvik, C. Delgado, et al. "Urban Agriculture as a Keystone Contribution Towards Securing Sustainable and Healthy Development for Cities in the Future." *Blue-Green Systems* 2, no. 1 (2019): 1-27. https://doi.org/10.2166/bgs.2019.931.

Soliman, Magdi R. I., Christopher T. Derosa, Howard W. Mielke, and Kofi Bota. "Hazardous Wastes, Hazardous Materials and Environmental Health Inequity." *Toxicology and Industrial Health* 9, no. 5 (1993): 901-12. https://doi.org/10.1177/074823379300900511.

Spence, Michael, Patricia Clarke Annez, and Robert M. Buckley. *Planning, Connecting, and Financing Cities – Now: Priorities for City Leaders*. Washington, DC: World Bank, 2013. https://openknowledge.worldbank.org/handle/10986/12238.

Stadt Köln. "Kölner Perspektiven 2030+ (English Summary)." (n.d.). www.stadt-koeln.de/mediaasset/content/pdf15/kp2030/kurzfassung_englisch.pdf.

Stahel, Walter R. "The Circular Economy." *Nature* 531, no.7595 (March 23, 2016): 435–38. http://dx.doi.org/10.1038/531435a.

Steg, Linda, and Charles Vlek. "Encouraging Pro-Environmental Behaviour: An Integrative Review and Research Agenda." *Journal of Environmental Psychology* 29, no. 3 (2009): 309-17.

Stengers, I. and Prigogine, I. *Order out of Chaos: Man's New Dialogue with Nature*. Brussels, Belgium: Verso, 2018. https://books.google.co.nz/books?id=Cm_nDwAAQBAJ.

Sullivan, C. A., J. R. Meigh, and A. M. Giacomello. "The Water Poverty Index: Development and Application at the Community Scale." *Natural Resources Forum* 27, no. 3 (2003): 189-99. https://doi.org/10.1111/1477-8947.00054.

Su, Tianyu, Maoran Sun, Zhuangyuan Fan, Ariel Noyman, Alex Pentland, and Esteban Moro. "Rhythm of the streets: a street classification framework based on street activity patterns." *EPJ Data Science* 11, no. 1 (2022): 43. https://doi.org/10.1140/epjds/s13688-022-00355-5.

Sun, L., J. Du, and Y. Li. "A New Method for Dividing the Scopes and Priorities of Air Pollution Control Based on Environmental Justice." *Environmental Science and Pollution Research* 28, no. 10 (2021): 12858–69. https://doi.org/10.1007/s11356-020-11160-w.

Surls, Rachel, Gail Feenstra, Sheila Golden, Ryan Galt, Shermain Hardesty, Claire Napawan, and Cheryl Wilen. "Gearing Up to Support Urban Farming in California: Preliminary Results of a Needs Assessment." *Renewable Agriculture and Food Systems* 30, no. 1 (2015): 33-42. https://doi.org/10.1017/S1742170514000052.

"10 Types of Urban Farming to Practice." 2021, accessed August 21, 2023. https://help.synnefa.io/articles/2021/11/19/10-types-of-urban-farming-to-practice.

Tapia, Carlos, Linda Randall, Shinan Wang, and Luciane Aguiar Borges. "Monitoring the Contribution of Urban Agriculture to Urban Sustainability: An Indicator-Based Framework." *Sustainable Cities and Society* 74 (2021): 103130. https://doi.org/10.1016/j.scs.2021.103130.

Tedesco, Silvia, Elena Montacchini, Roberto Giordano, and Federica Larcher. "Green Walls as Nature-Based Solutions for Urban and Building Resilience: A Case Study." (2019). www.sustainablemediterraneanconstruction.eu/en/rivista/2019-09/2019-09-132/.

"Construction Boosts Circular Economy – Demolition in Vattuniemi Shows the Way." 2024, accessed September 17, 2024. https://testbed.hel.fi/en/circular-economy/construction-boosts-circular-economy/.

"Apply for a Climate Adaptation Subsidy (for Rainwater Harvesting)." 2023, accessed August 15, 2023. www.denhaag.nl/en/subsidies/apply-for-a-climate-adaptation-subsidy-for-rainwater-harvesting-.htm.

The Nature Conservancy. "Beyond the Source: The Environmental, Economic and Community Benefits of Source Water Protection." (2017). www.nature.org/content/dam/tnc/nature/en/documents/Beyond_The_Source_Full_Report_FinalV4.pdf.

The Nature Conservancy. "Estimating the Water Supply Benefits from Forest Restoration in the Northern Sierra Nevada." (2015). www.researchgate.net/publication/305767082_Estimating_the_Water_Supply_Benefits_from_Forest_Restoration_in_the_Northern_Sierra_Nevada.

"Smart Water Meter Project Approved." 2021, accessed May 12, 2022. www.thenews.com.pk/print/917092-smart-water-meter-project-approved.

"About." 2024, accessed September 16, 2024. https://theoceancleanup.com.

"The Sponge Revolution." 2021, accessed September 15, 2024. www.thewirechina.com/2021/07/18/the-sponge-revolution/.

Thomas, Abdul Rashid. "Waste Collection Management Association Launched in Freetown." *The Sierra Leone Telegraph*, January 26, 2022. www.thesierraleonetelegraph.com/waste-collection-management-association-launched-in-freetown.

Thomas Budde Christensen. "Towards a Circular Economy in Cities: Exploring Local Modes of Governance in the Transition towards a Circular Economy in Construction and Textile Recycling." *Journal of Cleaner Production* (2021): 127058. https://doi.org/10.1016/j.jclepro.2021.127058.

Tjallingii, S. P. *Ecological Conditions: Strategies and Structures in Environmental Planning*. Wageningen: DLO Institute for Forestry and Nature Research (IBN-DLO), 1996. https://books.google.co.nz/books?id=ul7bAAAACAAJ.

Toralles, Christiano Piccioni. "Relationships Between Walkable Urban Environments and the Creative and Knowledge Economies." *IRSPSD International* 11, no. 1 (2023): 104–21. https://doi.org/10.14246/irspsd.11.1_104.

Tortajada, Cecilia, and Pierre van Rensburg. "Drink More Recycled Wastewater." *Nature* 577, no. 7788 (December 31, 2019): 26–28. https://doi.org/10.1038/d41586-019-03913-6.

UN. "Comprehensive Assessment of the Freshwater Resources of the World: Report of the Secretary-General." (1997). https://digitallibrary.un.org/record/231336?ln=en&v=pdf.

UN-HABITAT. "Slum Almanac 2015–2016." (2016). https://unhabitat.org/slum-almanac-2015-2016-0.

United Cities and Local Governments (UCLG). "Towards the Localization of the SDGs," Local and Regional Governments' Report Towards the 2019 HLPF, 3rd Report, Global Task Force of Local and Regional Governments (Barcelona: United Cities and Local Governments (UCLG), 2019). www.uclg.org/sites/default/files/towards_the_localization_of_the_sdgs_0.pdf.

United Nations Transforming Our World: The 2030 Agenda for Sustainable Development. (2015). Online verfügbar unter https://sdgs.un.org/, zuletzt geprüft am 21.08.2023.

United Nations Department of Economic and Social Affairs. "World Populations Prospects: Summary of Results." (2022). www.un.org/development/desa/pd/sites/www.un.org.development.desa.pd/files/wpp2022_summary_of_results.pdf.

United Nations Environment Program, (UNEP). *City-Level Decoupling: Urban Resource Flows and the Governance of Infrastructure Transitions.* Nairobi, Kenya: UNEP, 2013. www.unep.org/resources/report/city-level-decoupling-urban-resource-flows-and-governance-infrastructure.

United Nations Framework Convention on Climate Change (UNFCCC). *Nationally Determined Contributions under the Paris Agreement Synthesis Report by the Secretariat.* New York: UNFCCC, 2021. https://unfccc.int/sites/default/files/resource/cma2021_08E.pdf.

UNFCCC and Antonio Guterres. "Cities Are Where the Climate Battle Will Be Largely Won or Lost." *UN Climate Change News*, October 11, 2019. https://unfccc.int/news/guterres-cities-are-where-the-climate-battle-will-largely-be-won-or-lost.

UN-Water. "Un-Water Policy Brief on Climate Change and Water." (2019). www.unwater.org/publications/un-water-policy-brief-on-climate-change-and-water/.

UN-Water. "Water and Climate Change." 2020, accessed January 15, 2020. www.unwater.org/water-facts/climate-change/.

UN-Water. "Water and Jobs." (2016). https://unesdoc.unesco.org/ark:/48223/pf0000244040/PDF/244040eng.pdf.multi.

UN-Water. "Water Security and the Global Water Agenda." (2013). www.unwater.org/publications/water-security-global-water-agenda/.

UN-Water/WWAP (World Water Assessment Programme). "Nature-Based Solutions for Water." (2018). www.unwater.org/publications/world-water-development-report-2018.

"Cities and Climate Change." 2024, accessed September 20, 2024. www.unep.org/explore-topics/resource-efficiency/what-we-do/cities-and-climate-change#:~:text=At%20the%20same%20time%2C%20cities,contributors%20(IPCC%2C%202022).

"Medellín Shows How Nature-Based Solutions Can Keep People and Planet Cool." 2019, accessed August 15, 2023. www.unep.org/news-and-stories/story/medellin-shows-how-nature-based-solutions-can-keep-people-and-planet-cool.

UNESCO. "Education for Sustainable Developmen." (2012). https://sustainabledevelopment.un.org/content/documents/926unesco9.pdf.

UNESCO. *Managing Water under Uncertainty and Risk.* (2012). http://unesdoc.unesco.org/images/0021/002156/215644e.pdf.

UNESCO. "Sustainable Development Goals (Sdgs)." 2024, accessed September 23, 2024. www.unesco.at/bildung/bildung-2030/bildungsagenda-2030/sdgs.

United Nations. Report of the 51st Session of the United Nations Statistical Commission (March 3–6, 2020). E/2020/24–E/CN.3/2020/34. New York: United Nations. Available at: https://unstats.un.org/unsd/statcom/51st-session/documents/.

"Ziele Für Nachhaltige Entwicklung." (2021). www.un.org/depts/german/millennium/SDG%20Bericht%202021.pdf.

United Nations Department of Economic and Social Affairs. "World Urbanization Prospects: The 2018 Revision." (2019a). www.un-ilibrary.org/content/books/9789210043144.

"World Population Prospects 2019: Highlights." (2019b). www.un.org/en/desa/2018-revision-world-urbanization-prospects.

"Urban Innovative Actions (UIA)." Leidal Intermunicipal Association, (n.d.). https://uia-initiative.eu/en/uia-cities/leiedal-intermunicipal-association.

"Beneficial Reuse of Municipal Biosolids in Agriculture." 2017, accessed August 21, 2023. https://extension.uga.edu/publications/detail.html?number=SB27.

"Recycled Water." 2023, accessed August 21, 2023. https://urbanutilities.com.au/business/business-services/recycled-water.

"Fossil." 2024, accessed September 12, 2024. www.energy.gov/fossil.

"Source Water Protection." 2020, accessed March 4, 2020. www.epa.gov/sourcewaterprotection.

Urban Green Train. "Introduction into Urban Agriculture Concept and Types." (2023). https://ruaf.org/assets/2019/11/Module-1-Introduction-into-urban-agriculture-concept-and-types.pdf.

Urban Green Train. "Urban Agriculture Types/Production Systems and Short Food Chains." (2023). https://ruaf.org/assets/2019/11/Module-3-Urban-Agriculture-types-production-systems-and-short-food-chains.pdf.

US EPA. "How Wastewater Treatment Works … The Basics." (1998). www3.epa.gov/npdes/pubs/bastre.pdf.

"Stormwater Best Management Practice Bioretention (Rain Gardens)." (2021). www.epa.gov/system/files/documents/2021-11/bmp-bioretention-rain-gardens.pdf.

"Evaluating the Potential Benefits of Permeable Pavement on the Quantity and Quality of Stormwater Runoff." 2019, accessed August 15, 2023. www.usgs.gov/centers/upper-midwest-water-science-center/science/evaluating-potential-benefits-permeable-pavement.

"Rain Gardens and Bioswales." 2023, accessed August 15, 2023. https://extension.usu.edu/laep/research/nontraditional.

"Home." 2024, accessed September 17, 2024. www.velib-metropole.fr/en_GB.

Vale, David S., Miguel Saraiva, and Mauro Pereira. "Active accessibility: A review of operational measures of walking and cycling accessibility." *JTLU*. (2013):https://doi.org/10.5198/jtlu.2015.593.

van den Berg, Pauline E.W., Bojing Liao, Steef Gorissen, P.J.V. van Wesemael, and Theo A. Arentze. "The Relationship between Walkability and Place Attachment and the Mediating Role of Neighborhood-Based Social Interaction." *Journal of Planning Education and Research*, (2022): 0739456X2211181. https://doi.org/10.1177/0739456X221118101.

Vanhuyse, Fedra, Neal R. Haddaway, and Maryna Henrysson. "Circular Cities: An Evidence Map of Research Between 2010 and 2020." *Discover Sustainability* 2, no.1 (November 17, 2021): 1–17. https://link.springer.com/content/pdf/10.1007/s43621-021-00059-2.pdf.

Velasco Arevalo, Alexandra and Regine Gerike. "Sustainability evaluation methods for public transport with a focus on Latin American cities: A literature review." *International Journal of Sustainable Transportation*, (2023): 1–18. https://doi.org/10.1080/15568318.2022.2163208.

Verbeek, Thomas. "Unequal Residential Exposure to Air Pollution and Noise: A Geospatial Environmental Justice Analysis for Ghent, Belgium." *SSM – Population Health* 7 (2019): 100340. https://doi.org/10.1016/j.ssmph.2018.100340.

Vergragt, Philip J., Leonie Dendler, Martin De Jong, and Kira Matus. "Transitions to Sustainable Consumption and Production in Cities." *Journal of Cleaner Production* 134 (2016): 1–12.

Virginia Biosolids Council. "Biosolids Use for Urban Landscapes." (2019). www.virginiabiosolids.com/wp-content/uploads/2019/04/VBC_Urban-Landscapes.pdf.

Voskamp, I. M., and F. H. M. Van de Ven. "Planning Support System for Climate Adaptation: Composing Effective Sets of Blue-Green Measures to Reduce Urban Vulnerability to Extreme Weather Events." *Building and Environment* 83 (2015): 159–67. https://doi.org/10.1016/j.buildenv.2014.07.018.

Waag Futurelab. "Amsterdam Reflow Booklet." (2021). https://waag.org/en/article/amsterdam-reflow-booklet/.

Wahba, Sameh N. "Can Cities Bounce Back Better from COVID-19? Reflections from Emerging Post-Pandemic Recovery Plans and Trade-Offs." *Environment & Urbanization*, 34, no. 2 (2022). https://doi.org/10.1177/09562478221102867.

Wahba, Sameh, Silpa Kaza, and Kremena Ionkova. "A New Phenomenon – Realizing Economic Growth While Cutting Waste. HOW?" *Sustainable Cities Blog*, November 12, 2019. https://blogs.worldbank.org/sustainablecities/new-phenomenon-realizing-economic-growth-while-cutting-waste-how.

Wandl, Alexander, Verena Balz, Lei Qu, Cecilia Furlan, Gustavo Arciniegas, and Ulf Hackauf. "The Circular Economy Concept in Design Education: Enhancing Understanding and Innovation by Means of Situated Learning." *Urban Planning* 4, no 3 (2019): *Facilitating Circular Economy in Urban Planning*. https://doi.org/10.17645/up.v4i3.2147.

Wang, Fu, Chang Tan, Miaohan Li, Dengjun Gu, and Huini Wang. "Research on Traffic Design of Urban Vital Streets." *Sustainability* 14, no. 11 (2022): 6468. https://doi.org/10.3390/su14116468.

Wang, Luqi and Chen Wen. "The Relationship between the Neighborhood Built Environment and Active Transportation among Adults: A Systematic Literature Review." *Urban Science* 1, no. 3, (2017): 29. https://doi.org/10.3390/urbansci1030029.

Wang, Rui, Hong Wu, and Robert Chiles. "Ecosystem Benefits Provision of Green Stormwater Infrastructure in Chinese Sponge Cities." *Environmental Management* 69, no. 3 (January 12, 2022): 558–75. https://doi.org/10.1007/s00267-021-01565-9.

Wang, Zheng, Yue Huang, Tie Liu, Chanjuan Zan, Yunan Ling, and Chenyu Guo. "Analysis of the Water Demand–Supply Gap and Scarcity Index in Lower Amu Darya River Basin, Central Asia." *International Journal of Environmental Research and Public Health* 19, no. 2. (2022). https://doi.org/10.3390/ijerph19020743.

Wang, Zhiyong, Dick Ettema, and Marco Helbich. "Objective environmental exposures correlate differently with recreational and transportation walking: A cross-sectional national study in the Netherlands." *Environmental Research* 194, (2021): 110591. https://doi.org/10.1016/j.envres.2020.110591.

Wasfi, Rania, Madeleine Steinmetz-Wood, and Yan Kestens. "Place matters: A longitudinal analysis measuring the association between neighbourhood walkability and walking by age group and population center size in Canada." *PLoS One* 12, no. 12 (2017): e0189472. https://doi.org/10.1371/journal.pone.0189472.

Water Supply & Sanitation Collaborative Council. "Public Funding for Sanitation. The Many Faces of Sanitation Subsidies." (2009). https://sswm.info/sites/default/files/reference_attachments/EVANS%20et%20al%202009%20Public%20Funding%20for%20Sanitation%20Subsidies.pdf.

Waterwise. "H2eco Behavioural Research (Phase 10)." (2019). www.waterwise.org.uk/knowledge-base/h2eco-behavioural-research-phase-10/.

Waterwise. "Investigating the Impact of Water Efficiency Educational Programmes in Schools: A Scoping Study." (2012). www.waterwise.org.uk/wp-content/uploads/2018/02/Investigating-the-impact-of-water-efficiency-educational-programmes-in-schools_final.pdf.

WCED Report of the World Commission on Environment and Development: Our Common Future. (1987). Online verfügbar unter www.un-documents.net/wced-ocf.htm, zuletzt geprüft am 21.08.2023.

West 8, & RHDHV. *Solicitation for Concept Design Schemes of Public Space of the Ecological Flood Control Levee around the Starting Area in Xiong'an New District (Hebei Province, China), Vol. 8*. Rotterdam, the Netherlands: West 8, 2018.

West, J. Jason, Aaron Cohen, Frank Dentener, Bert Brunekreef, Tong Zhu, Ben Armstrong, Michelle L. Bell, et al. "What We Breathe Impacts Our Health: Improving Understanding of the Link between Air Pollution and Health." *Environmental Science & Technology* 50, no. 10 (2016): 4895–904. https://doi.org/10.1021/acs.est.5b03827.

Whittle, Nathalie. "Welcome to the 15 Minute City." *Financial Times*, July 17, 2020. www.ft.com/content/c1a53744-90d5-4560-9e3f-17ce06aba69a.

Wielemaker, Rosanne C., Jan Weijma, and Grietje Zeeman. "Harvest to Harvest: Recovering Nutrients with New Sanitation Systems for Reuse in Urban Agriculture." *Resources, Conservation and Recycling* 128 (2018): 426–37. https://doi.org/10.1016/j.resconrec.2016.09.015.

"Cradle to Cradle." 2024. https://mcdonough.com/cradle-to-cradle/.

Williams, J. *Circular Cities: A Revolution in Urban Sustainability*. London: Taylor & Francis, 2021. https://books.google.co.nz/books?id=JcMfEAAAQBAJ.

Williams, Jo. "Circular Cities: Planning for Circular Development in European Cities." *European Planning Studies* 31, no. 1 (2023): 14–35.

Williams, Joanna. "Circular Cities: Challenges to Implementing Looping Actions." *Sustainability* 11, no. 2 (2019): 423.

Williams, Joanna. "Circular Cities." *Urban Studies* 56, no. 13 (2019): 2746–62.

"World Urbanization Prospects." OECD iLibrary, accessed October 20, 2023. www.oecd-ilibrary.org/content/publication/527e5125en/#:~:text=Globally%2C%20more%20people%20live%20in,is%20projected%20to%20be%20urban.

Wittwer, Rico, Regine Gerike, and Stefan Hubrich. "Peak-Car Phenomenon Revisited for Urban Areas: Microdata Analysis of Household Travel Surveys from Five European Capital Cities." *Transportation Research Record* 2673, no. 3, (2019): 686–99. https://doi.org/10.1177/0361198119835509.

Wong, T. and R. Brown. "Transitioning to Water Sensitive Cities: Ensuring Resilience through a New Hydro-Social Contract." 11th International Conference on Urban Drainage Edinburgh, Scotland, UK, 2008.

Wong, T. H., and R. R. Brown. "The Water Sensitive City: Principles for Practice." [In English]. *Water Science and Technology* 60, no. 3 (2009): 673-82. https://doi.org/10.2166/wst.2009.436.

World Bank. *High and Dry: Climate Change, Water, and the Economy*. Washington, DC: World Bank, 2016b. https://openknowledge.worldbank.org/handle/10986/23665.

World Bank. "Improving Waste Management and Resource Efficiency: The Ningbo Experience." *Results Briefs*, April 27, 2021. www.worldbank.org/en/results/2021/04/27/improving-waste-management-and-resource-efficiency-the-ningbo-experience.

World Bank. *Kitakyushu Model Subsector: Interplay between Solid Waste and Urban Flood Risk*. Washington, DC: World Bank, 2017. https://openknowledge.worldbank.org/handle/10986/30950.

World Bank. *Results-Based Financing for Municipal Solid Waste, Urban Development Series*. Washington, DC: World Bank, 2014. https://documents1.worldbank.org/curated/en/237191468330923040/pdf/918610v20WP0FM0BE0CATALOGED0BY0WED0.pdf.

World Bank. The World Bank Annual Report 2013: End Extreme Poverty, Promote Shared Prosperity (Vol. 1 of 3): Main Report (English) (Washington, DC: World Bank, 2013). http://documents.worldbank.org/curated/en/947341468338396810.

World Bank. "Doing More with Less – Smarter Subsidies for Water Supply and Sanitation." (2019). www.worldbank.org/en/topic/water/publication/smarter-subsidies-for-water-supply-and-sanitation.

"This Chart Shows the Impact Rising Urbanization Will Have on the World." 2022, accessed September 18, 2024. www.weforum.org/agenda/2022/04/global-urbanization-material-consumption/.

"Aqueduct Projected Water Stress Country Rankings." 2015, accessed September 15, 2024. www.wri.org/data/aqueduct-projected-water-stress-country-rankings.

World Bank and International Monetary Fund. *Global Monitoring Report 2013: Rural–Urban Dynamics and the Millennium Development Goals*. Washington, DC: World Bank and IMF, 2013. https://documents.worldbank.org//en/publication/documents-reports/documentdetail/720451468171242999.

World Bank Group. *Investing in Urban Resilience: Protecting and Promoting Development in a Changing World*. Washington, DC: World Bank Group, 2016. https://openknowledge.worldbank.org/handle/10986/25219.

World Health Organization. "Circular Economy and Health: Opportunities and Risks." (2018). https://apps.who.int/iris/bitstream/handle/10665/342218/9789289053341-eng.pdf?sequence=1.

"Regional Office for Europe. Circular economy and health: opportunities and risks." (2018). https://apps.who.int/iris/handle/10665/342218.

Wortmann, C., A. M. Anne Magdalene Syré, A. Grahle, and D. Göhlich. "Analysis of Electric Moped Scooter Sharing in Berlin: A Technical, Economic and Environmental Perspective." *World Electric Vehicle Journal* 12, (2021): 3: 96. https://doi.org/10.3390/wevj12030096.

Wyes, Henry W. "Hazardous Waste: Its Impact on Human Health in Europe." *Toxicology and Industrial Health* 13, nos. 2–3 (1997): 109–19. https://doi.org/10.1177/074823379701300202.

Zeng, Zhao, Junguo Liu, and Hubert H. G. Savenije. "A Simple Approach to Assess Water Scarcity Integrating Water Quantity and Quality." *Ecological Indicators* 34 (2013): 441–49. https://doi.org/10.1016/j.ecolind.2013.06.012.

Zhao, J., L. Gladson, and K. Cromar. "A Novel Environmental Justice Indicator for Managing Local Air Pollution." [In English]. *International Journal of Environmental Research and Public Health* 15, no. 6 (2018). https://doi.org/10.3390/ijerph15061260.

Zhou, D., C. Y. Zhao, and Y. Tian, "Review on Thermal Energy Storage with Phase Change Materials (PCMs) in Building Applications." *Applied Energy* 92 (2012): 593–605. lhttps://doi.org/10.1016/j.apenergy.2011.08.025.

Index

For EU product safety concerns, contact us at Calle de José Abascal, 56–1°,
28003 Madrid, Spain or eugpsr@cambridge.org.

www.ingramcontent.com/pod-product-compliance
Ingram Content Group UK Ltd.
Pitfield, Milton Keynes, MK11 3LW, UK
UKHW050937280825
462323UK00008B/249

* 9 7 8 1 0 0 9 2 4 9 4 5 4 *